WALES A PHOTOGRAPHER'S JOURNEY DAVID WILSON

GRAFFEG

For Mum and Dad

Published by Graffeg

ISBN 9781905582594

Graffeg, 16 Neptune Court, Vanguard Way,
Cardiff Bay CF24 5PJ Wales UK
www.graffeg.com

Wales – A Photographer's Journey, David Wilson
Author David Wilson

Designed and produced by Peter Gill & Associates
www.petergill.com

A CIP Catalogue record for this book is available from the British Library.

CONTENTS

GRIFF RHYS JONES

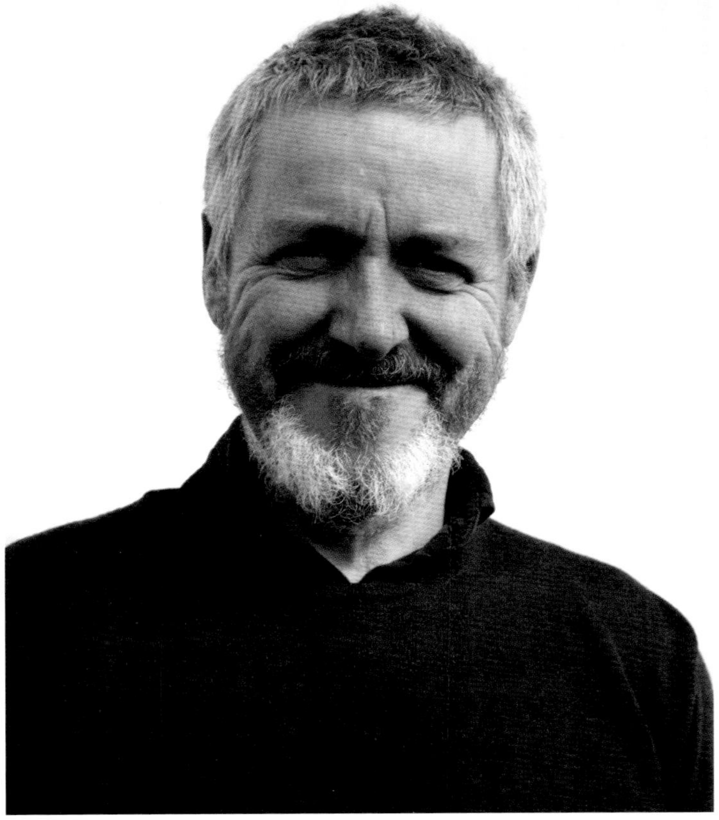

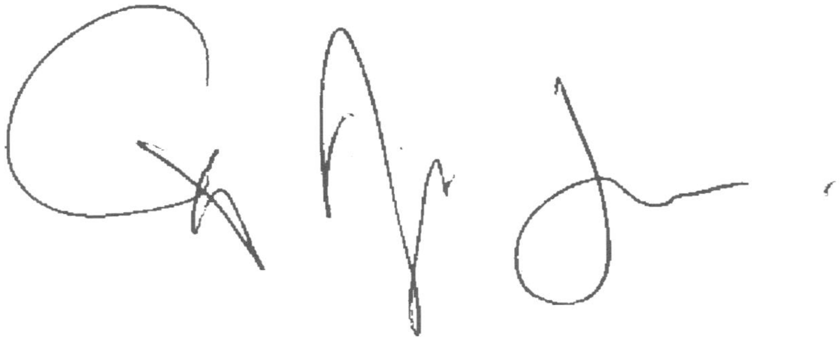

Knock-kneed and shock-waved sheep; a copse, white-feathered with frost; wet foreshores, black seas and white skies; corrugated iron, fuzzy mist and telegraph poles – David Wilson's photographs don't flatter Wales, but by God they capture her essence. You have to look at these pictures with your metaphorical coat on. You feel the cold searching sun and the scouring wind and enjoy the harsh abstractions and the bare outlines. These are powerful images. They remind us that rural Wales has a stark and demanding beauty. She may be handsome, but she is certainly raw.

Sometimes, as I drive to Pembrokeshire (David's home turf) passing Cardiff at the half-way mark of the tarmac river that leads to Fishguard, I wonder whether the five hour journey might have got me to the Caribbean or the Alps or another more upholstered bolt-hole. But past Goodwick on the by-roads that will take me to Trehilyn, I forget all that. I am gripped again. The landscape charges away towards St Davids. It is topped by crusted ice age remnants. It waves through islands of light. I love it.

FOREWORD

It is startling. The green boggles. The sky seems fresh and adventurous. The clouds are luminous, even when ragged. It is called 'a particular landscape' in one guide book and David has often captured this ethereal world and its singularity. But it is hardly unique. North to the Cambrian Mountains and up to Snowdonia, around the coast, or into the heart of the Brecon Beacons, there are hundreds of thousands of distinctive, glowing vistas in Wales. They are rarely cosy, only intermittently grandiose, often washed with rain and shafted by bleak sun. David has fixed a moment in them all and he has made me see that the human involvement, which so often seems untidy, frazzled or insecure, is also touching and beautiful. Modern stuff has an edge of decay. The cottages cringe into the hills. The undergrowth wraps itself around abandoned cars. The corrugated sides of a painted chapel buckle. Not always particularly old and rarely impressively new, David captures the way that people add to but seldom dominate the landscape. The atmosphere itself remains by far the strongest element. It's the weather, you see. If light is the main component of any great photograph, then David adds the refractions of early morning and late seasons and captures the feeling of the damp air itself.

On the wall of my bedroom in Melin Trehilyn is one of his photos. It is of a badly painted blue shed door and a rusty modern petrol pump in a frame of old stone wall. The paint and the metal, scumbled by the weather, have colour and charm. But I look at it a lot. It is far more than a coincidence of decay and patina. David recognised that the pitted surfaces, the tinge of rust and the hopeful blaze of colour all talk of the weather and world and the resistance to it. The pump has its story and that is the story of Welsh Wales.

There is more of his unflinching and perceptive eye in this great collection. Wrap up warm, pull up your metaphorical collar and enjoy David Wilson's authentic, bracing, beautiful Wales.

DAVID WILSON

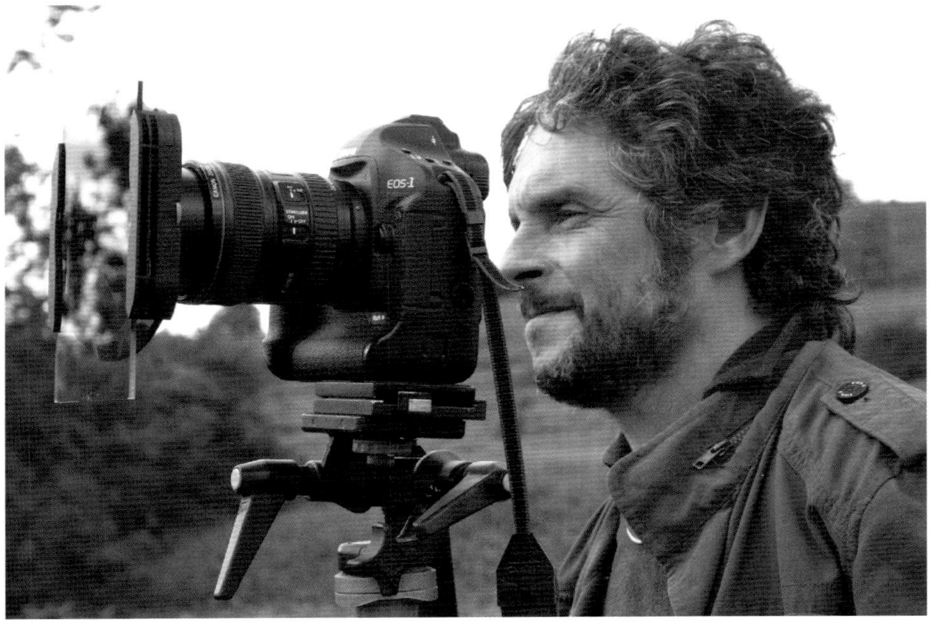

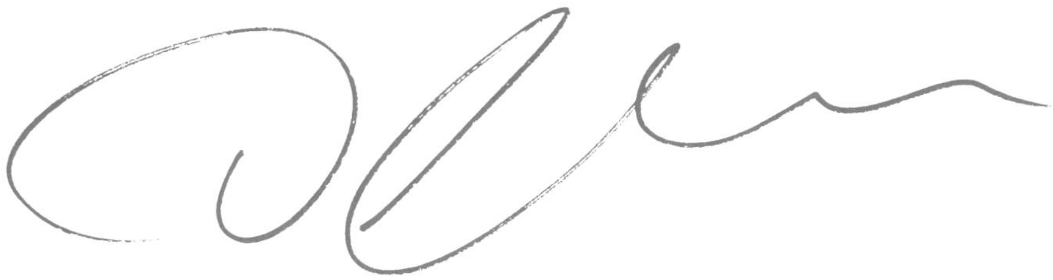

Wales could hardly be described as a big country, but what it lacks in size it certainly makes up for with its wealth of breathtaking landscapes and the enchanting stories to be found within them. Indeed, if the measure of a nation's land mass were determined by the impact of its vistas then Wales would be truly continental in proportion. It's all here: cloud-piercing mountain peaks; rugged, storm-lashed coastlines; ancient woodlands; medieval castles; meandering river valleys; remnants of past industrial glory; isolated farms. The Welsh landscape not only offers a vision of the picturesque, it tells the story of a nation.

For those of us with a yearning to discover its many charms, Wales is wonderfully accessible, compact and eminently suited to exploration. On a photographic excursion or a sight-seeing trip, vast swathes of the country can be squeezed into a day-long adventure.

The borders of Wales have remained pretty much static for well over a thousand years. The nation has been blessed with a feeling of age-old constancy; rooted to a land that has been definably ours for countless generations. In comparison a number of European nations have seen their frontiers regularly redrawn down through the centuries. Within living memory some modern countries did not even exist.

INTRODUCTION

The Welsh language and its distinct Celtic culture have shaped and defined this small country on the very periphery of Western Europe. There is an ancient and epic tale to tell, and a pedigree reaching far back into the mists of time. That story is inextricably connected to the landscape, be it the folk-lore of the forests, a disused slate mine or an impregnable fortress perched high up on a rocky knoll. As a nation our history is etched into the land.

It dawned on me from the outset that I could never hope to fit the entirety of this narrative in to a single book. All I could hope for was to embark on my own particular journey; a personal homage to my homeland, if you like. I hope that the resulting collection of images is representative of Wales; that people will identify with the varied landscapes and the environments influenced by man that are captured in this book.

As a landscape photographer I am aware of the need to evolve, to explore new ways of presenting my work to an audience. In this book I have incorporated the mini photo-essay, an approach that affords an in-depth appreciation of a locality, allowing me to communicate more fully the intimate story within a particular landscape. The combination of images and text in each essay builds an appreciable narrative of a specific location or area, allowing readers to immerse themselves in the journey that I took.

Every photographer has a particular style that defines their work, a way of photographing that shines out from the imagery either overtly or as a subtle theme. In my work I strive wherever possible to reflect evidence of human interaction with the landscape: a hill farm; a remote chapel; telegraph poles strung out along a rain-soaked road. People's experience of the landscape almost inevitably includes elements introduced by man and that is what I attempt to portray. Importantly, I think this approach enables the viewer to better connect with the photograph and the narrative within it.

Logistically, my previous book, *Pembrokeshire* was quite straight forward. It is where I live and always have lived. I know the area intimately. I knew what I wanted to photograph and exactly how and where to go to get to it. This project was a different proposition. Photography on a much broader scale, it demanded an expeditionary approach; planned routes and focus. It was, though, a hearty adventure and in many cases a leap into the unknown. Blind alleys were encountered and glorious surprises fell into my lap.

The opportunity to explore and photograph my native land led to a most joyful odyssey. I have been blessed with so many everlasting memories: encountering a host of warm and trusting people; happening upon tiny crooked churches; capturing remote farms with the trickle of rainwater running down my back; tucking into a pit-stop lunch while gazing in awe at a looming mountain range; creeping gingerly in the car along snow-covered roads; brushing through centuries-old doorways wondering who had gone before me. It has been a journey of simple pleasures and twisting routes. And the result of these not inconsiderable delights is this book; my take on Wales.

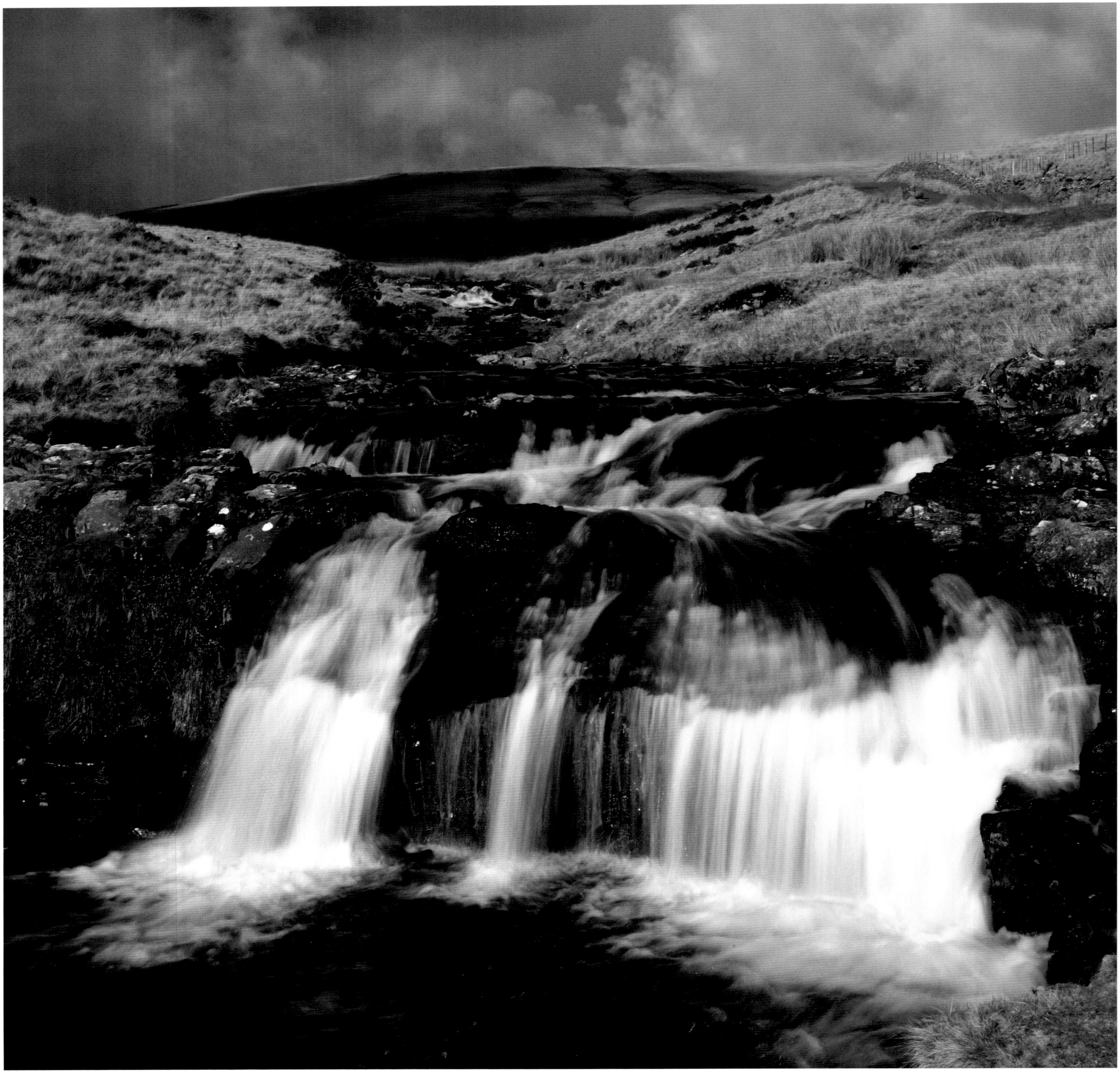

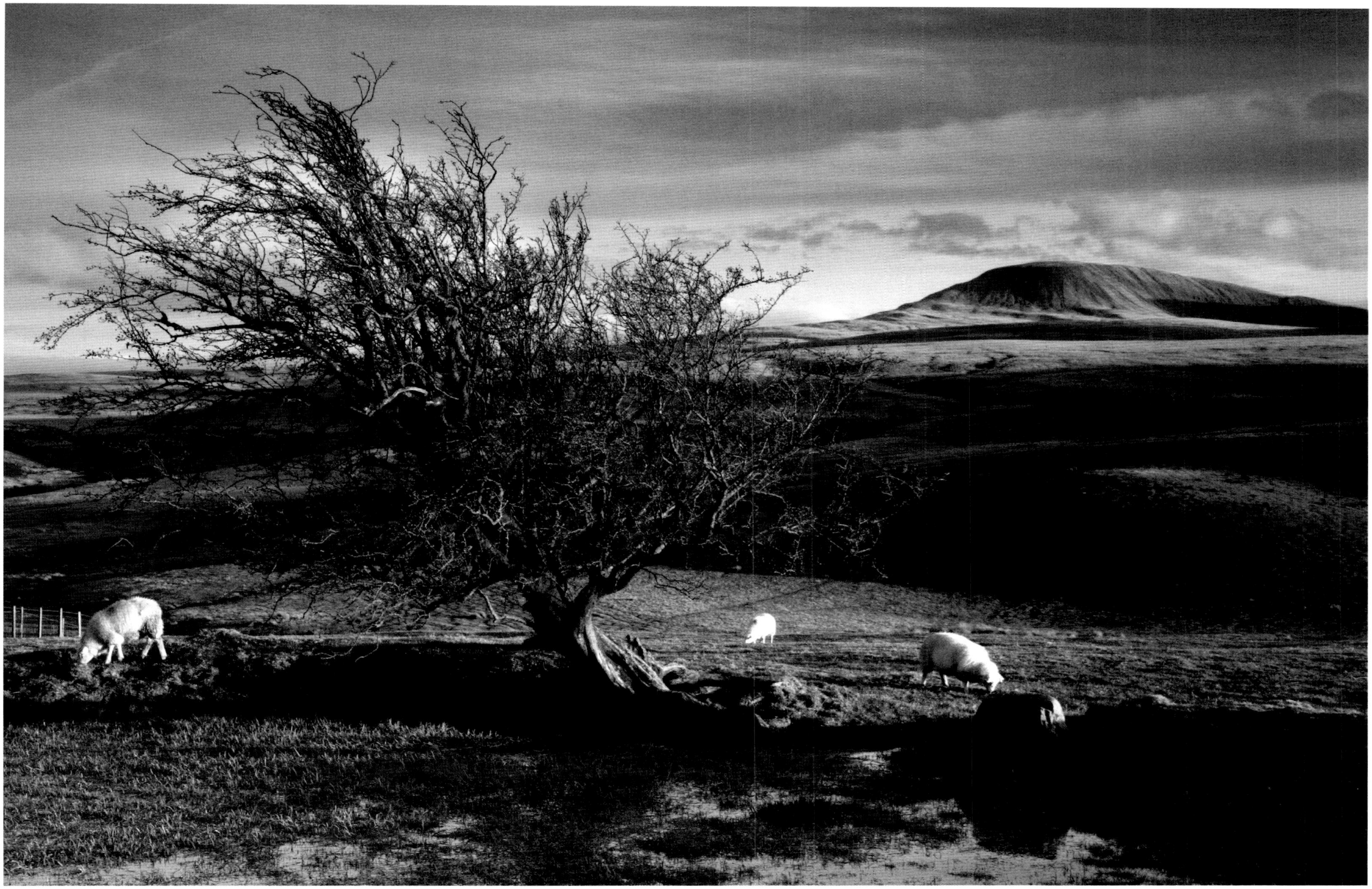

01 BLACK MOUNTAIN, BRECON BEACONS

The Black Mountain stands at the western edge of the Brecon Beacons. I drove via Brynamman and Glyntawe, eventually arriving where the embryonic River Tawe cascades over a waterfall. Moel Feity loomed behind at 591 metres (1,938 ft). A world away, it seems, the very same river flows leisurely through Swansea and into the Bristol Channel. Waterfalls possess a raw elemental power. A slow shutter speed accentuates that relentless flow, capturing the streaky movement of the water.

The afternoon was slipping away and the light with it, so on I went to the road that runs adjacent to Fan Foel and Picws Du. A barren landscape was punctuated by a solitary crooked tree, a still pond and some grazing sheep with the peak of Fan Foel at 781 metres (2,562 ft) in the distance. Within minutes the sun had ducked ever westwards and the direct light with it. (Map C5)

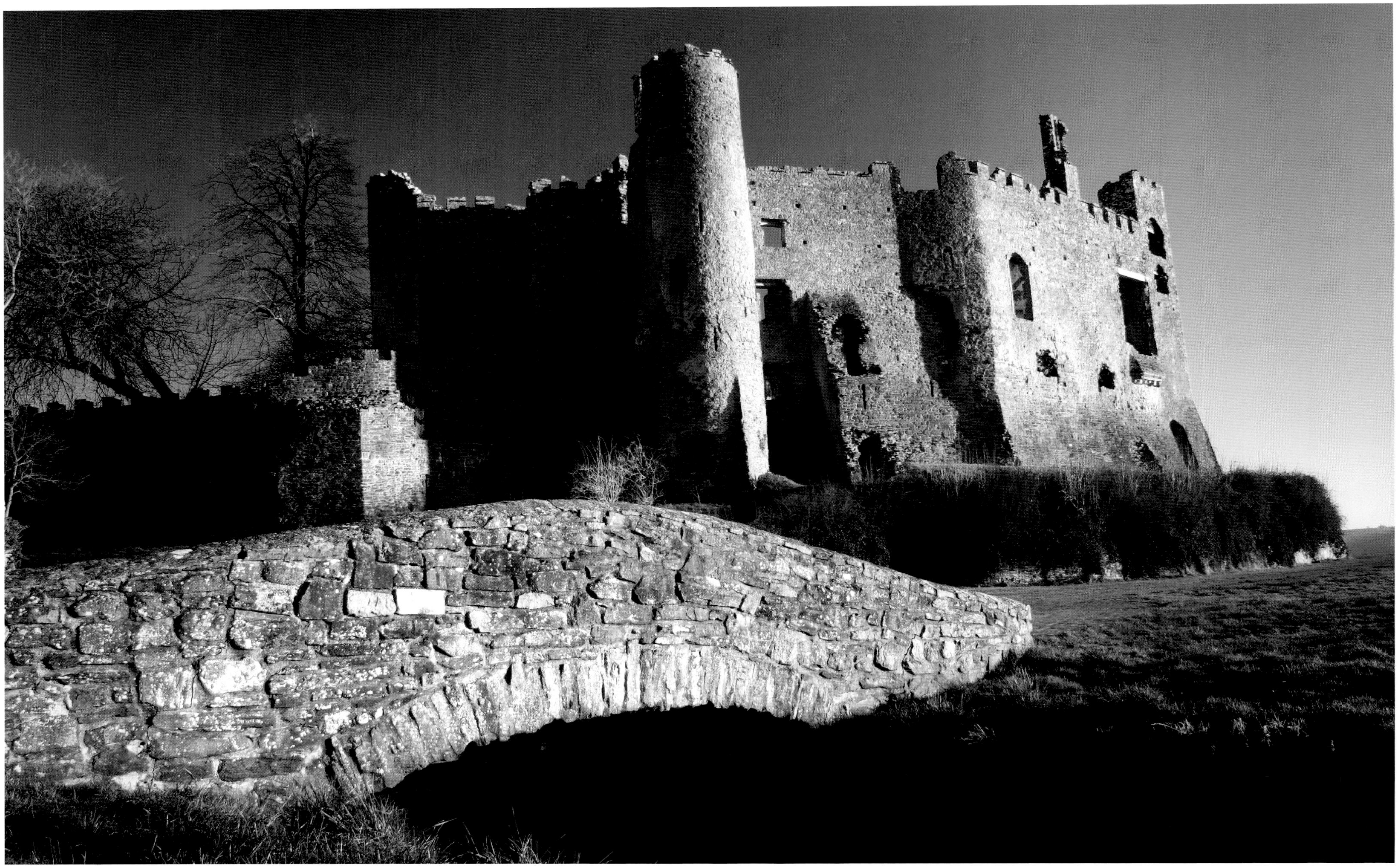

Above: Laugharne Castle
Right: Laugharne Bookshop prior to restoration

02 LAUGHARNE, CARMARTHENSHIRE

Laugharne's most famous former resident, the poet Dylan Thomas, lived with his wife Caitlin and their children in the Boathouse by the river's edge. In his writing shed, with its glorious views over the estuary, he penned some of his most celebrated works – in between the occasional saunter round the corner to Brown's Hotel. In October 1953 he left for a tour of America, never to return. He died in New York on 9 November.

Once a favoured haunt of retired sea captains, the town has experienced something of a renaissance in recent years. Rather fittingly it now hosts an annual literary festival drawing large, bookish crowds. The aged and crumbling exteriors of some of its fine houses have been re-rendered and spruced up, undergoing that most modern of phenomenons, the 'makeover'. The town boasts a robust identity, its isolation near the tip of the estuary imbuing it with a resilient sense of community. This is a town with character. (Map B6)

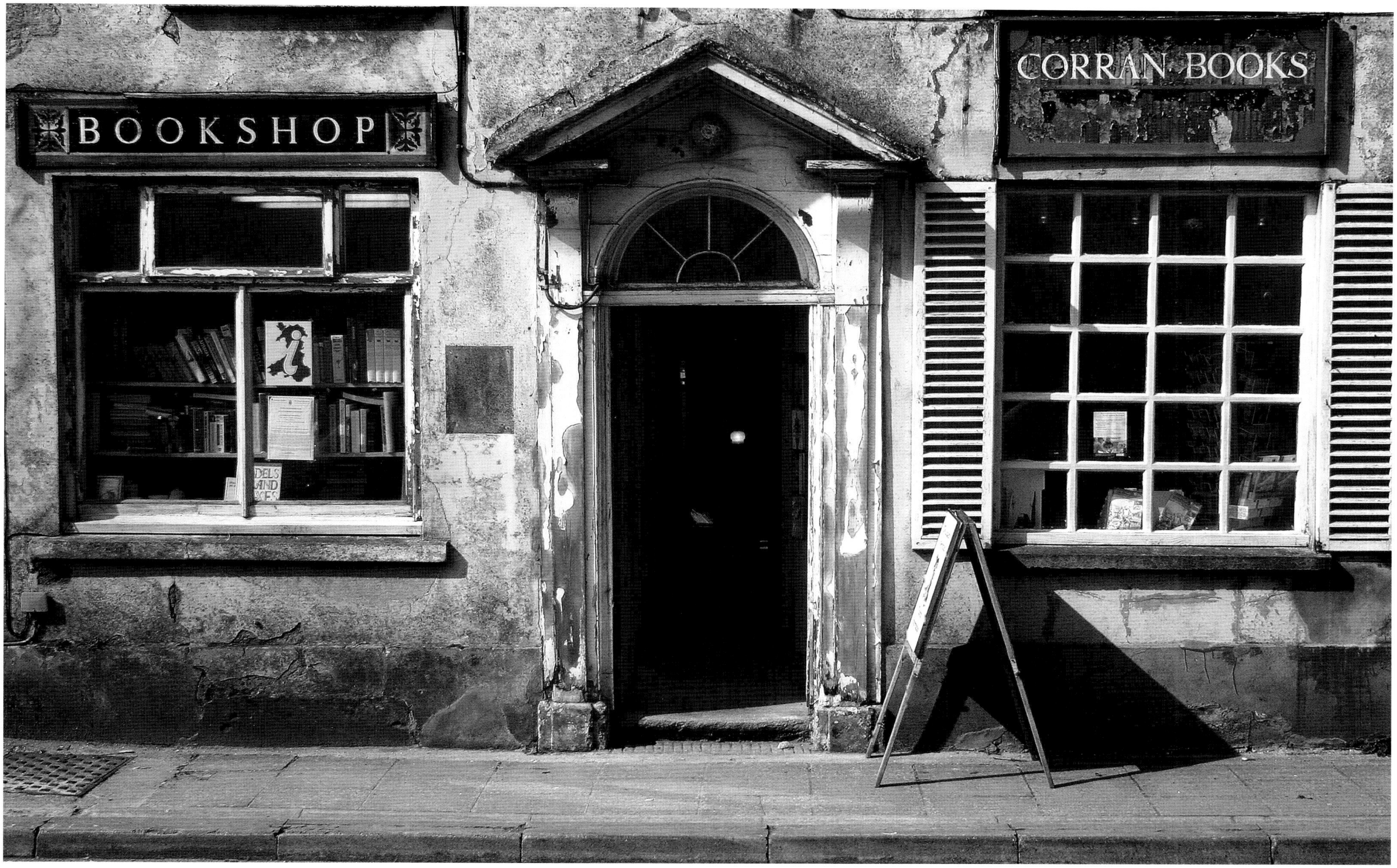

02 Laugharne, Carmarthenshire

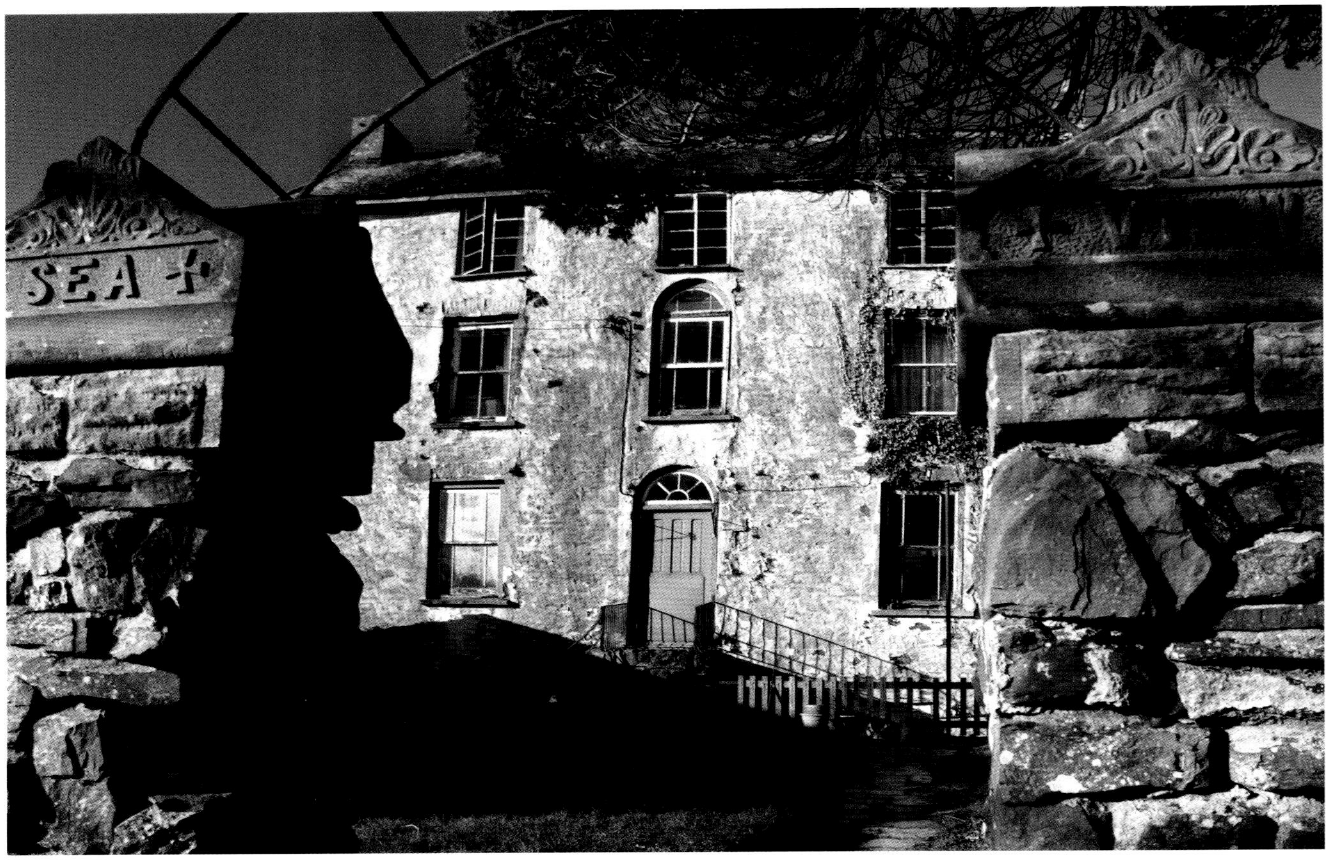

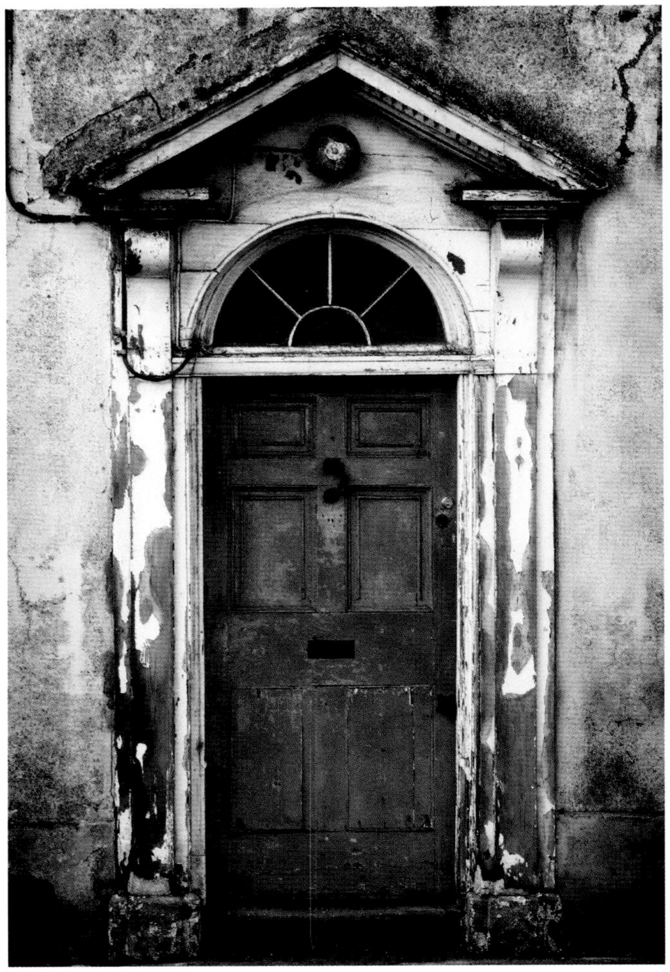

Above: Sea View prior to restoration
Above right: Laugharne Bookshop doorway prior to restoration
Right: The Boathouse
Opposite: Dylan Thomas' writing shed

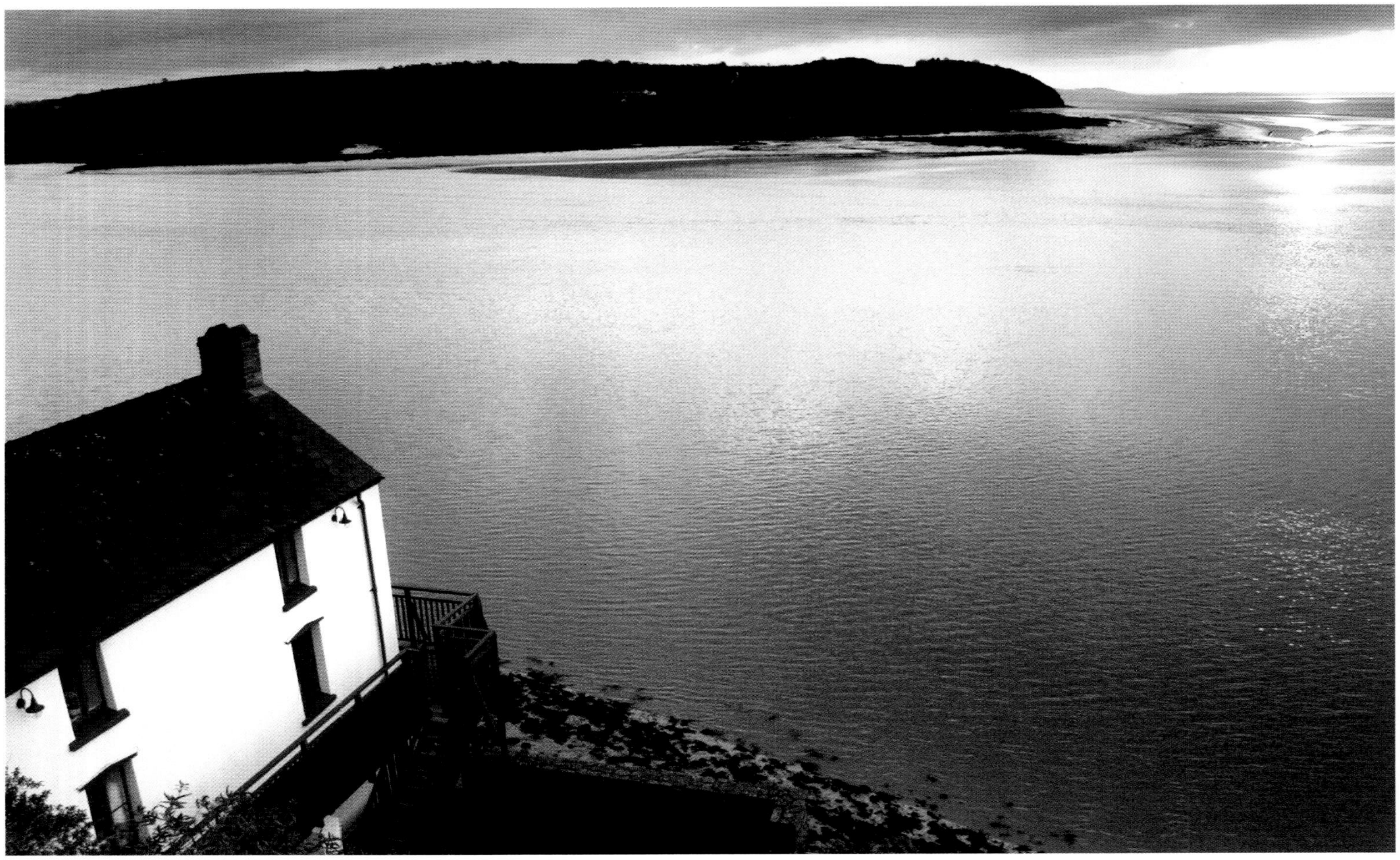

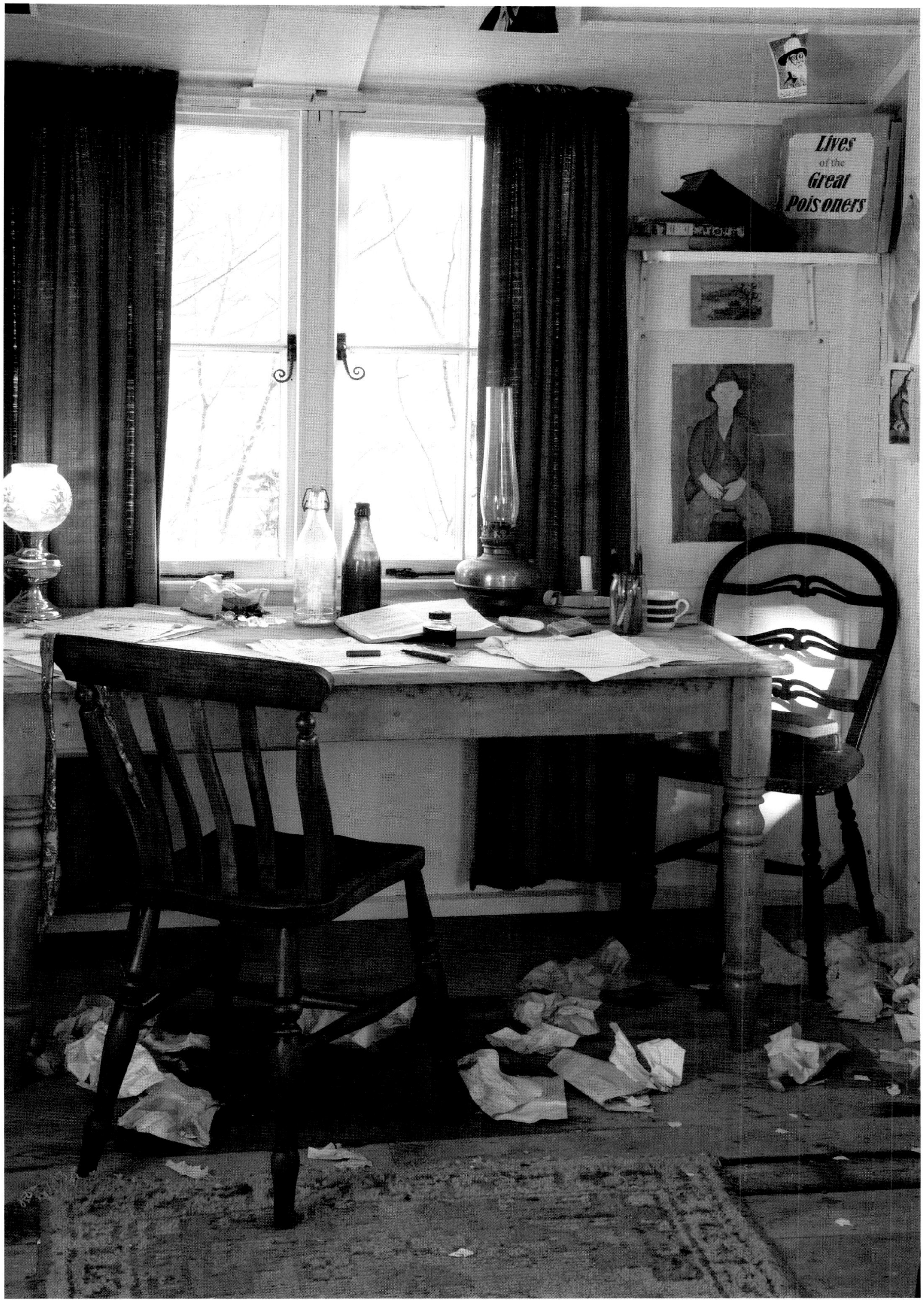
Lives
of the
Great
Poisoners

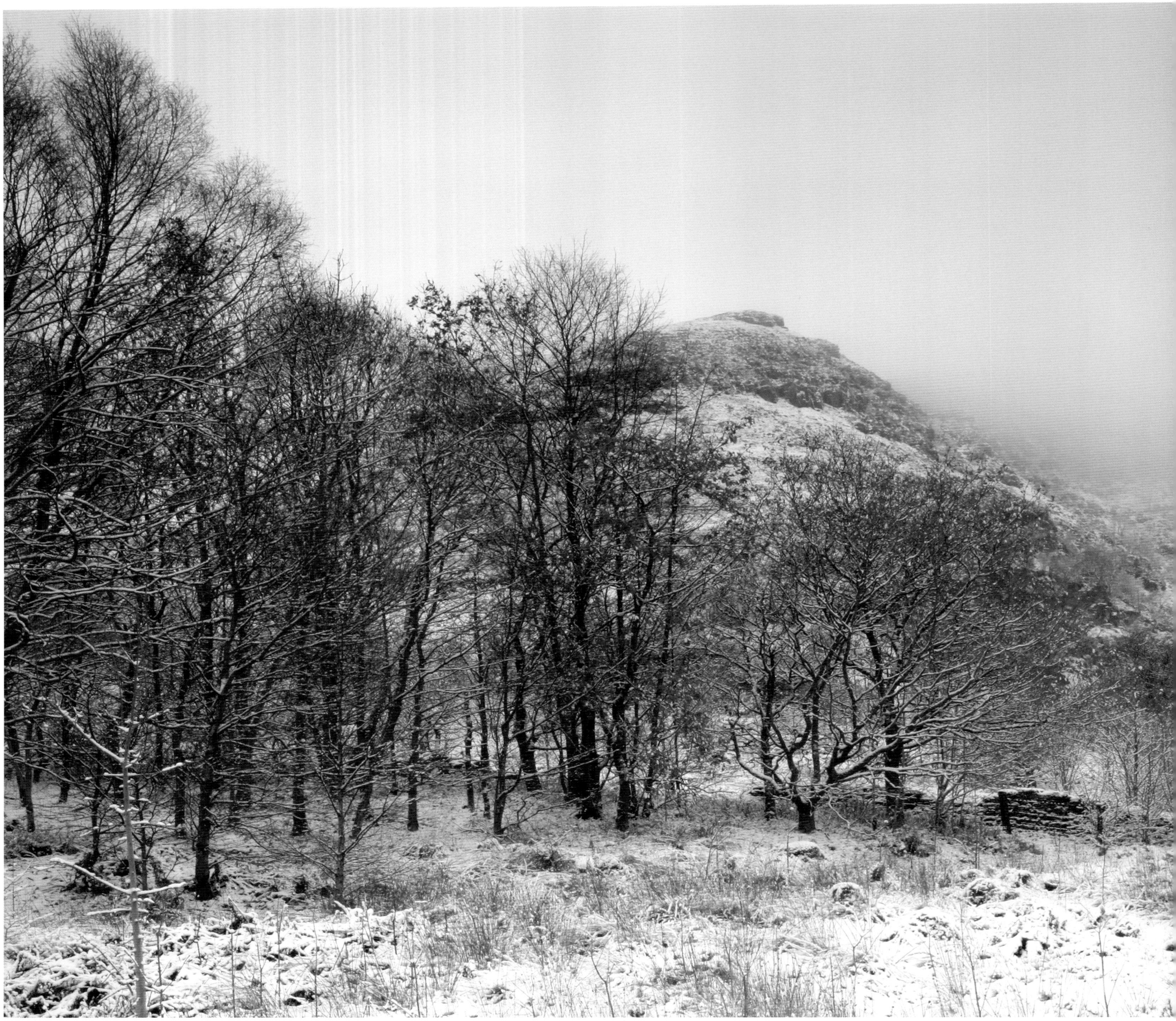

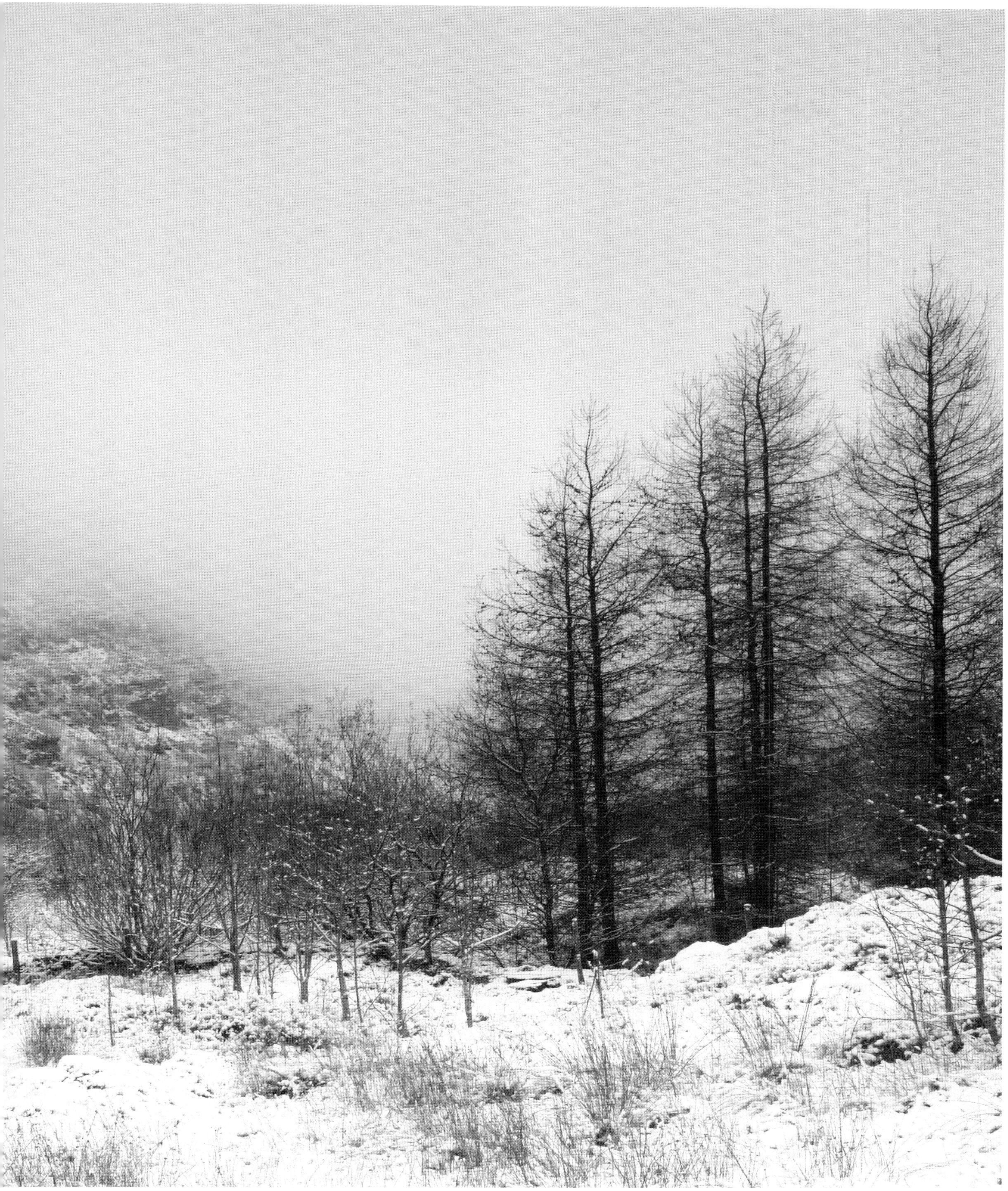

03 CRAIG CERRIG-GLEISIAD, BRECON BEACONS

On this day I had been photographing the starkness of bare trees in Dinefwr Park, Llandeilo, against a fresh fall of snow. As I packed up my gear I remembered seeing this composition at Craig Cerrig-gleisiad a few weeks previously, and how it had lacked a certain something to lift it.

So off I trundled along the A40 back to this spot a couple of miles from the Storey Arms outdoor education centre near Brecon. As I suspected, the snow had worked its magic. Compositionally I was drawn to the way in which the trees frame the scene, inviting you through the gap and onwards to explore the mountains. (Map D5)

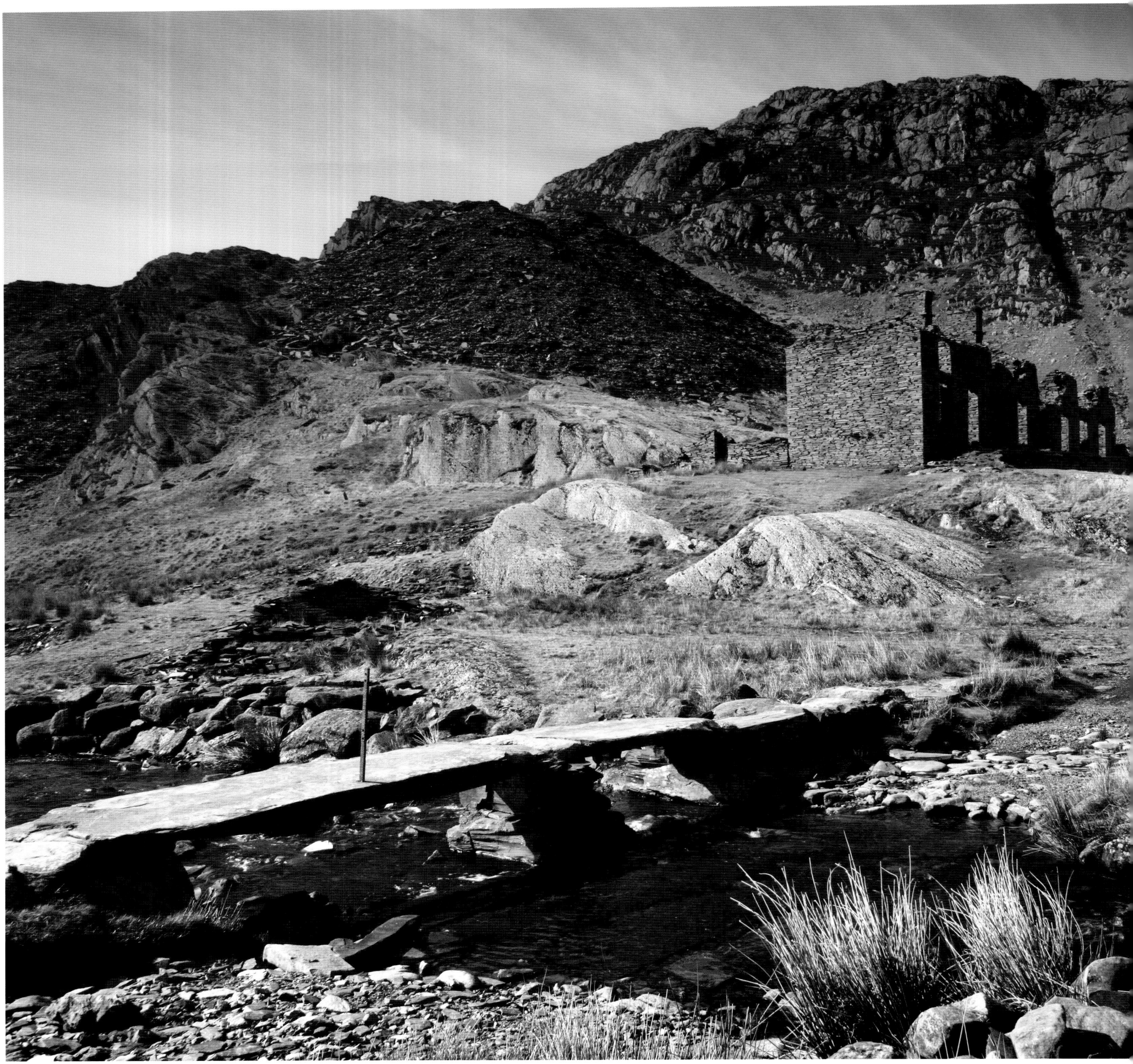

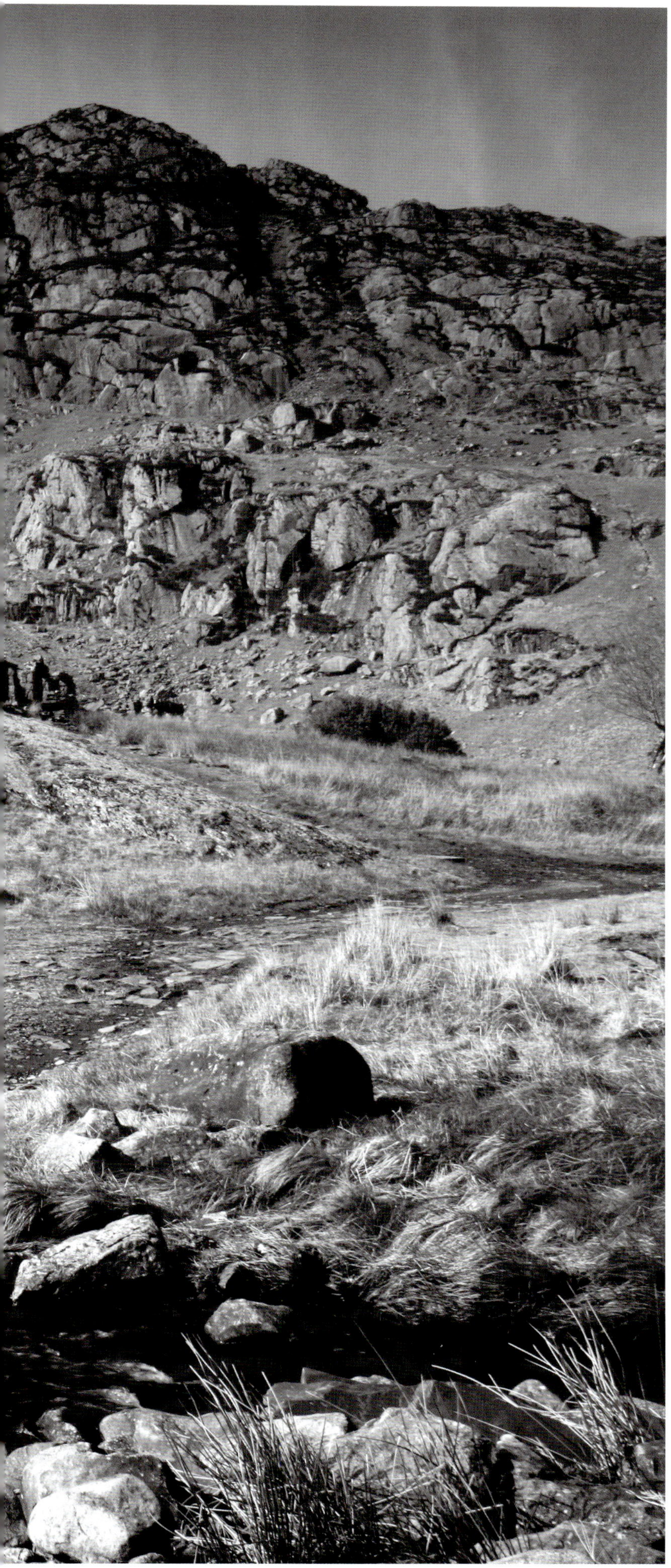

04 CWMORTHIN SLATE MINE, NEAR BLAENAU FFESTINIOG

Laden down with equipment, my wife Anna and I enjoyed a pleasant slog up to Cwmorthin Mine, near Blaenau Ffestiniog. Reaching the lake, we lay down on a bed of springy moss by the water's edge. Closing my eyes I immersed myself in the most beautiful silence, broken only by the twittering of birds. I could have lain there for hours in the early spring sunshine, but photography beckoned. For the workers who once extracted the slate I doubt there would have been much time for such quiet contemplation.

Apart from the slag heaps of discarded material, the landscape remains unscarred as the slate was mined from underground caverns and tunnels. It was an unforgiving existence, bristling with ever-present danger. Winters spent cooped up in those grim barracks wouldn't have been very luxurious either. Today that life seems quite austere, but it would have been their normality, albeit a harsh one. No doubt in a hundred years some modern occupations will be seen as equally hard. Time changes our perceptions, I suppose.

There is always an eerie feeling strolling around former industrial sites such as Cwmorthin. Where once there was an energised sense of purpose, a well-directed operation requiring the input of countless individuals, there is now total peace and quiet. The derelict buildings stand in the hush of the landscape, silent witnesses to a thousand conversations. You enter these shells and imagine the chattering of miners about to head home for a couple of days. Above all, though, I find it a chastening experience, making me thankful for my way of life compared to theirs. (Map C2)

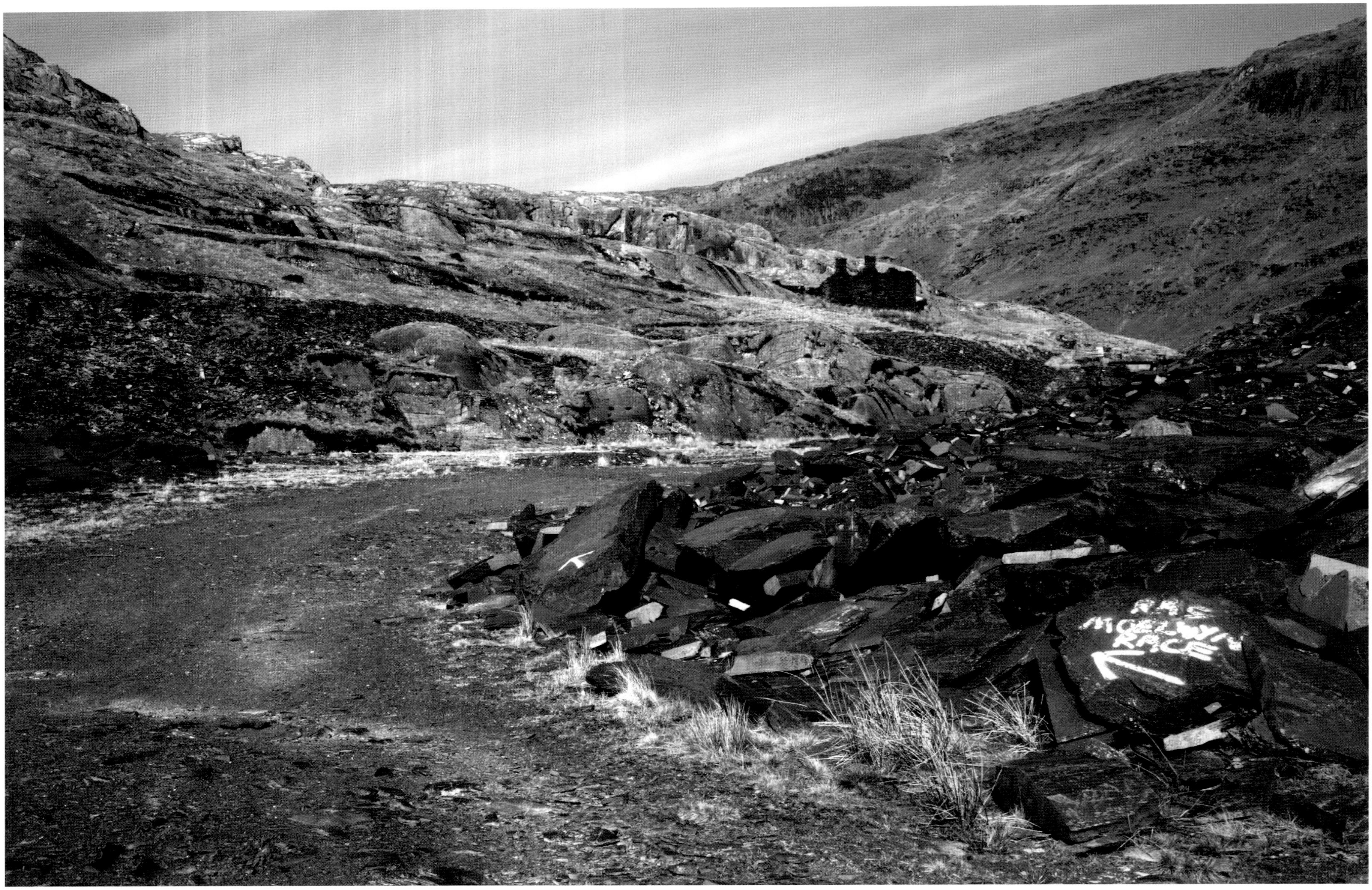
RAS
MOELWYN
RACE

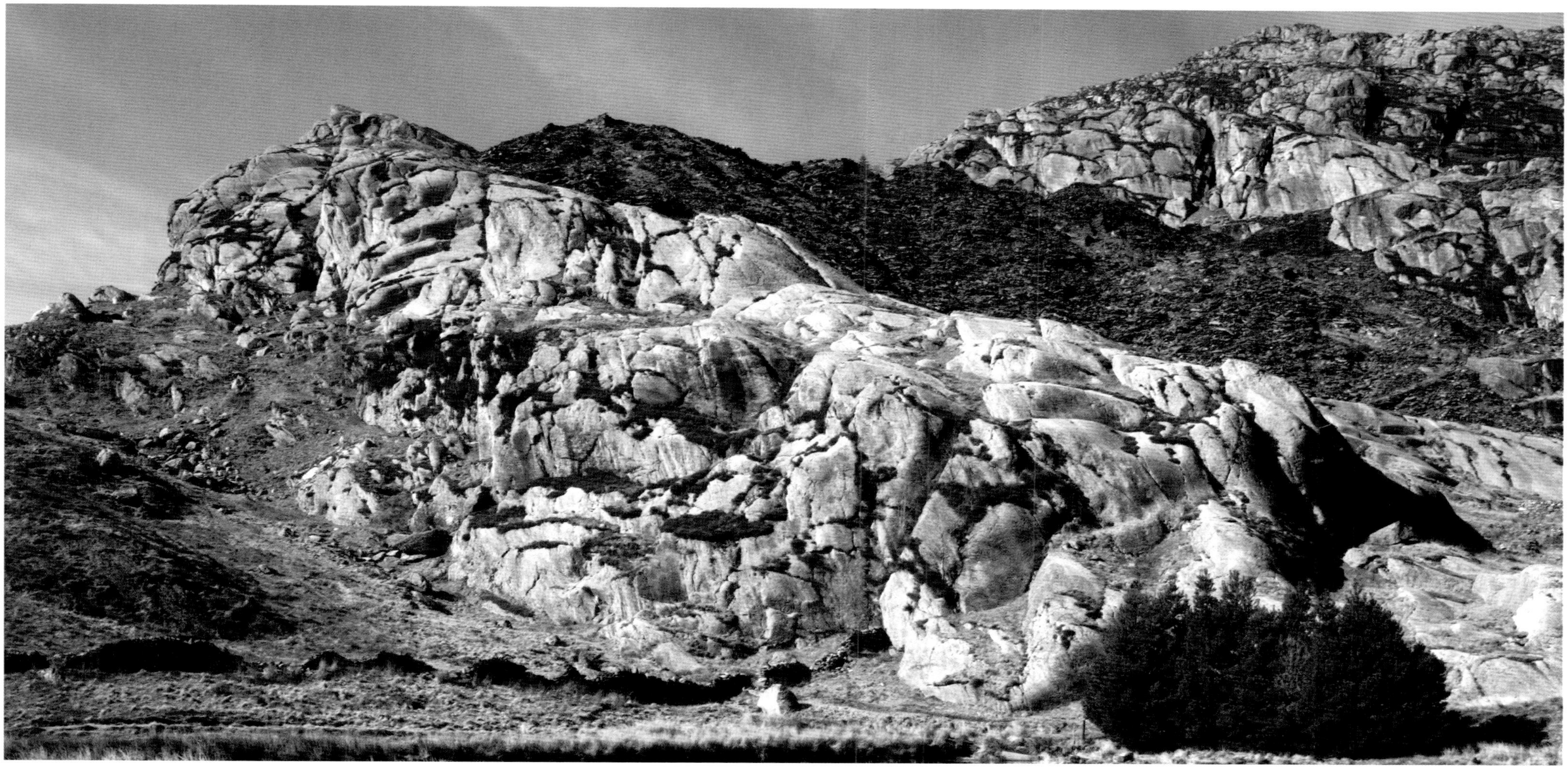

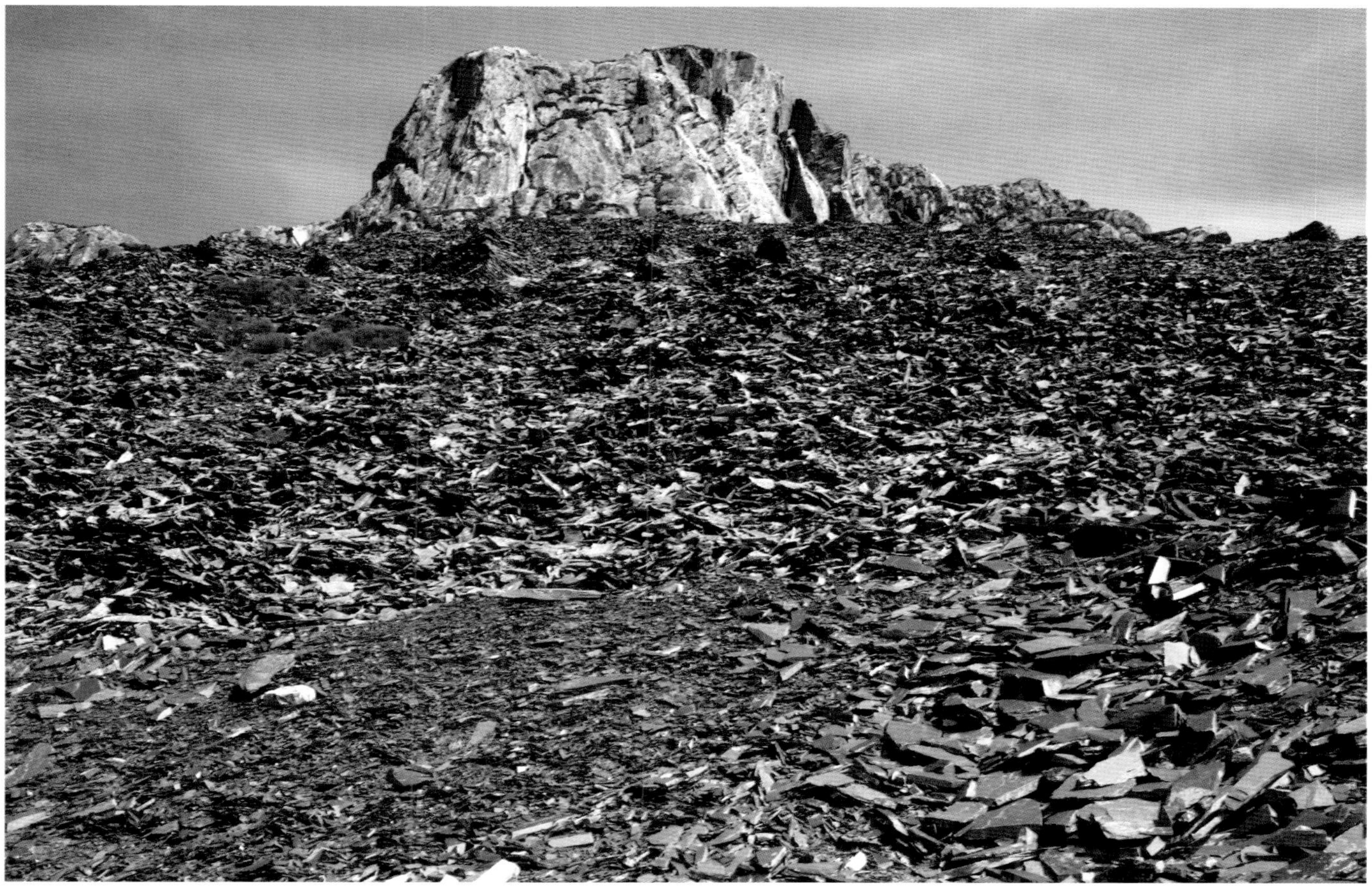

04 Cwmorthin Slate Mine, near Blaenau Ffestiniog

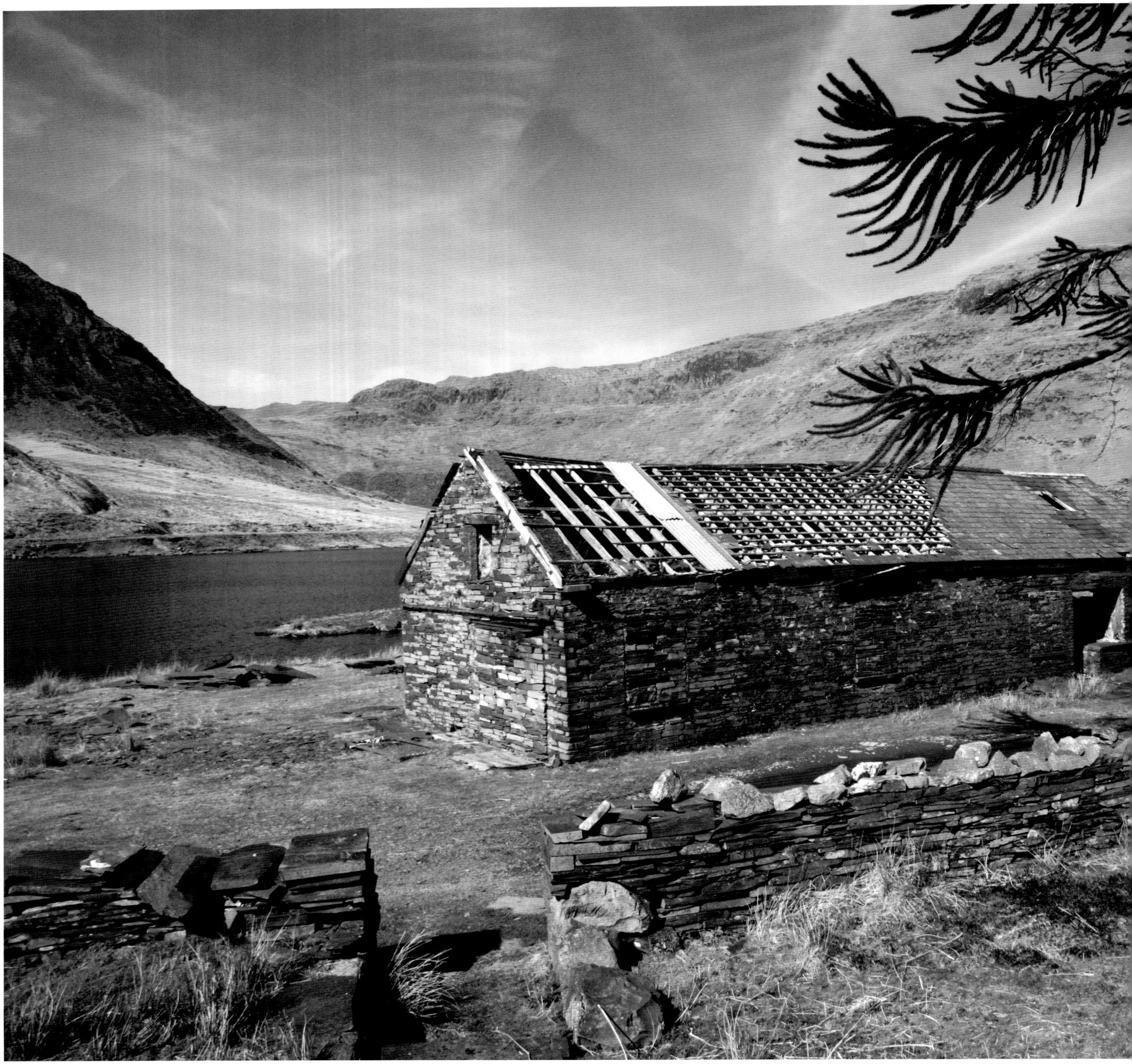

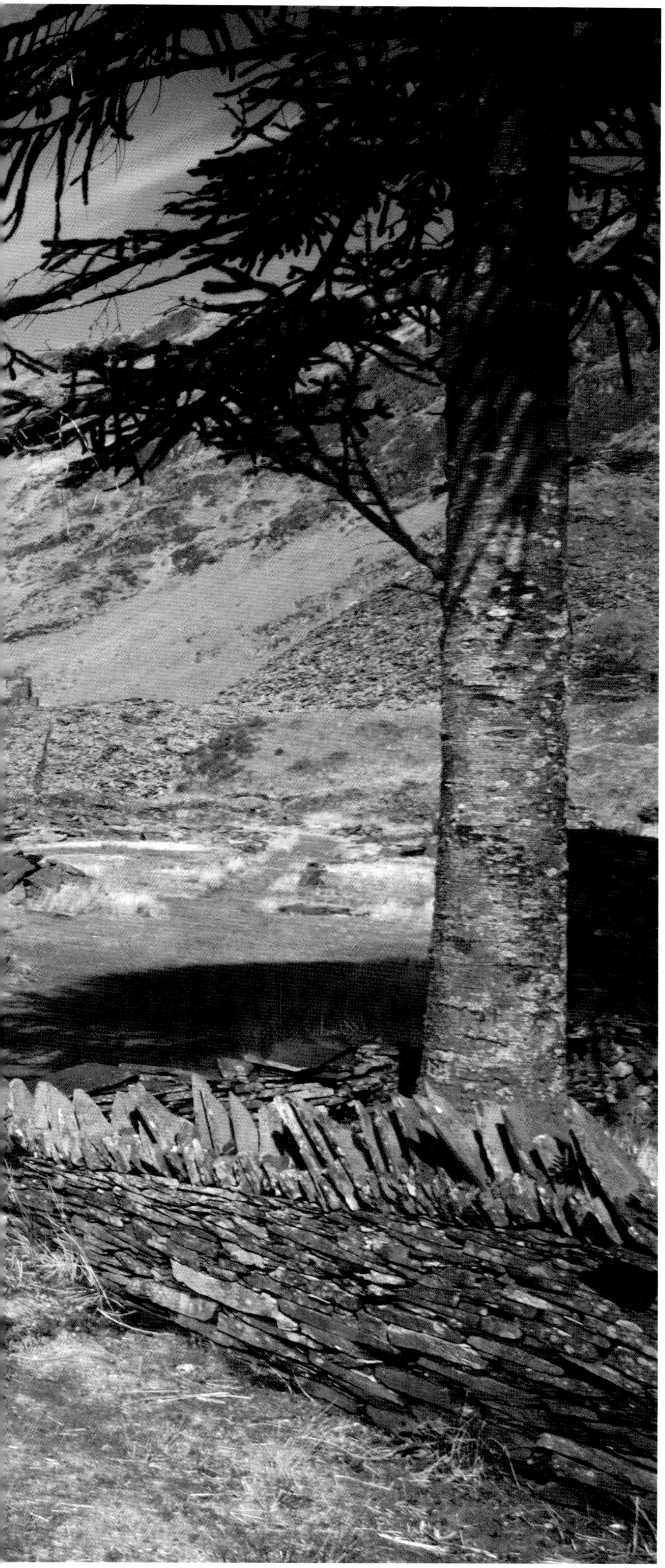

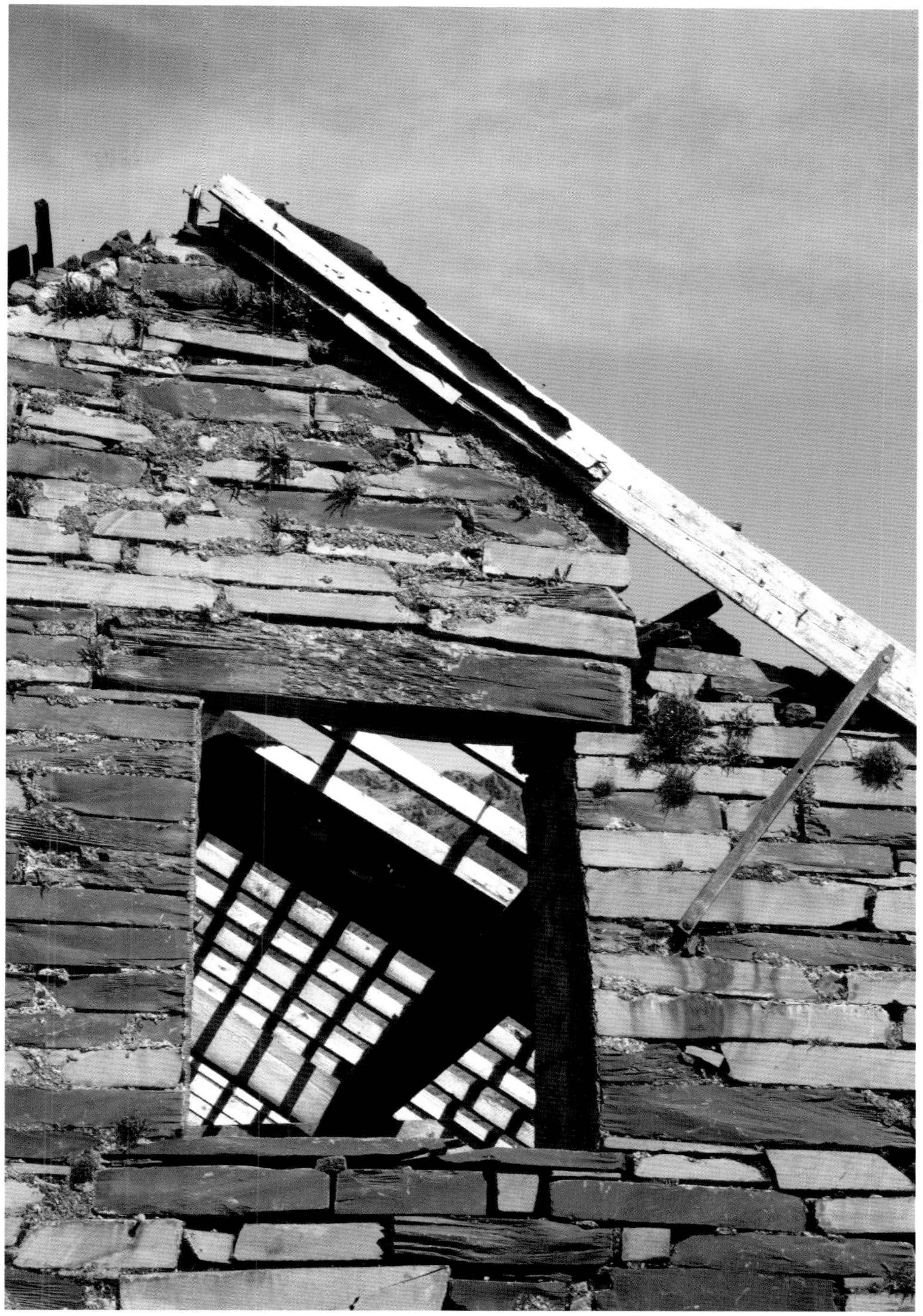

04 Cwmorthin Slate Mine, near Blaenau Ffestiniog

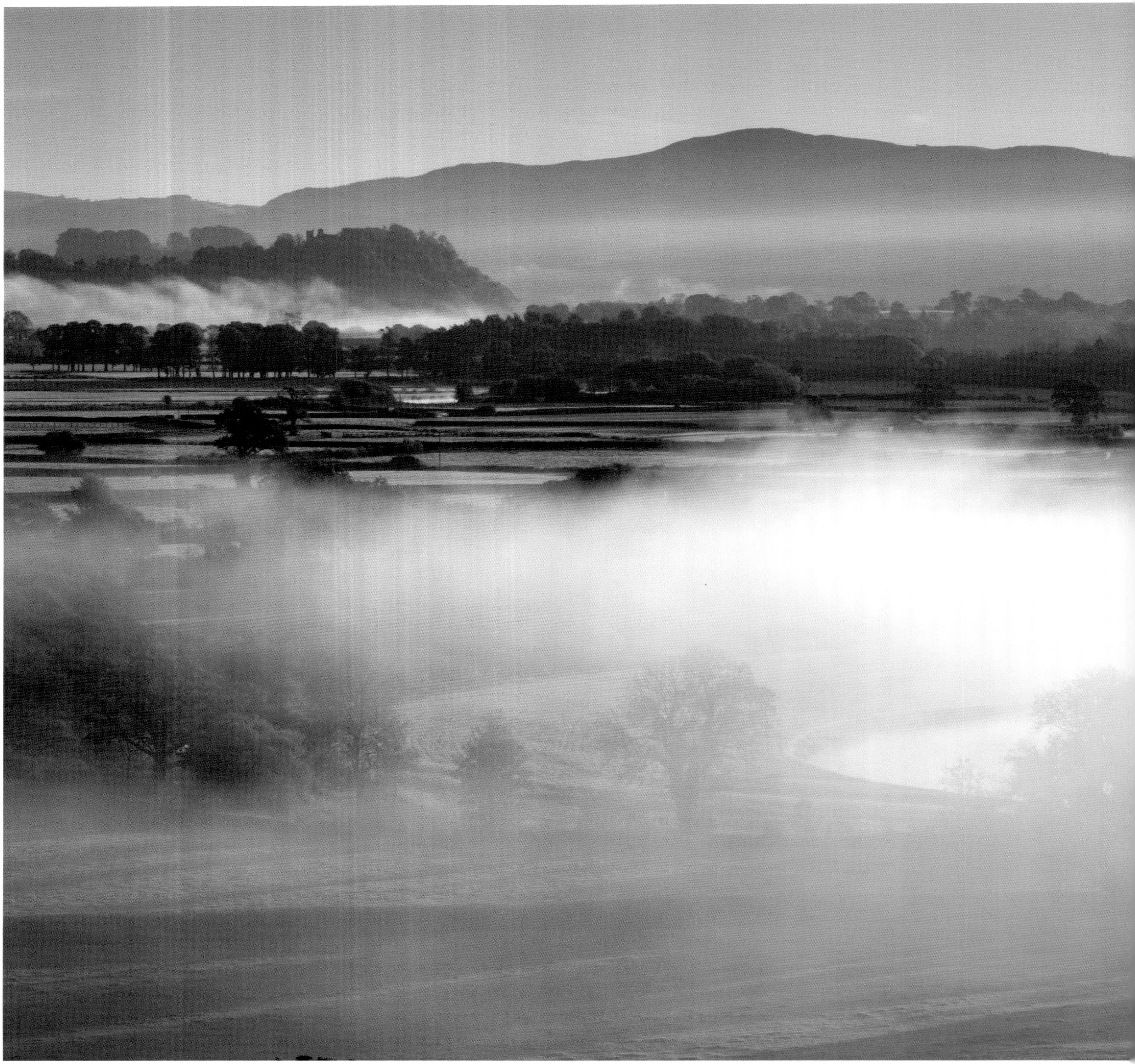

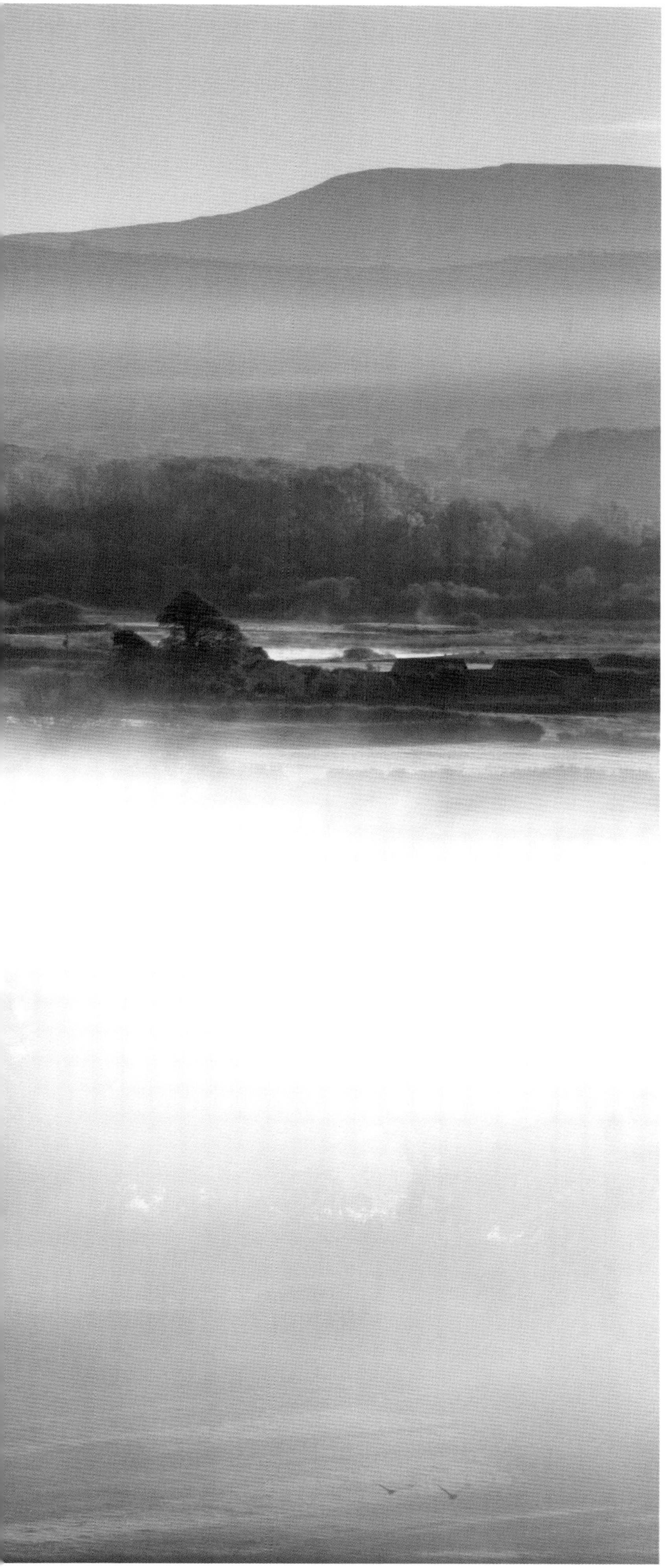

05 TOWY VALLEY, CARMARTHENSHIRE

I took an early morning walk up to Dryslwyn Castle in the Towy Valley, from where you get the most rewarding views towards Dinefwr Castle and Llandeilo. Autumn was slipping into winter and there was a decent frost on the ground. The weather forecast had hinted at sun and, sure enough, within minutes of reaching the top up it came. A combination of the Towy Valley, frost and sun usually results in mist. Dryslwyn gives you the necessary elevation for a long distance photograph, but is not so high that you begin to lose that sense of connection with the landscape. There was an uplifting solitude being up there so early in the morning; just me and the view – and the many ghosts from the castle's past!

But there was no time for romantic musings, as I wanted to get back down to the valley floor to see what else I could photograph: the landscape photographer's imperative. This sense of urgency paid off, as from Cilsan Bridge I got a haunting view of a group of trees enveloped in a swirling mist. (Map C5)

Left: Towards Llandeilo from Dryslwyn Castle
Overleaf: View from Cilsan Bridge

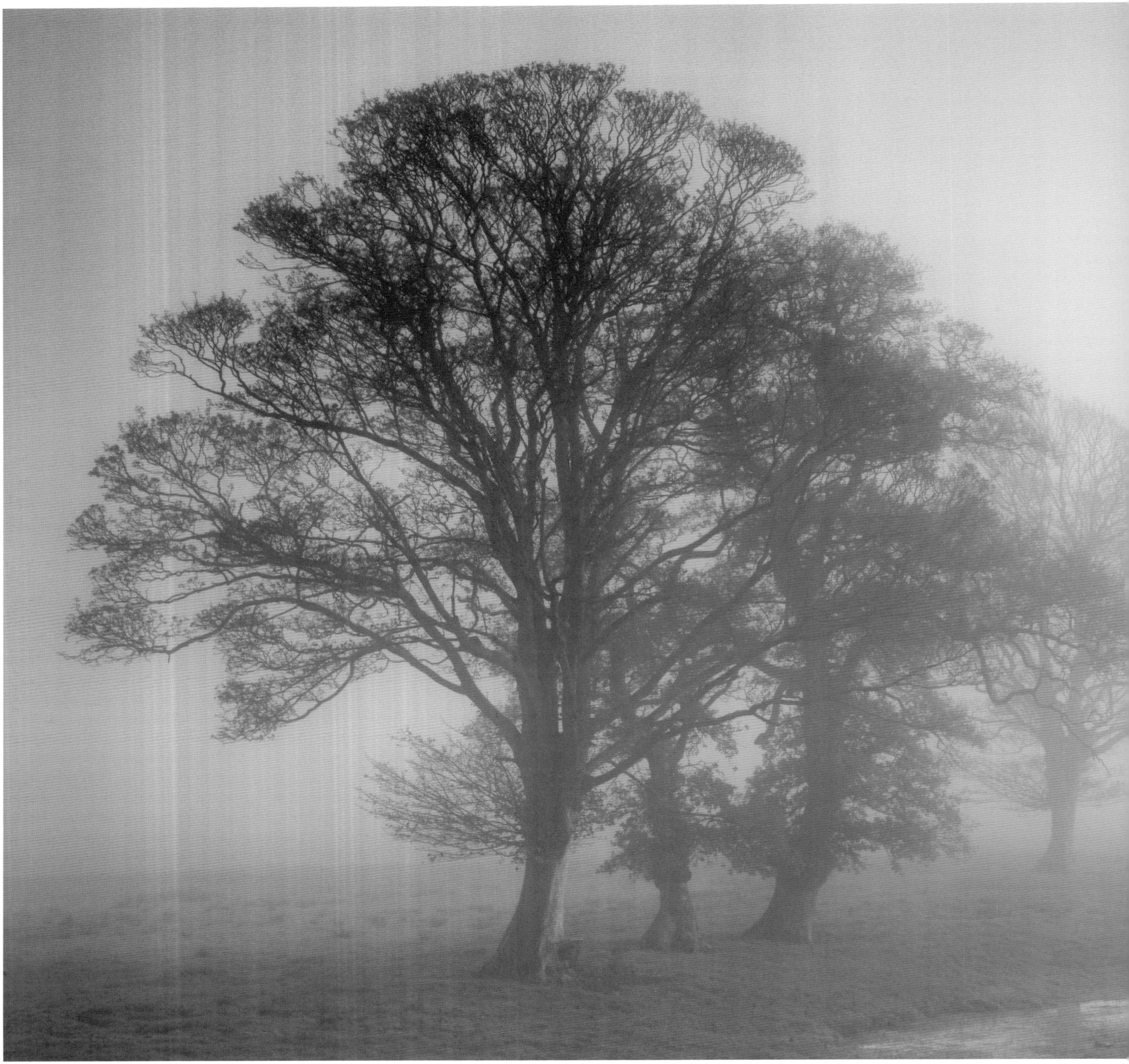

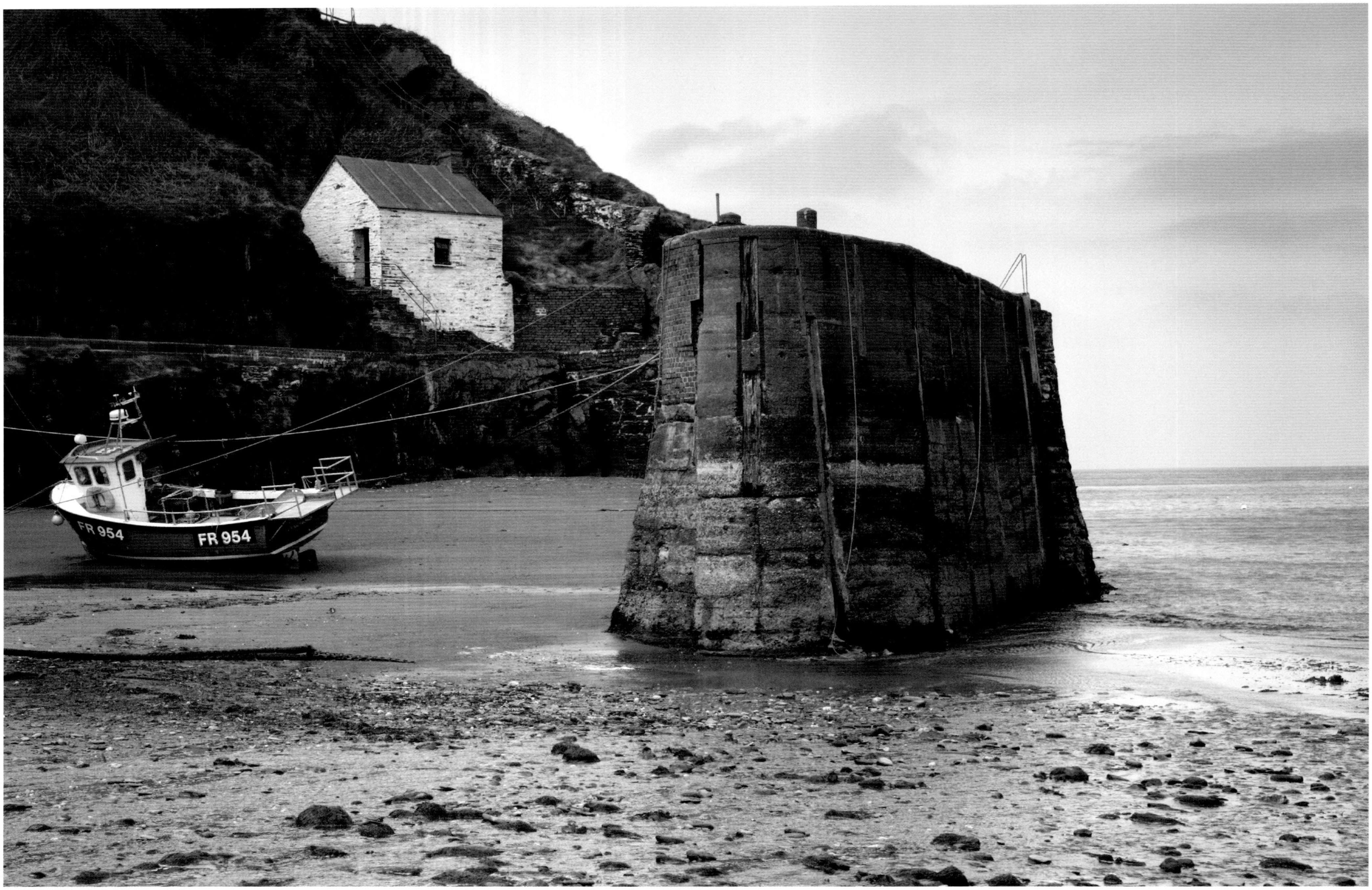

06 PORTHGAIN HARBOUR, PEMBROKESHIRE

Porthgain is a picturesque harbour village nestling into the rugged north coast of Pembrokeshire. During the tourist season it attracts more than its fair share of visitors, drawn by the prospect of a hearty, often bracing, walk along the cliff-tops, culminating perhaps in a well deserved pint and a spot of lunch. An after dinner slump is enlivened by a leisurely browse around the resident art galleries: a perfect way to let a few hours slip from your grasp.

For all its tourist credentials though Porthgain is a busy working harbour, landing lobster, crab and other shellfish. Evidence of this endeavour is everywhere to see; stacked lobster pots, waterproof leggings, ropes and buoys. What particularly drew me was the industrious relationship of the fishing boats, the whitewashed harbourmaster's house and the imposing and indestructible breakwater. (Map A5)

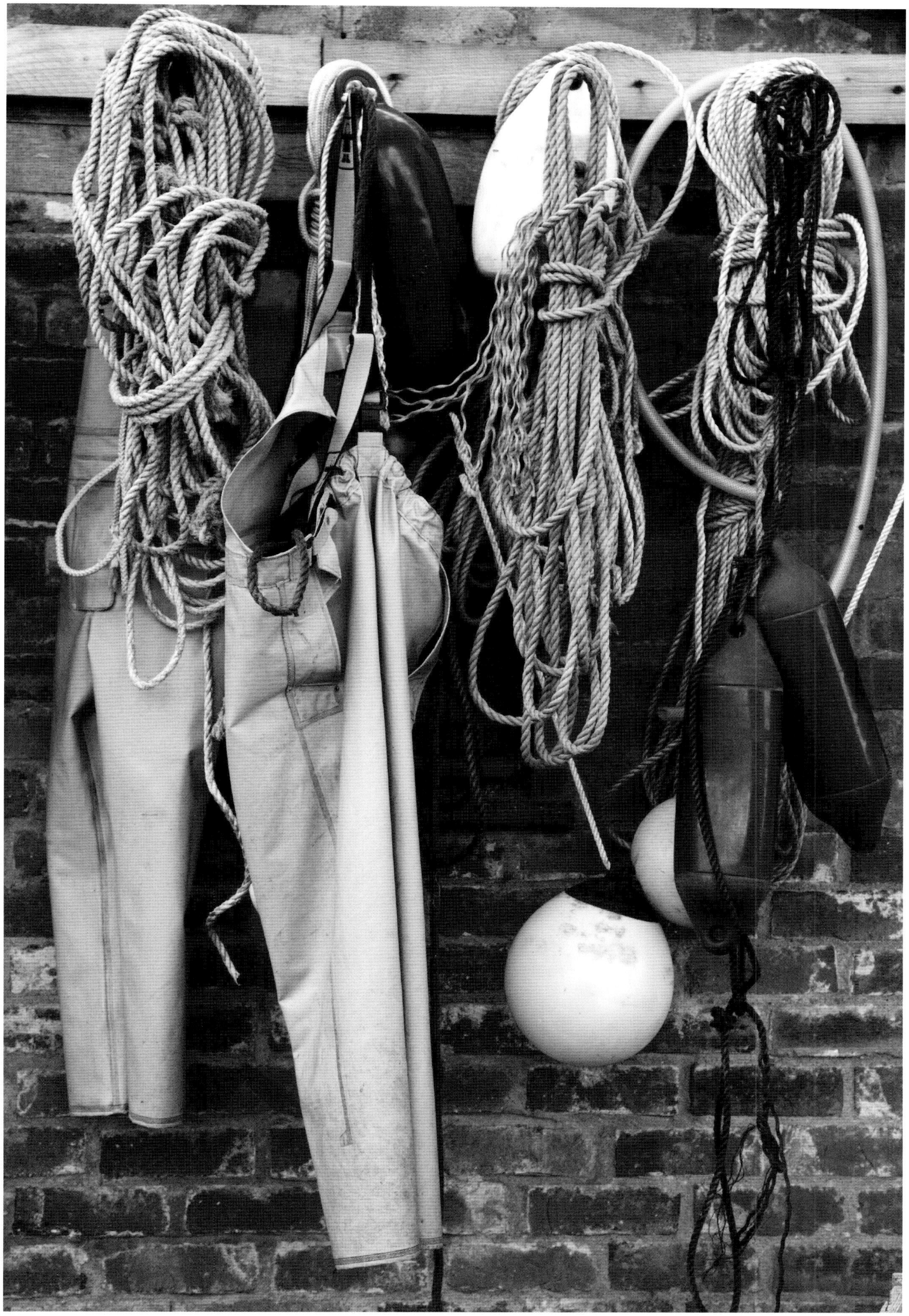

06 Porthgain Harbour, Pembrokeshire

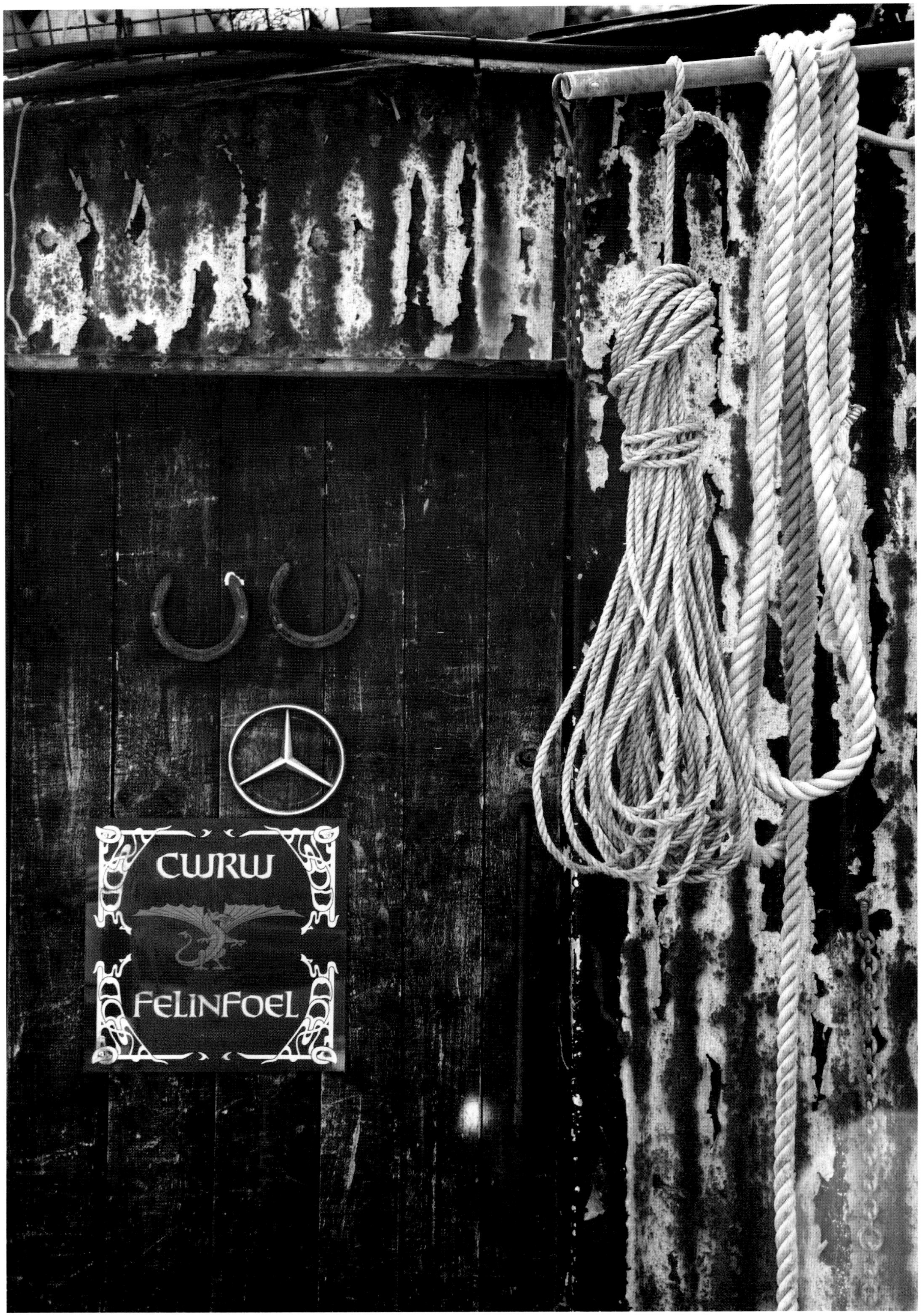
CWRW
FELINFOEL

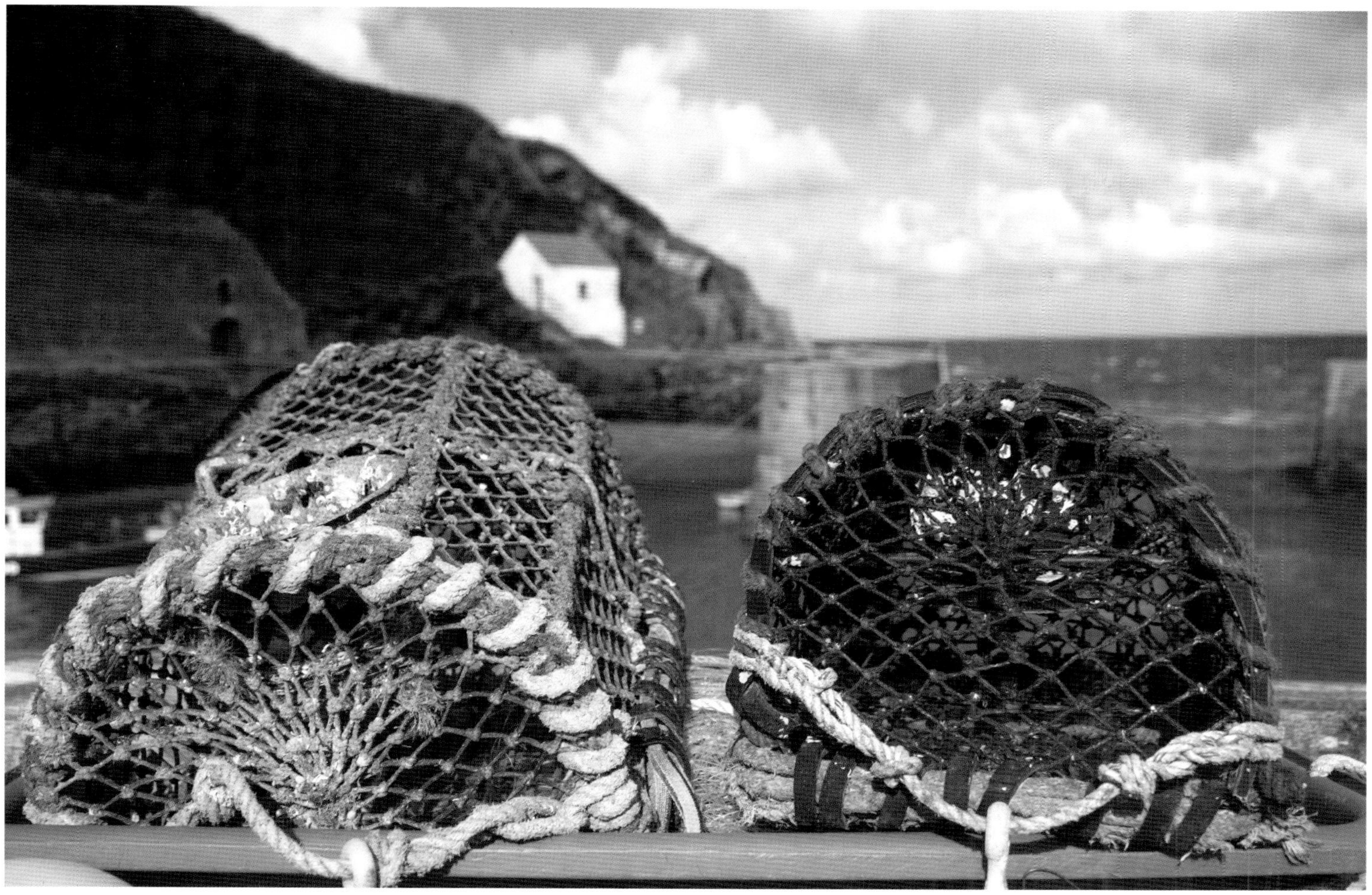

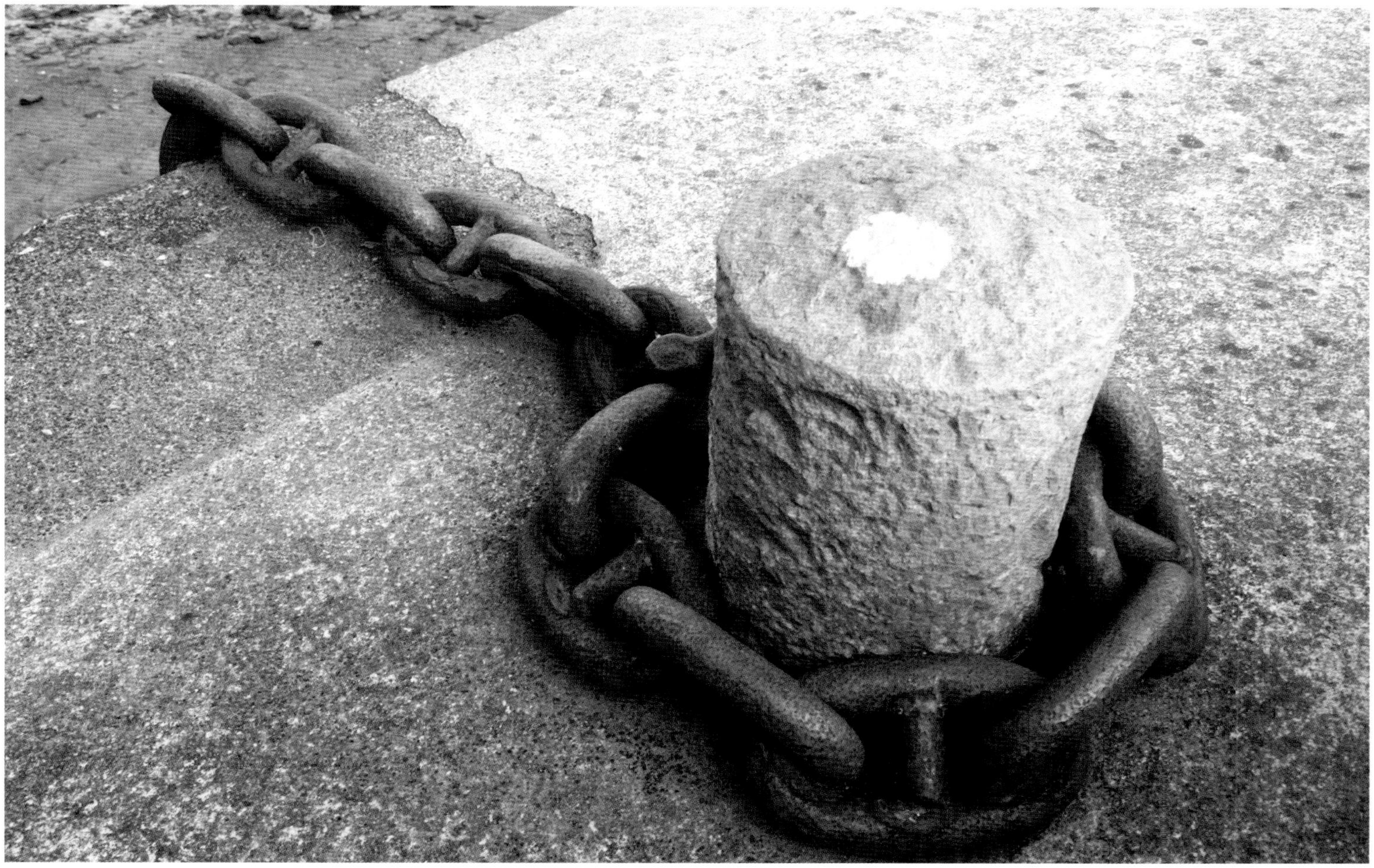

06 Porthgain Harbour, Pembrokeshire

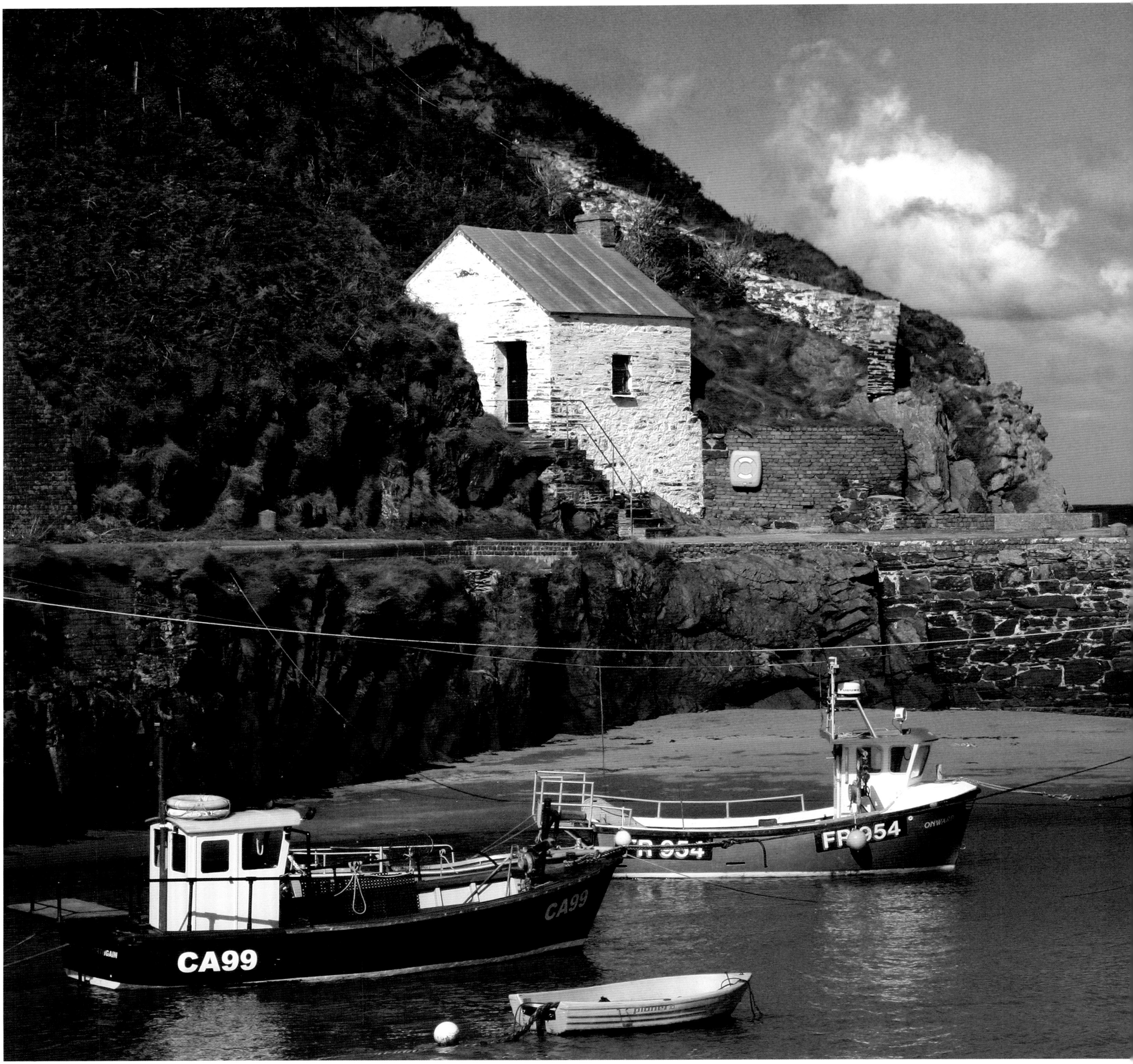
CA99
CA99
FR954
ONWARD

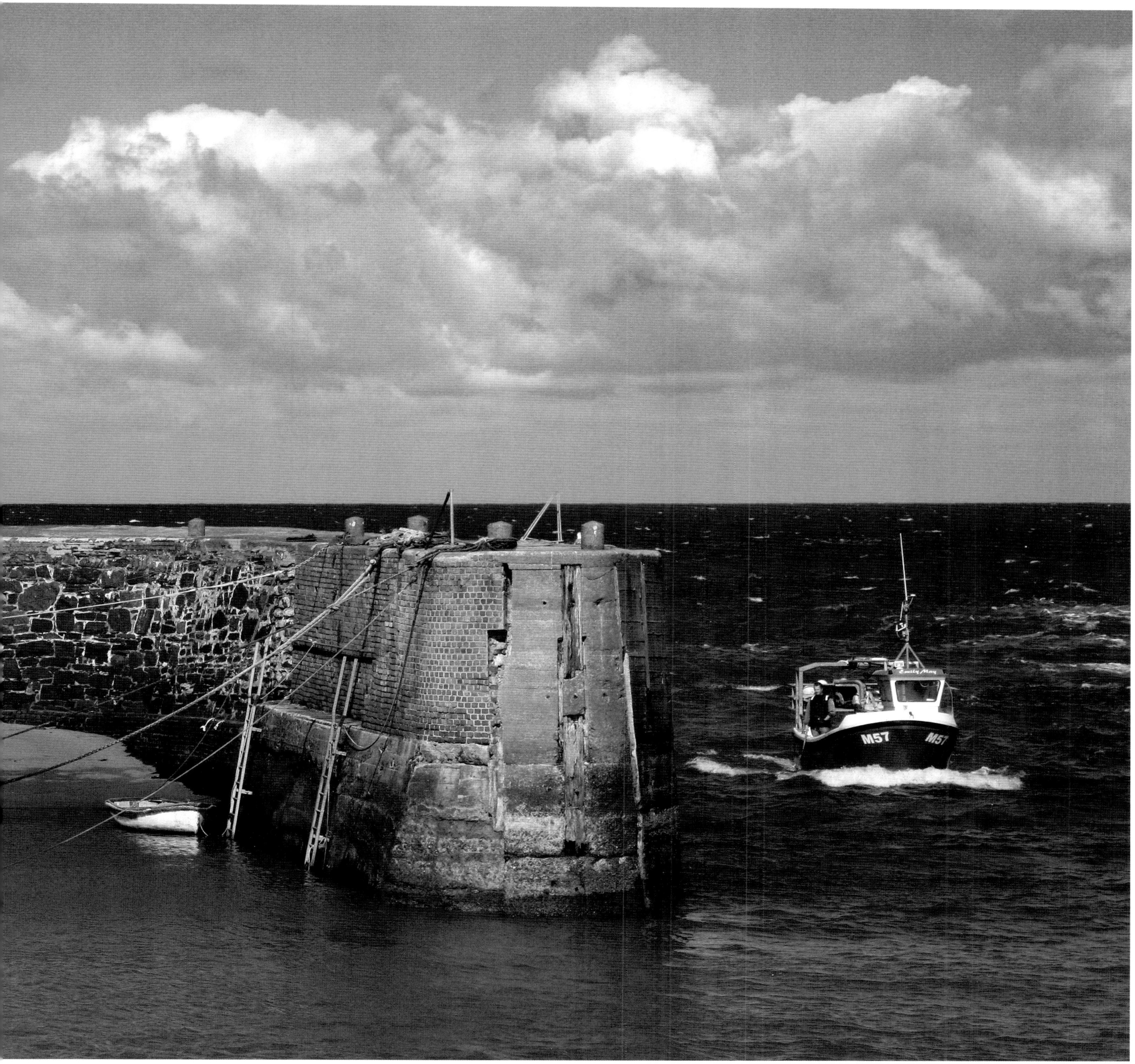

06 Porthgain Harbour, Pembrokeshire

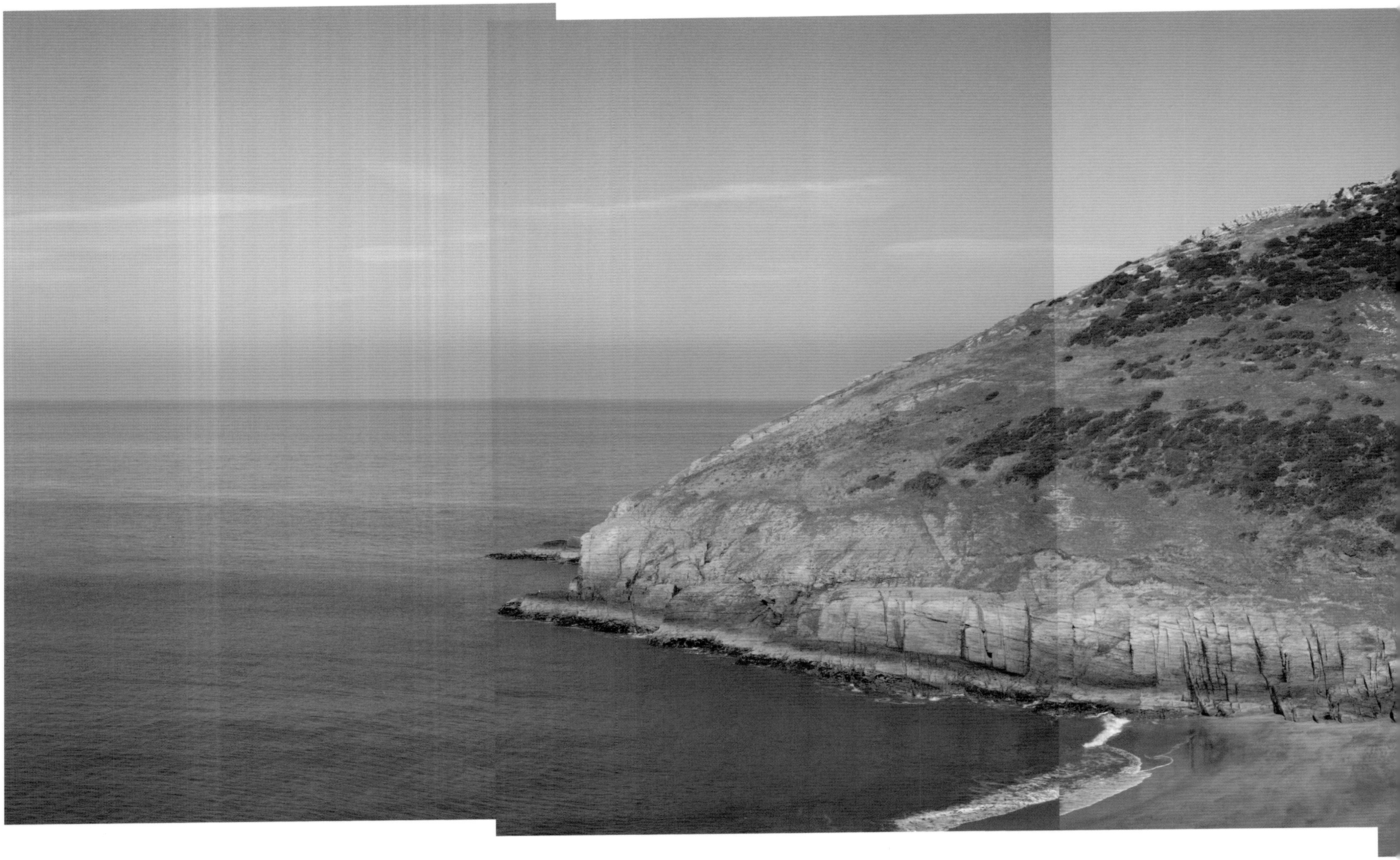

07 MWNT, CEREDIGION

Approaching Eglwys y Grog at Mwnt you get a real sense of what a medieval pilgrim must have felt like, making his way over the hill towards St Davids. Foot-sore and weary, Eglwys y Grog would have provided rest and sustenance for the onward journey to the city.

There is a splendid isolation to this ancient building, evoking a mystical Christian aura. Its whitewashed exterior huddles for shelter behind a sturdy earth and stone enclosure. Its stark white walls form powerful shapes in the landscape, lending themselves perfectly to monochrome photography.

Behind the church looms the hill known as Foel y Mwnt. In 1155 a force of Flemings landed nearby. Never the most welcome of visitors in those days, they were put to the sword by local warriors. Legend has it that their bones lie just beneath the surface of the sandy headland, which might explain the dog I saw digging furiously! (Map B5)

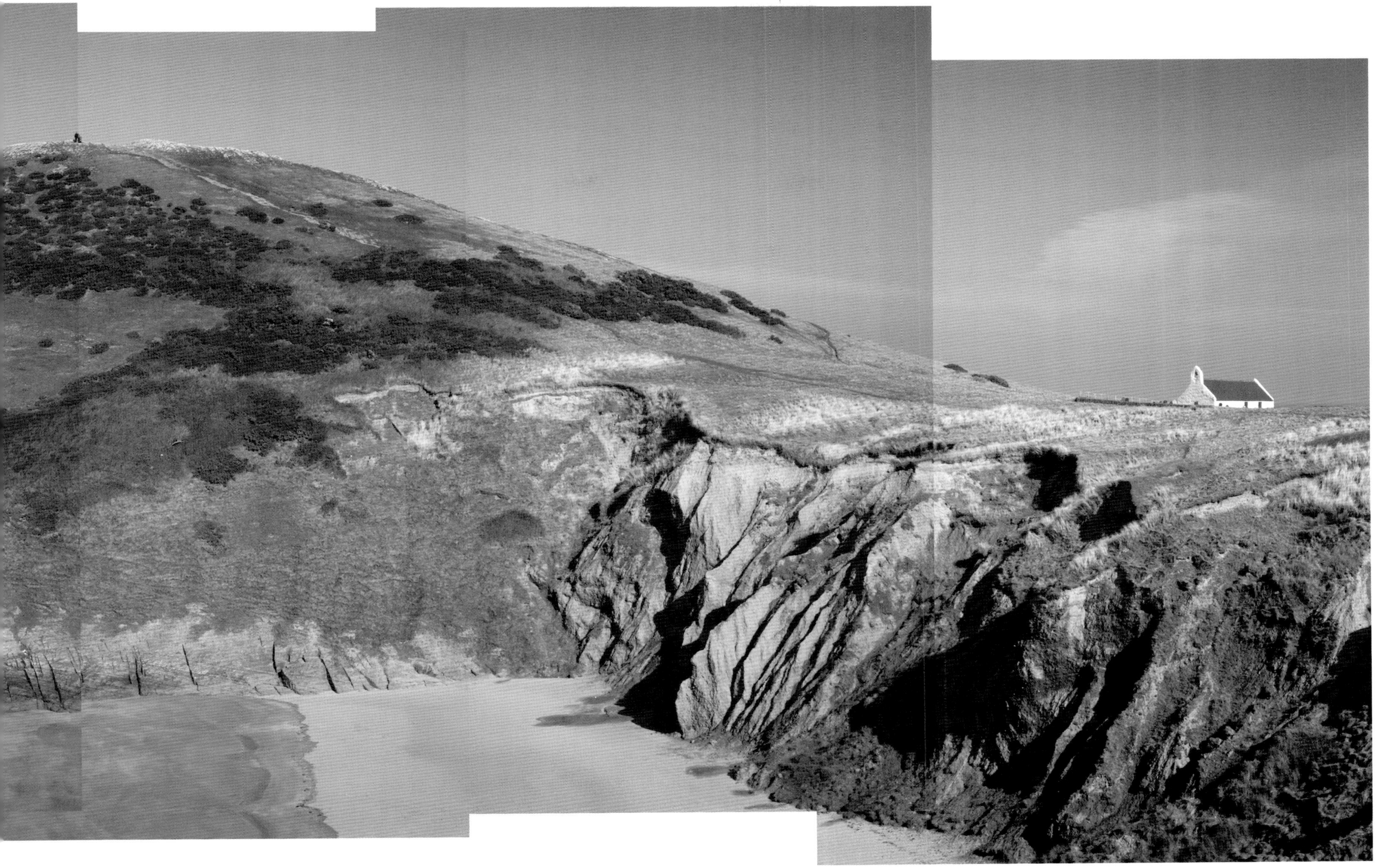

Foel y Mwnt, Eglwys y Grog and the beach at Mwnt

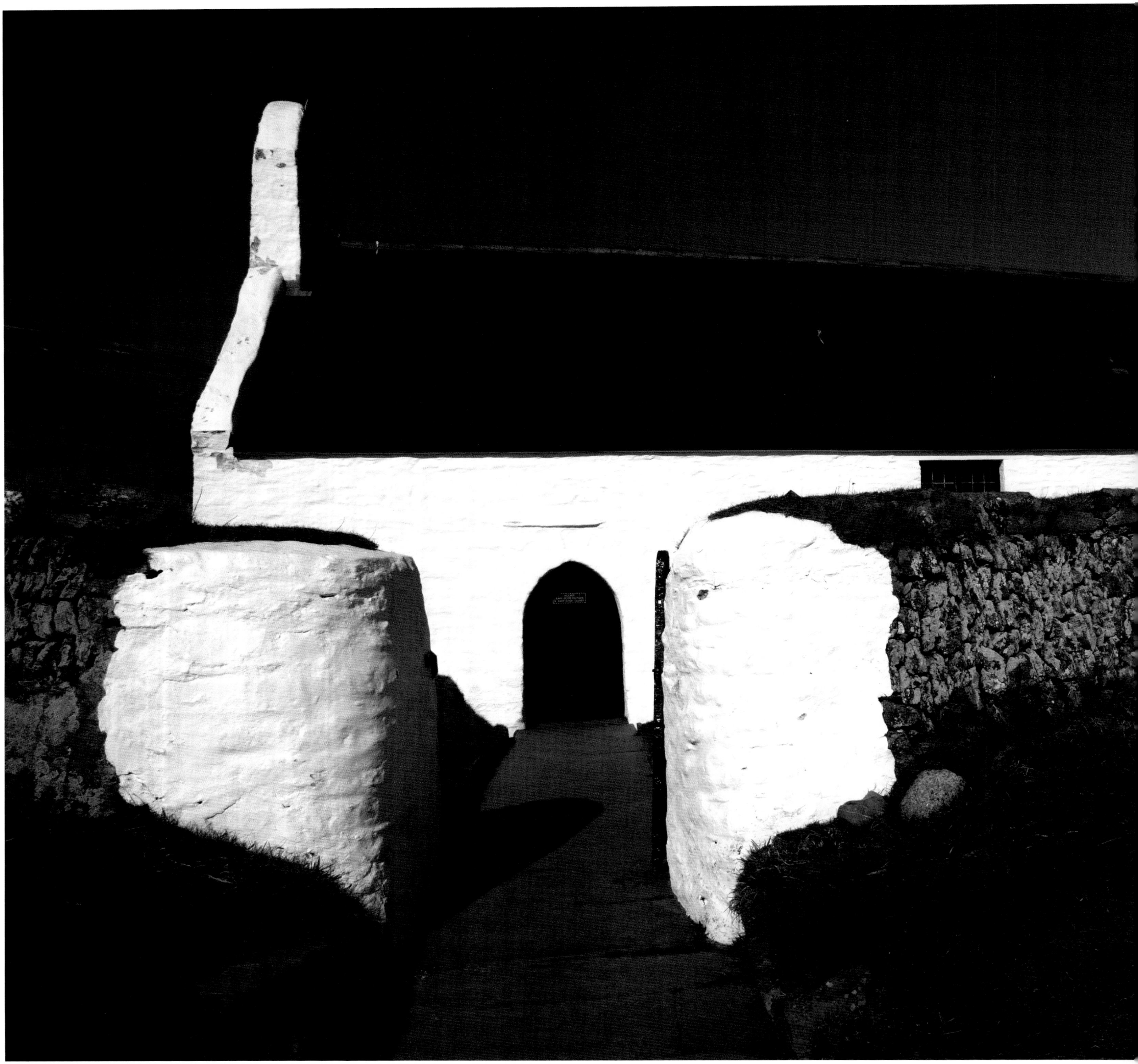

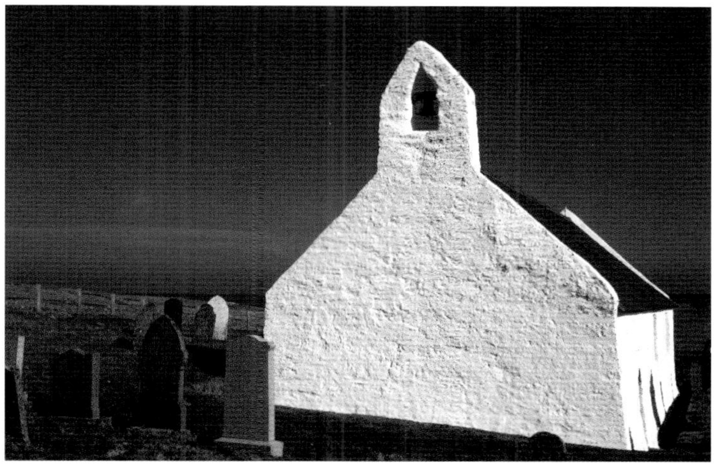

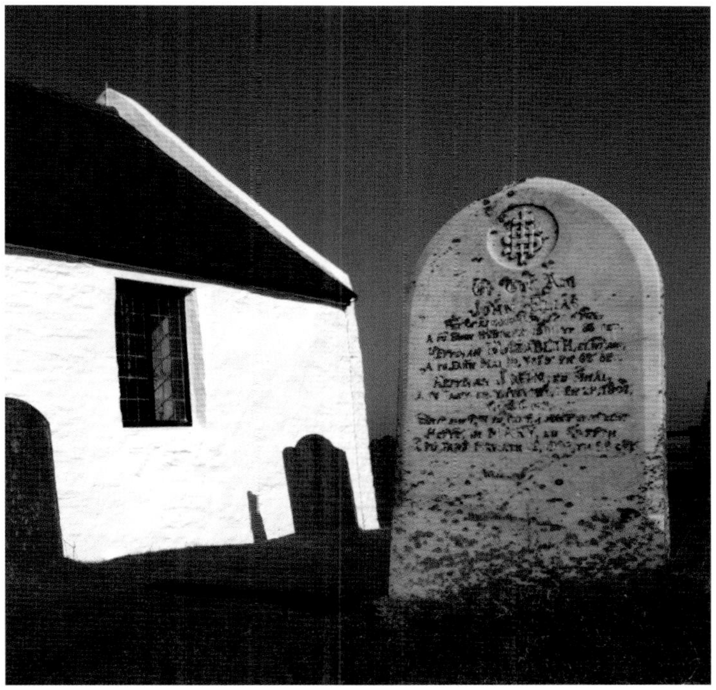

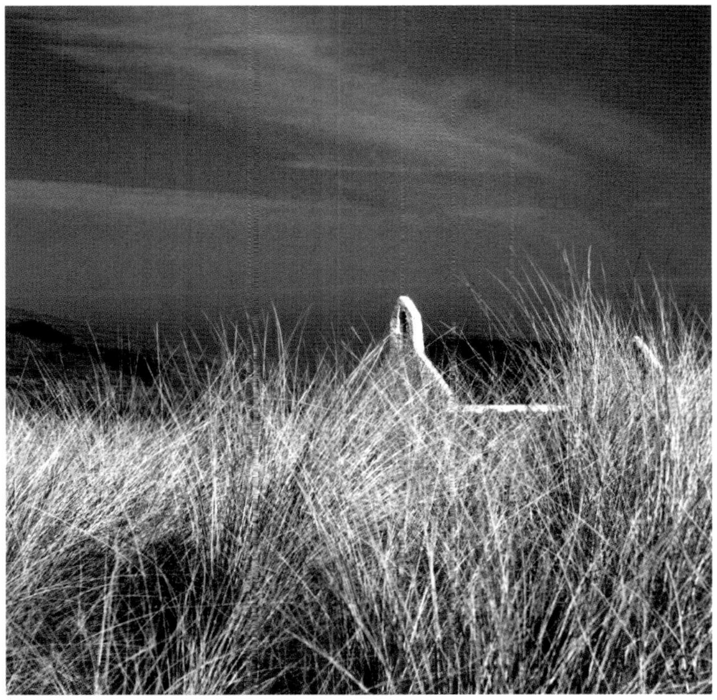

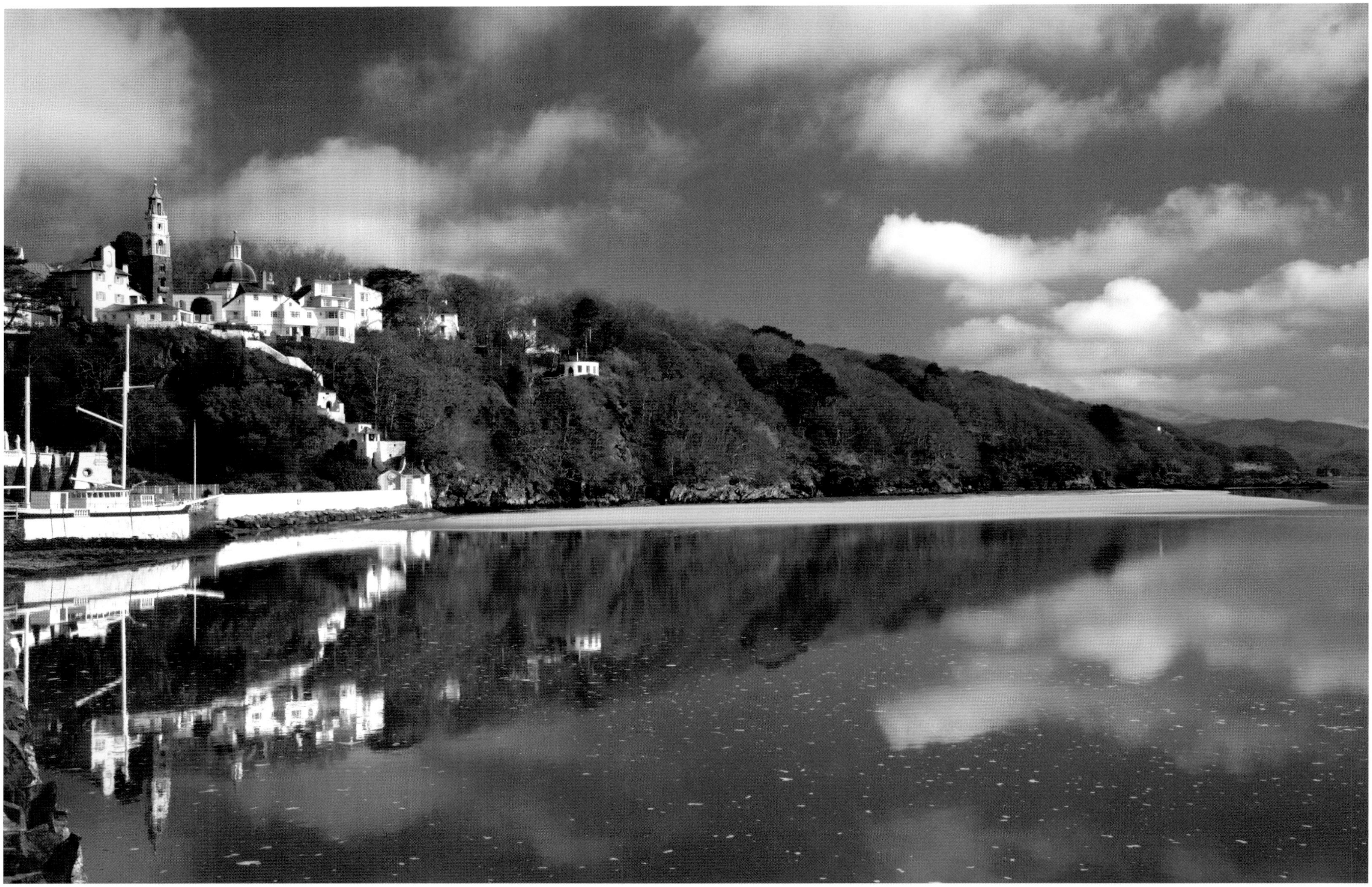

08 PORTMEIRION VILLAGE, SNOWDONIA

I was born in the mid-1960s and have vague recollections of *The Prisoner*, starring Patrick McGoohan and mostly involving large inflatable white balls rolling along the sands of the estuary. Suffice it to say I was a bit too young to get it. Set in the fantastical Italianate surroundings of Clough Williams-Ellis's Portmeirion, it was one of the iconic TV programmes of the era.

For the Welsh it is almost an expected act of homage to visit Portmeirion. It sits there in the national psyche along with Snowdon and other must-see destinations. I happened to visit the day before the annual *Prisoner* convention, where devotees of the programme descend on this enclave of unreality to meet like-minded fans. I found it all very intriguing; hoards of people with their fervent love for a TV show aired decades ago. I also found Portmeirion fascinating. It is a place that defies categorisation and is unlike any other place I have ever visited, which made for a confusing yet enjoyable day out.

Having toured Tuscany and married in Amalfi, near Naples, I welcomed the opportunity to immerse myself in the sensation, if not the actuality, of Italy and perhaps re-ignite some memories. From so many angles it felt very Italian, which really lifted the spirits. All that was missing was the raucous Latin hustle and bustle. Some describe it as being a touch wacky. Personally I thought of it as the beautiful realisation of one man's dream to create something truly memorable. (Map C2)

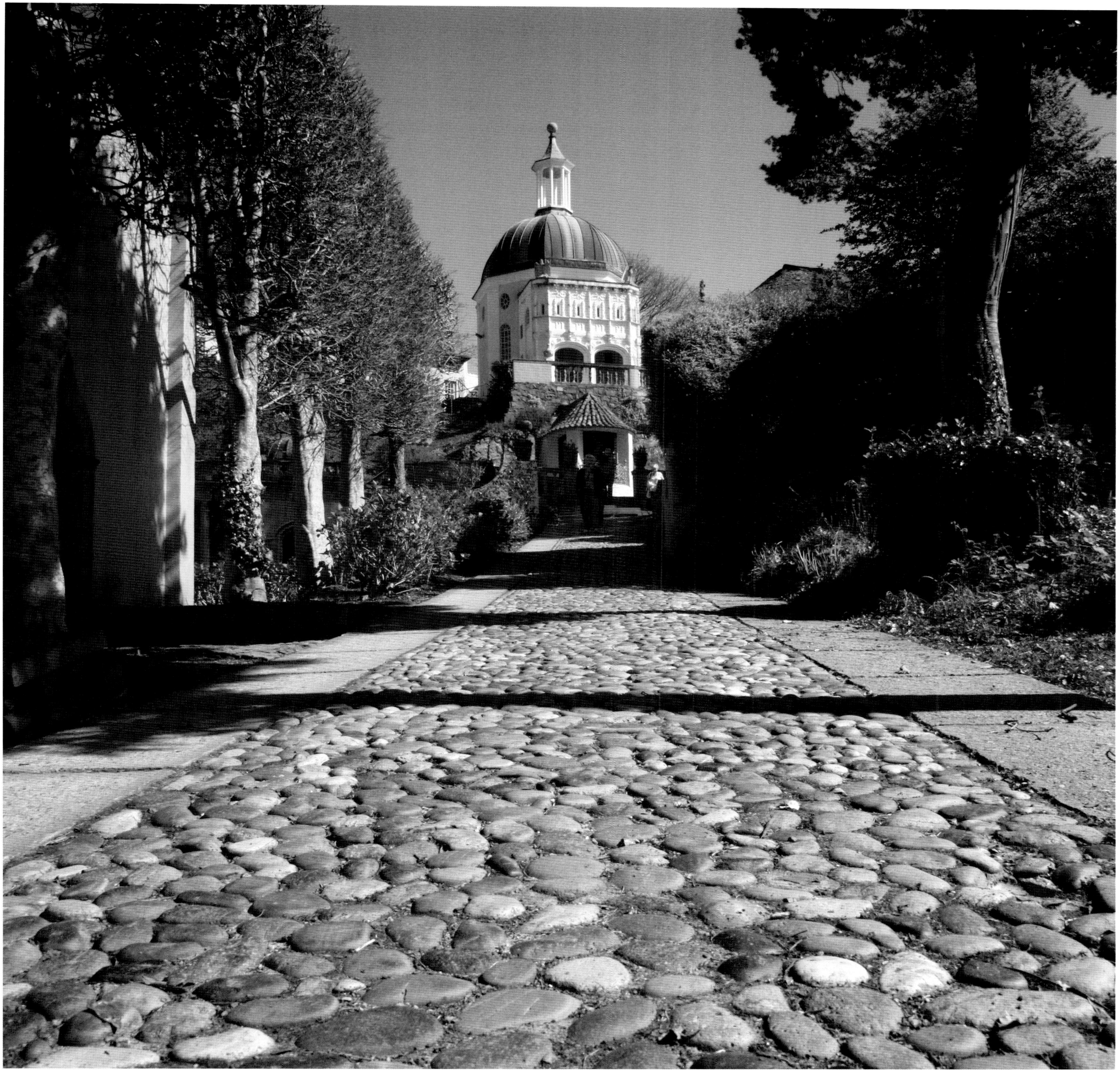

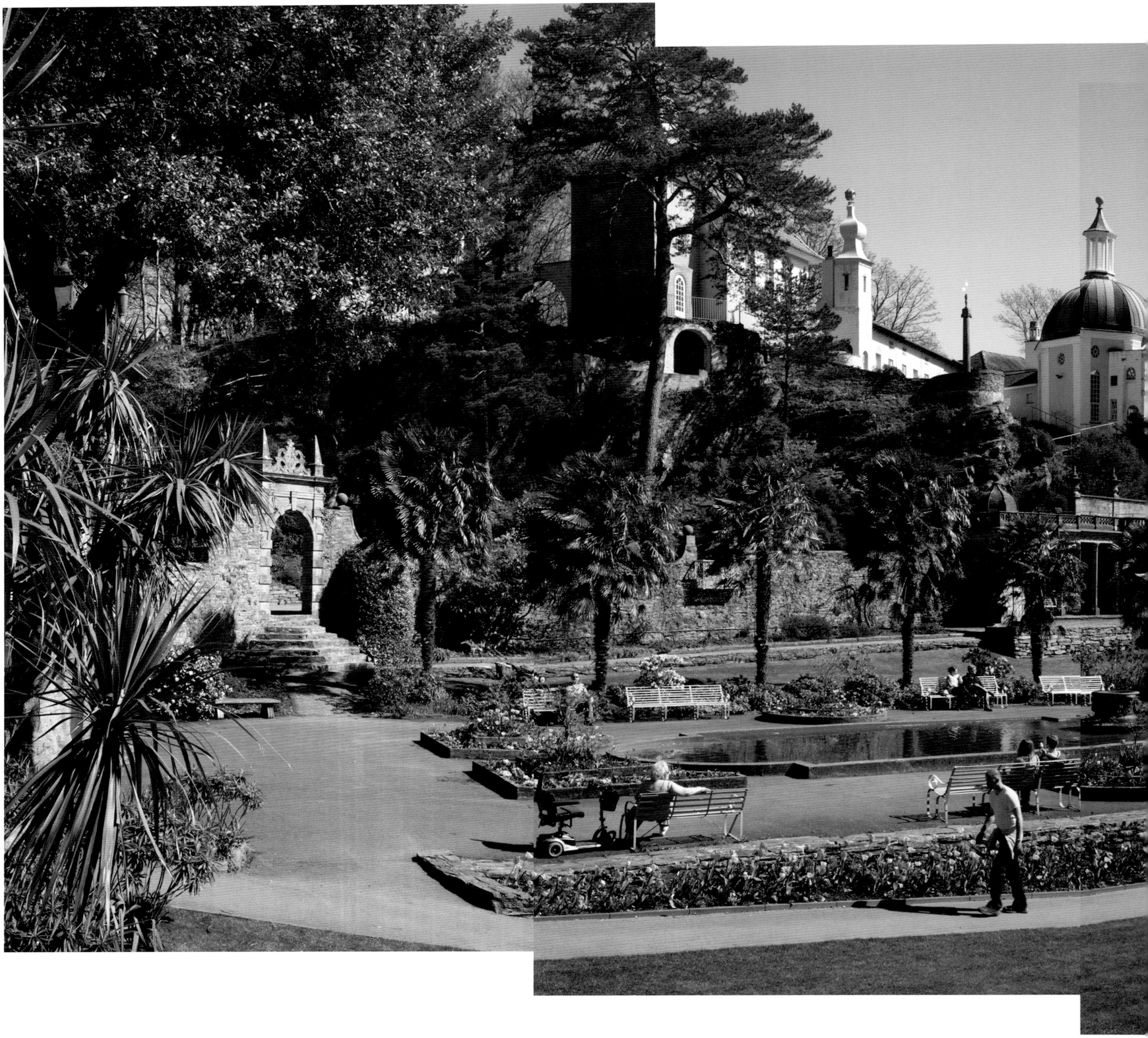

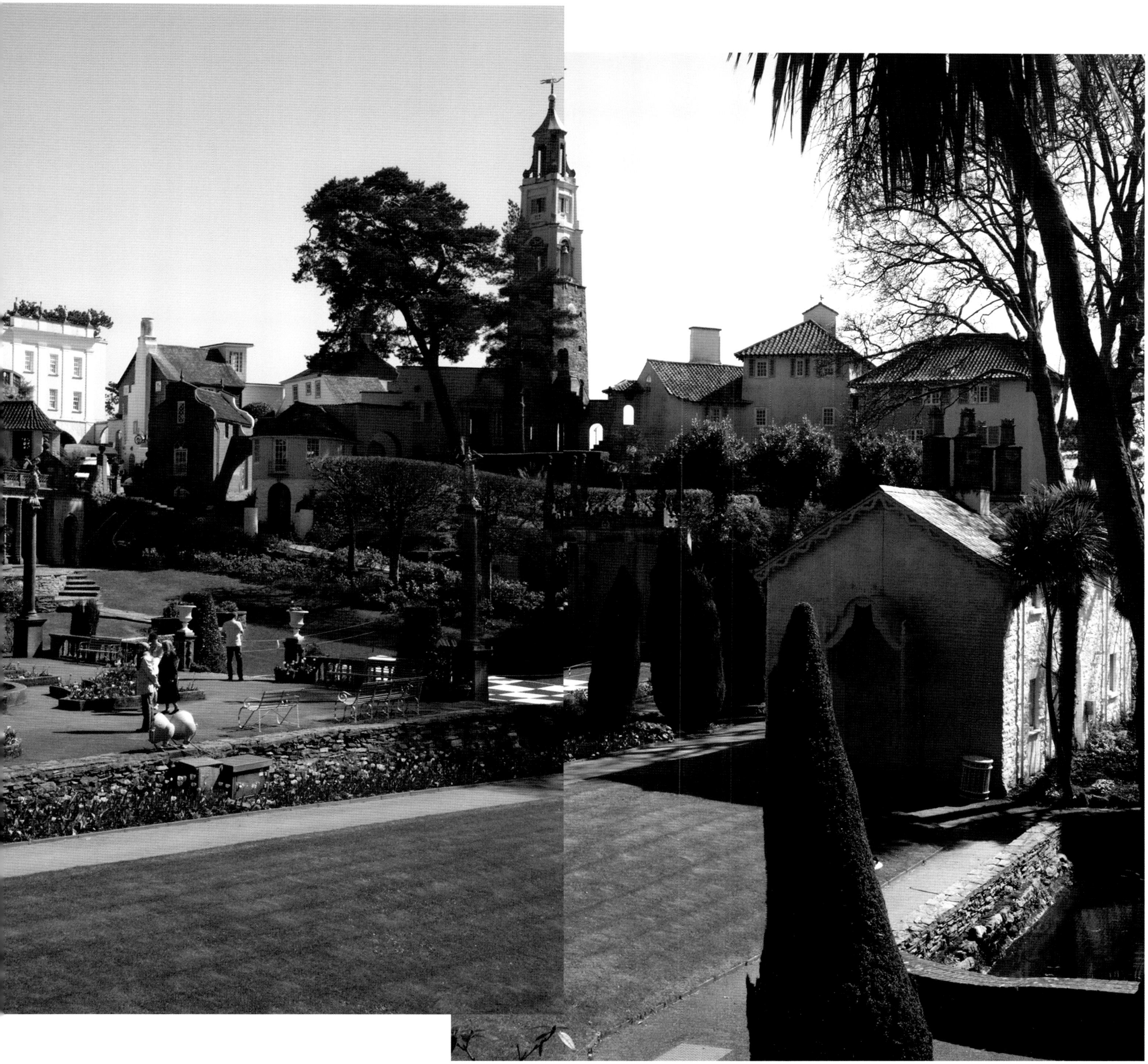

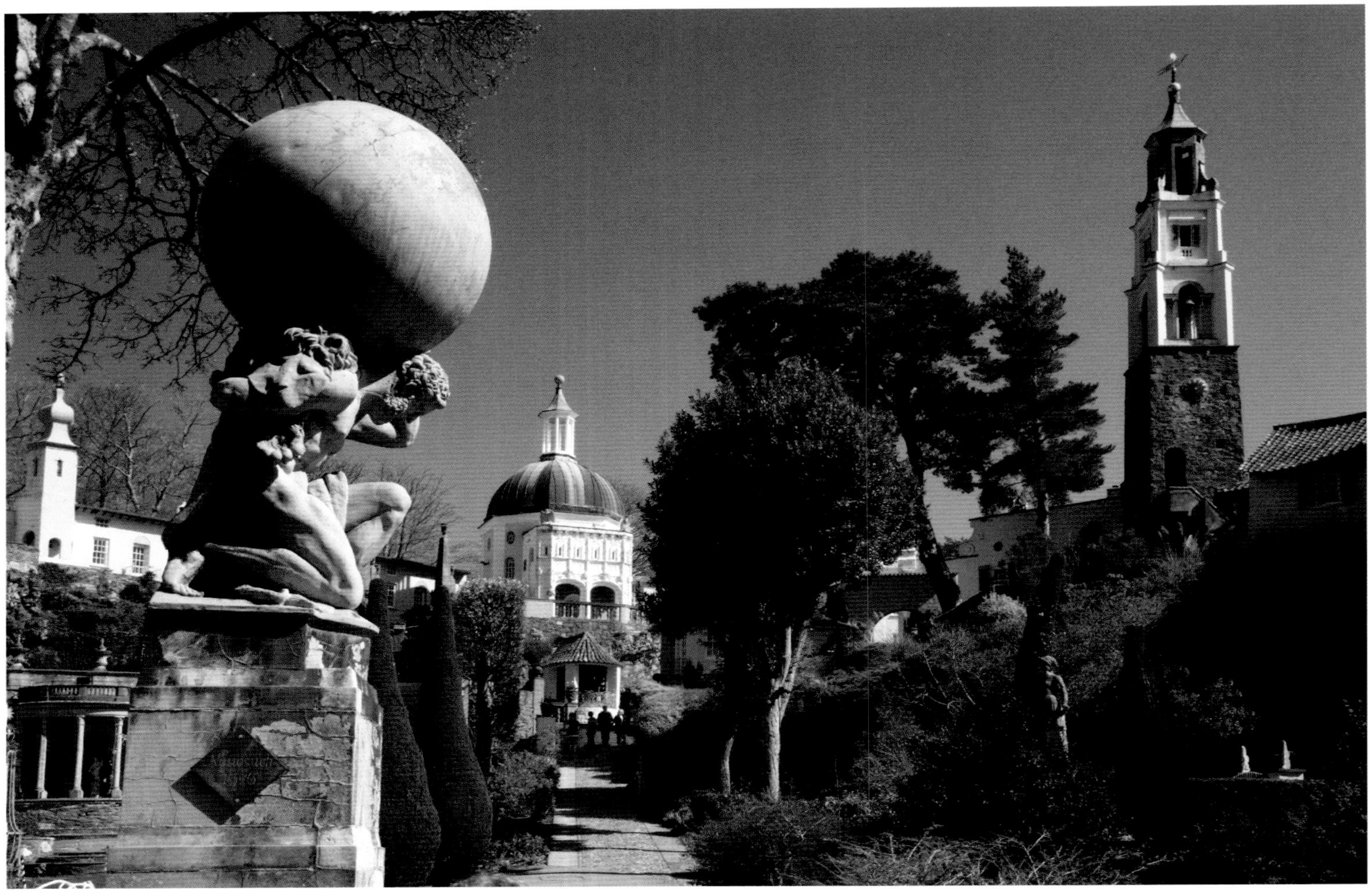

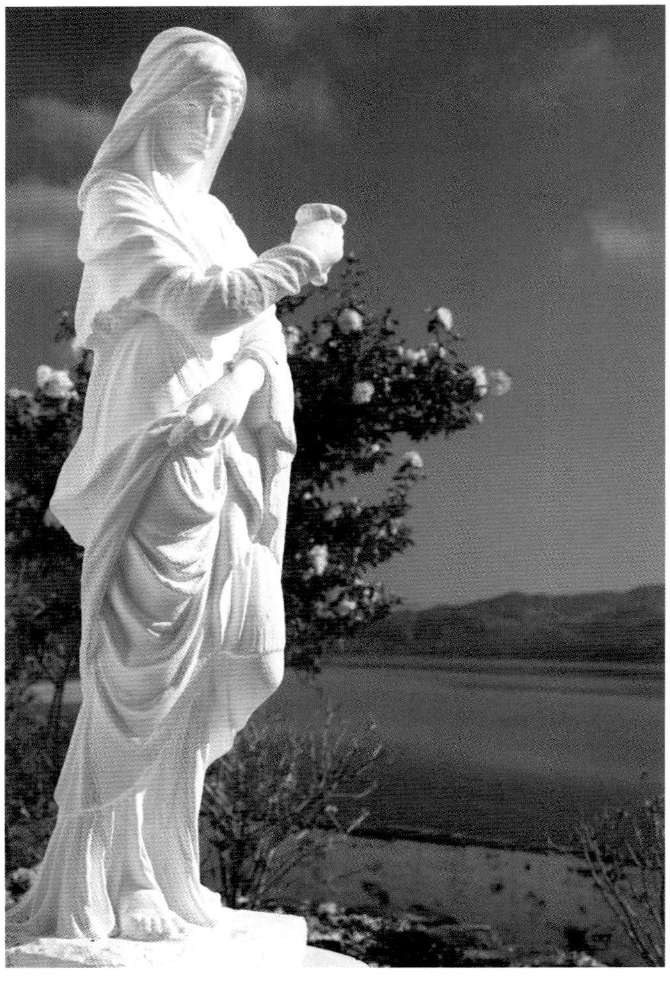

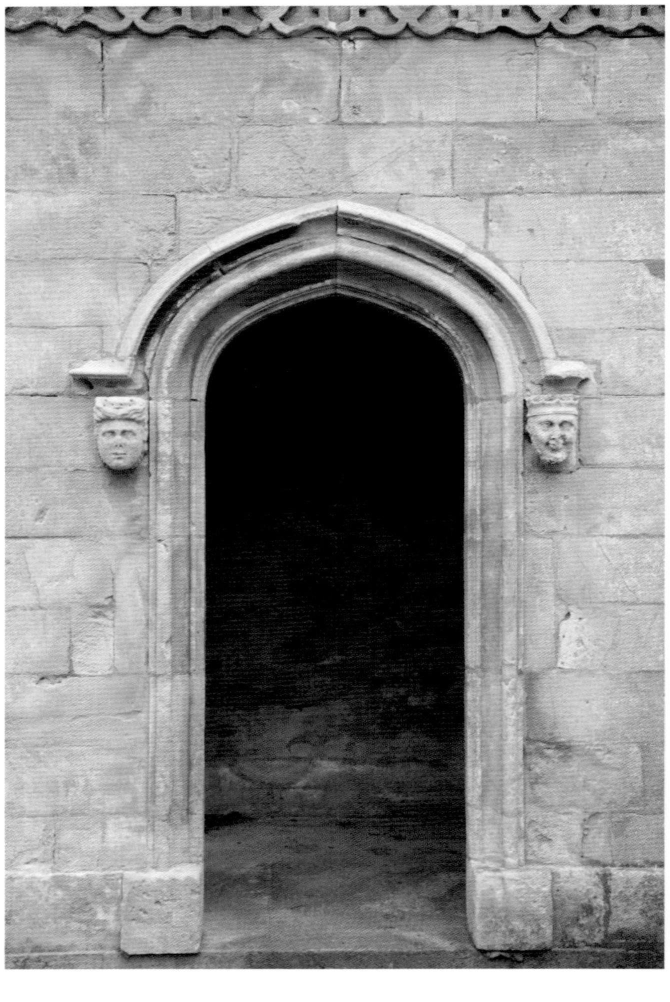

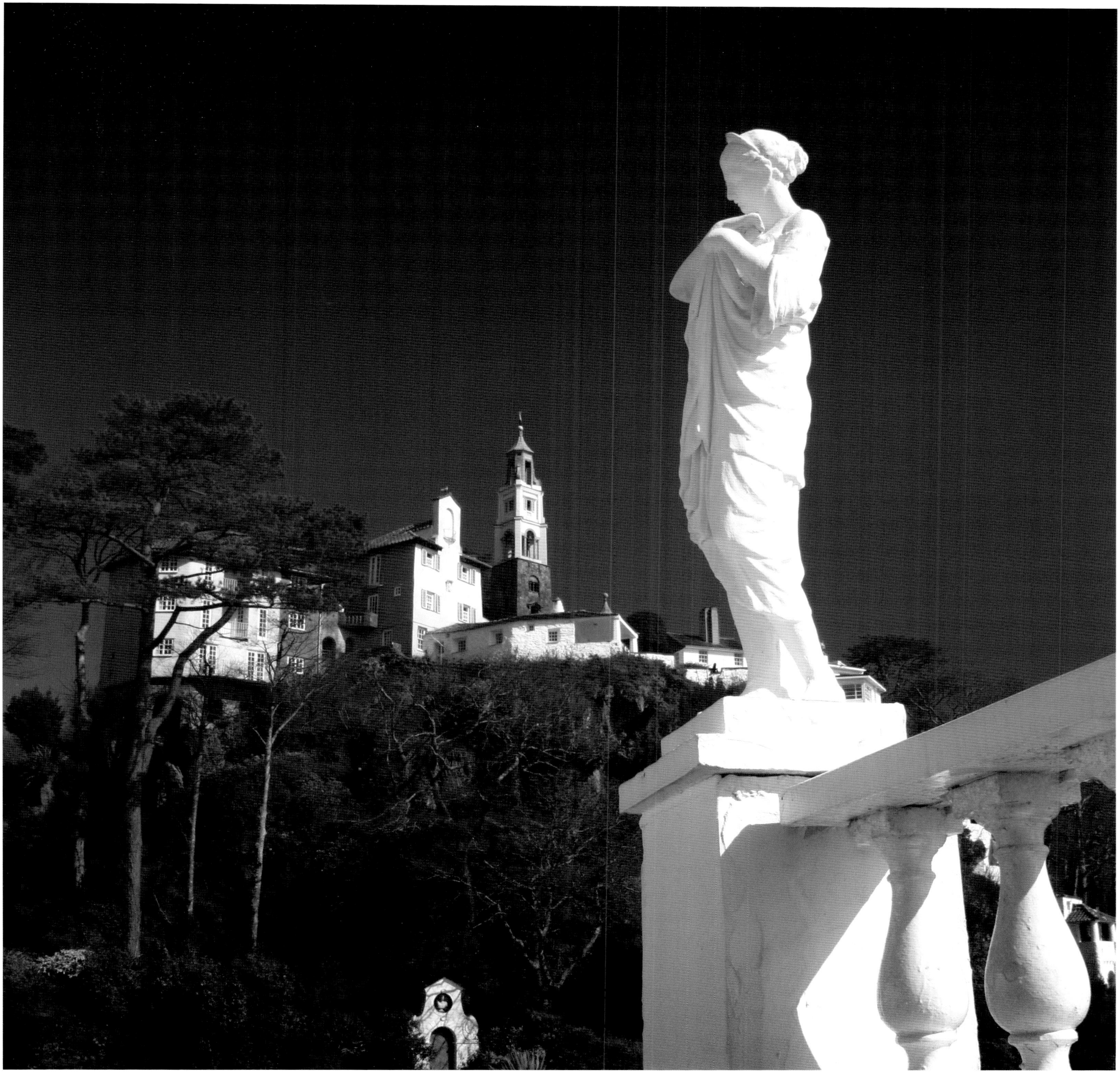

09 TOWARDS PEN Y FAN & CORN DU, BRECON BEACONS

It was a late winter's afternoon when I took this photo of Pen y Fan and Corn Du from many miles away on the neighbouring Black Mountain. A dark sky was threatening over the twin peaks while the patchwork of fields in the foreground basked in sunshine.

Taken with a long lens to compress the elements in the composition, I like the transition from managed farmland to untamed peaks. Images such as this work best in the winter months when the air is cleaner and long-range visibility good. (Map D5)

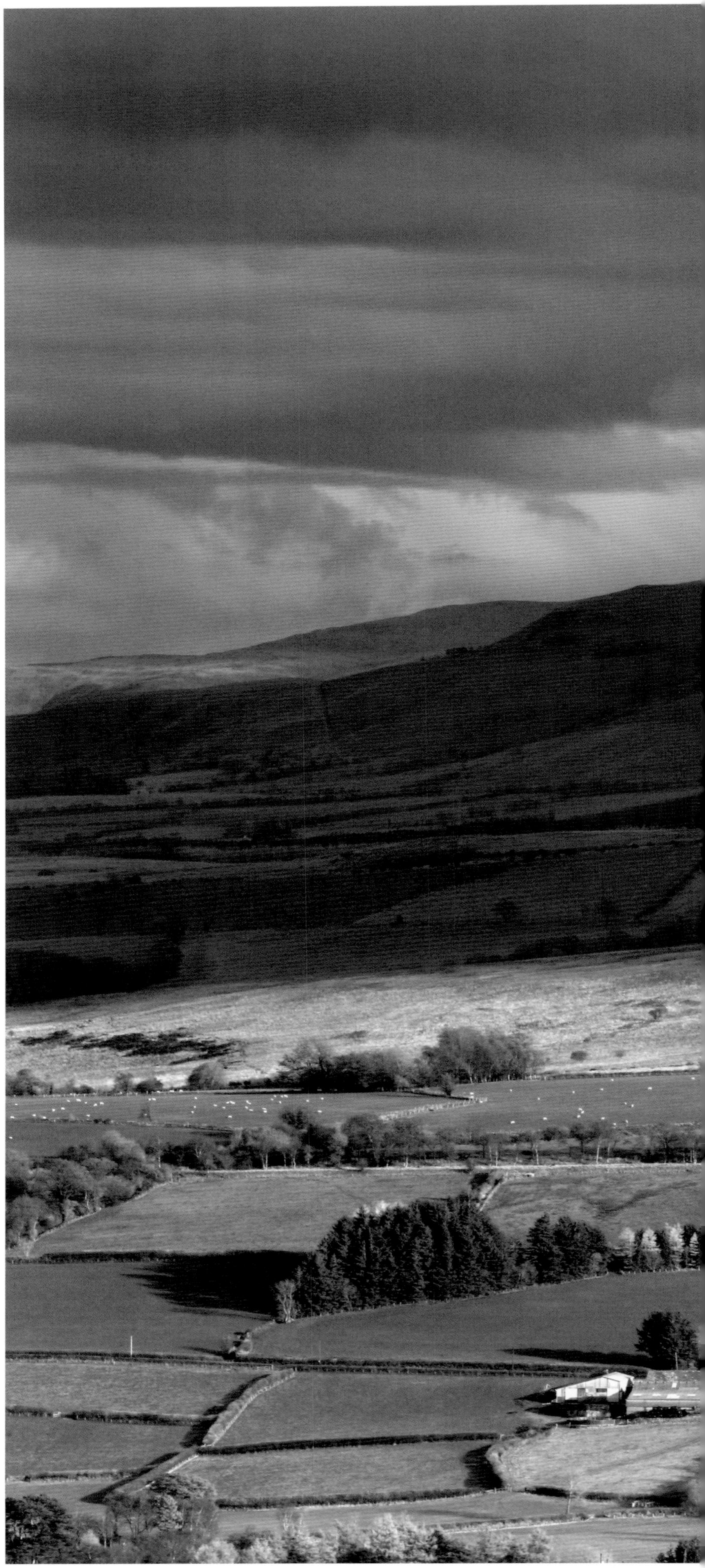

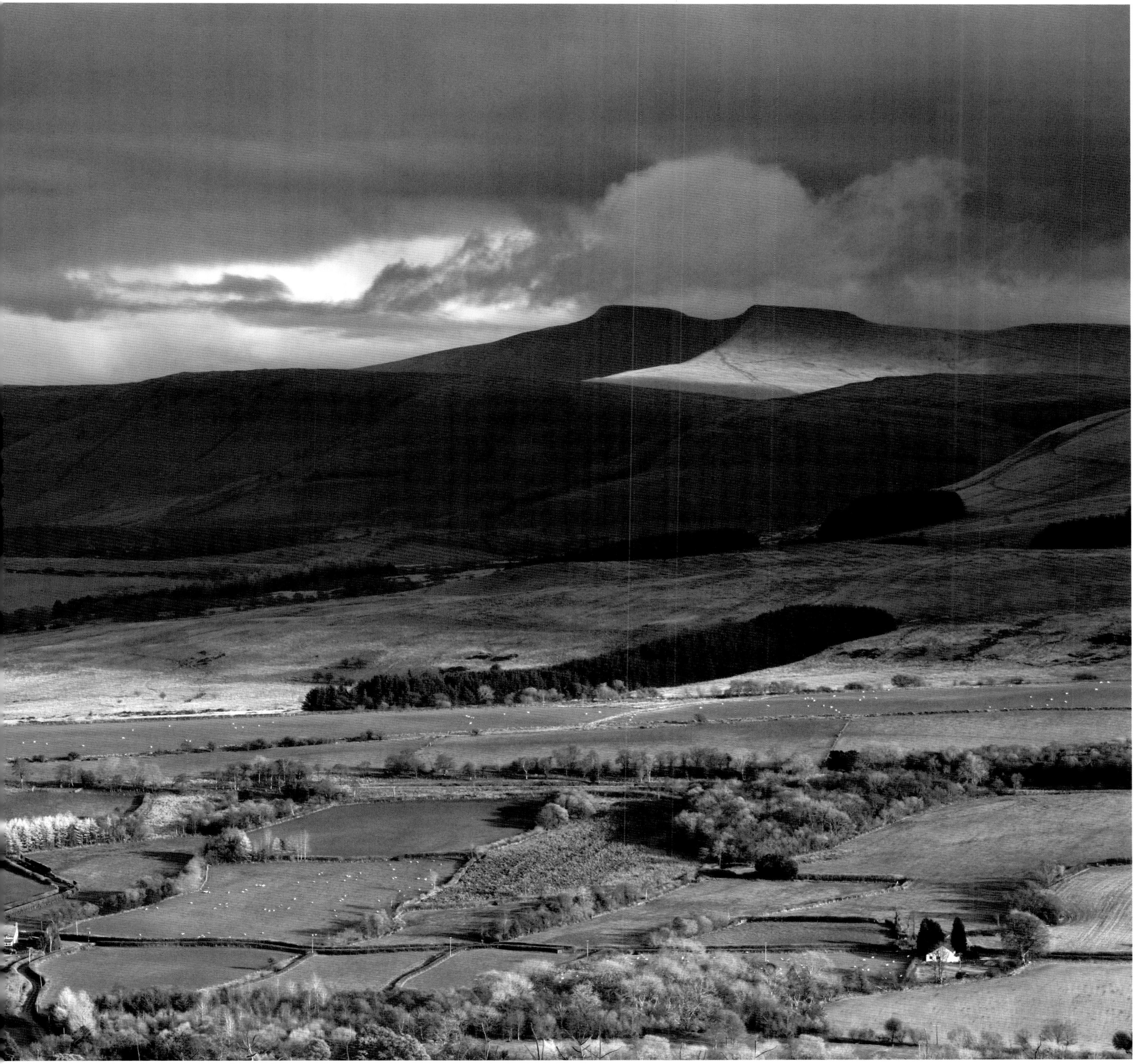

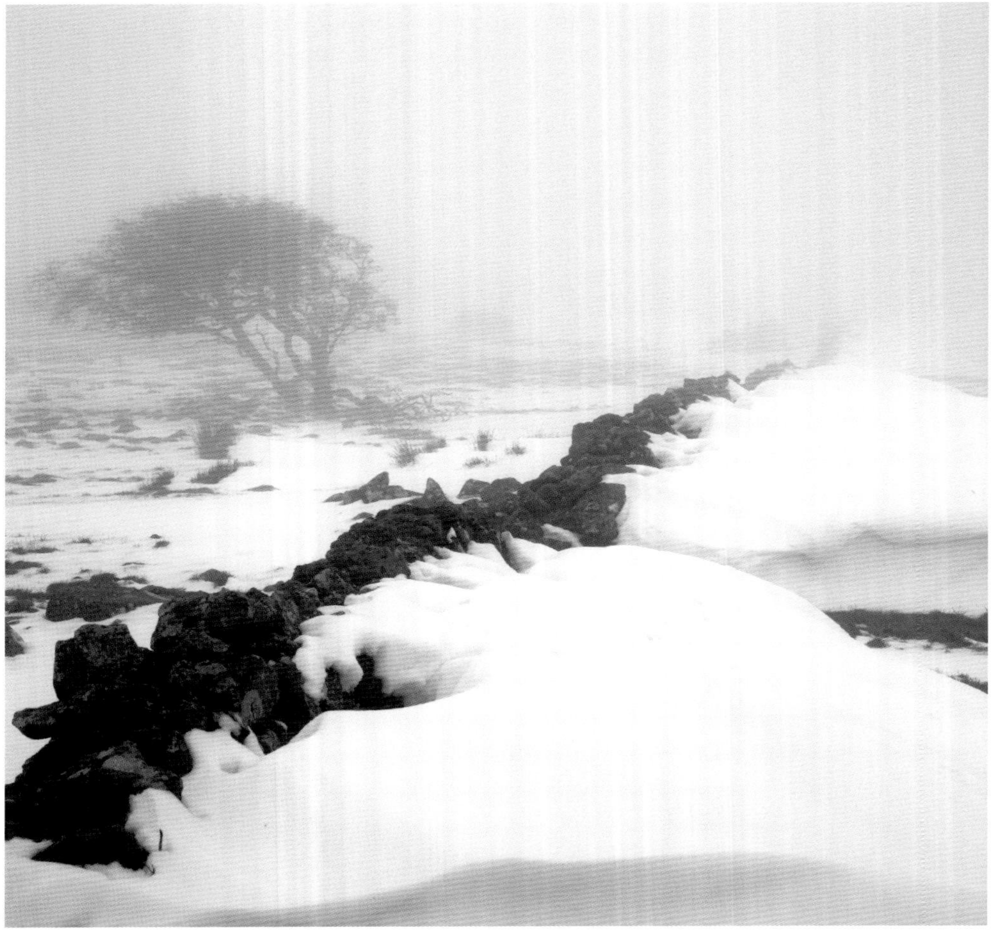

10 A PEMBROKESHIRE WINTER

Pembrokeshire is usually spared severe winters. It could be something to do with being a peninsula and having the Gulf Stream flowing by, but don't quote me on that. Consequently snow is something of an event; a bit of a novelty.

The image of Maenclochog village is timeless. The absence of cars or modern street signage makes it evocative of winter-time in the 1950s or just about any era during the past century. I was drawn to the three pine-ends seemingly connected to one another by the telegraph pole. The veil of mist shrouding this collection of images was a fortunate addition.

I returned to the 'Abandoned Farm' in the Preseli Hills which I had photographed three years previously. The intervening years had taken their toll, with the outbuilding attached to the house having almost entirely collapsed.

I happened upon a simple composition of a snow-drift, a dry-stone wall and a wind-bent tree: the Preseli Hills at their most desolate yet bleakly stunning.

A group of people emerging from a cluster of trees at Scolton Manor provided a useful scaling device. (Map B5)

Above: Snow-drift & dry-stone wall
Right: Maenclochog
Overleaf: The 'Abandoned Farm'
Pages 48–49: Scolton Manor

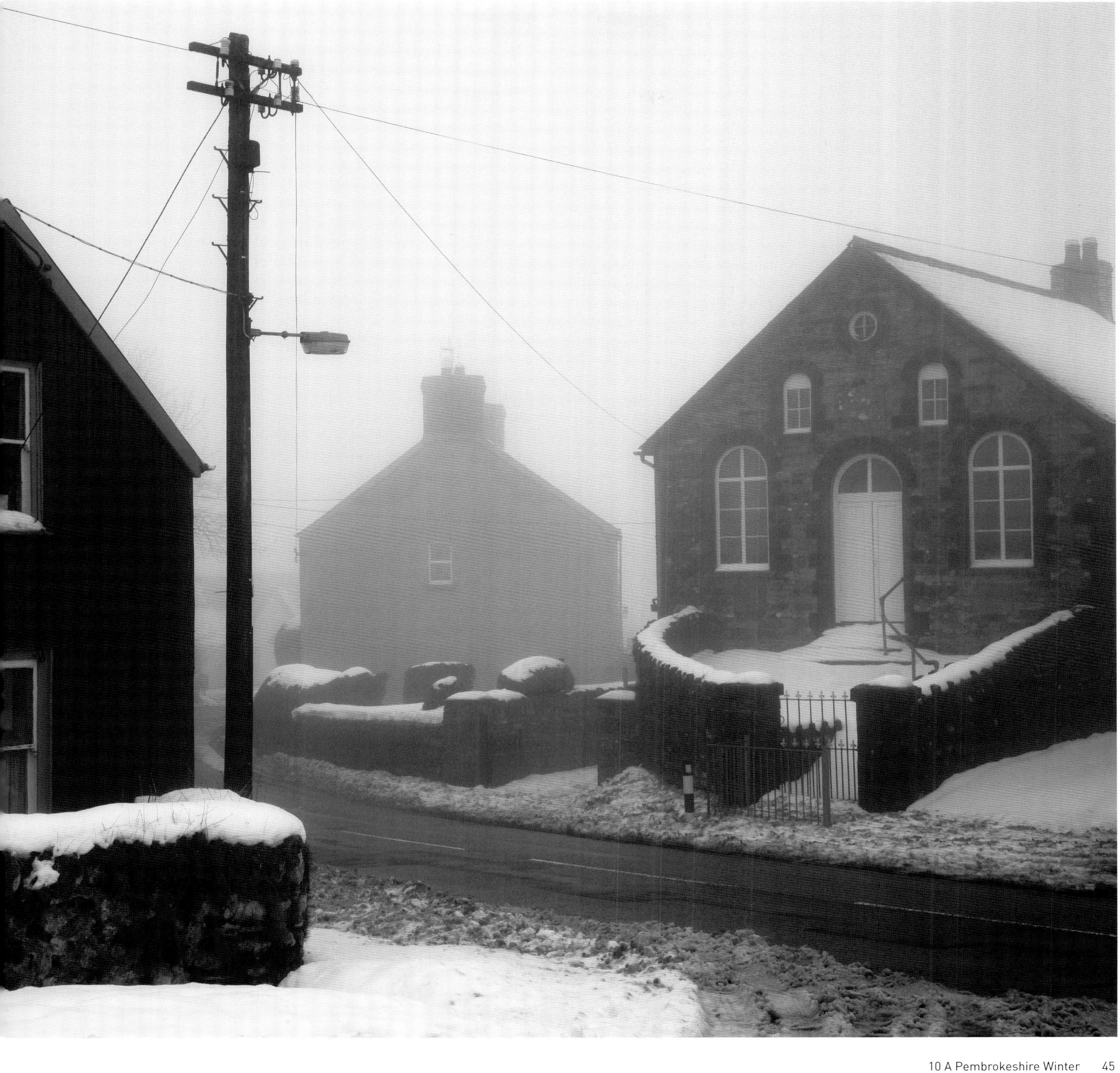

10 A Pembrokeshire Winter

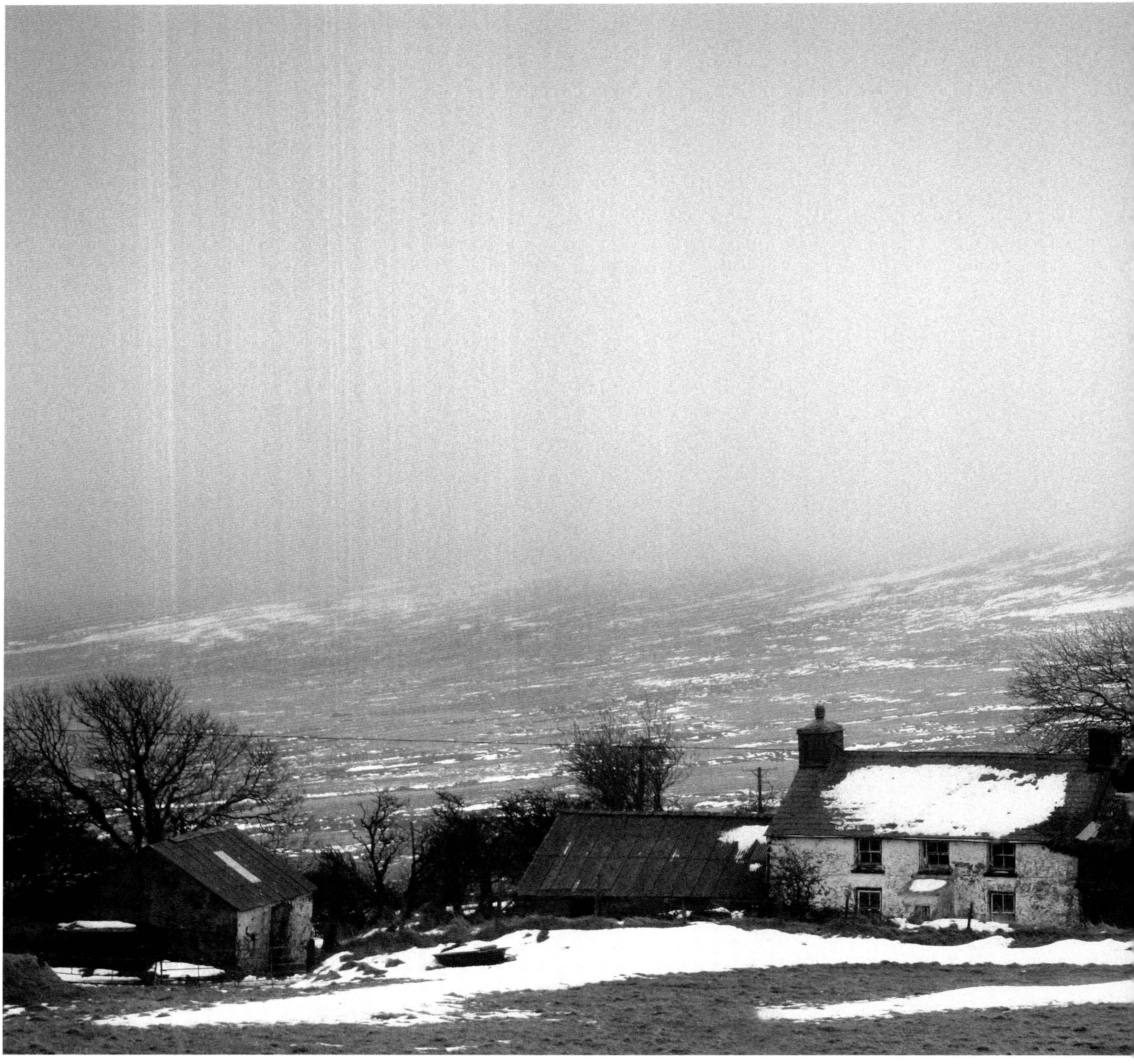

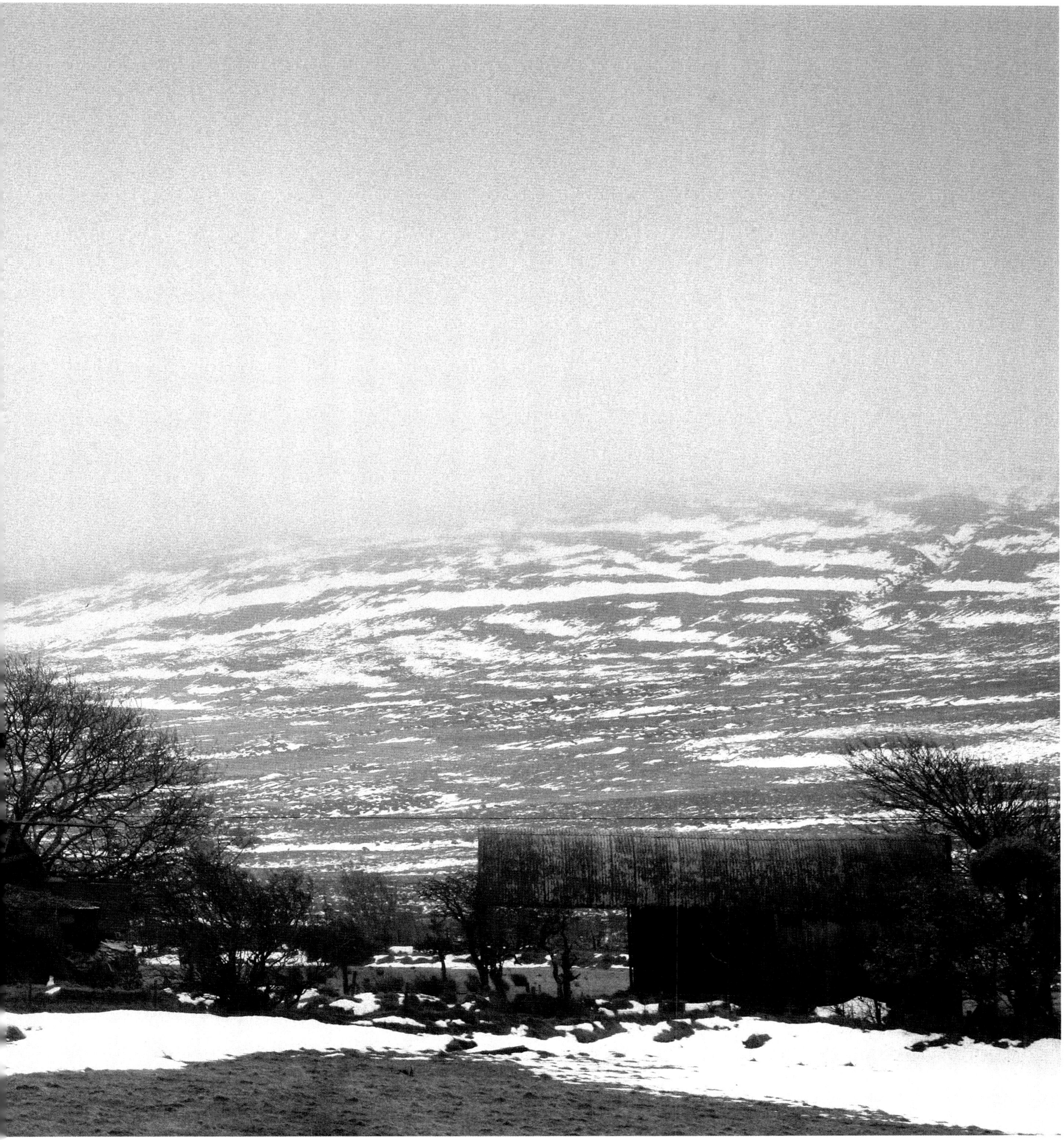

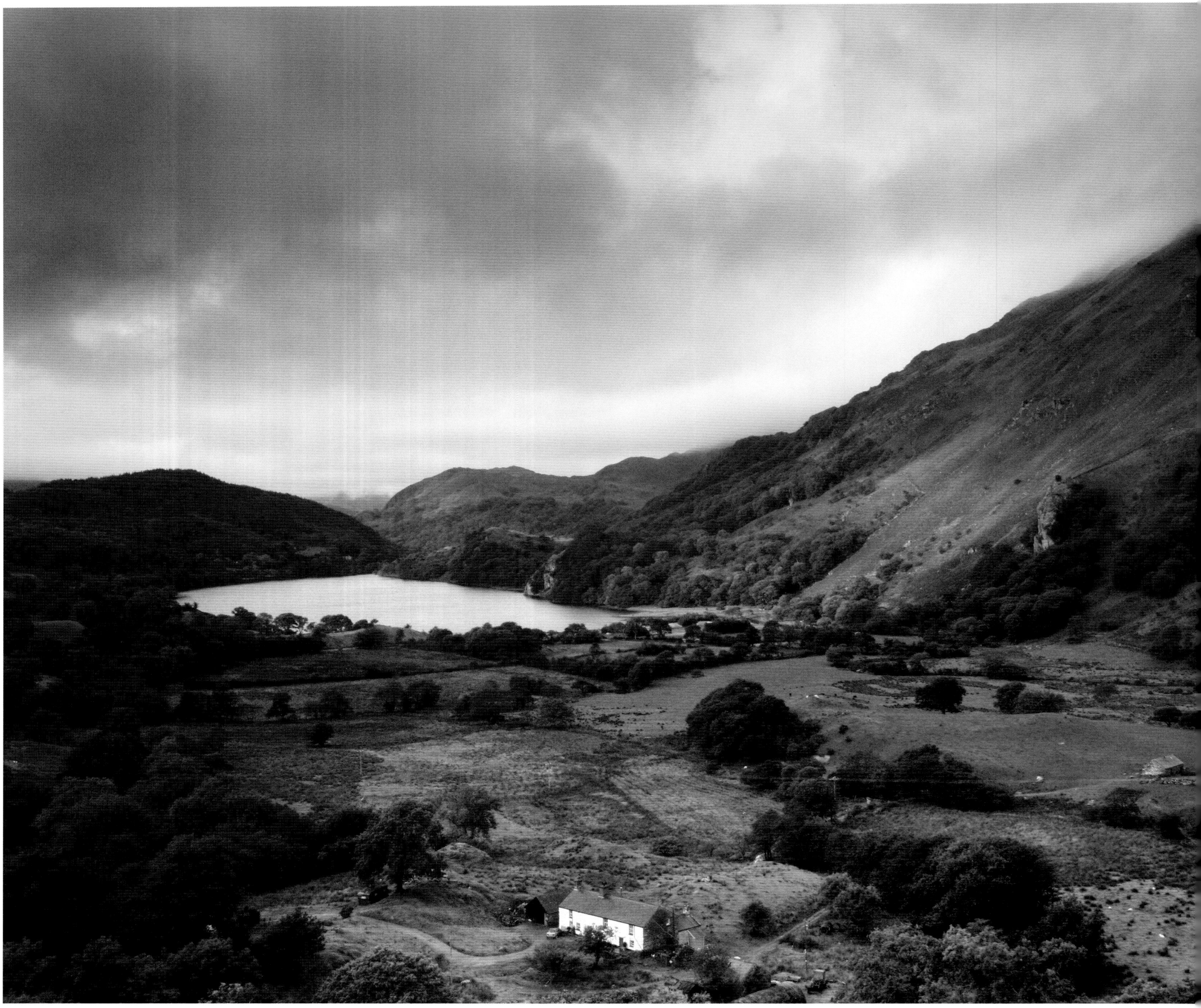

Above: Nant Gwynant with Hafod Rhisgl in the foreground

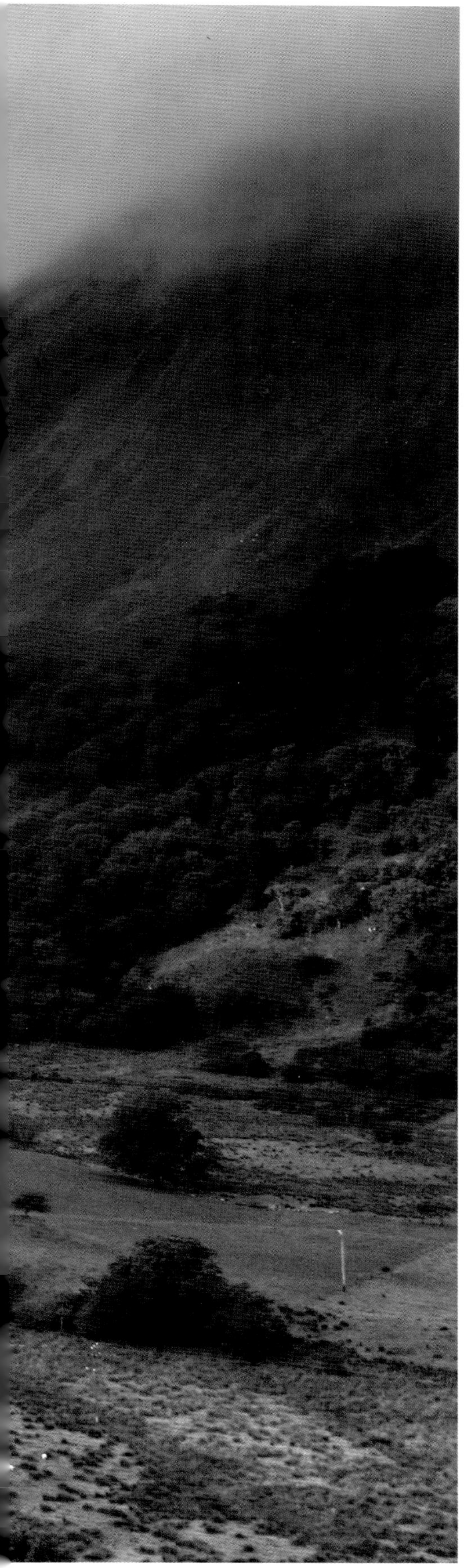

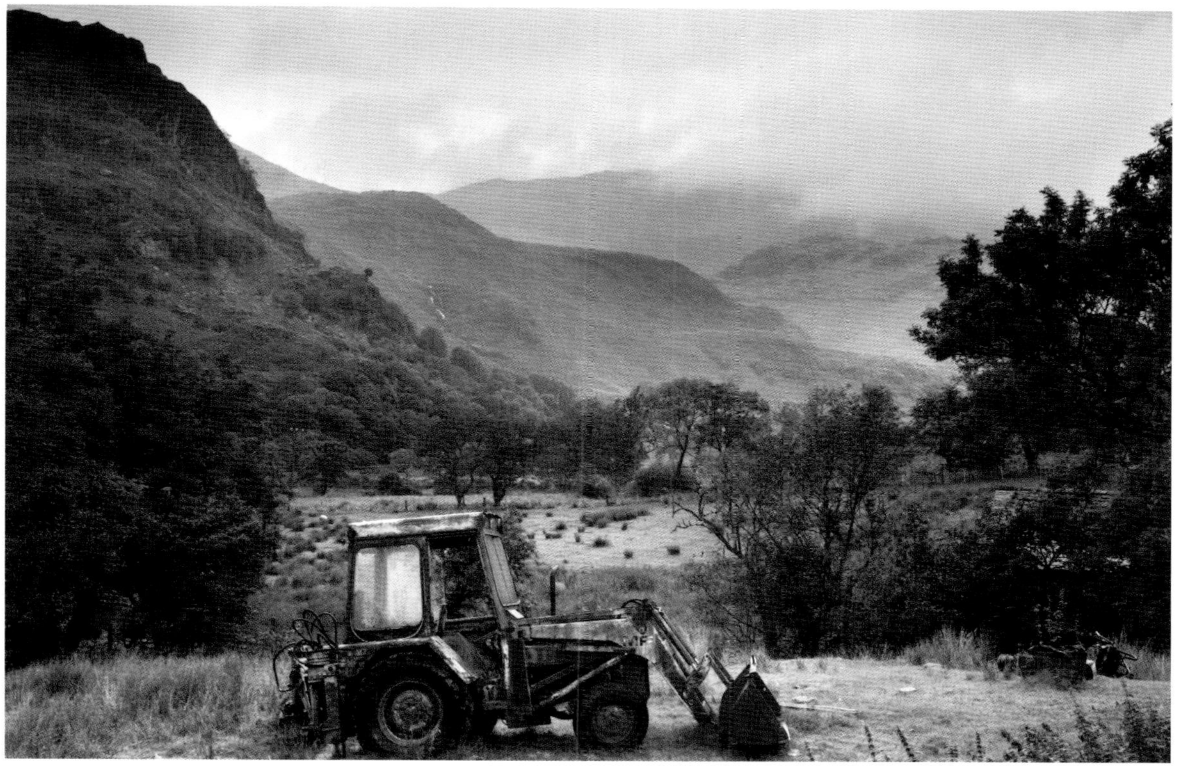

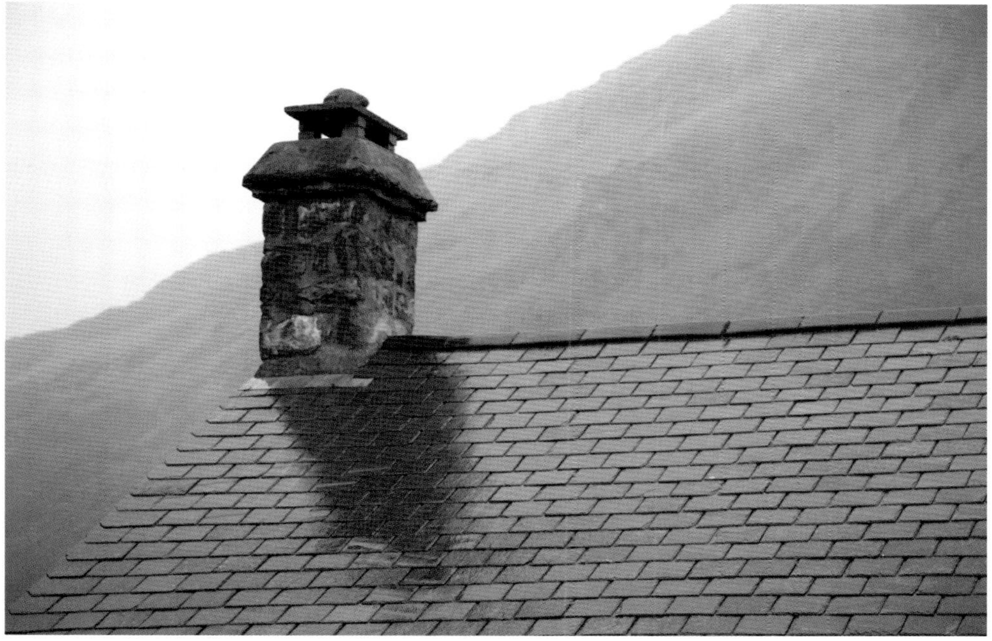

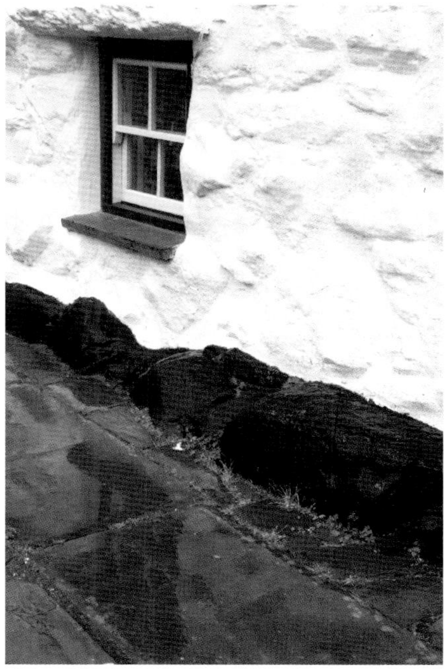

11 HAFOD RHISGL, NANT GWYNANT, SNOWDONIA

Standing on a rocky promontory overlooking Nant Gwynant, I spied a farm in the valley which looked inviting. So down I went to Hafod Rhisgl.

Situated about half a mile from Llyn Gwynant, this farm has a long history. The current occupants are the Williams family, who have farmed Hafod Rhisgl for several generations since William Williams first arrived in 1799.

On this particular day the farmhouse and valley looked very atmospheric – in other words, it was raining heavily. Thankfully Anna proved herself adept at holding a large golfing umbrella over me while I shot the images.

For me the idyllic surroundings were enhanced by an old caravan, with its best days behind it, and a digger parked up in a field. I found the incongruity of these man-made objects dropped into this beguiling landscape quite intriguing. It was all part of the intimate narrative of this wonderful farm and what made photographing it so enjoyable. (Map C2)

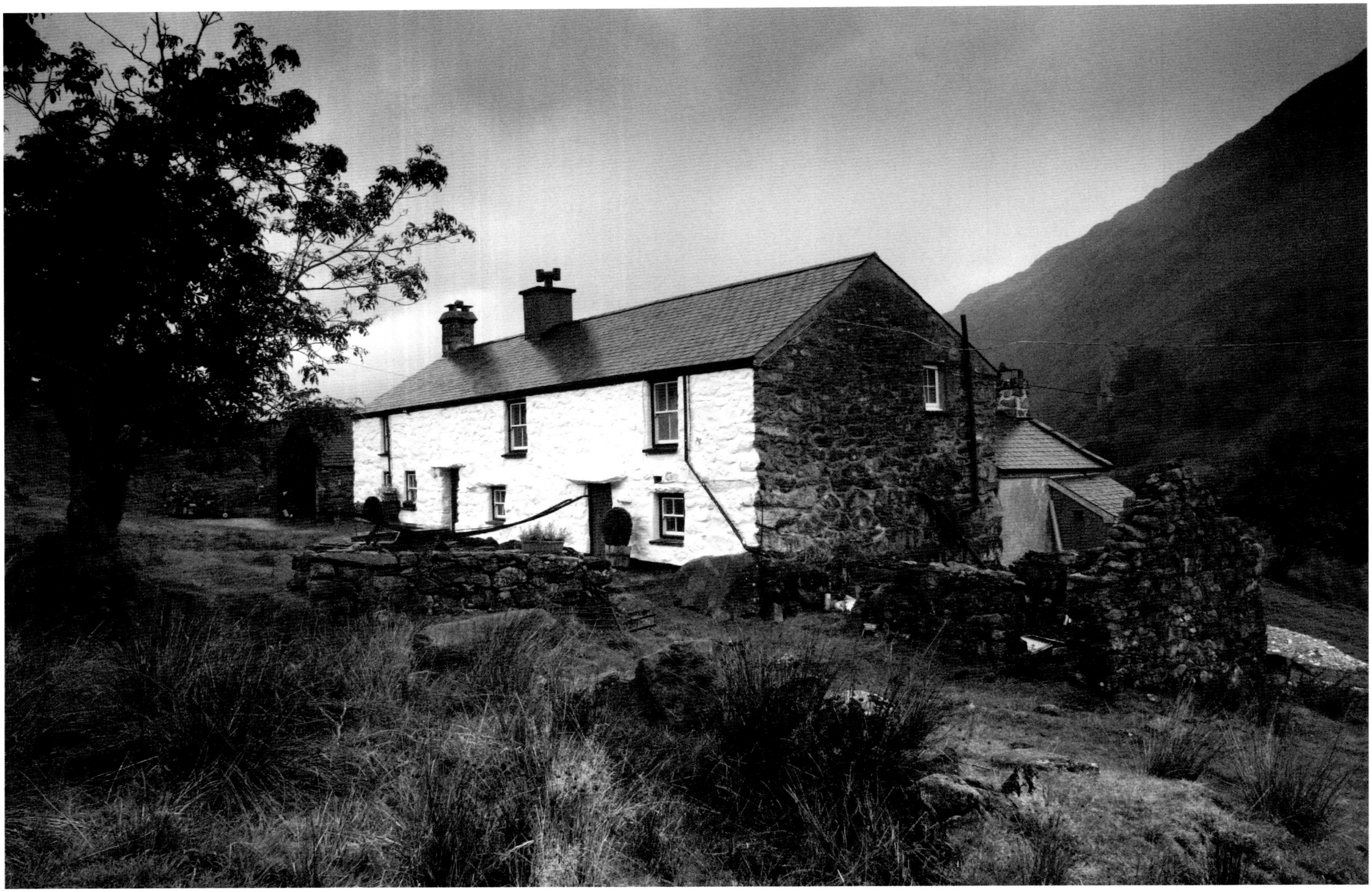

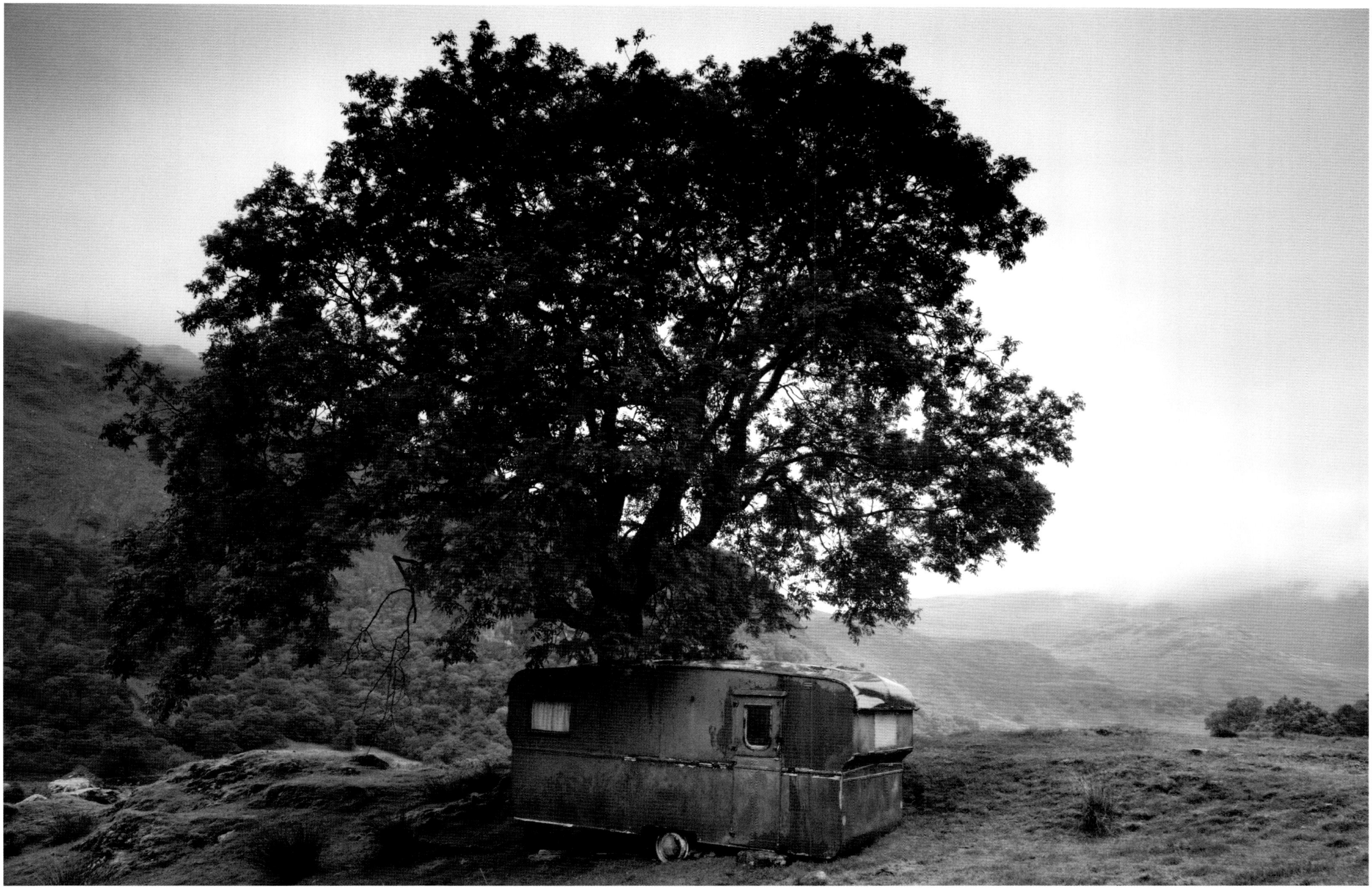

11 Hafod Rhisgl, Nant Gwynant, Snowdonia

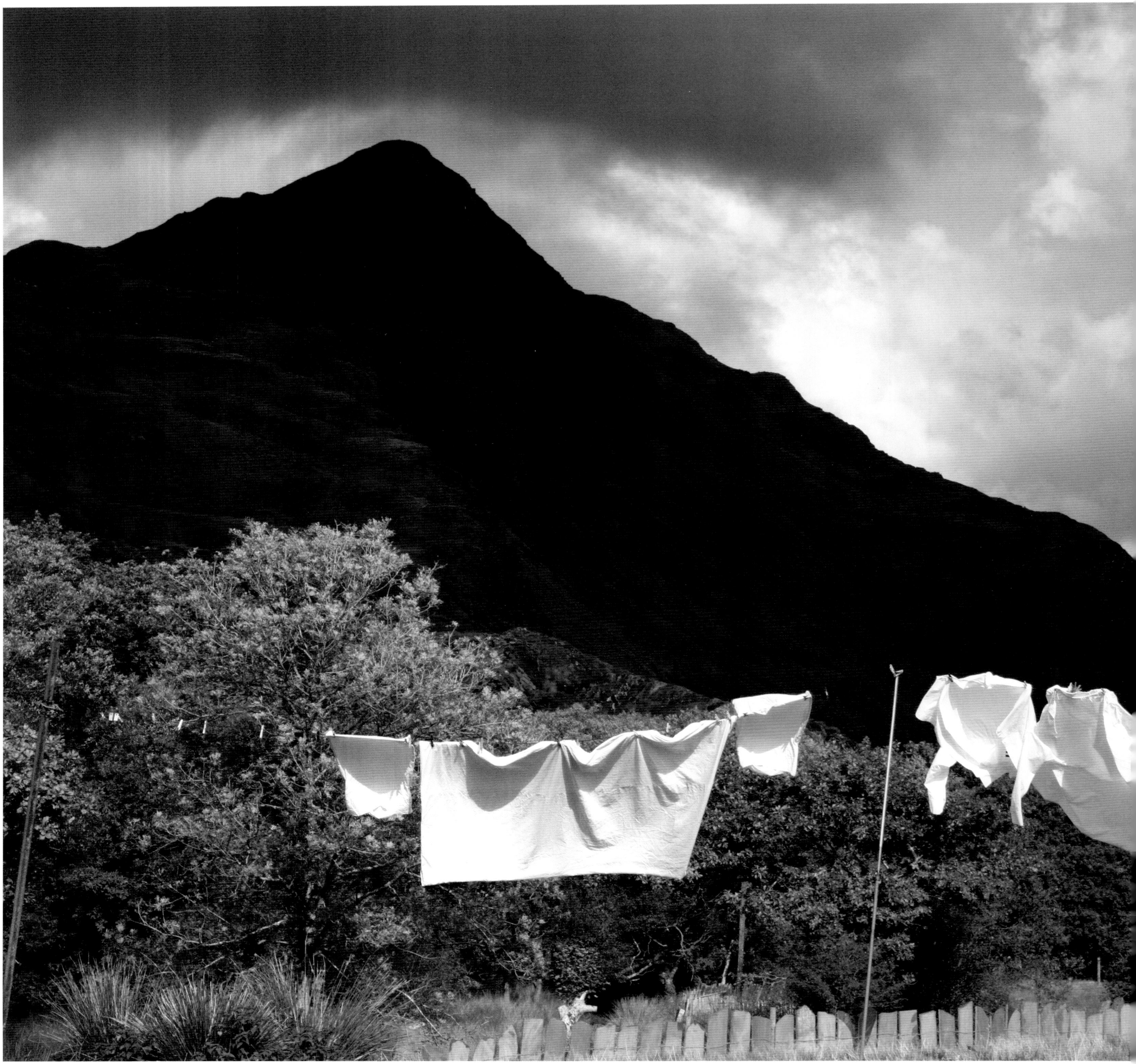

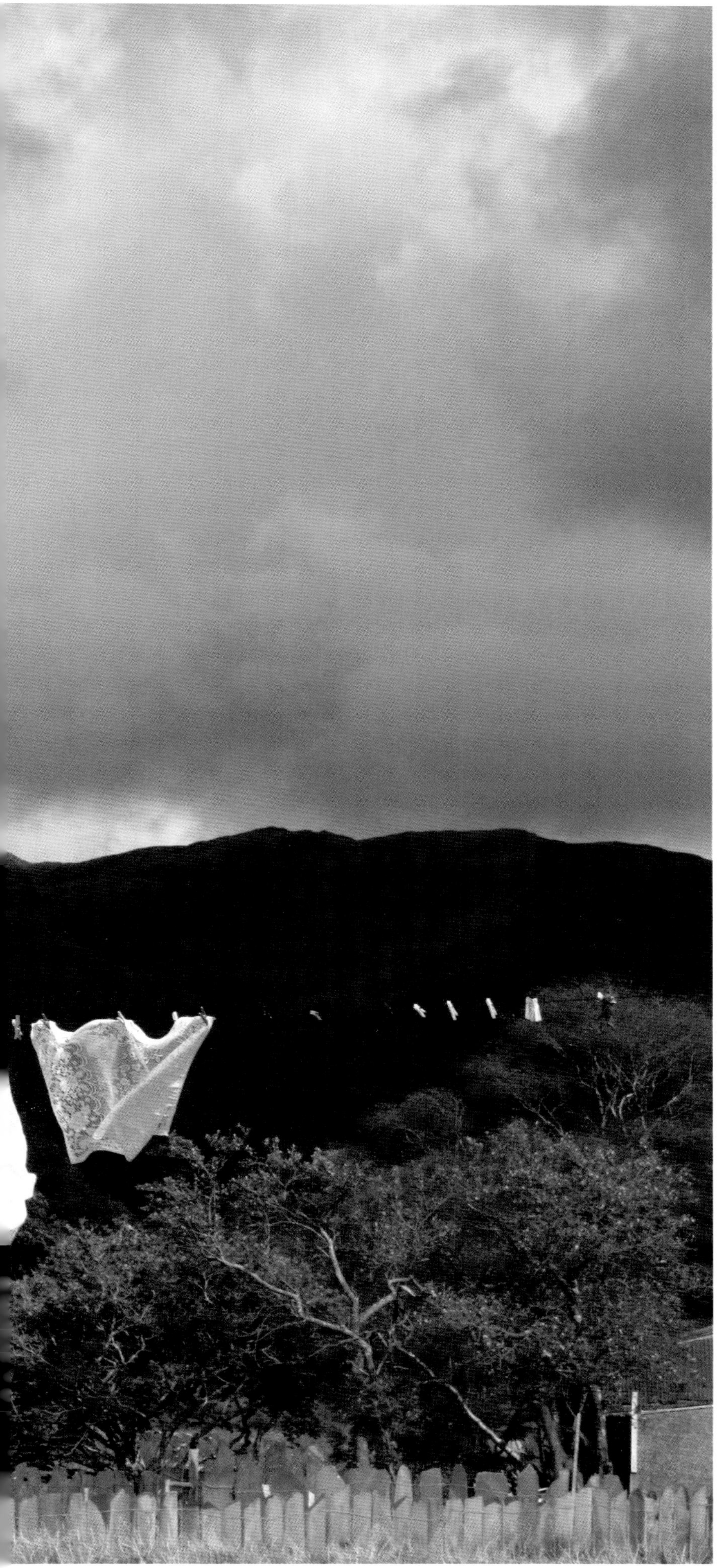

12 MYNYDD CNICHT FROM CROESOR, SNOWDONIA

From the village of Croesor you get the perfect view of shapely Cnicht, a 689 metre (2,260ft) high peak that dominates this tiny community. Croesor is something of a cul-de-sac, situated at the top end of a valley off the Beddgelert to Penrhyndeudraeth road. Cnicht is certainly not the highest mountain in Wales but with its sobriquet 'The Welsh Matterhorn', it sparked my curiosity and so off I went to take a closer look.

While strolling around the village I saw a line of washing flapping energetically in the breeze. As I glanced the sun disappeared behind some clouds, throwing the mountain completely into shade. The washing remained brightly lit: a eureka moment, albeit a fleeting one. I bagged the shot and seconds later the sun was bathing the mountain again. The image works as there is a stark contrast between the clothing and the dark brooding outline of the mountain. It also helps that it was a white wash!
(Map C2)

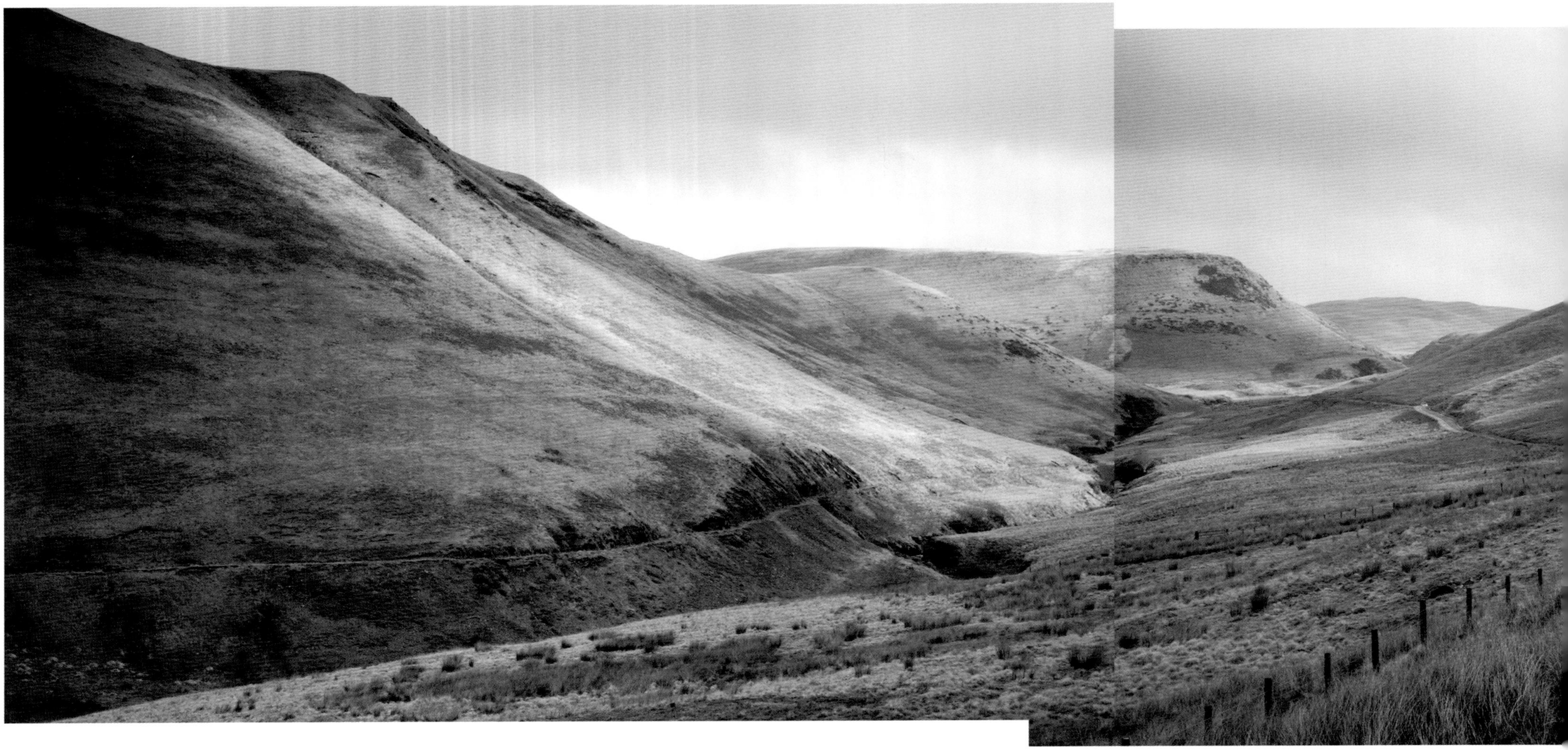

13 ELAN VALLEY, MID WALES

It's easy to call an enjoyable journey a 'great road-trip'. I do it myself constantly. But to call the drive down the Elan Valley a great road-trip is possibly to under-sell it. This drive offers a riot of jaw-droppingly handsome landscape. It is a distillation of Wales at its very best – sweeping river gorges, scattered farms, spectacular peaks and shimmering reservoirs. As a landscape photographer it is as close to viewfinder heaven as it is possible to get.

A couple of miles after leaving Cwmystwyth, I climbed out of one valley and descended into the valley of the River Elan. Almost immediately I spotted a farm with boarded-up windows, an invitation I can never resist. Abergwngu sits in a picturesque setting with the fledgling Elan trickling past its front door. Wherever my travels take me in Wales I seem to encounter such deserted farms. For me they exude a more poignant air than say an empty terraced house or closed-down shop. These farms often have long family histories with generations cultivating the land. Then one day, for whatever reason, it all comes to an end.

A little way along from Abergwngu the ever-widening Elan is abruptly swallowed up by the Craig Goch Reservoir. Constructed in the late nineteenth century, this initial reservoir feeds down in quick succession through others before eventually terminating at the Caban-coch Reservoir near Elan Village. Evergreen forests carpet the hills and mountains, tumbling right down to the water's edge. Peering into the impenetrable blackness it's easy to forget that at one time the River Elan cascaded through deep ravines bordered by native woodland, and past country houses and farms. Then the civil engineers and an army of navvies turned up to confine it all to the depths. My arrival at the Caban-coch Reservoir marked the end of a glorious day's photography. It had indeed been one of the 'great road-trips'. (Map C4)

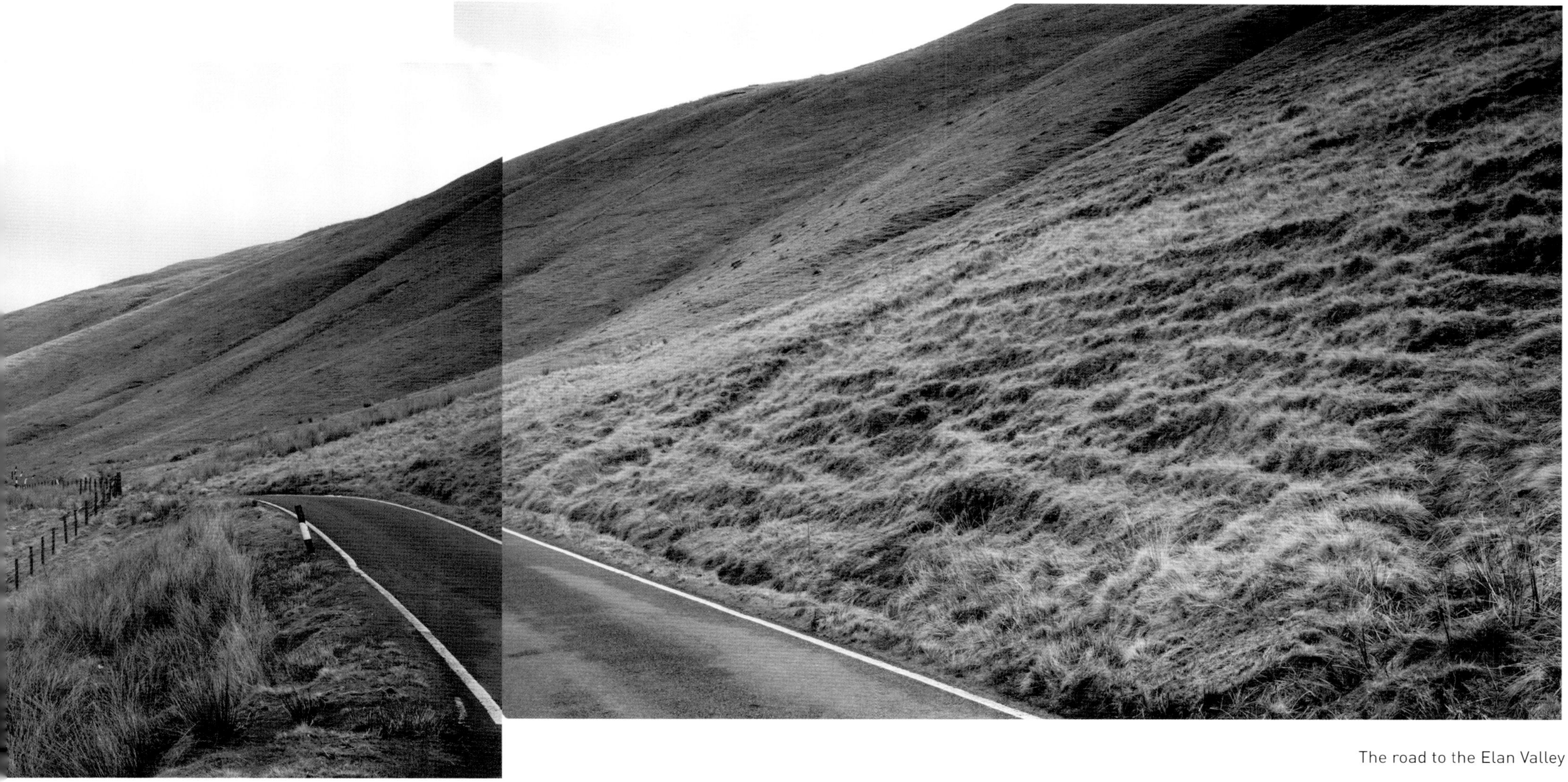

The road to the Elan Valley

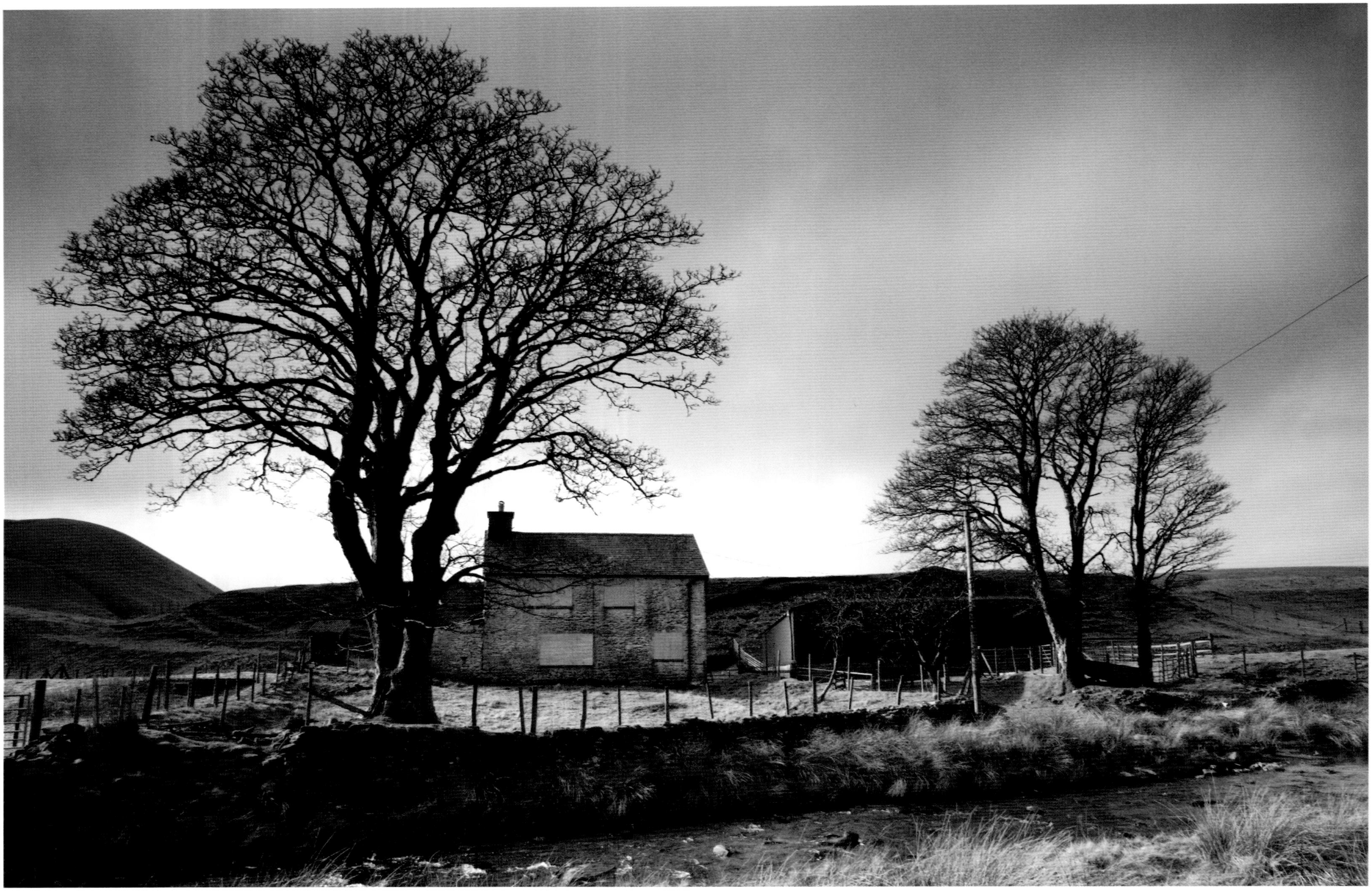

Abergwngu Farm

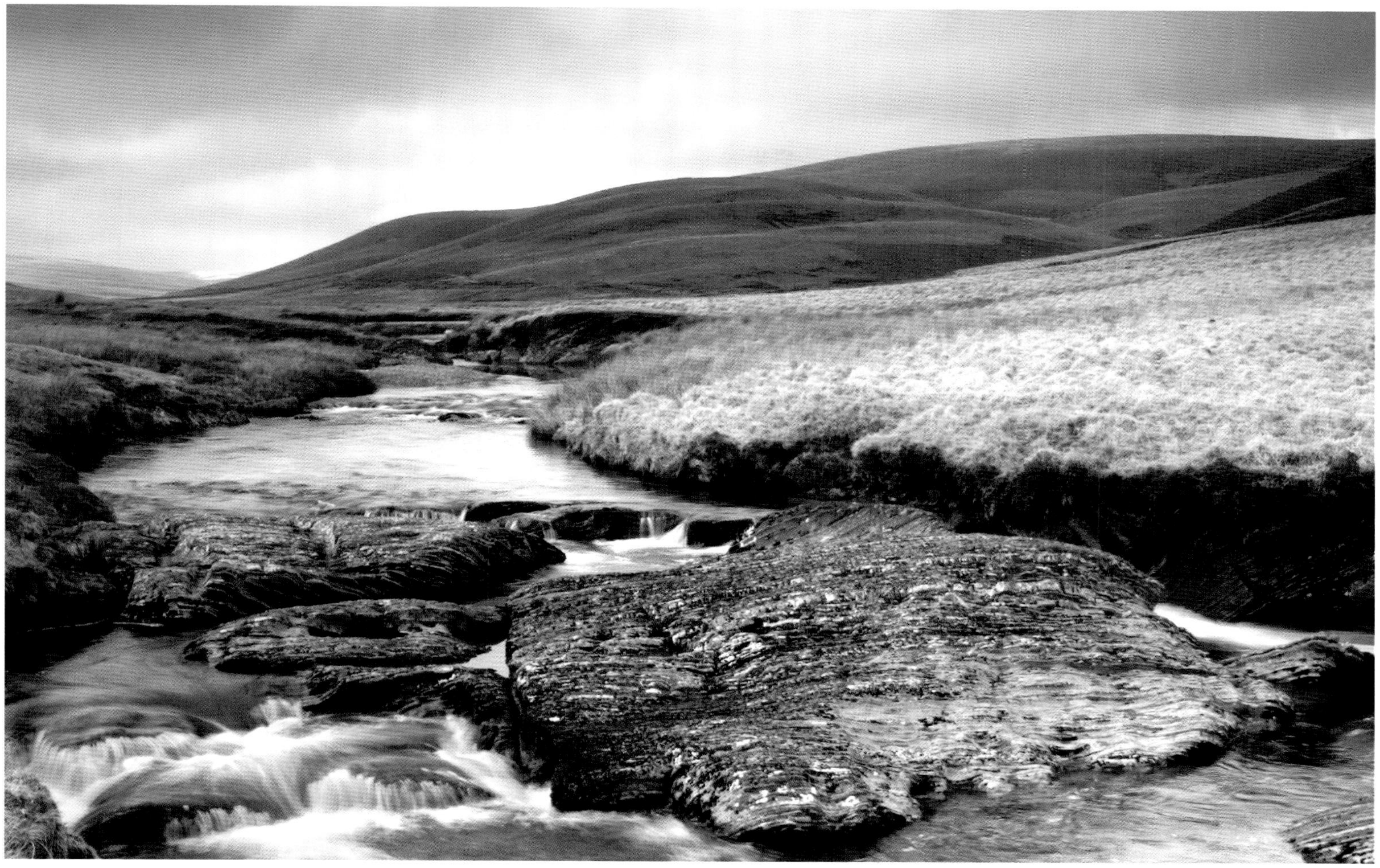

Above: The River Elan

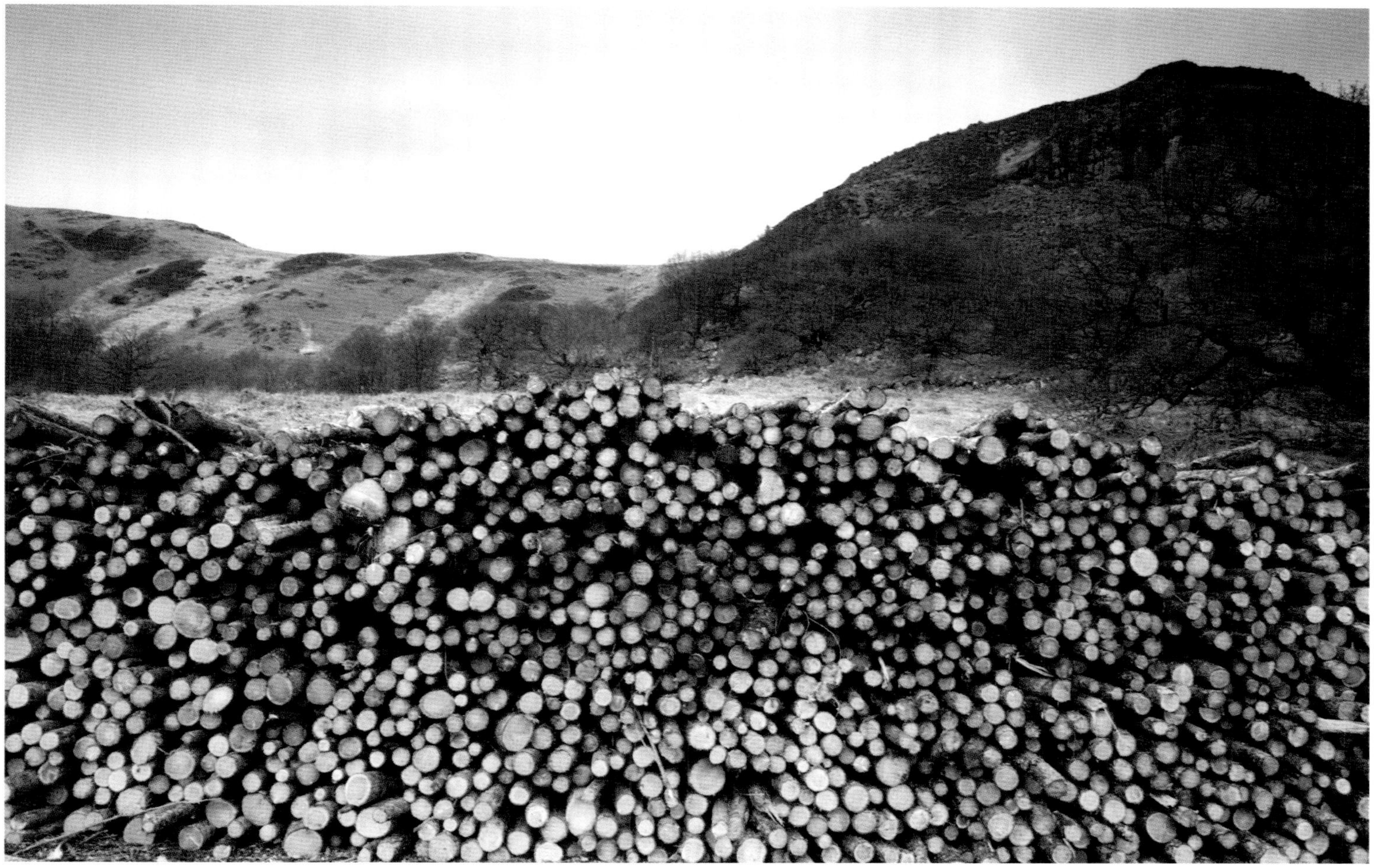

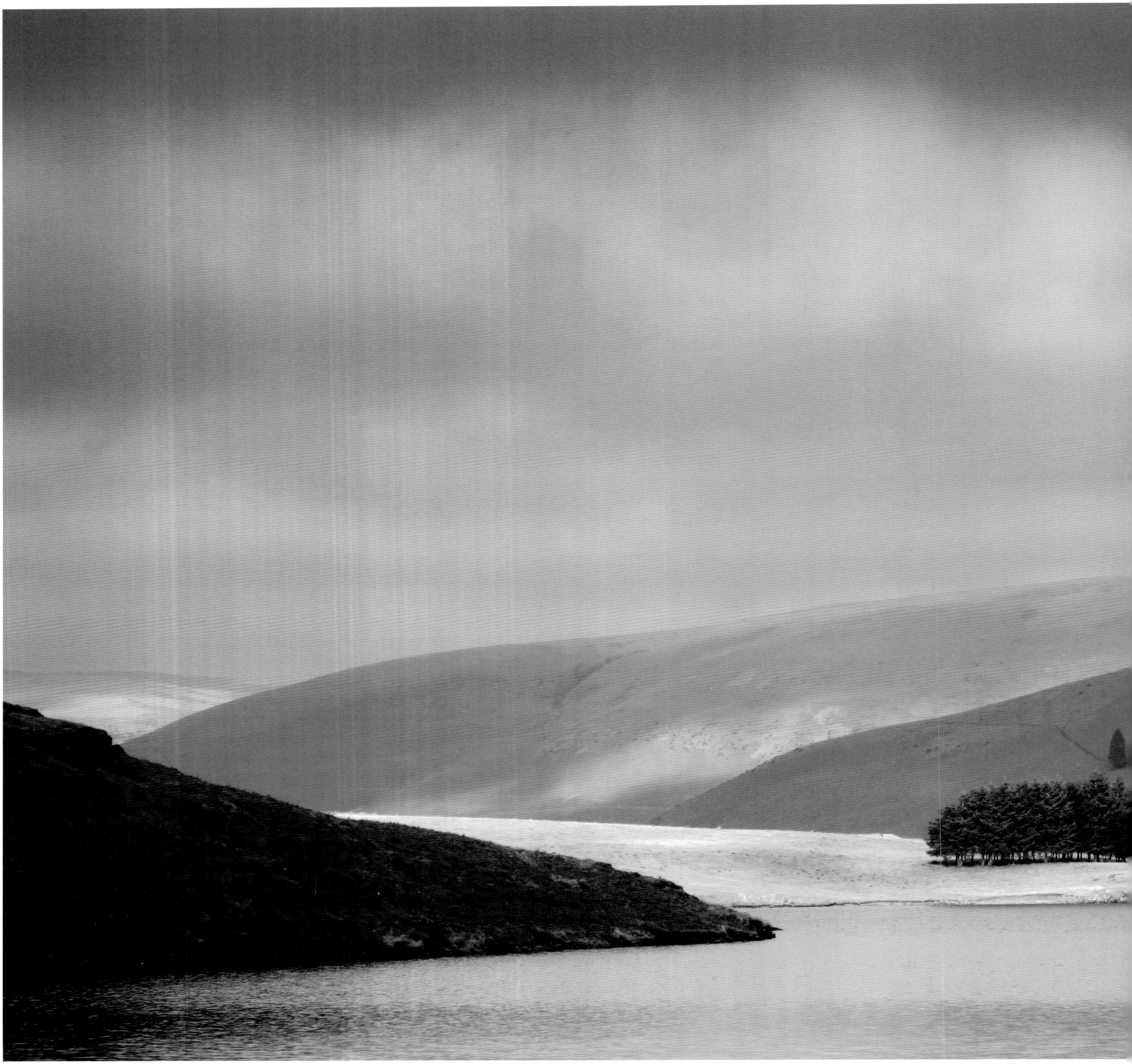

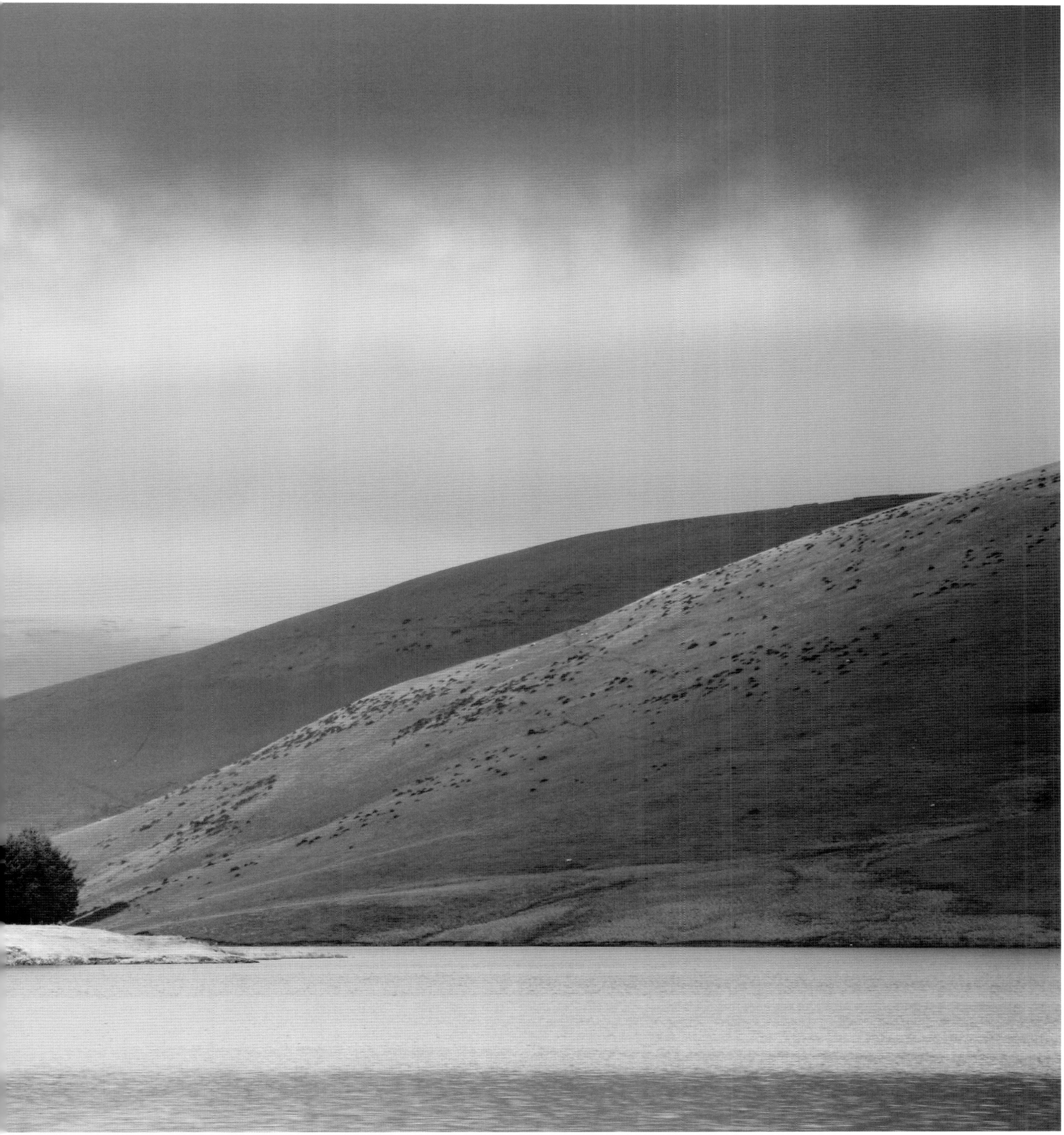

13 Elan Valley, Mid Wales

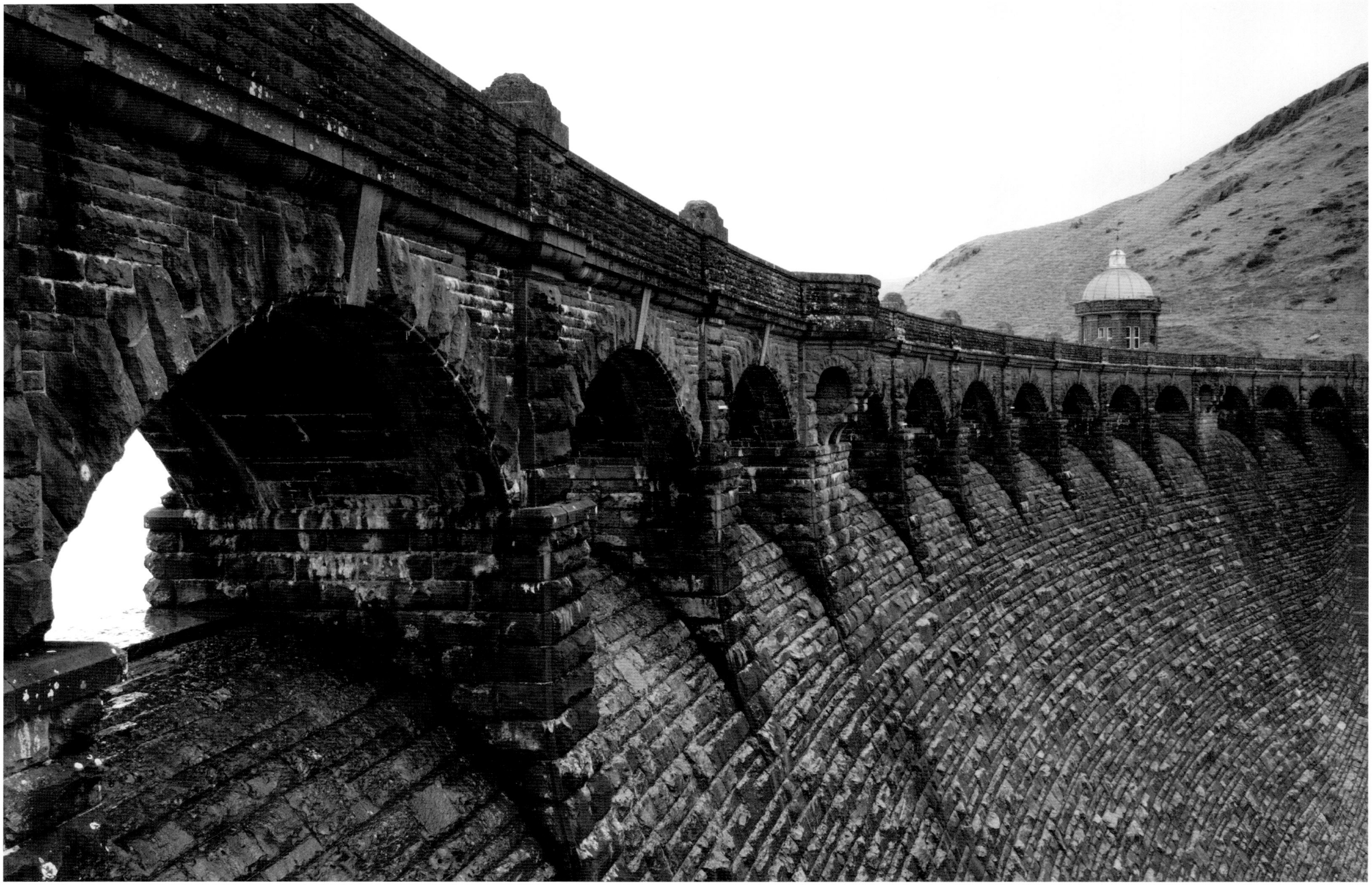

Above / Previous page: Craig Goch Reservoir

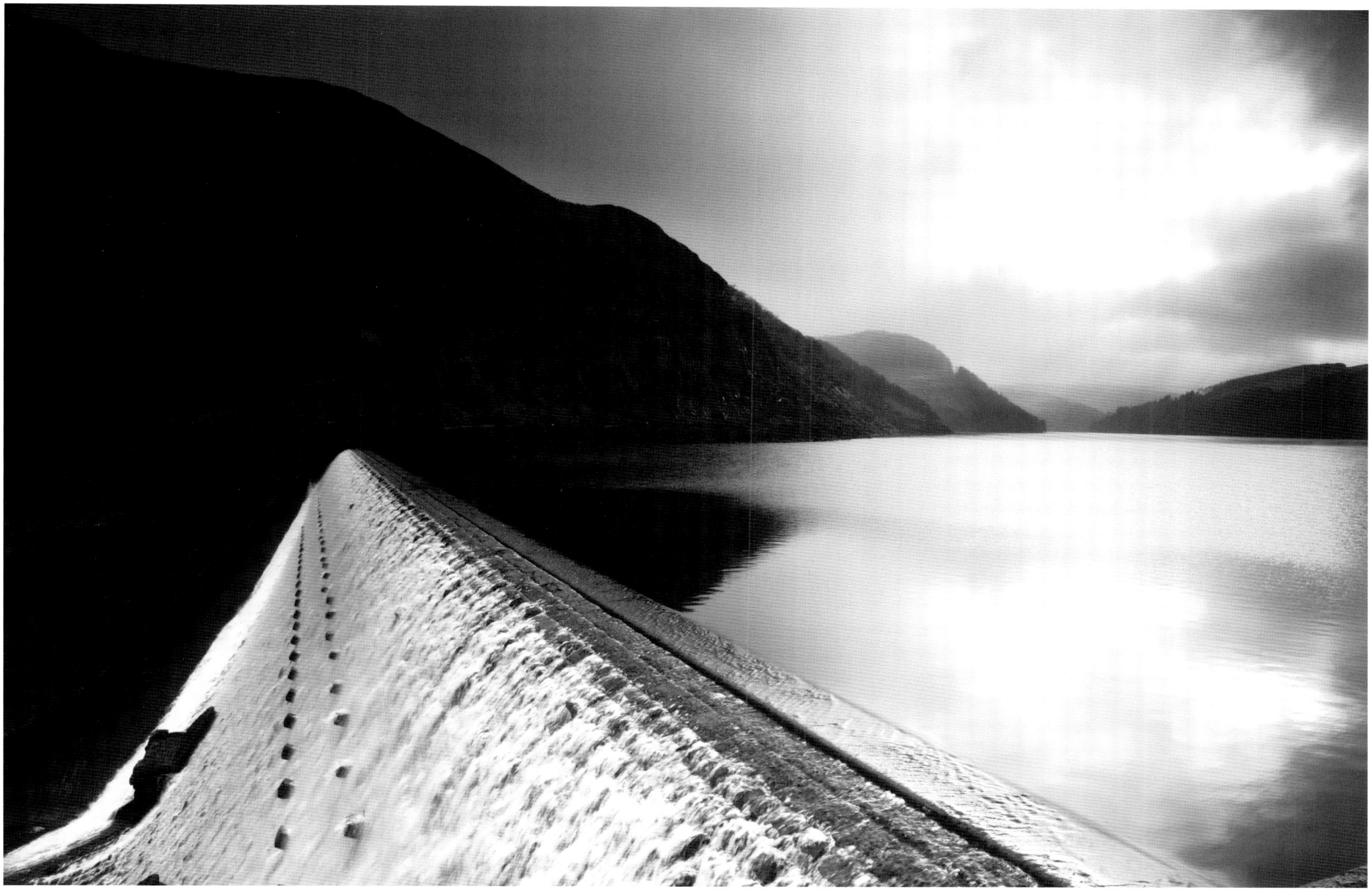

Caban-coch Reservoir

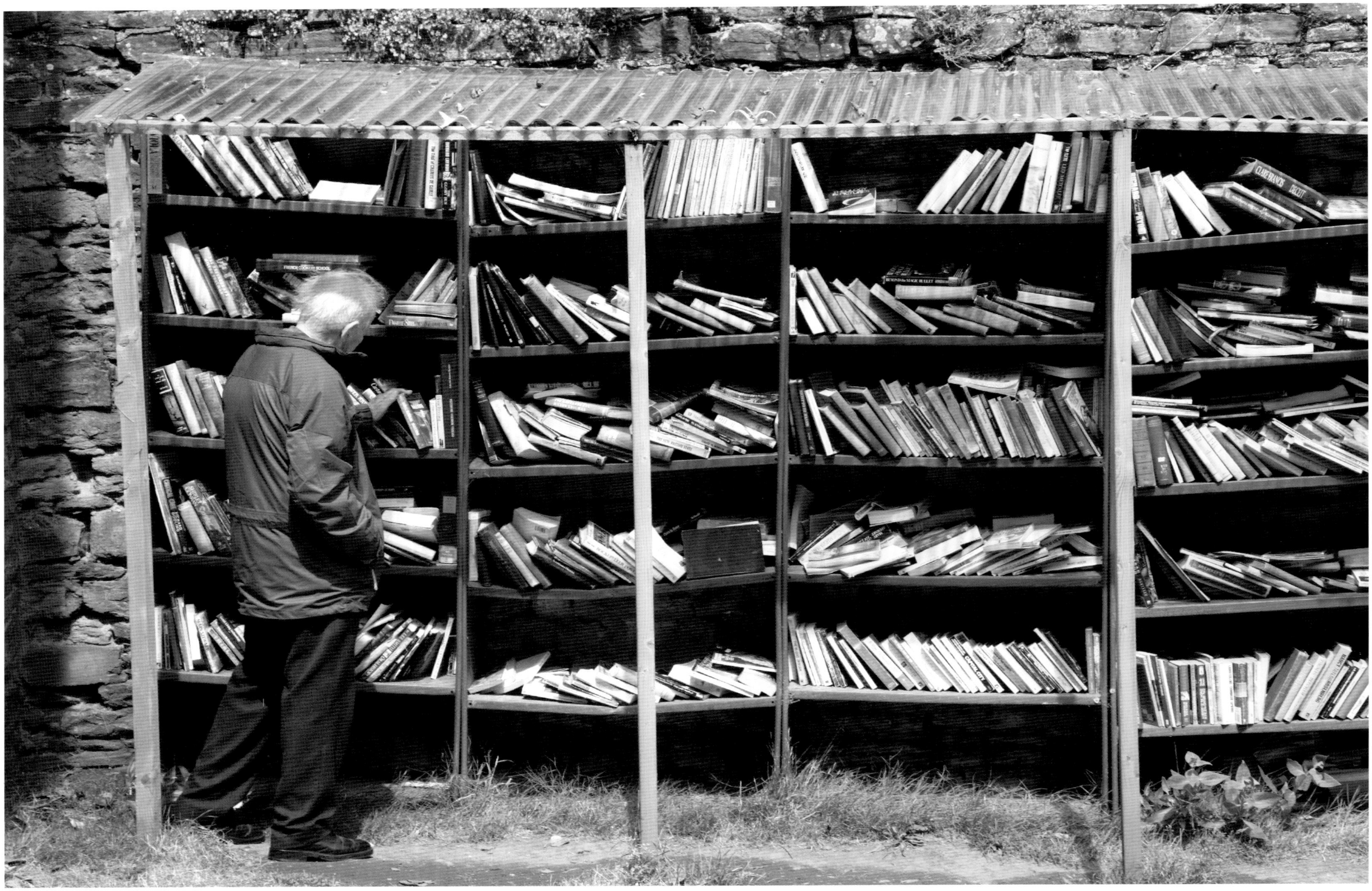

14 HAY-ON-WYE, POWYS

A lot has been written about the predicted demise of the printed book. Apparently the physical book cannot compete with the portable screen with its access to thousands of books at the press of a key. Try telling that to the booksellers of Hay-on-Wye. The trade is most definitely alive and well and this market town is living proof.

If you are a book lover, which I am, the pure joy of picking up a volume and eagerly flicking through its pages is heavenly. For me, a computer screen could never compete with that sense of satisfaction.

I avoided visiting Hay during the yearly book festival as I wanted to photograph the shops themselves, not the throngs. During my life certain shop frontages have acted like magnets to me: toy shops when I was a kid (obviously); motorcycle showrooms in my youth when I fancied myself as Britain's answer to Evel Knievel (a short-lived and ultimately painful interlude); and nowadays book and antique shops.

Bookshops, particularly the independents, often project a character which is a joy to photograph. The most novel (please excuse the pun), experience was strolling into the grounds of the Hay Castle Bookshop. The open-air honesty section comprises row-upon-row of metal shelving displaying thousands of books, all exposed to the elements. Pick a book, leave your money in the box, and enjoy. (Map D5)

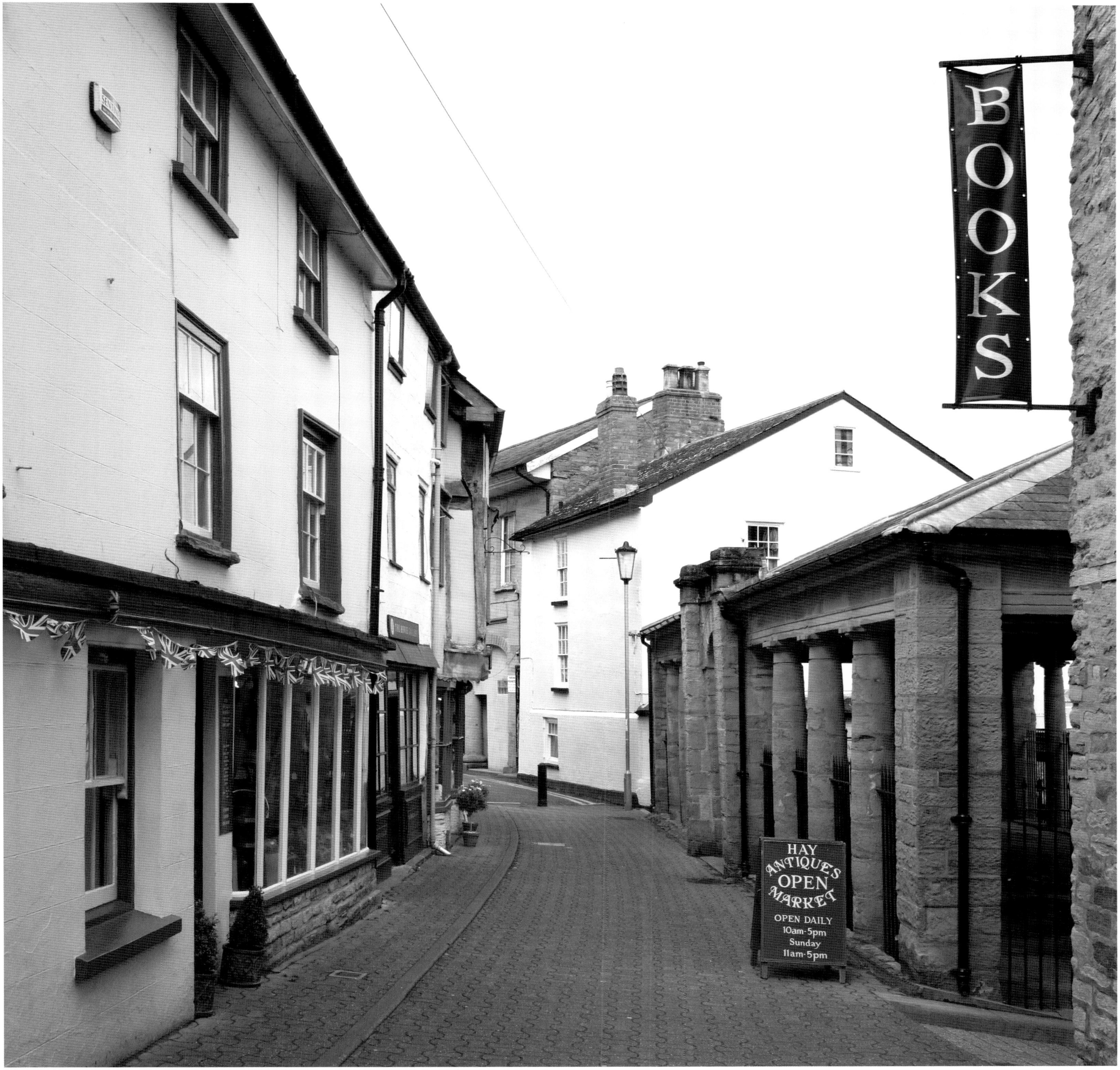

14 Hay-on-Wye, Powys

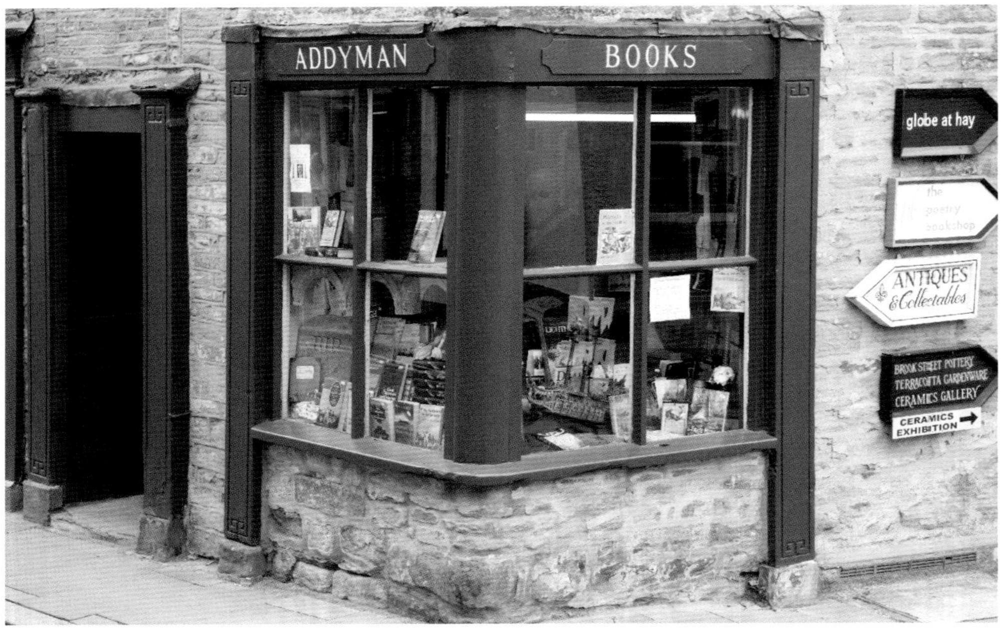
ADDYMAN
BOOKS
globe at hay
ANTIQUES & Collectables
BROOK STREET POTTERY
TERRACOTTA GARDENWARE
CERAMICS GALLERY
CERAMICS EXHIBITION

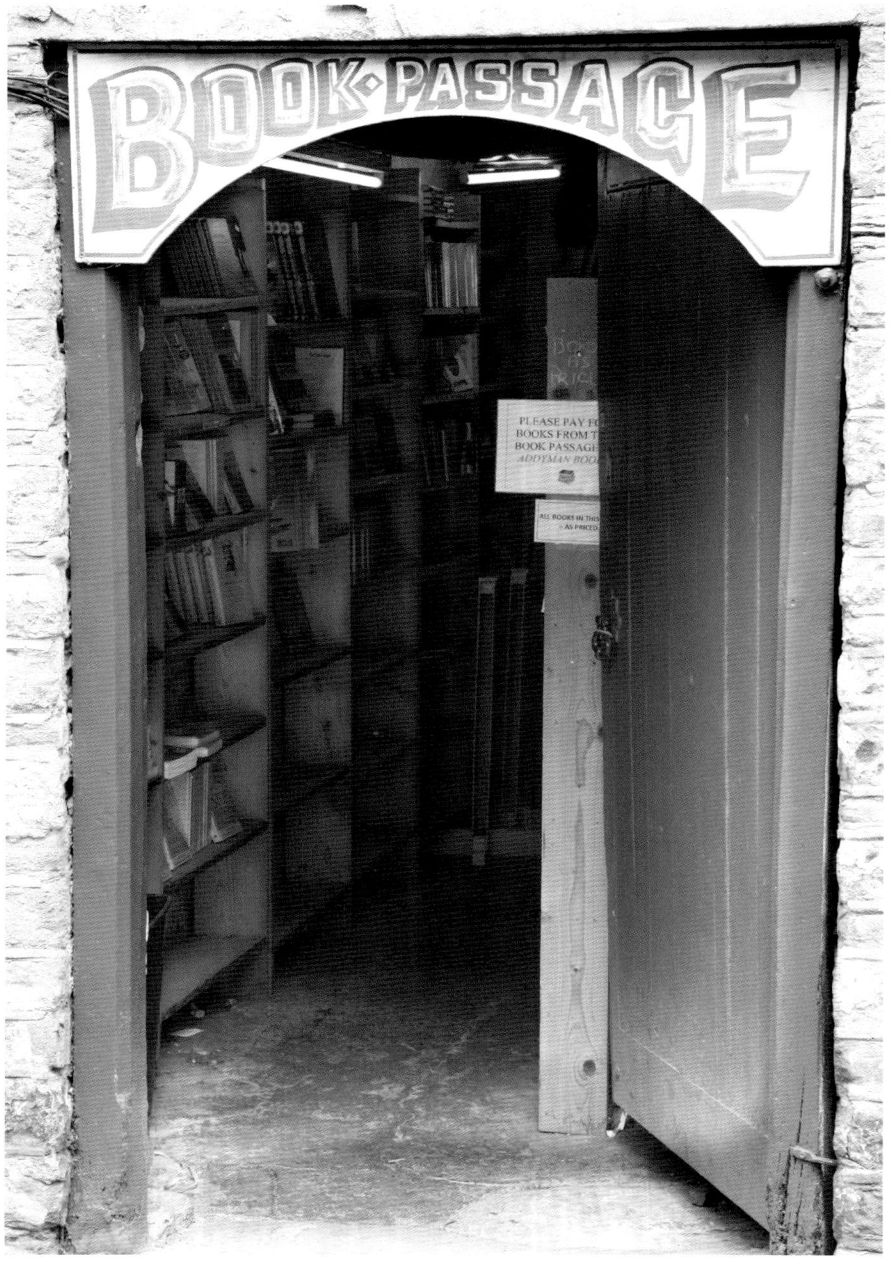
BOOK·PASSAGE

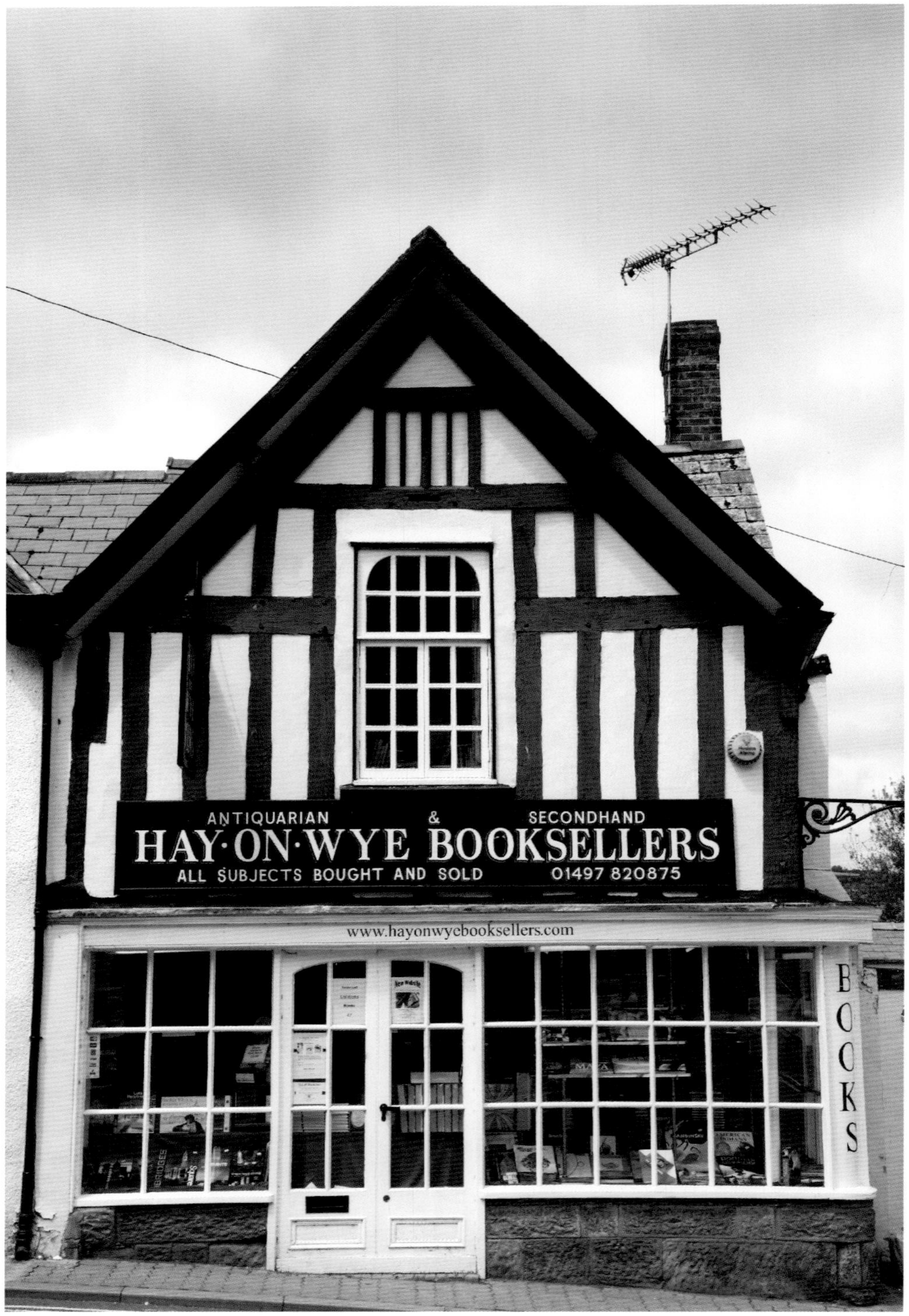
ANTIQUARIAN & SECONDHAND
HAY·ON·WYE BOOKSELLERS
ALL SUBJECTS BOUGHT AND SOLD 01497 820875
www.hayonwyebooksellers.com
BOOKS

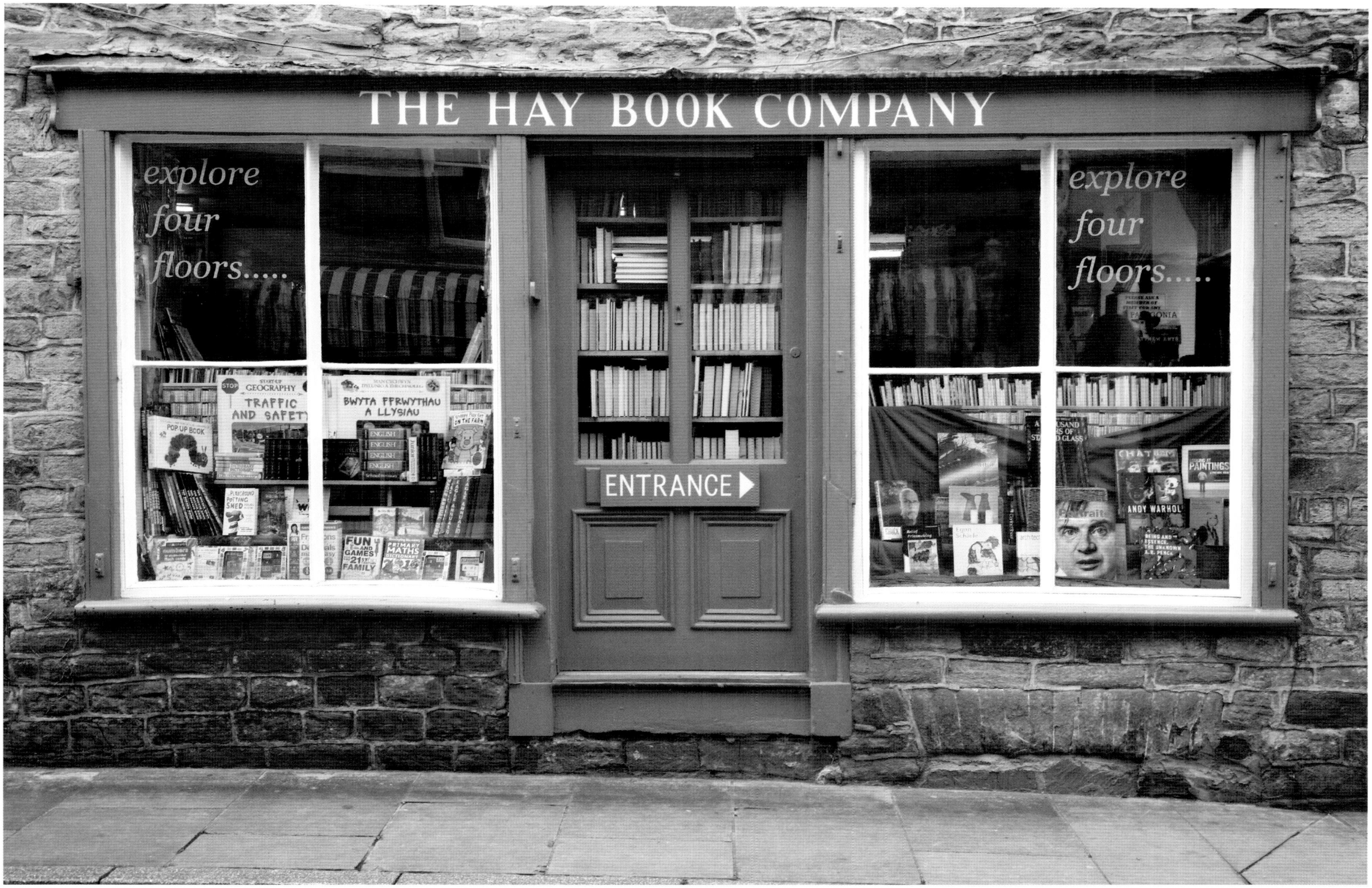
THE HAY BOOK COMPANY
explore
four
floors.....
ENTRANCE
explore
four
floors.....
GEOGRAPHY
TRAFFIC
AND SAFETY
BWYTA FFRWYTHAU
A LLYSIAU
POP UP BOOK
ANDY WARHOL
PAINTINGS

15 FRESHWATER WEST, PEMBROKESHIRE

One of the most westerly and so wildest beaches in Pembrokeshire, 'Fresh West', as it is known locally, has caught Hollywood's eye. Scenes from both Russell Crowe's 'Robin Hood' and 'Harry Potter and the Deathly Hallows' were filmed here.
There was no sign of any film crews on this winter's day when the elements were brutal and the wind howled in off the sea, accompanied by the occasional blast of sideways rain. I didn't hang around long! (Map A6)

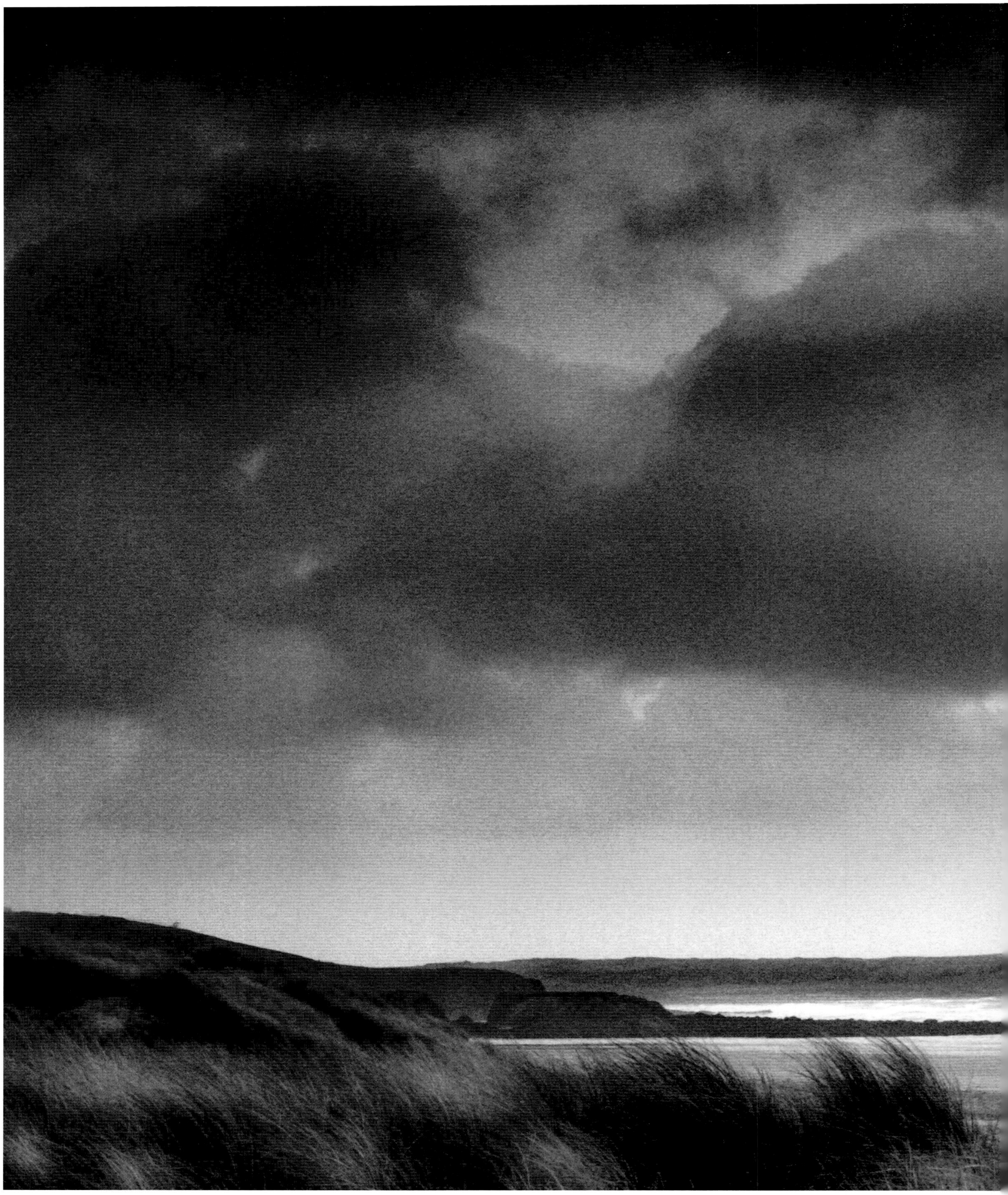

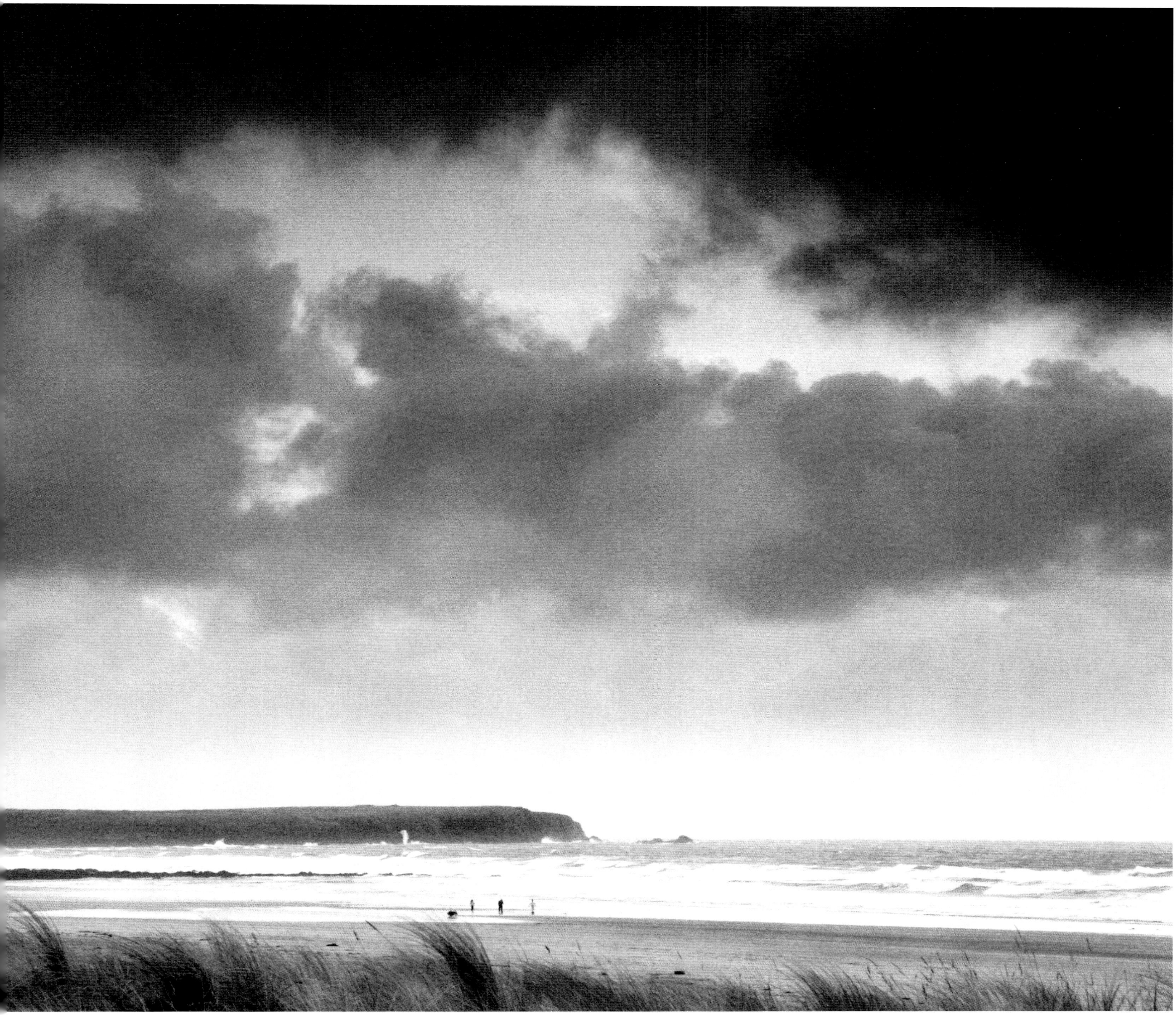

15 Freshwater West, Pembrokeshire

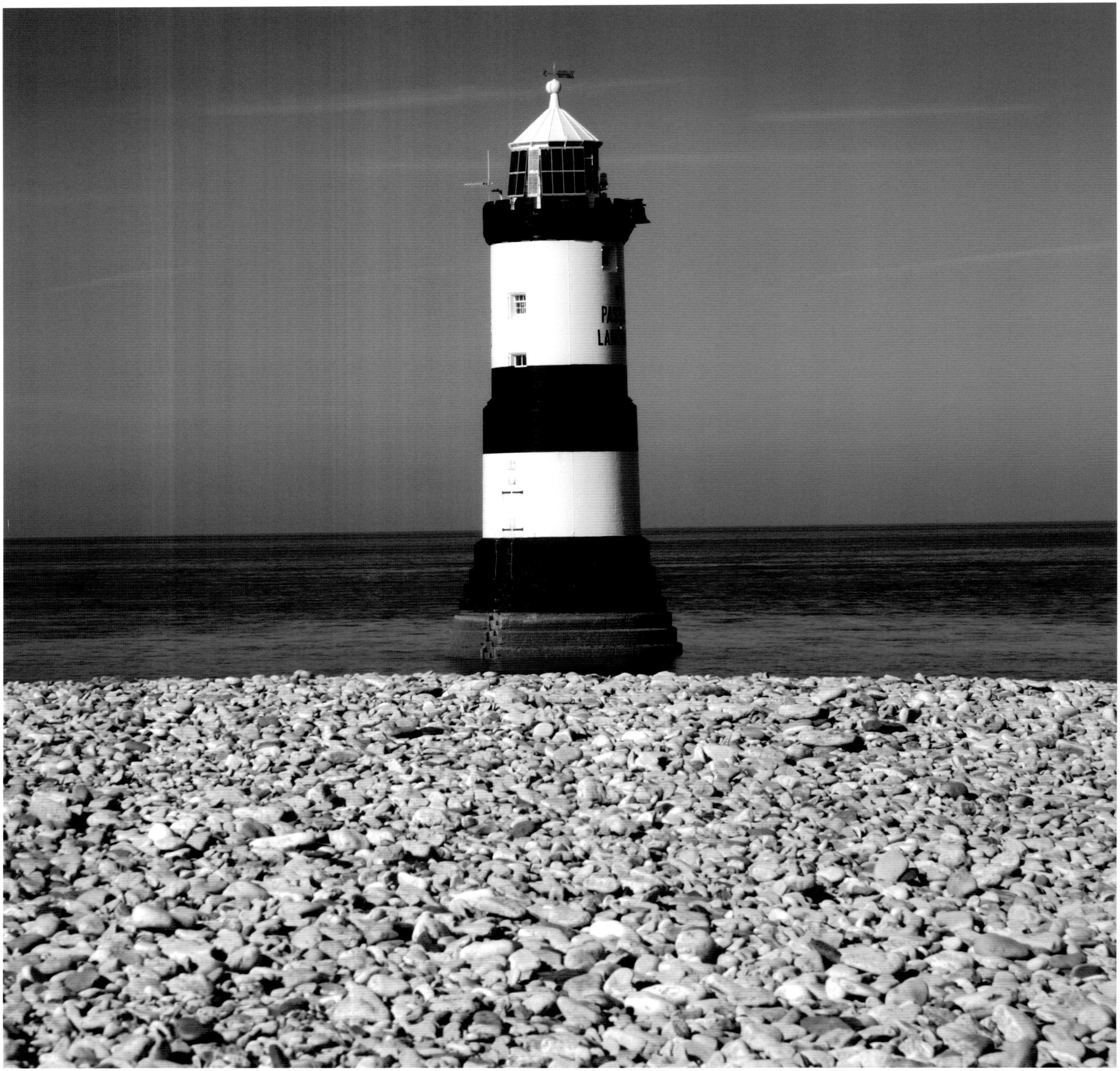

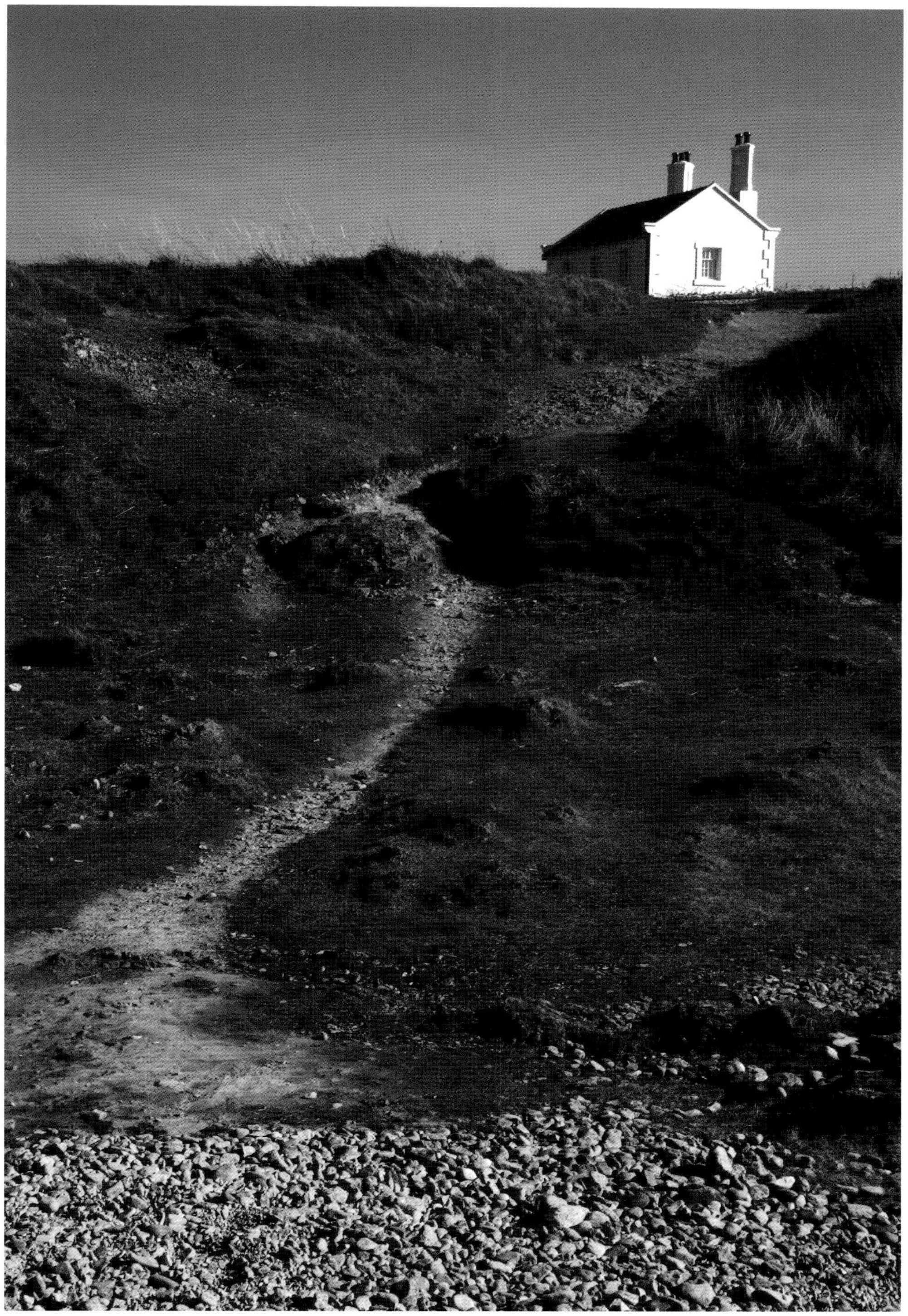

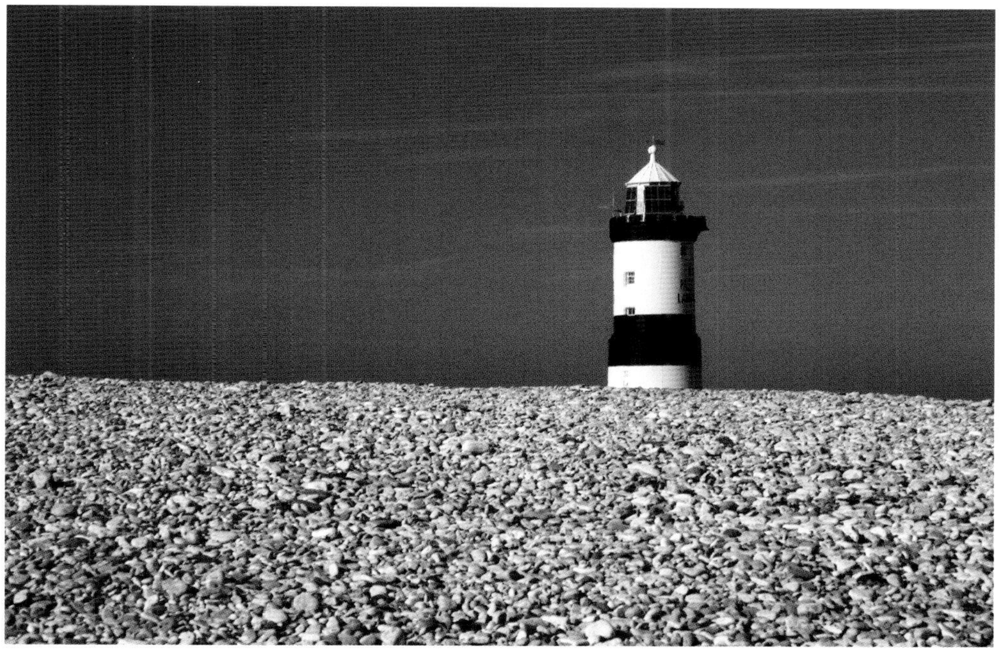

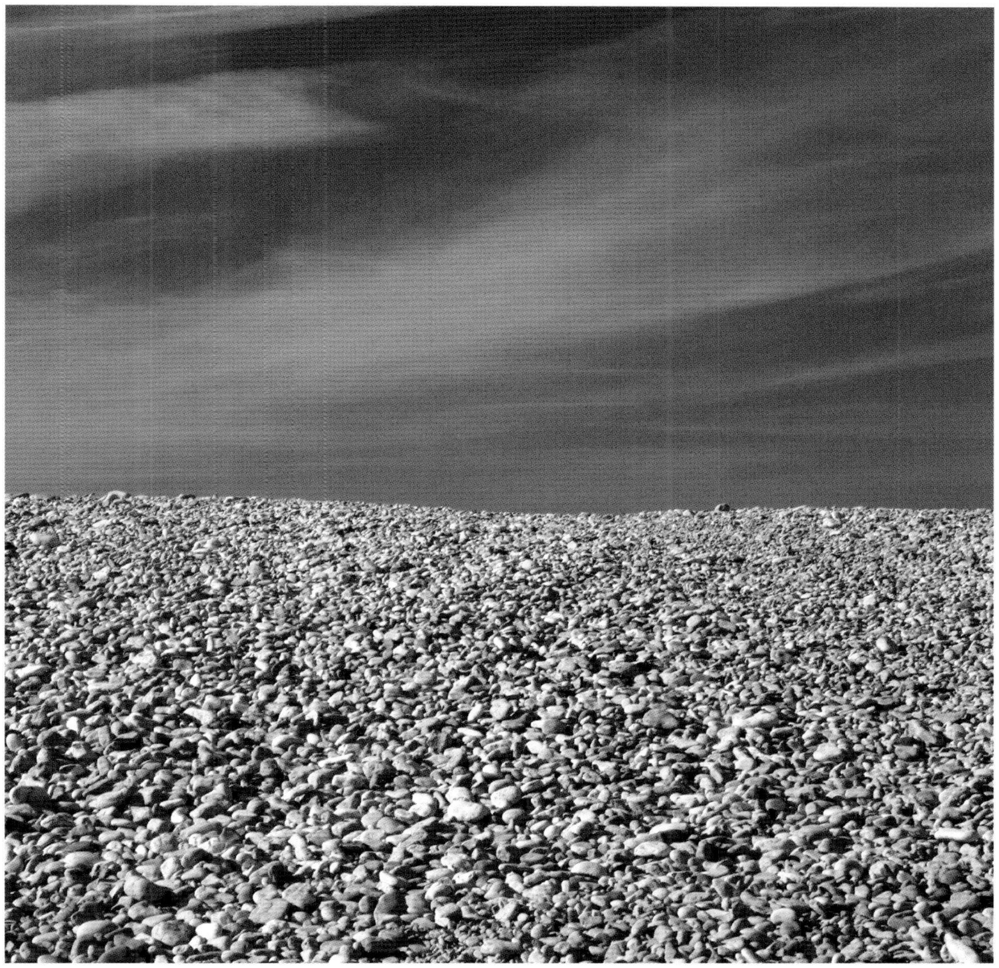

16 PENMON POINT, ANGLESEY

I arrived late afternoon at Penmon Point after a long hot day photographing Portmeirion village. It was a relief to exchange the stifling still heat of earlier for a lilting sea breeze, and the salty tang on the air reinvigorated me. The lighthouse slowly reveals itself as you ascend a large pebble embankment. After taking some photographs I sat on the crest of the embankment gazing out to sea. It was a perfect way to eke out the last light of the day. (Map C1)

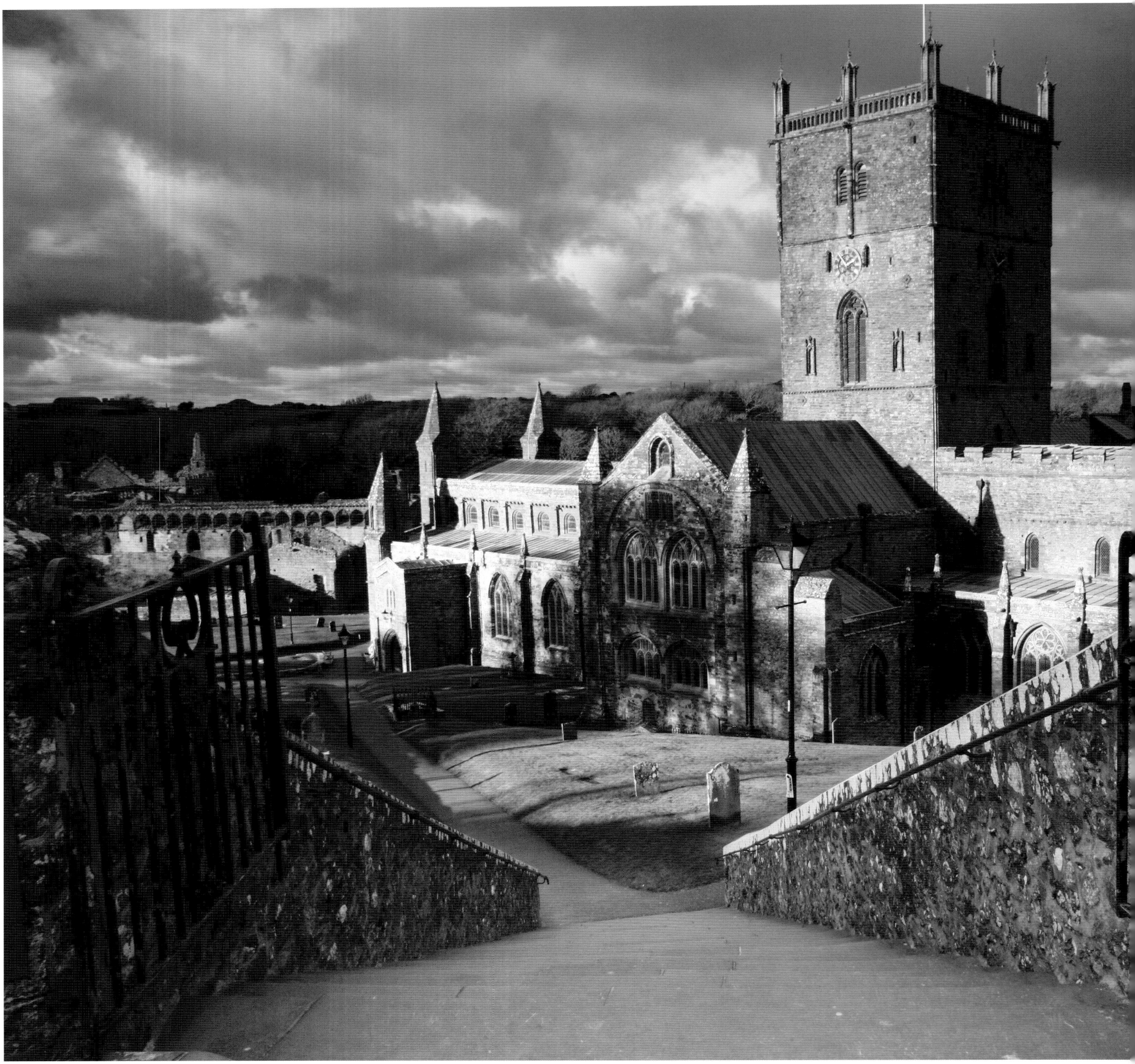

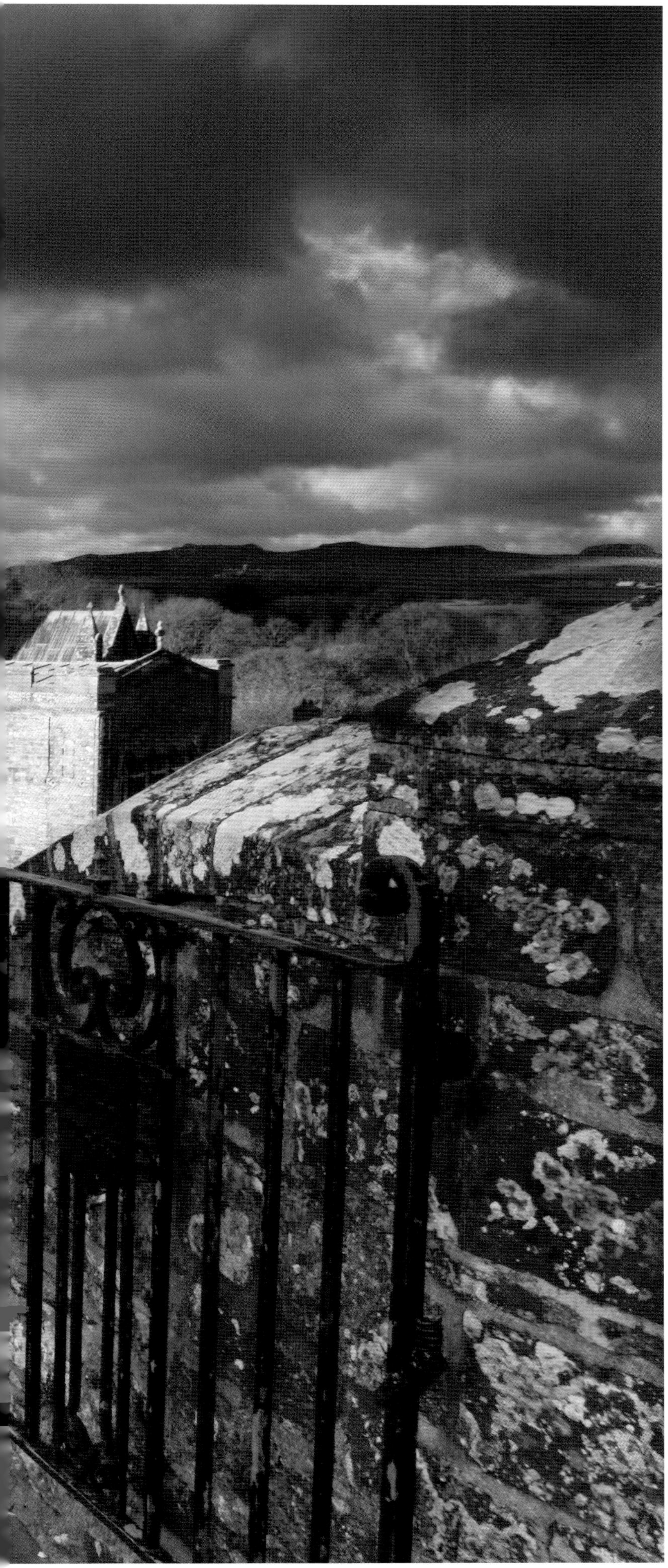

17 ST DAVIDS CATHEDRAL, PEMBROKESHIRE

By virtue of its cathedral dedicated to the patron saint of Wales, St Davids is Britain's smallest city. Cathedrals can often feel vast and impersonal; cavernous spaces that make it difficult for you to connect with the fabric of the building. St Davids Cathedral, though, welcomes you with its smaller-scale intimacy. This cosiness is reflected in the city itself and indeed, standing on Cross Square, you can imagine yourself in a large village.

There is a pleasing simplicity to the cathedral. The lack of over-embellishment invests the building with an added sense of purity. Not being prone to any form of worship myself, I can well imagine it a fulfilling experience to pray there devoid of too many visual distractions. I found the ceiling of the cathedral particularly enchanting; a beautifully carved, ornate and rare wooden structure erected in the sixteenth century. Looking up at it I marvelled at the artisan skills of the craftsmen who produced it.

It was wintertime and the sun's arc was low in the sky, its weak rays shining horizontally through the windows. A number of objects and fixtures were brought to life; an illuminated pulpit, a carved wooden screen with the dappled pattern of leaded windows projected onto it, light refracting off candlesticks on an altar table, a crucifix picked-out on the ceiling.

I spent a few hours photographing the interior of the cathedral and I can genuinely vouch for the sense of serenity I felt on leaving. All the small concerns of life were banished, at least for a little while anyway. (Map A5)

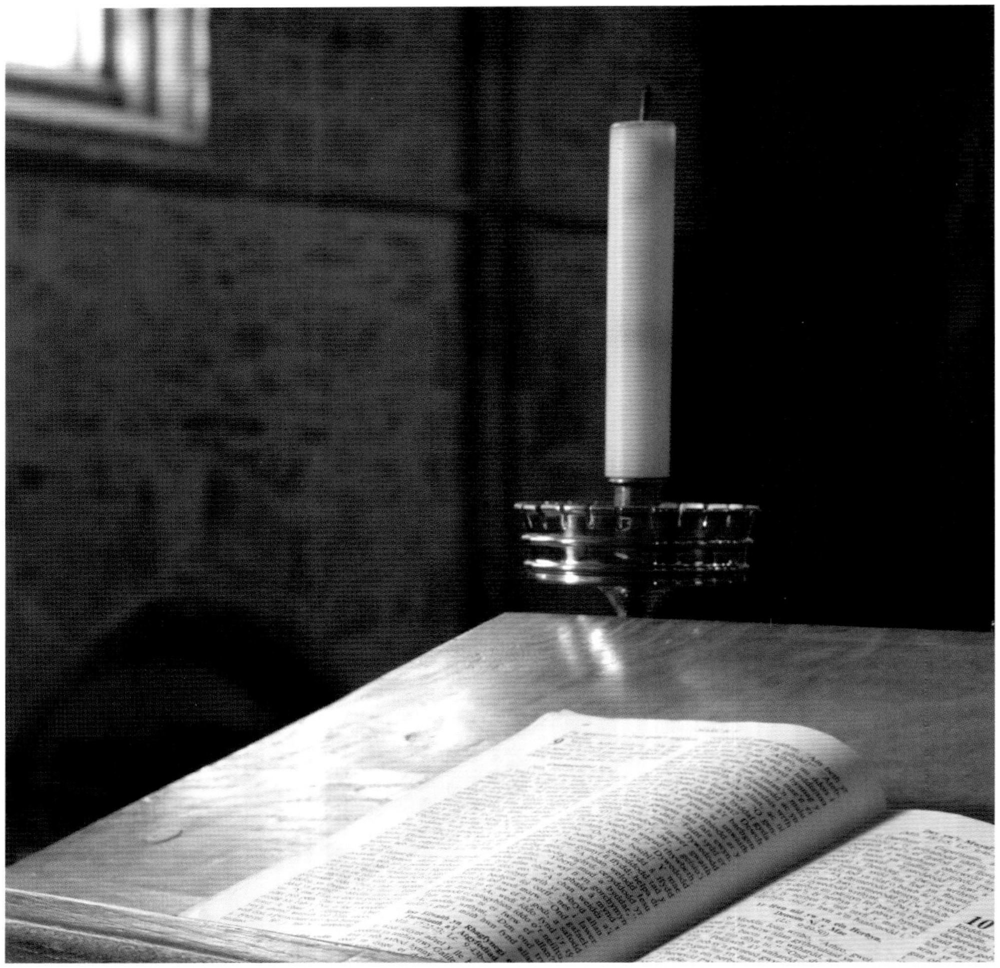

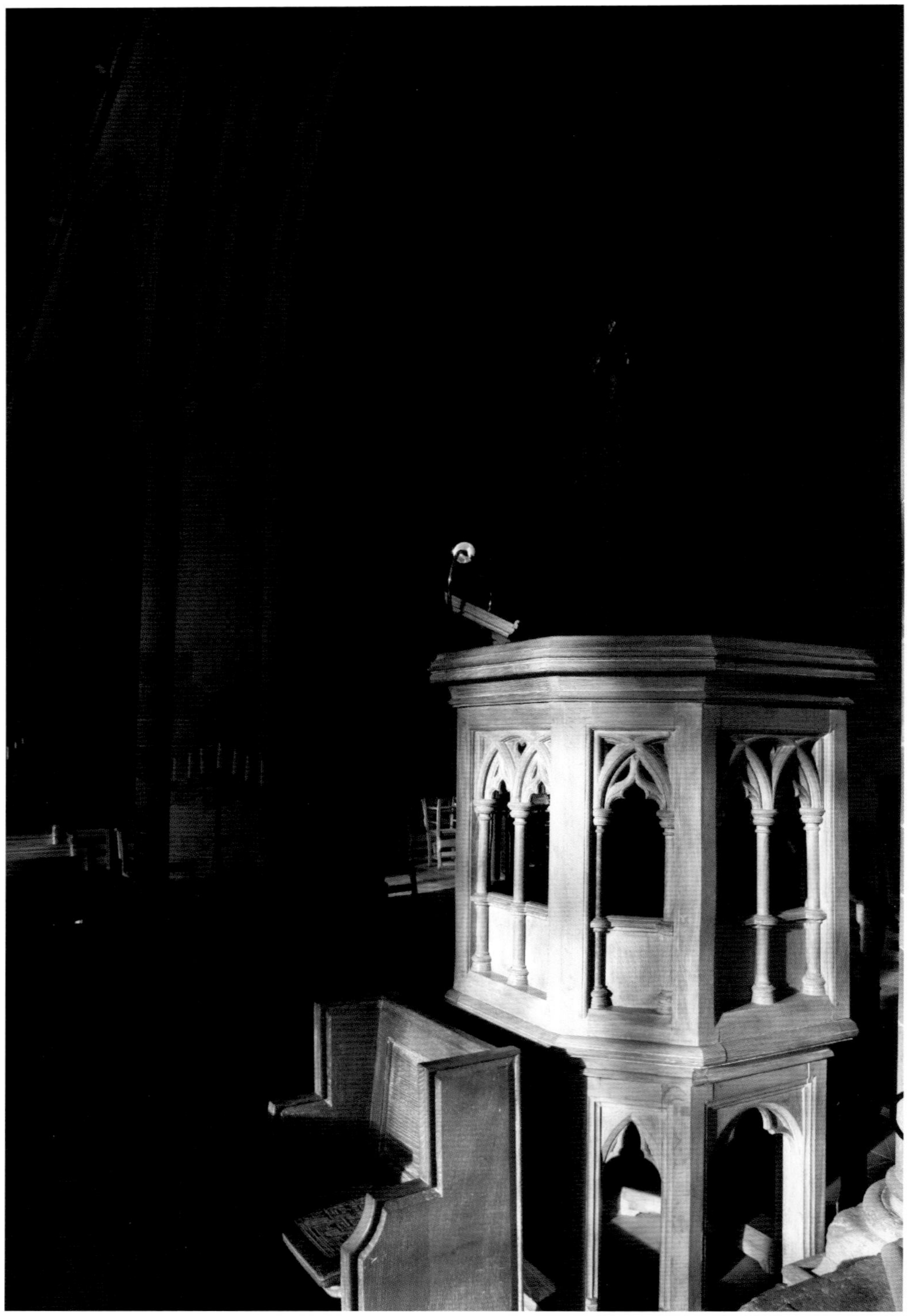

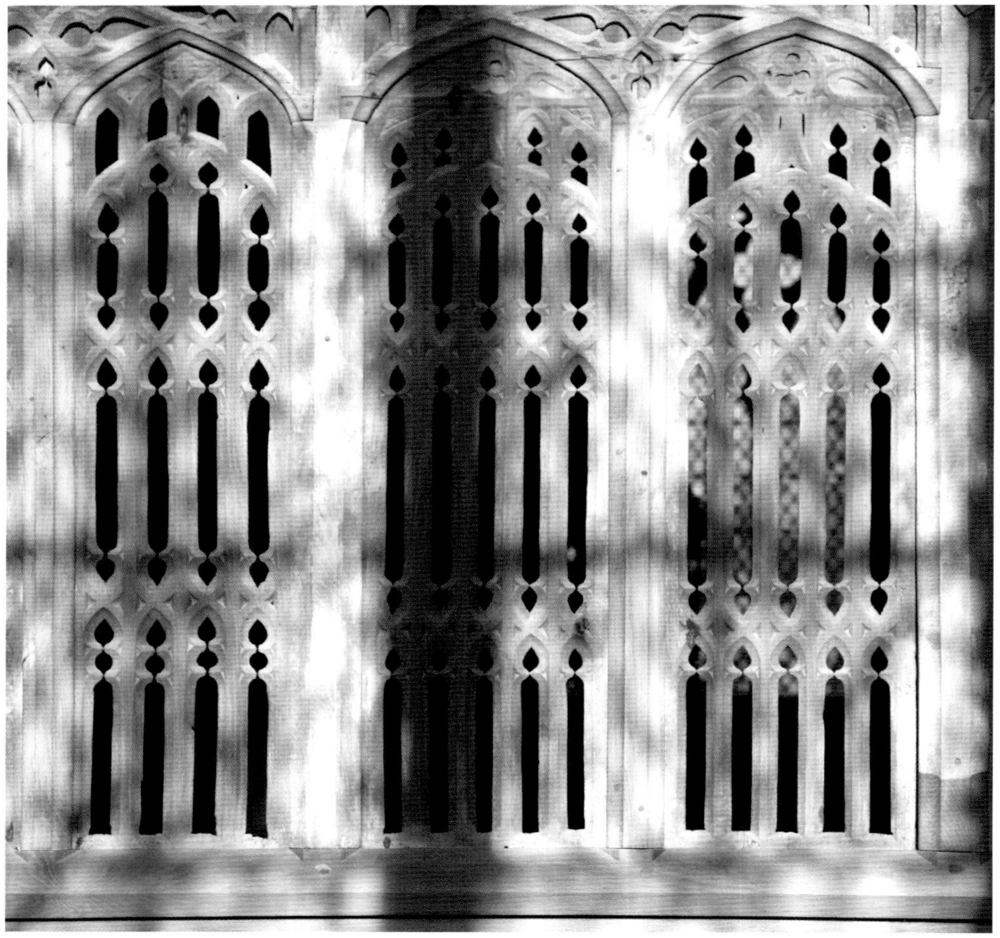

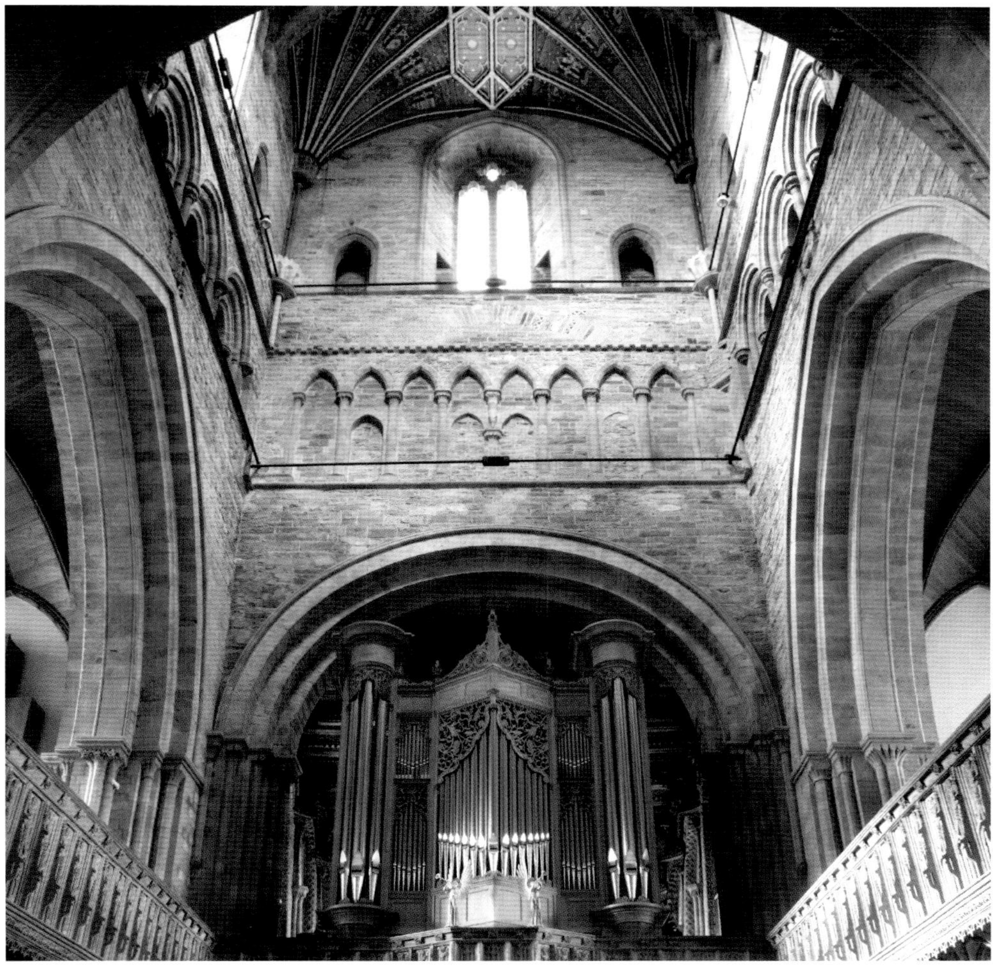

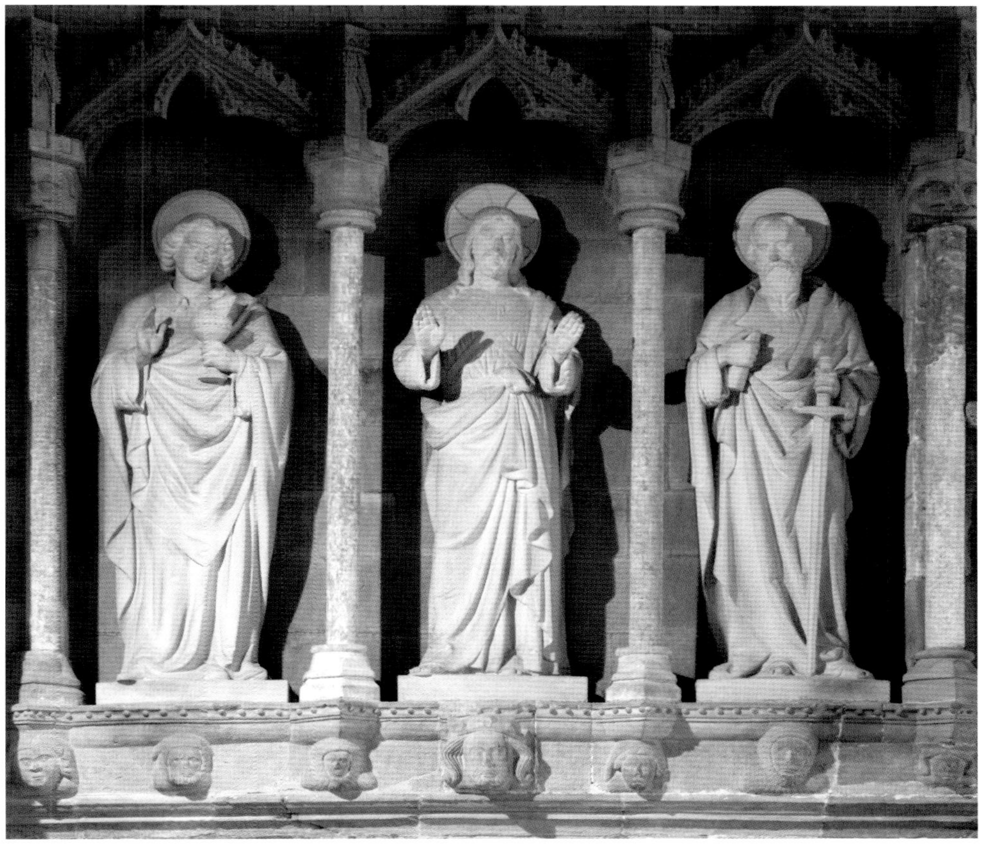

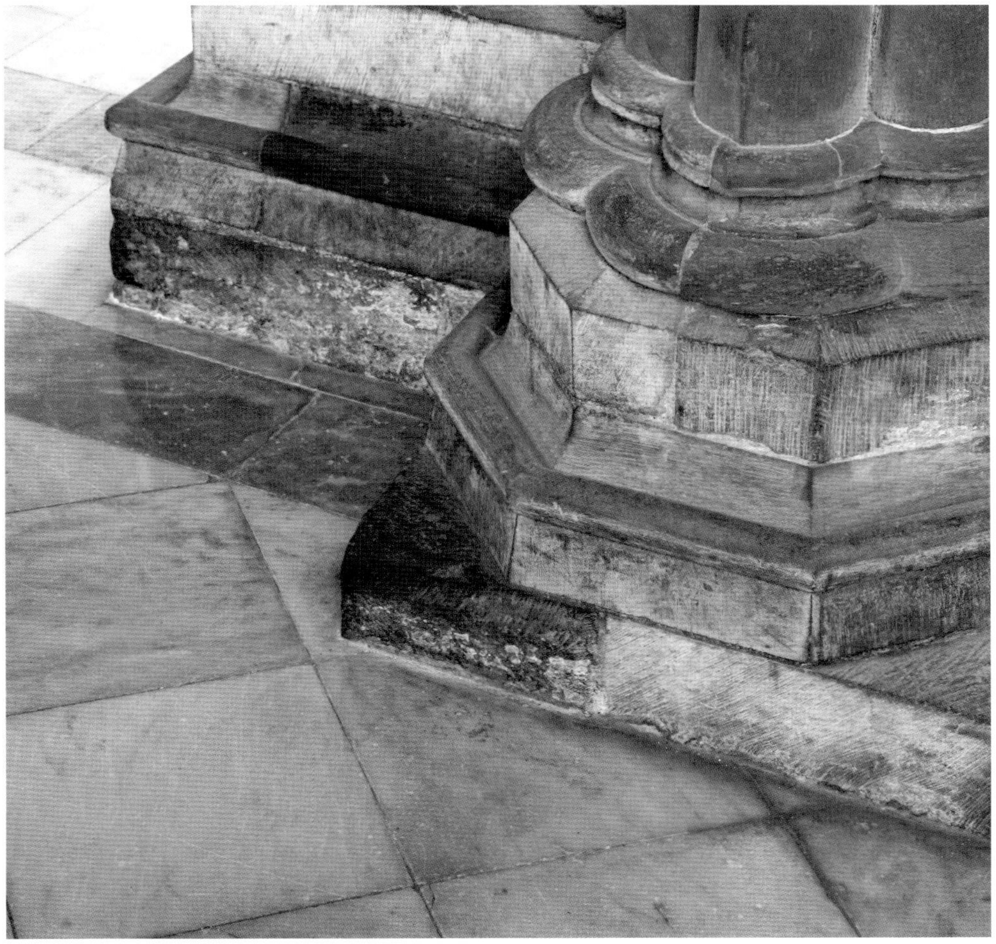

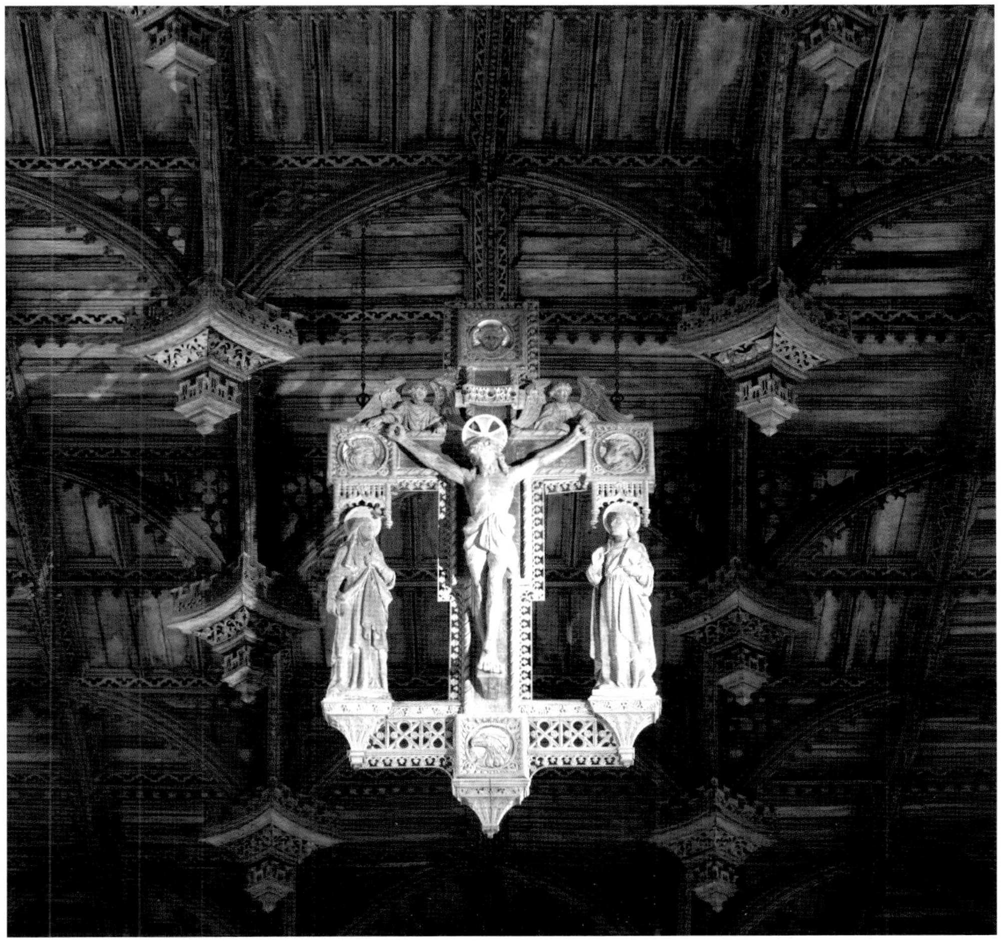

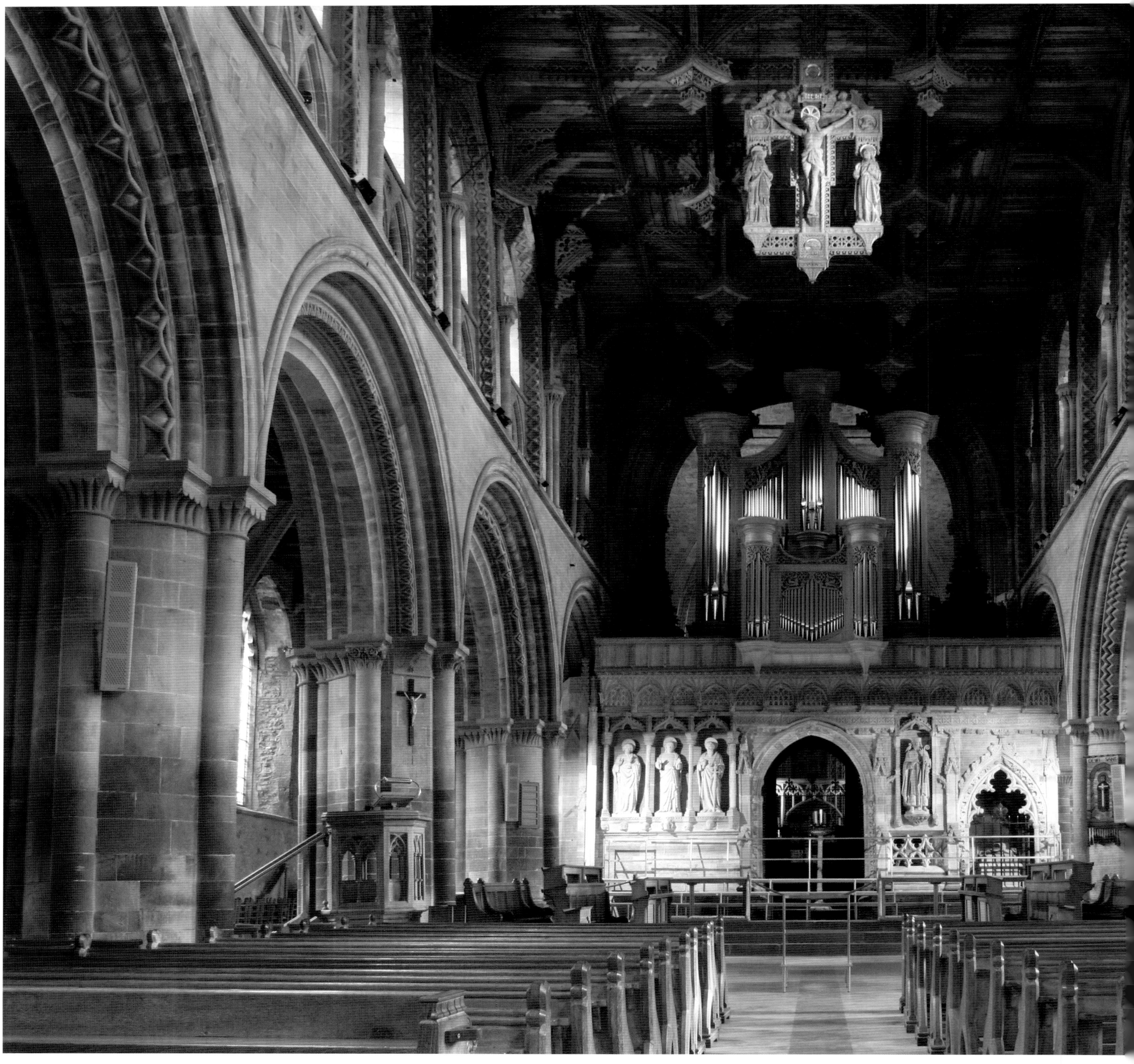

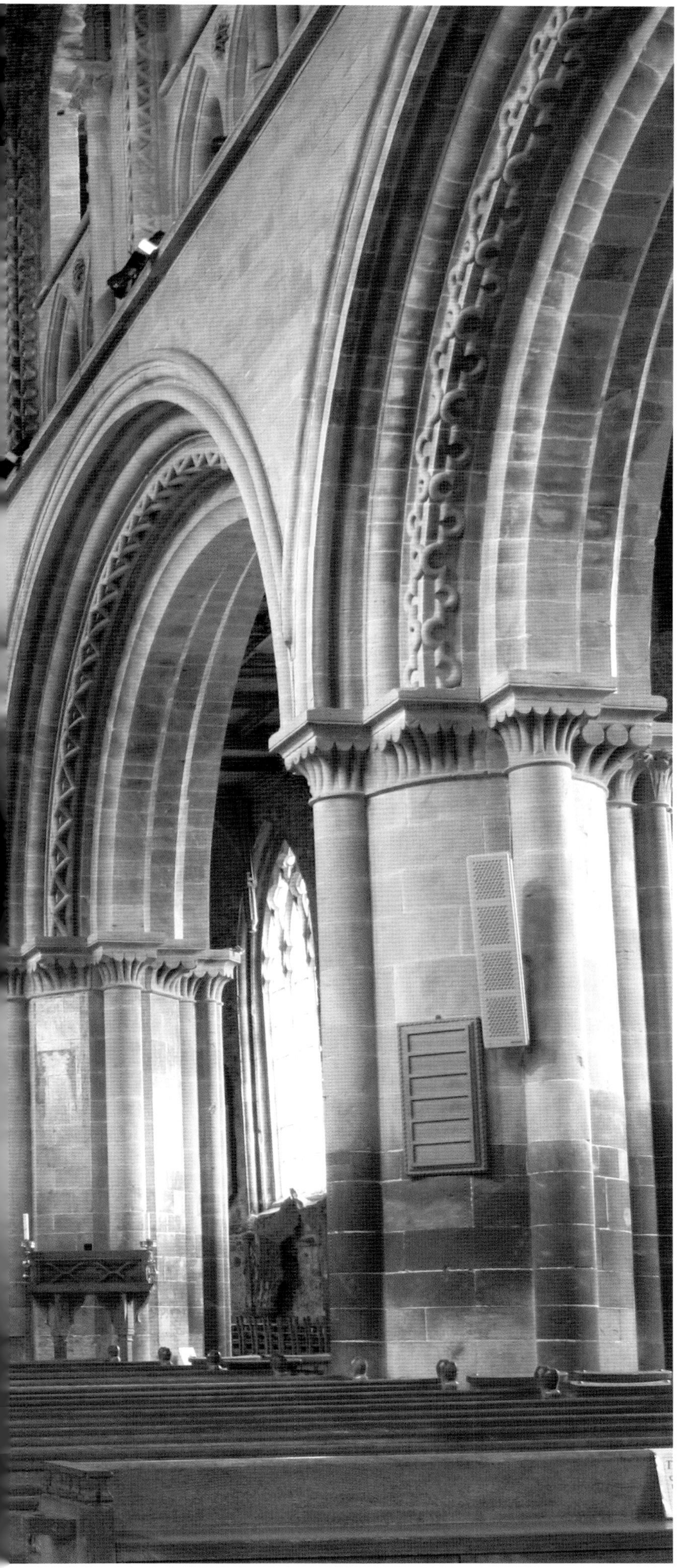

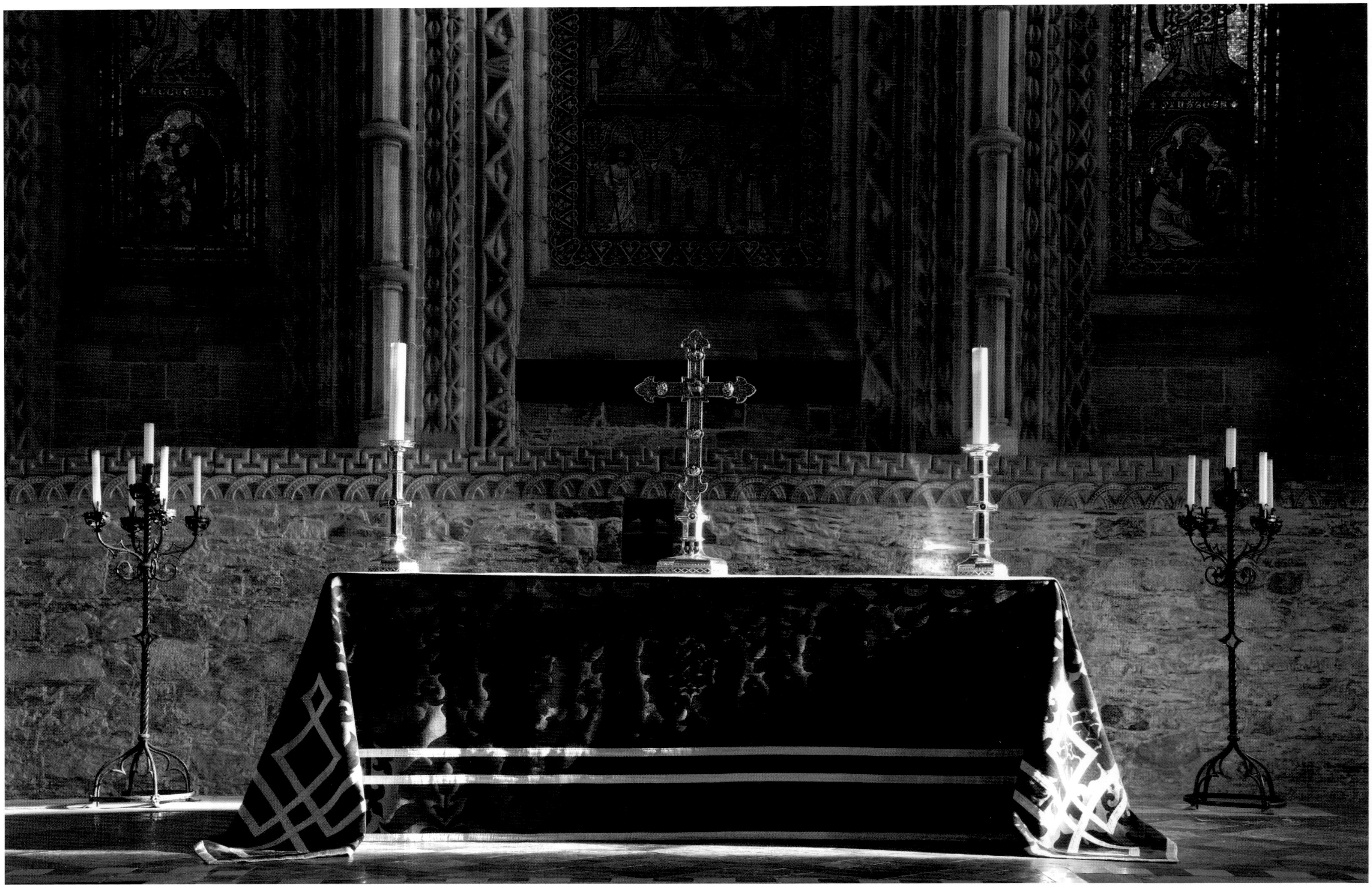

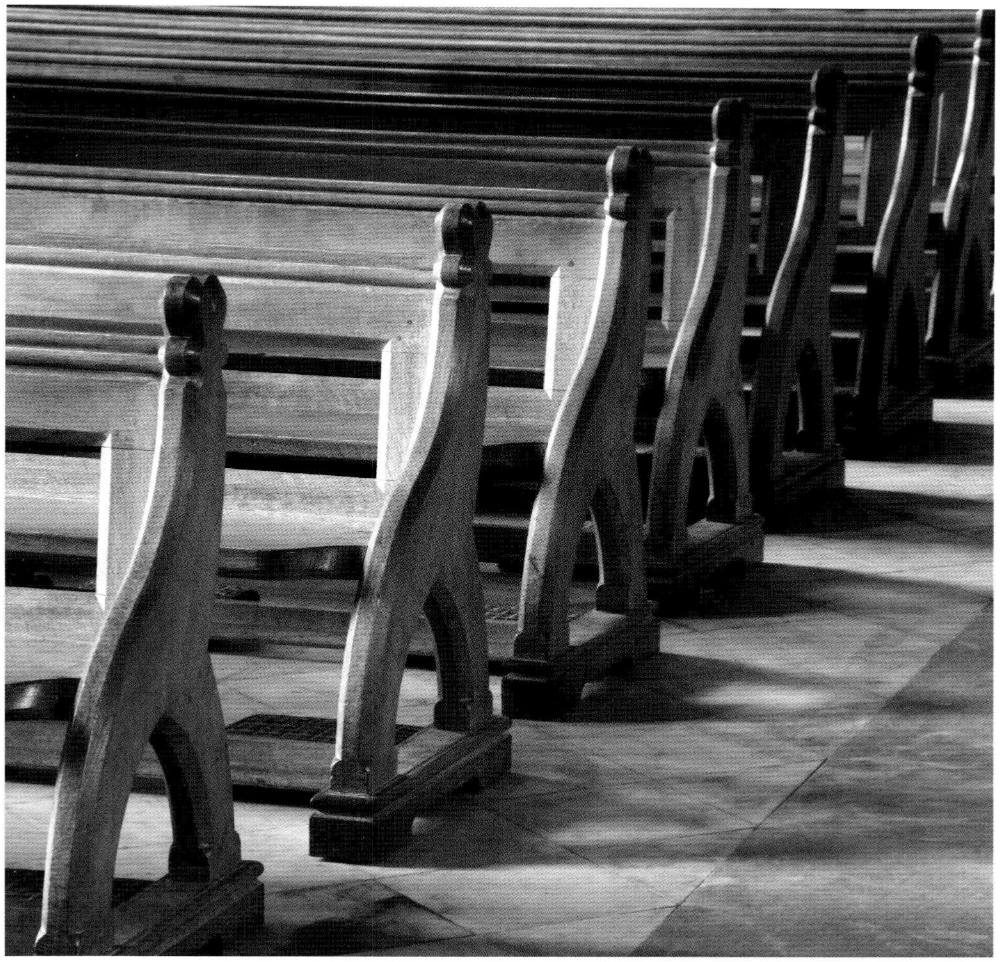

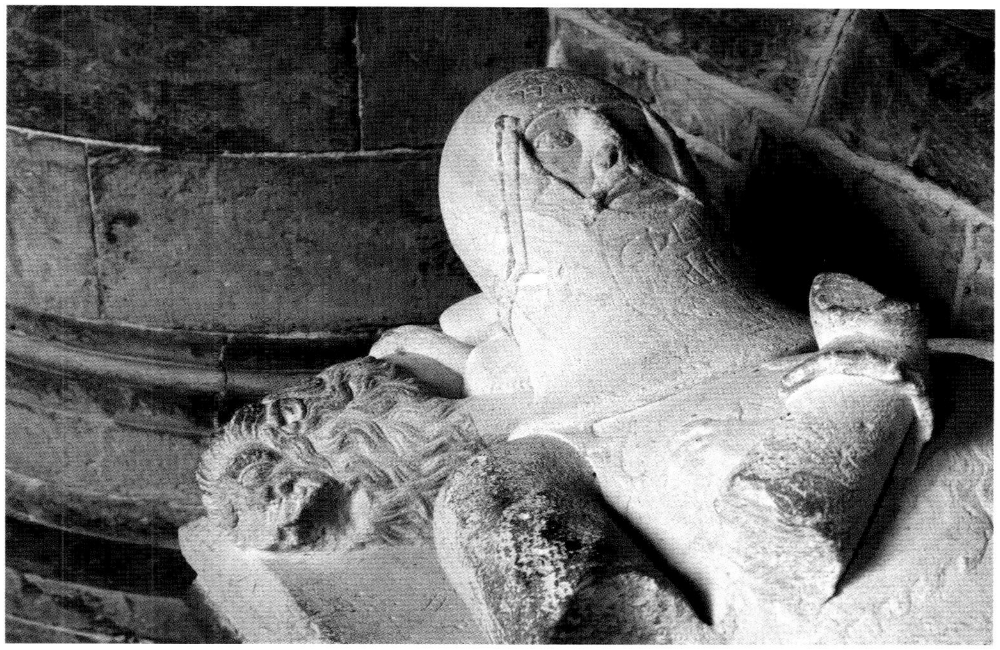

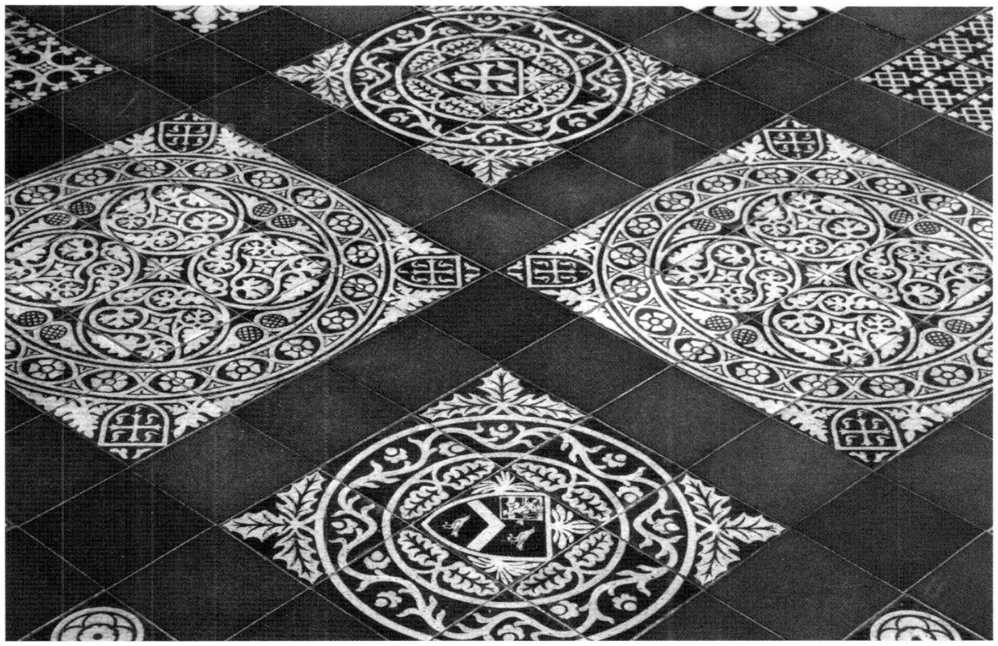

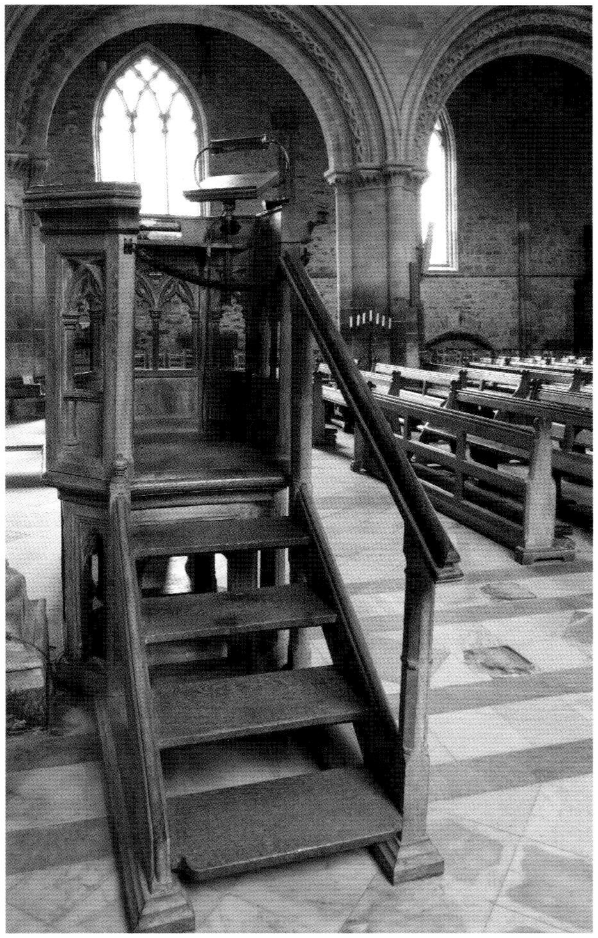

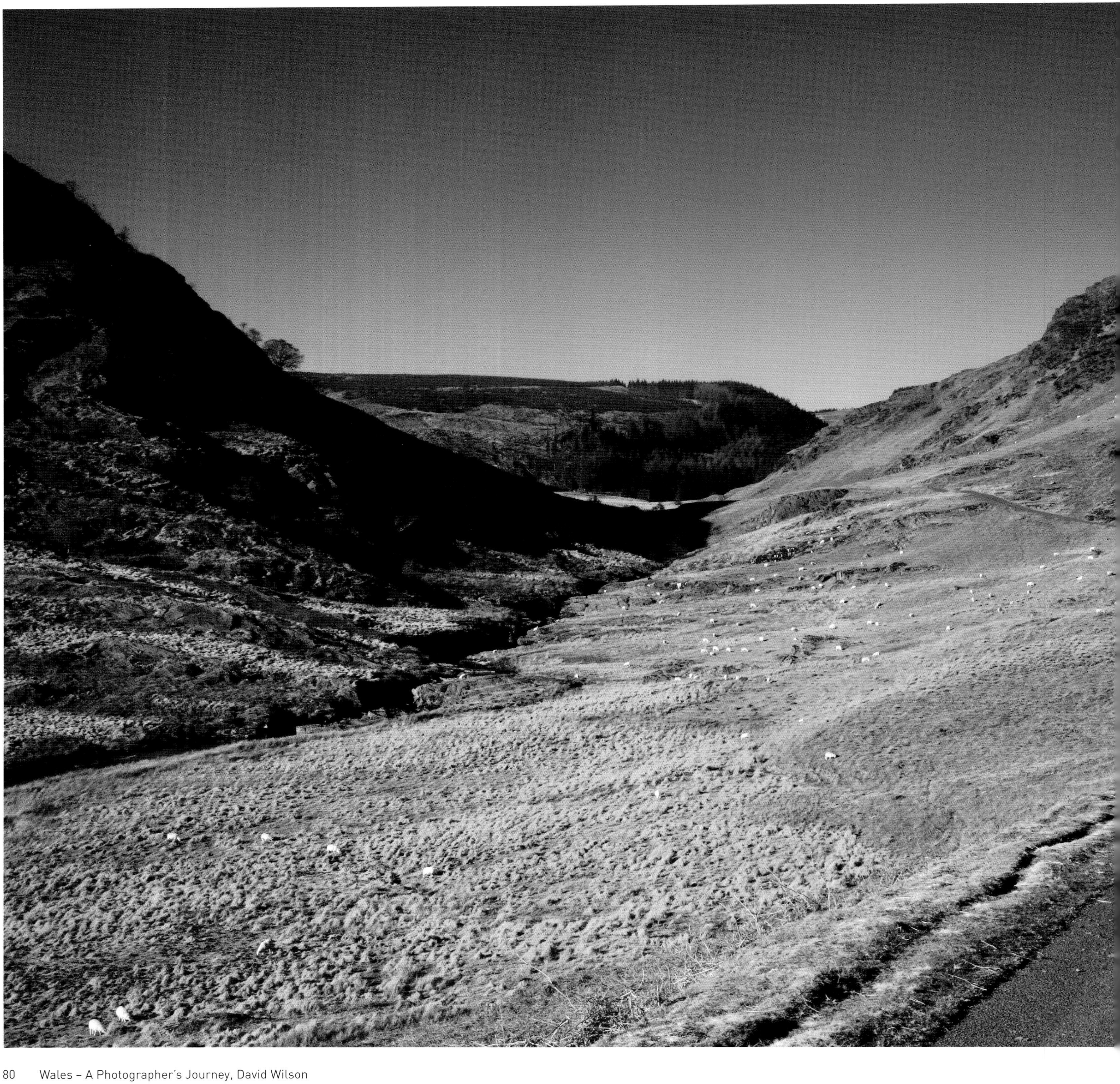

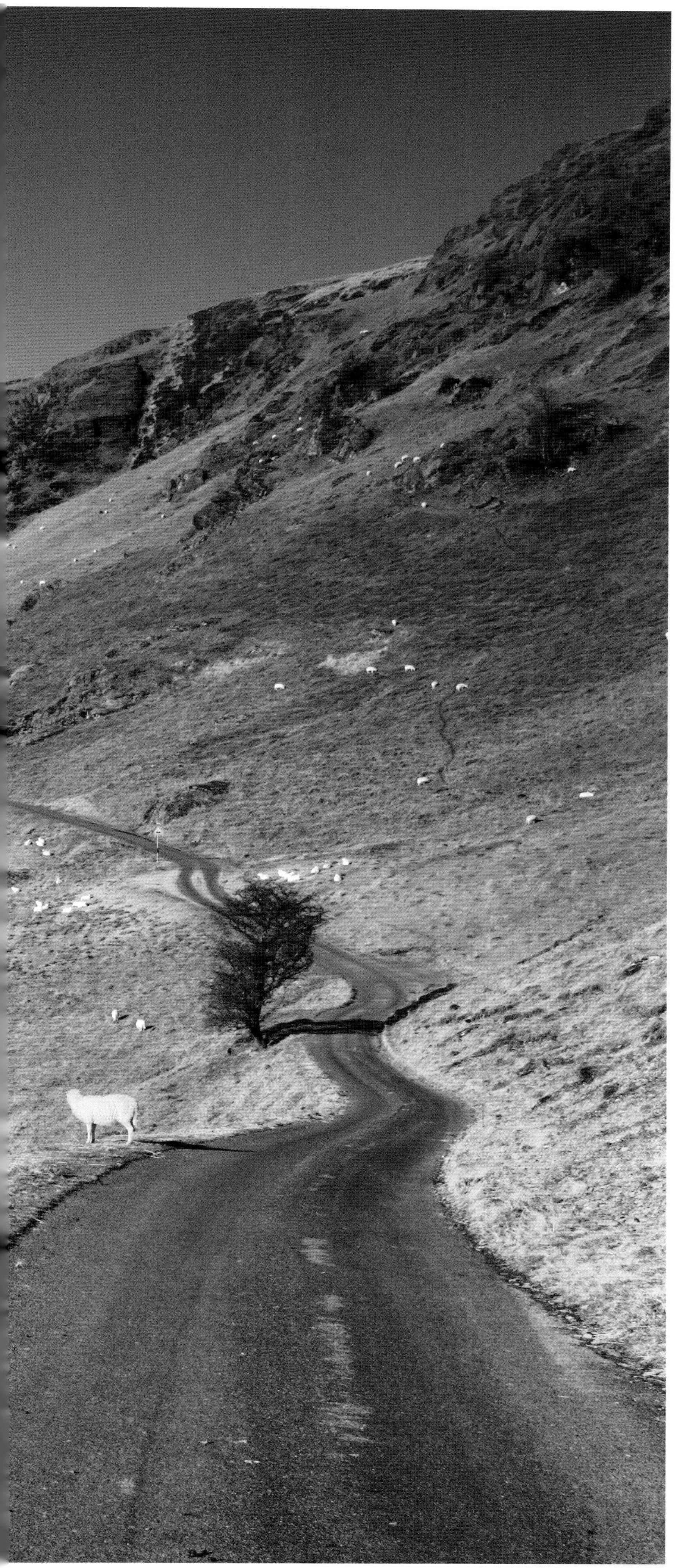

18 ABERGWESYN PASS TO TREGARON, CEREDIGION

Retracing the old drovers' route from the Abergwesyn Pass back to Tregaron filled me with an enormous sense of awe for the people who trod this way with their livestock heading for market in England. Covering an average of 15 miles (24km) a day, it was a life endured by hardy people with resolve and determination.

As I drove along, I encountered a large and dispersed flock of sheep, the majority of which were lying down either side of the road, seemingly basking in the sunshine.

I stopped and got out fully expecting them to scatter, which is the usual response. But no, they stood up and began converging on me from every direction. I felt almost Messianic! Very quickly I was penned in against the car boot surrounded by dozens of densely packed sheep – quite surreal!

The exit from the pass was via the appropriately named Devil's Staircase, a perilously steep road peppered with hairpins. On parts of the road permanently shaded from the sun, sheets of black ice clung to the surface, making it an anxious ascent.

Once out of there, the Cambrian Mountains open out into vast plains of grassland stretching as far as the eye can see, punctuated only by the odd cluster of evergreen trees. What an inspiring sight it must have been to see hundreds of head of cattle munching their way across this Welsh desert. A few miles further on I came across an old phone kiosk, incongruent in the wilderness. The perfect spot for lunch and a few scribbled notes. After a reinvigorating pasty I was on my way towards Cwm Berwyn and my eventual destination of Tregaron. (Map C5)

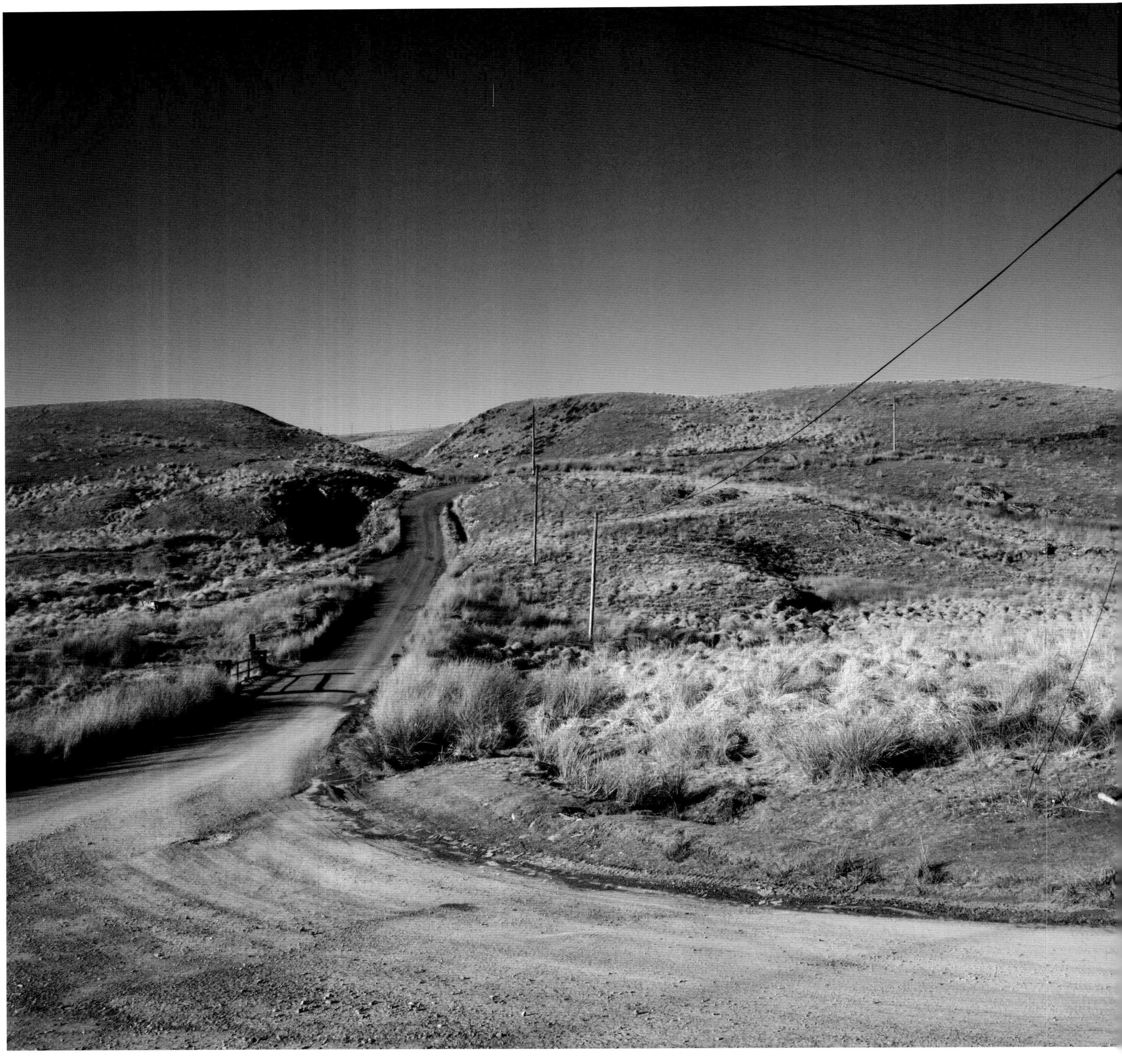

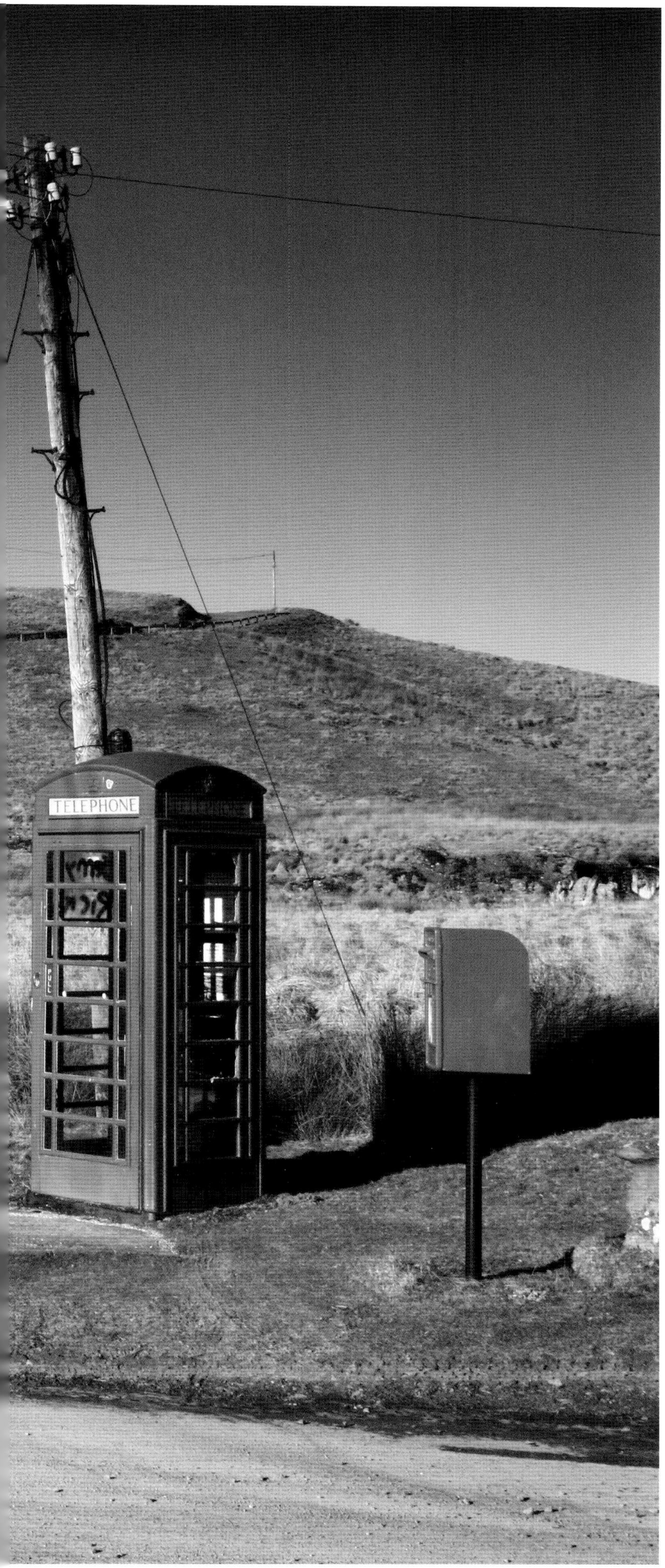

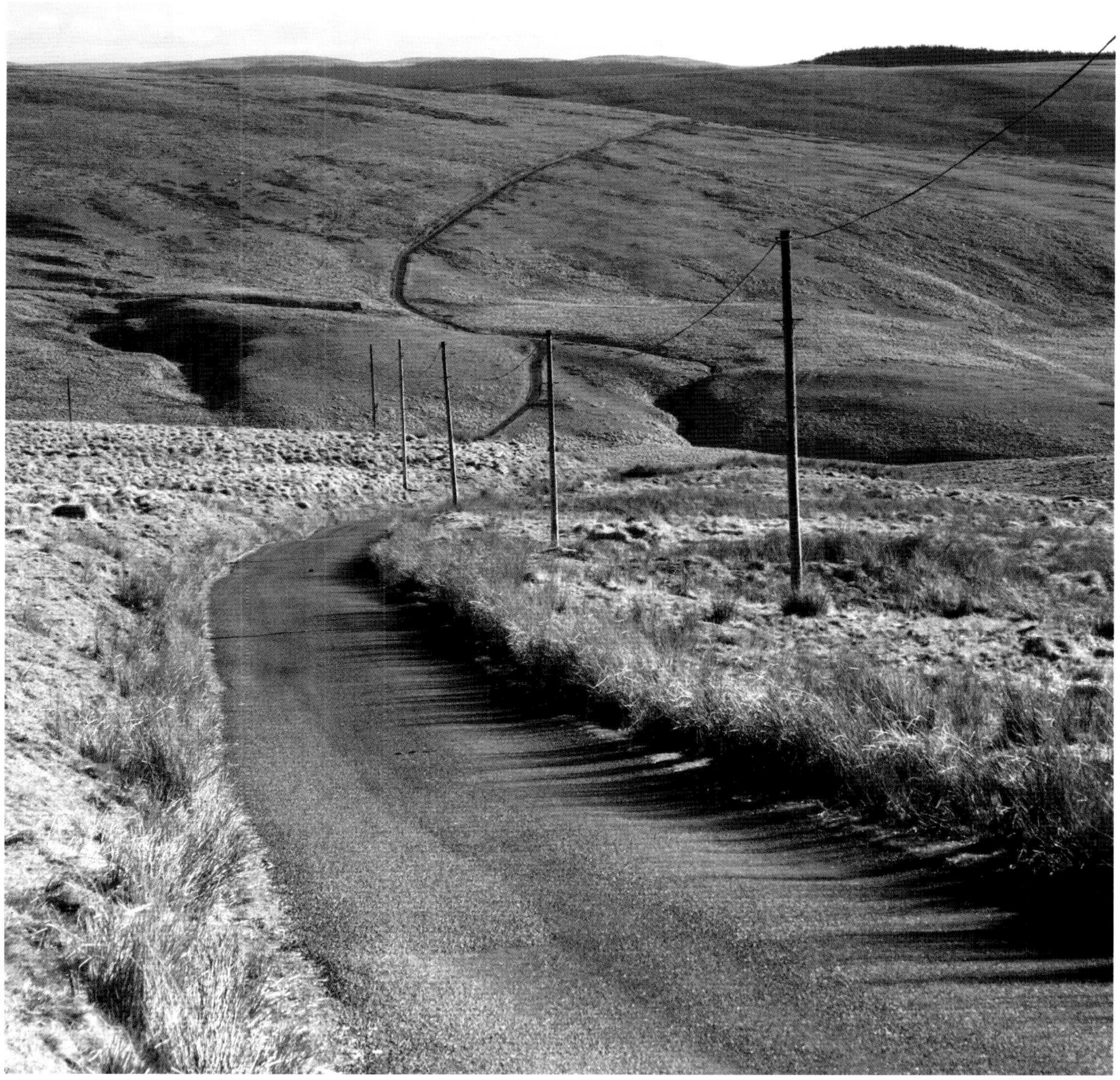

Left: The perfect spot for lunch
Above: Looking back on my route

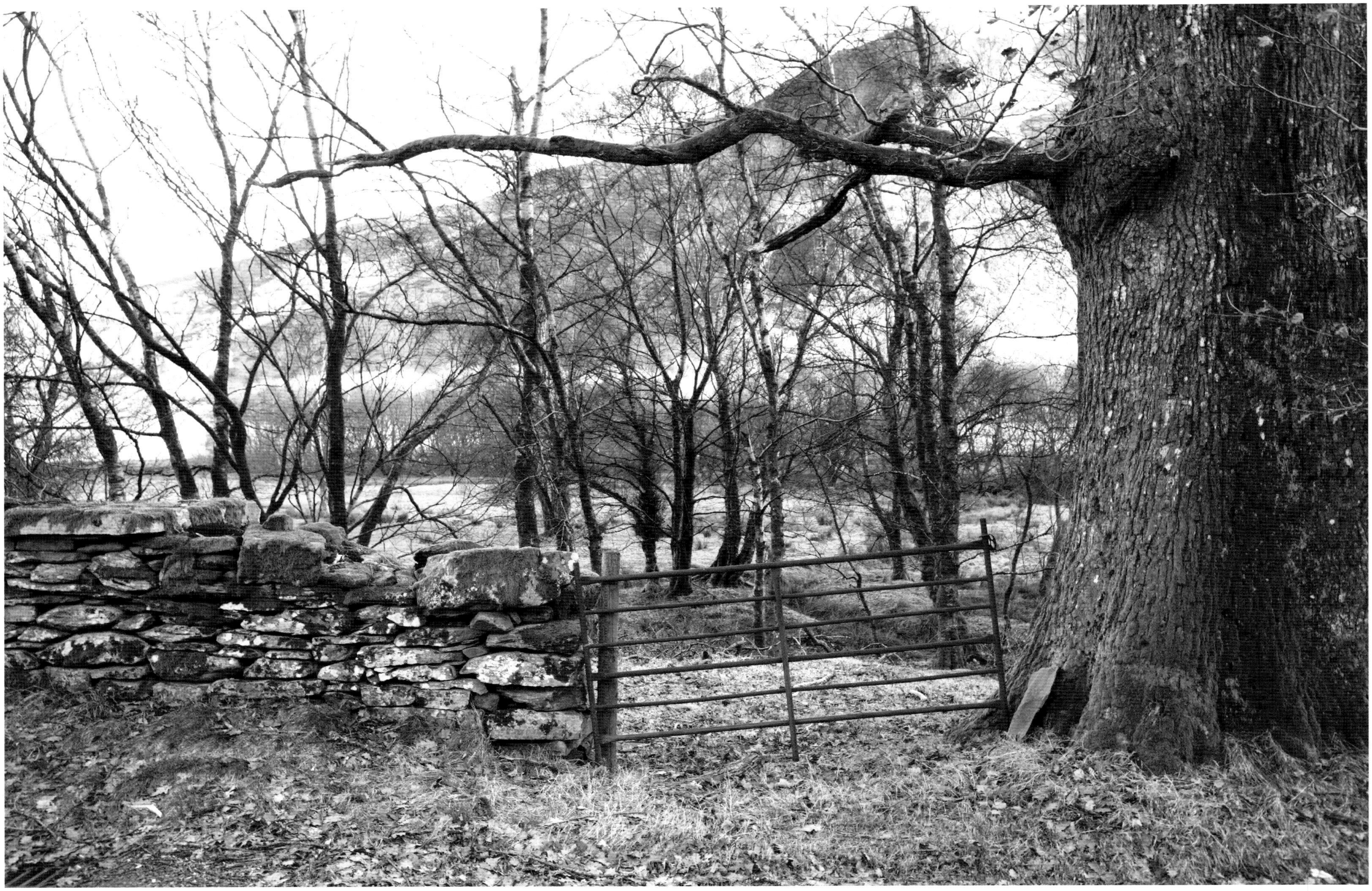

Above: Cwm Berwyn

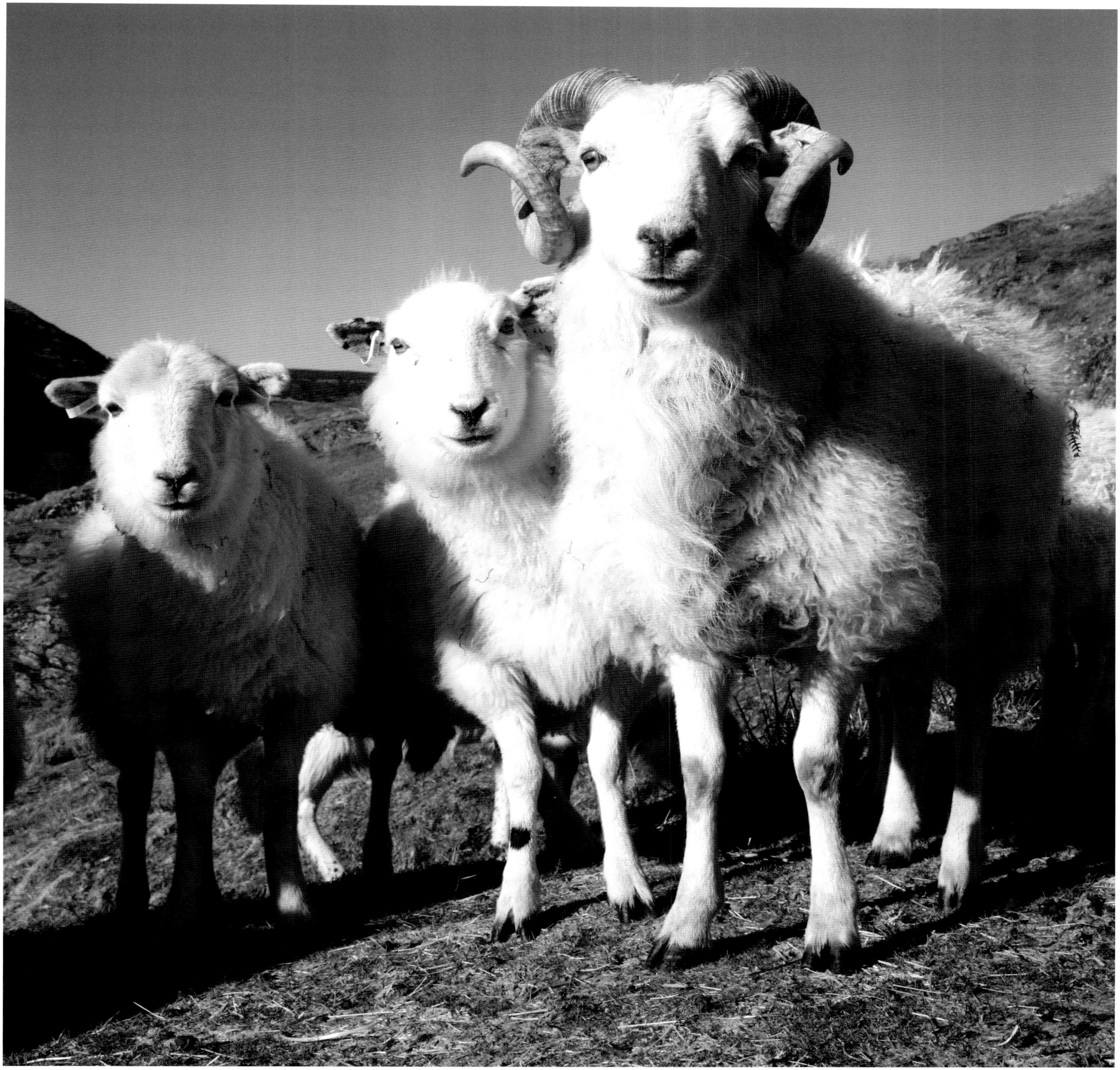

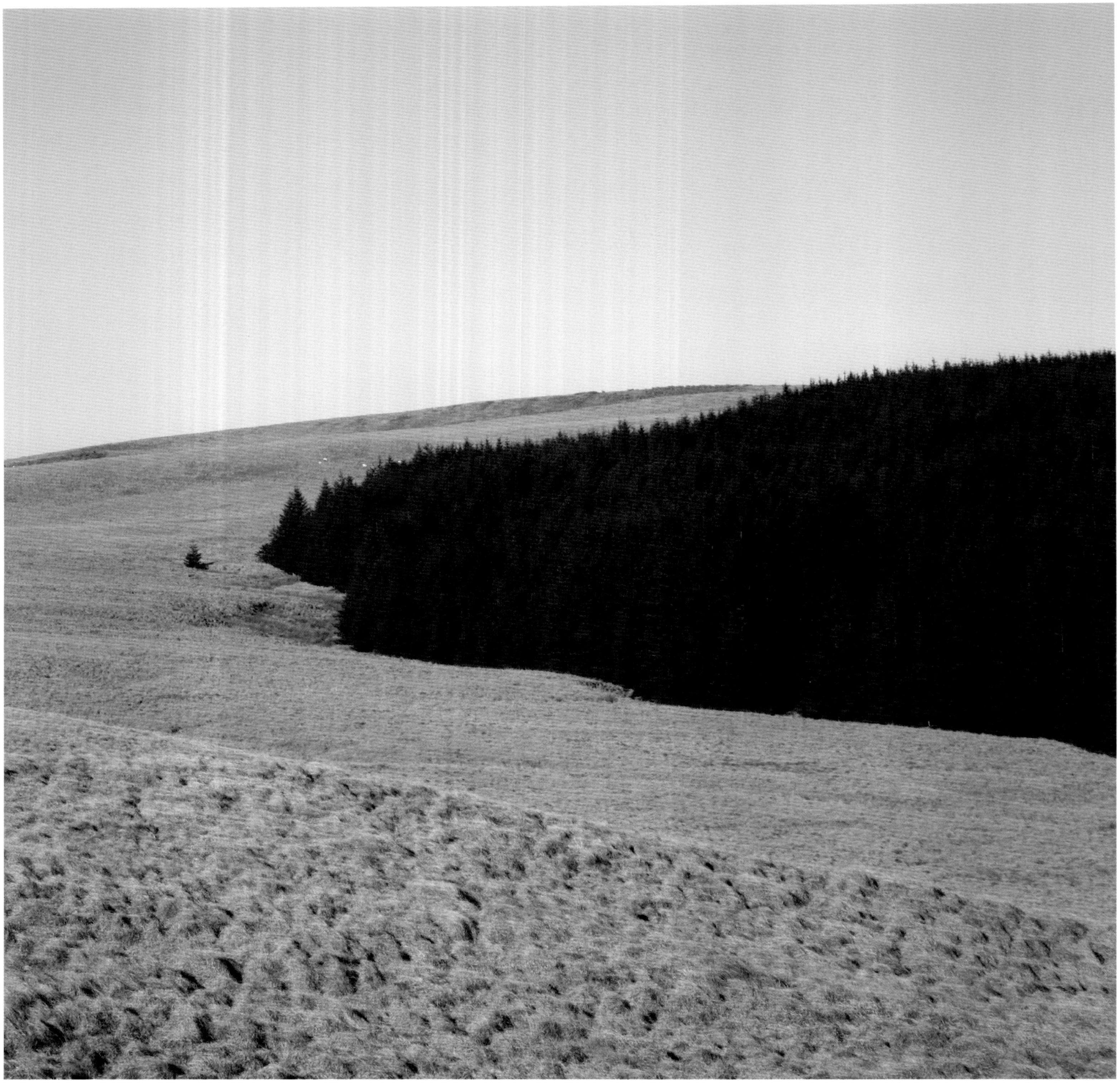

Above: Rolling grasslands

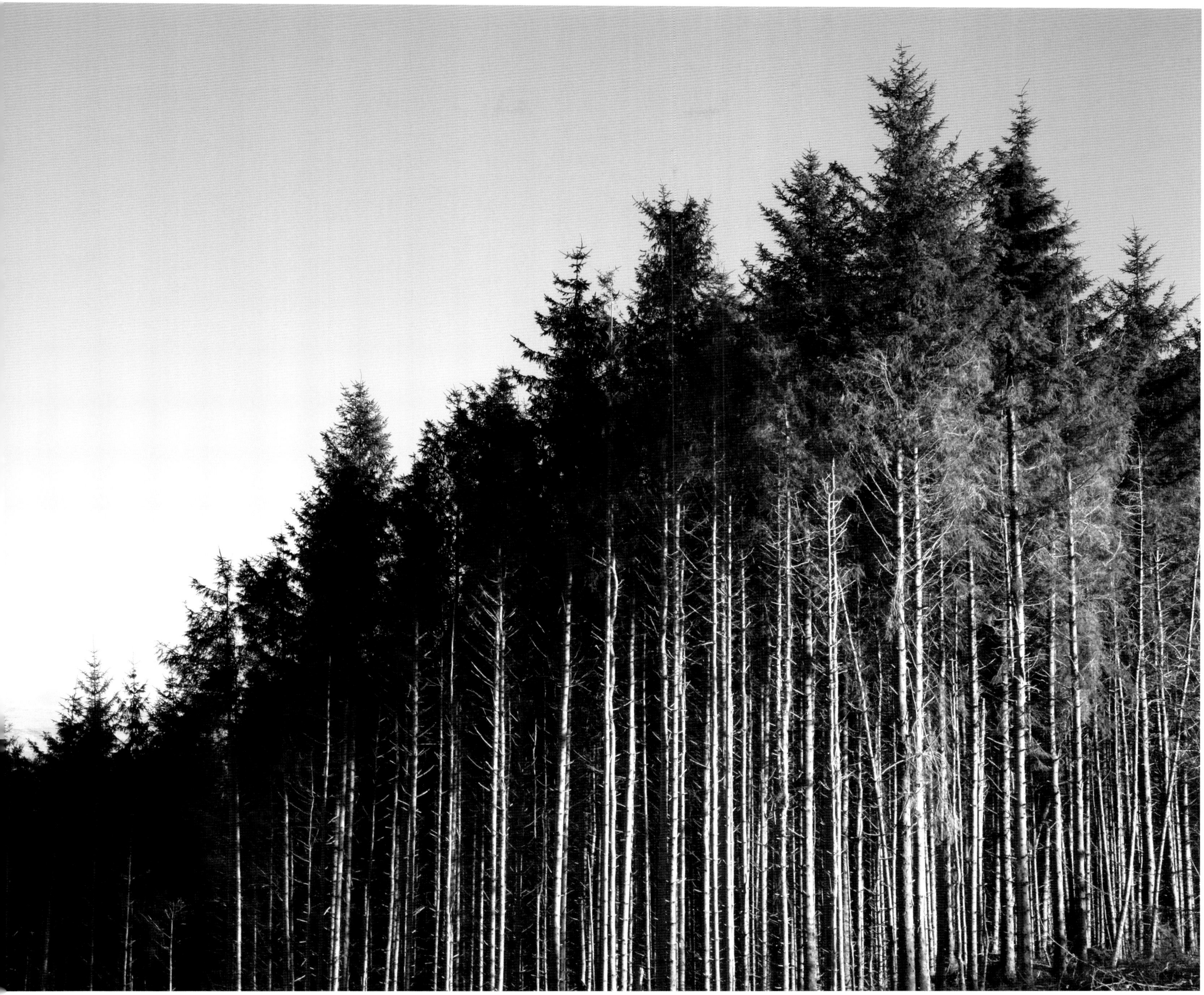

18 Abergwesyn Pass to Tregaron, Ceredigion

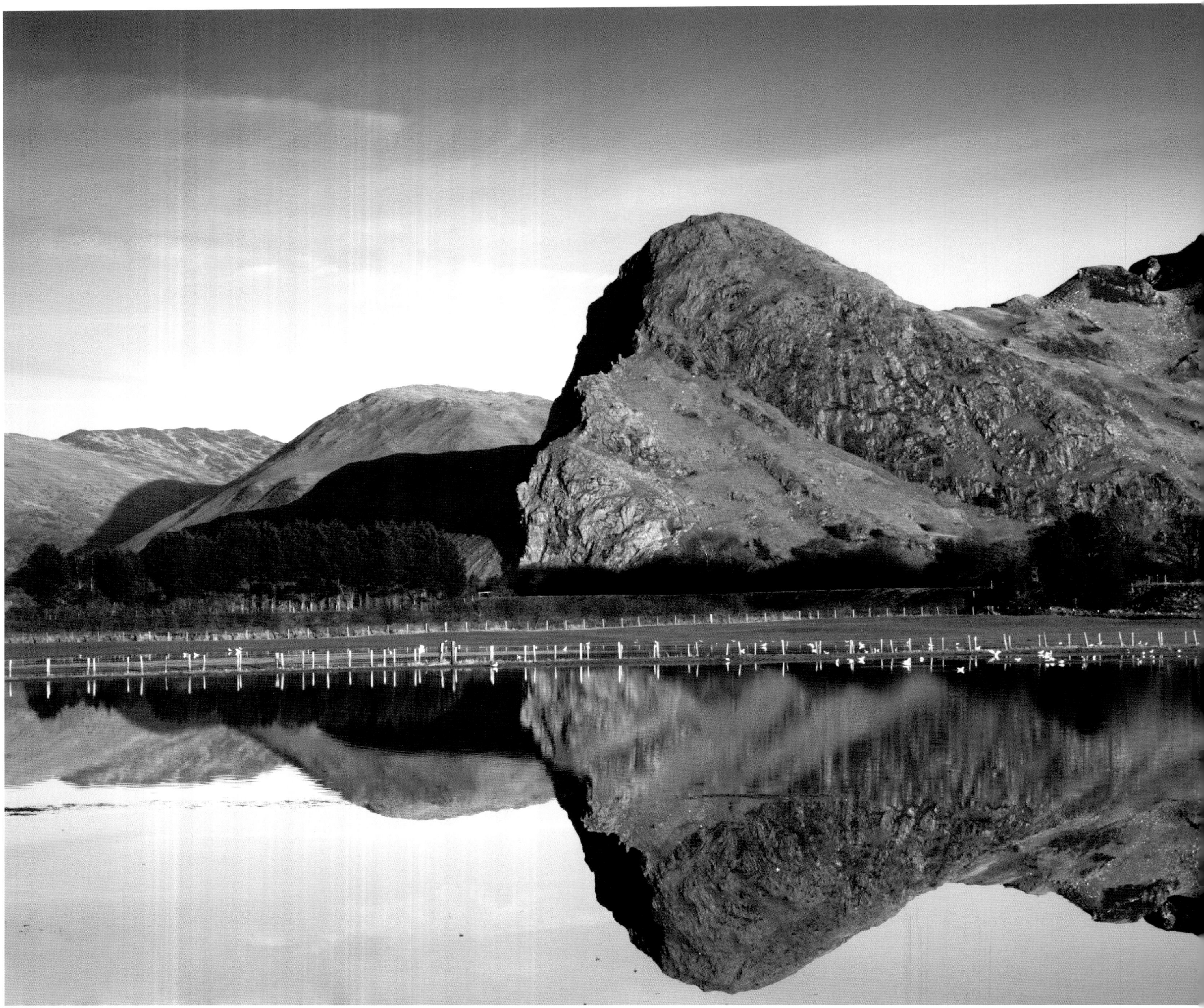

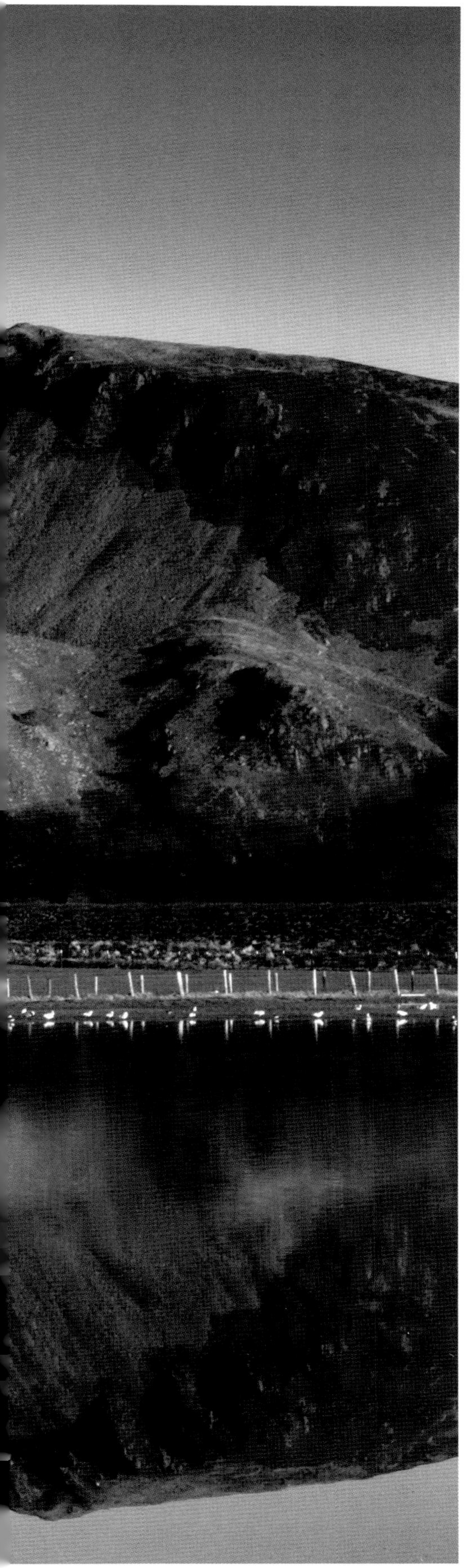

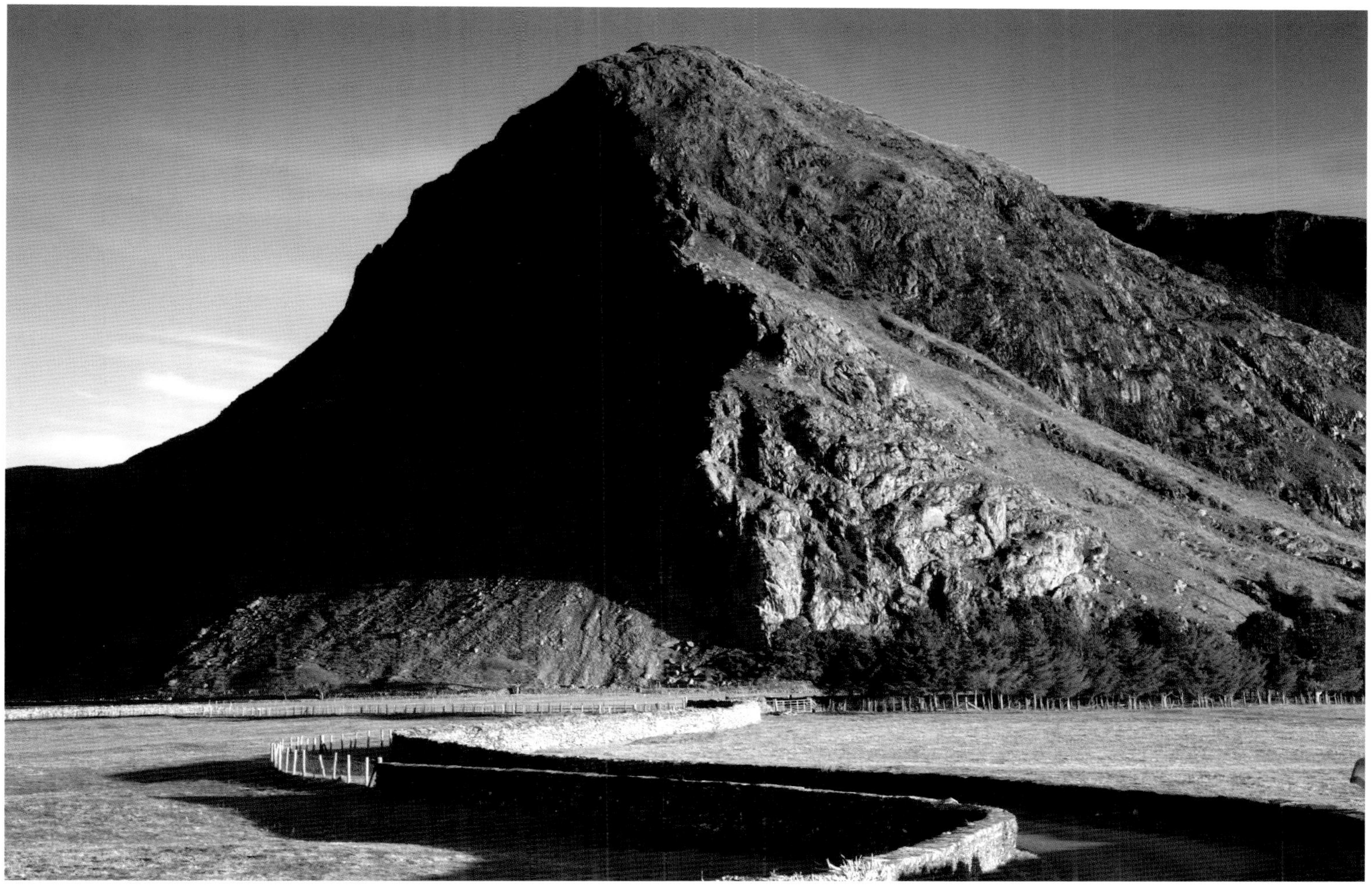

Left / Above: Craig yr Aderyn
Overleaf: Castell y Bere

19 DYSYNNI VALLEY, SNOWDONIA

Rising to a proud 258 metres (856 ft), Craig yr Aderyn (Birds' Rock) is situated in the Dysynni Valley a few miles inland from Tywyn on the Cardigan Bay coast. At one time the sea lapped its base, but these days the tidal reach has receded considerably and the valley is now given over to farming. It is an incredibly striking lump of rock, erupting as it does from a billiard table of level pasture. Its name derives from the cormorants that still perch on top, oblivious to the disappearance of the shoreline.

Recently melted snow and heavy rain had flooded parts of this low-lying valley, possibly convincing the cormorants that the sea had returned. Castell y Bere, a mile further up the valley also benefited from this sense of reflected glory. Built by Llywelyn the Great, Prince of Gwynedd in the early thirteenth century, the castle is now a romantic ruin shrouded by trees atop its rocky outcrop. (Map C3)

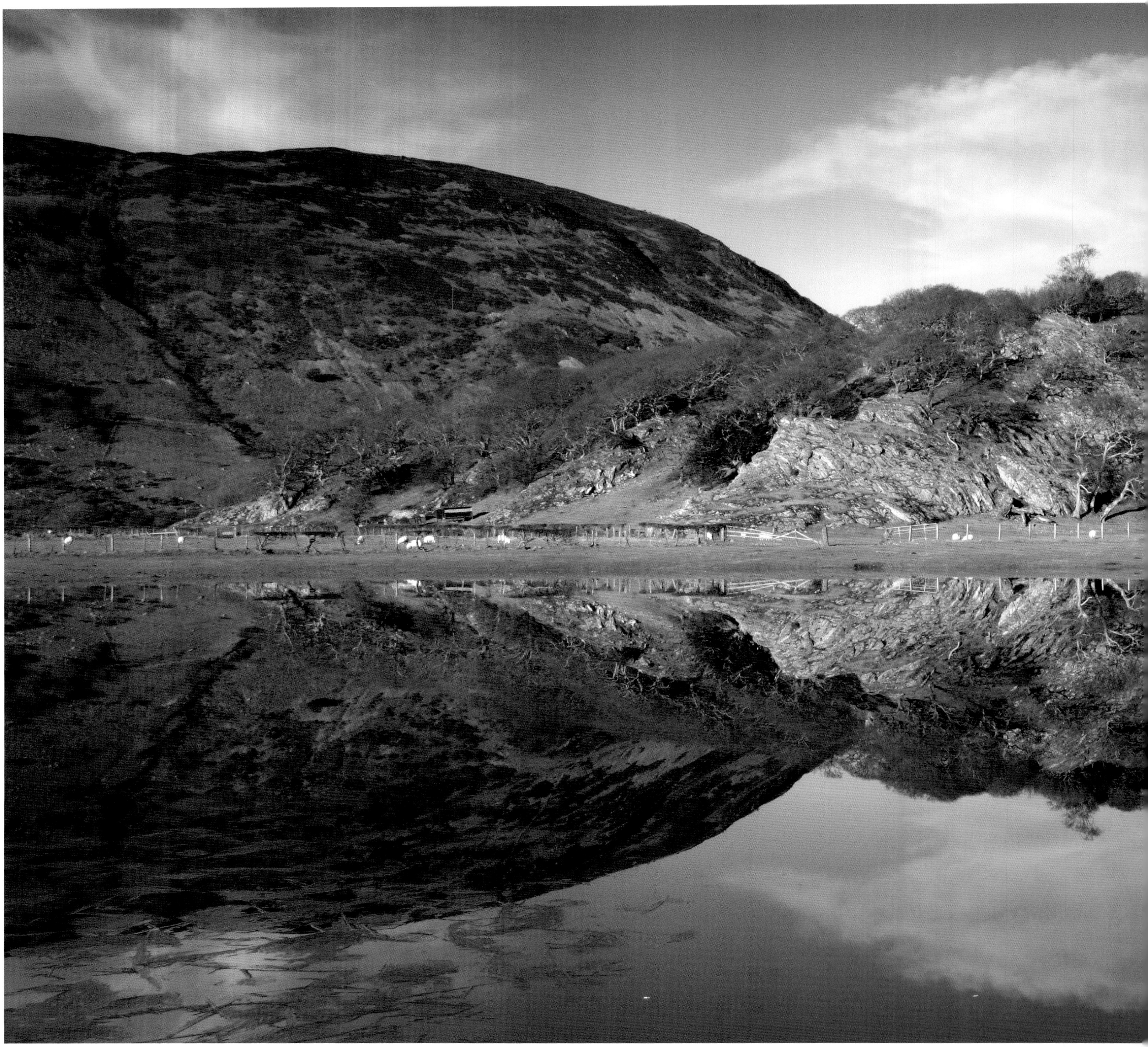

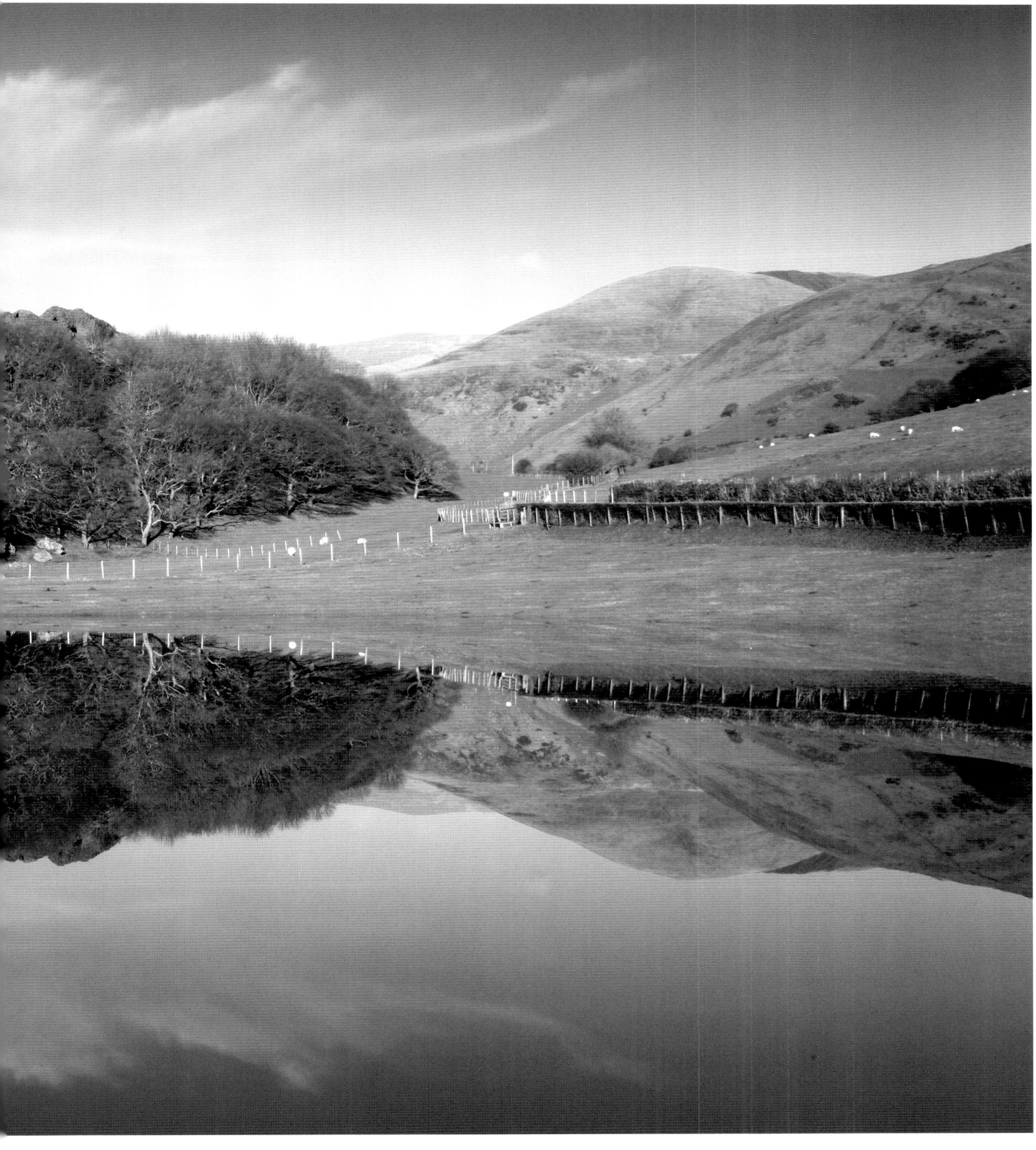

19 Dysynni Valley, Snowdonia

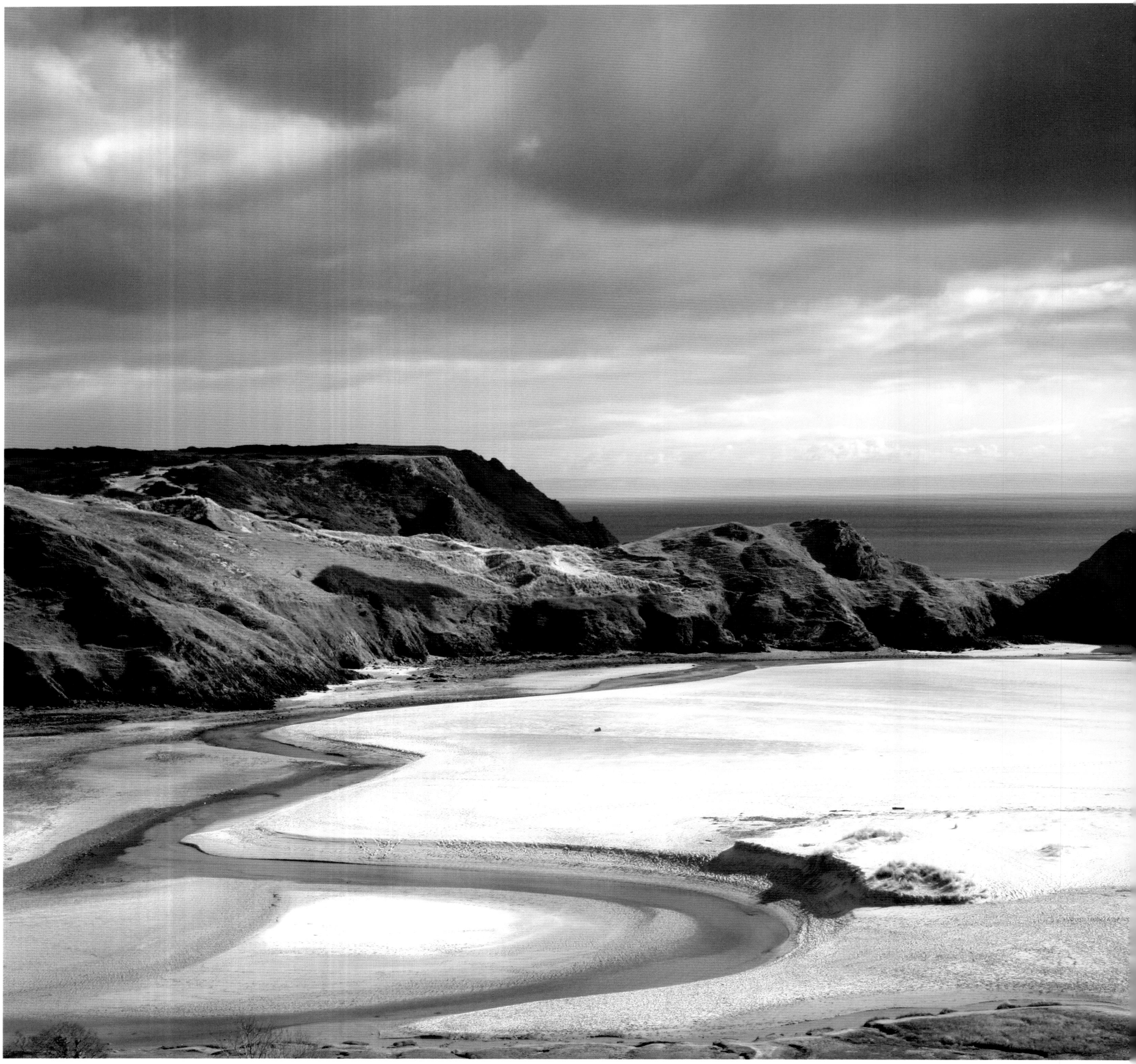

20 THREE CLIFFS BAY, GOWER

Wales has an enviable coastline boasting an abundance of stunning bays and beaches. As a native of Pembrokeshire I have enjoyed countless dreamy days spent on an array of great stretches of sand. This was my first visit to Three Cliffs Bay and I had high hopes for this jewel of the Gower. Film-set perfect, it confirmed everything I had been led to expect; a secluded bay with the meandering Pennard Pill snaking past the three pinnacles and out to sea. It was February and the weather had been very changeable; driving rain one moment, gentle sunshine the next. This may explain why the beach was deserted – just the way I like it!
(Map C6)

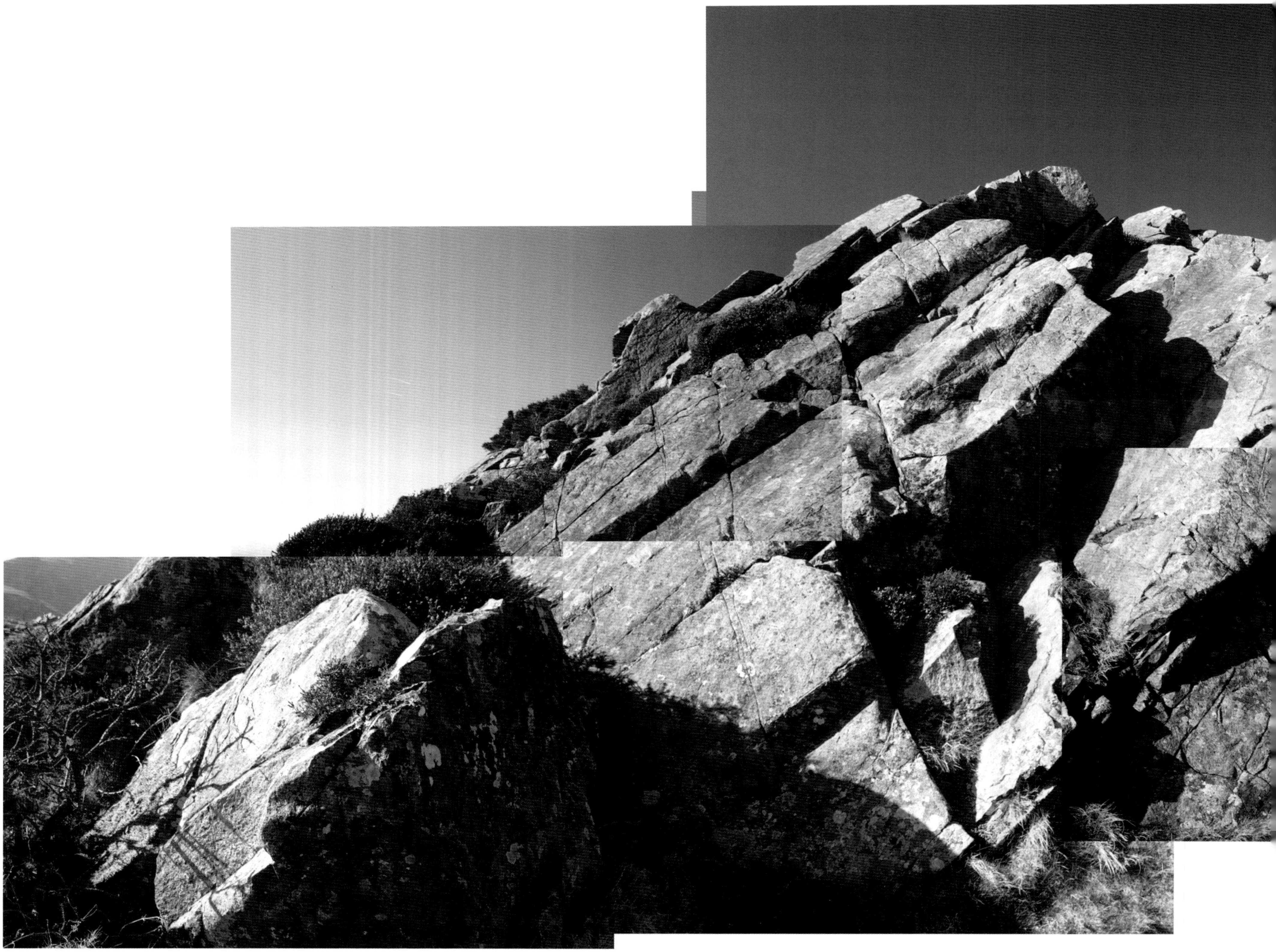

Rock formation on Garn Fawr

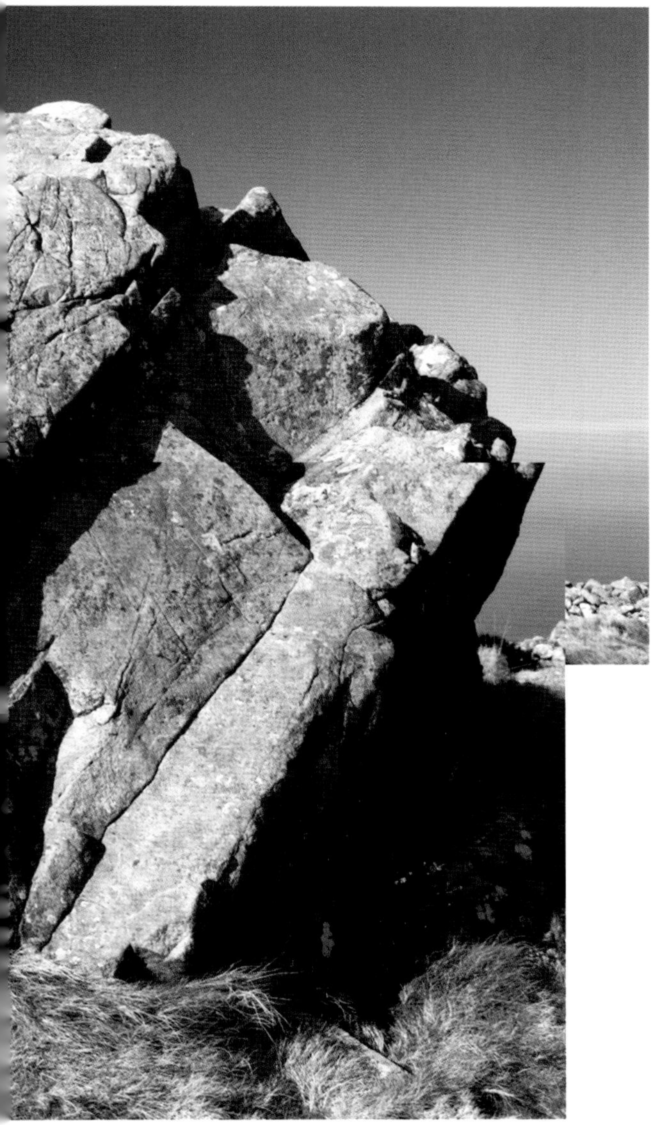

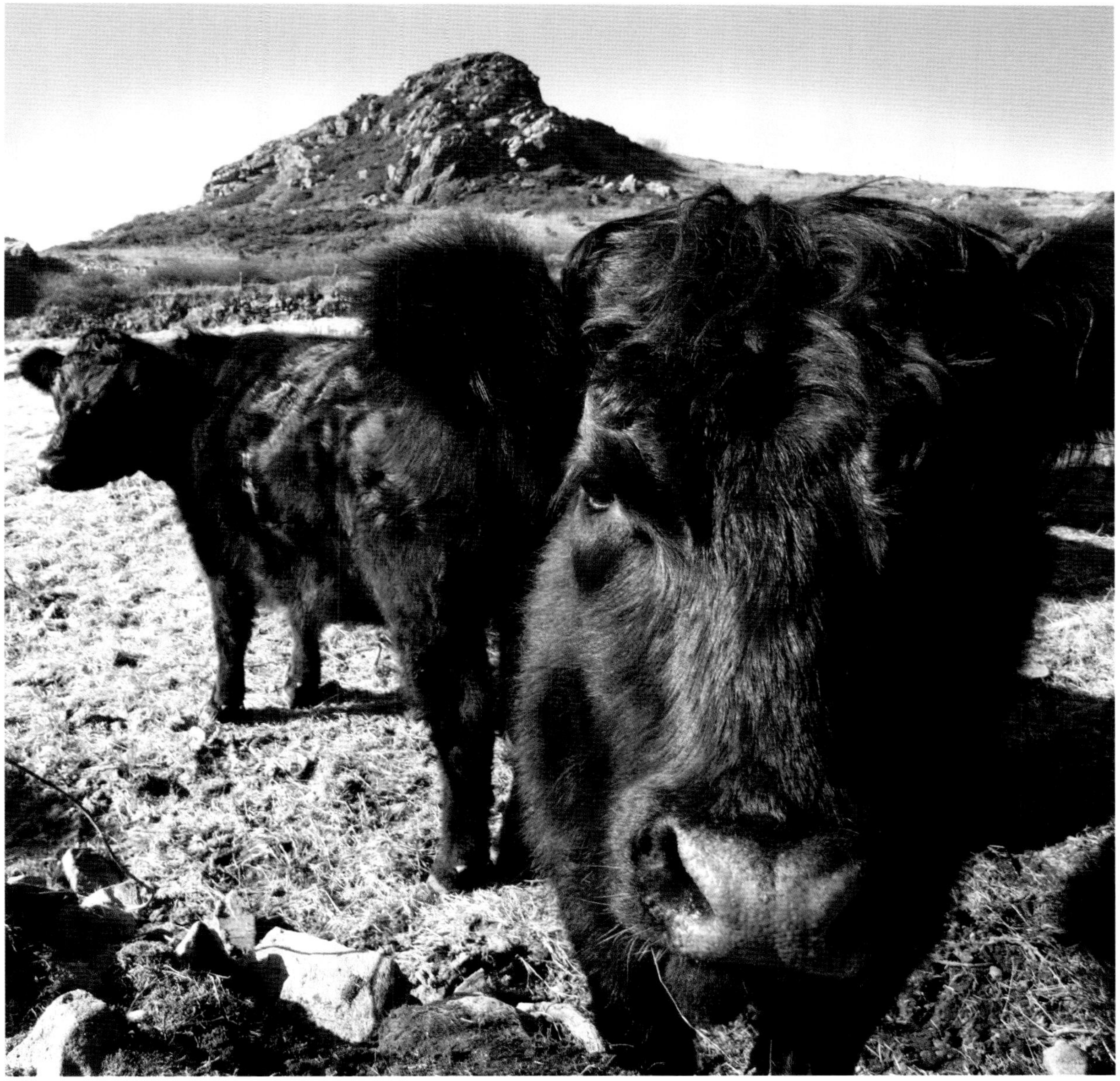

Cattle at the foot of Garn Fawr

21 STRUMBLE HEAD, PEMBROKESHIRE

Many visitors to Pembrokeshire sum up the charm of the county in a single word – 'unspoilt'. It is one of many affectionate appraisals, all of which conjure up the essence of what makes this tiny piece of Wales such a magical destination. And certainly for me, Strumble Head falls into the category of being 'unspoilt'.

I am not suggesting for one moment that this rugged headland has been frozen in aspic. Of course modern life has encroached, which is to be welcomed. In the howling depths of winter double-glazing and central heating have become essential. But what I love about this promontory are its high-banked hedges, meandering lanes, cottages that seem to duck down out of the scything winds, rusting hulks of cars, fields parcelled out generations ago and still farmed by the same families.

If you like, it all adds up to a sense of seamless continuity in a world of constant change. And the best place to view this miniature kingdom? Atop Garn Fawr. It delivers boundless views down to St David's Head in the west and, on a crystal clear day, the peaks of Snowdonia are just visible away up in the north. (Map A5)

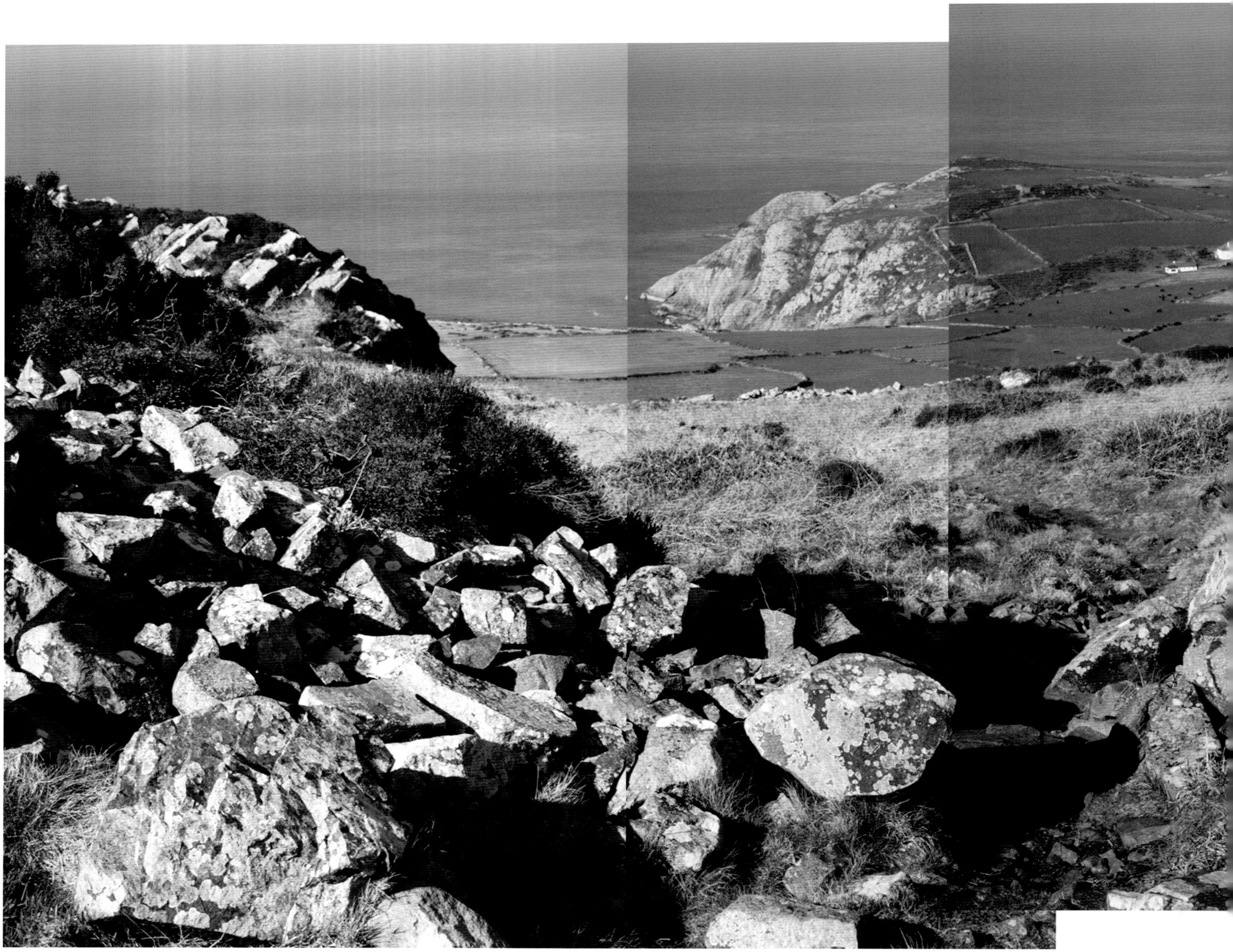

Above: Strumble Head seen from the top of Garn Fawr
Overleaf: Capel Harmoni, close to Strumble Head

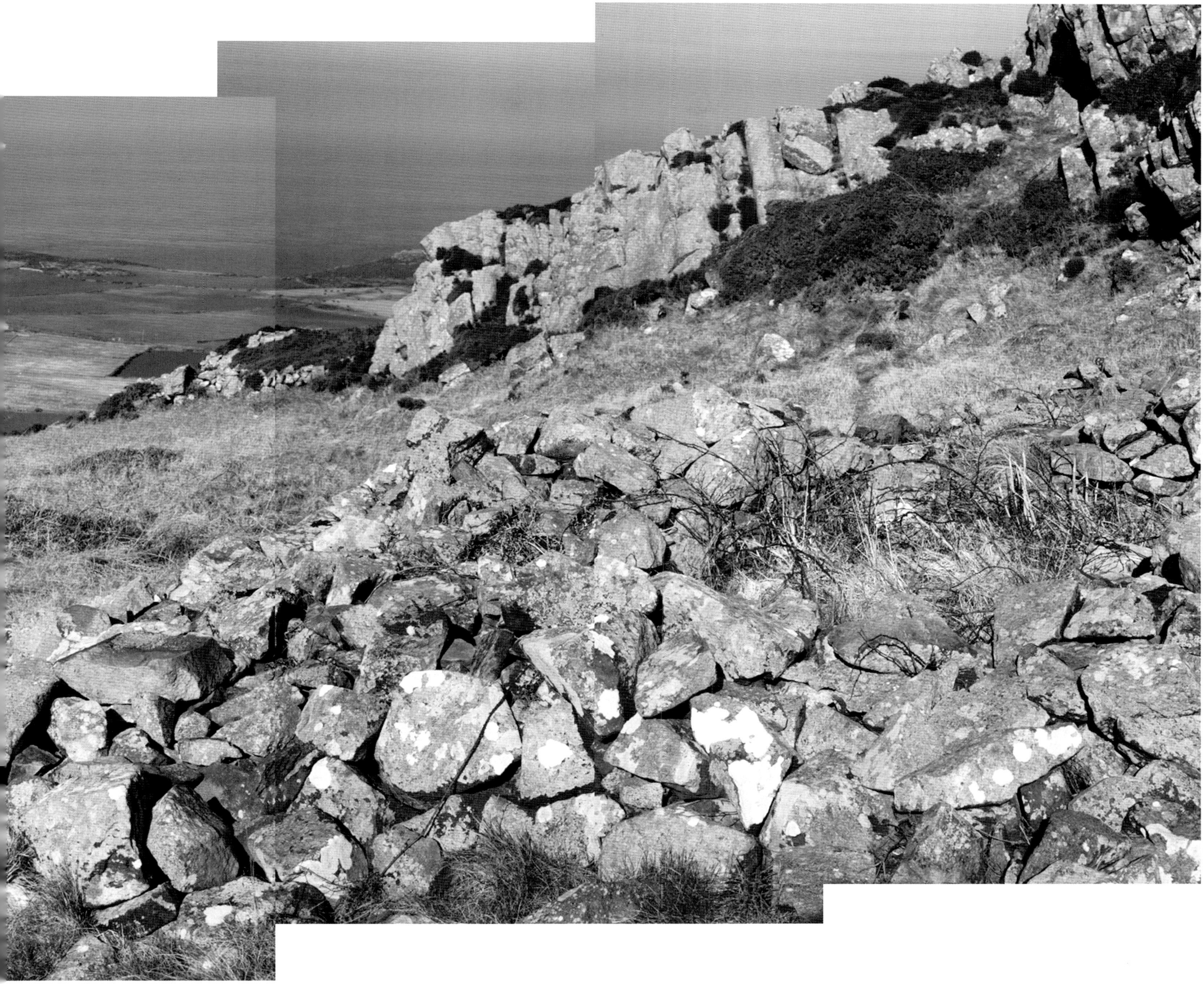

21 Strumble Head, Pembrokeshire

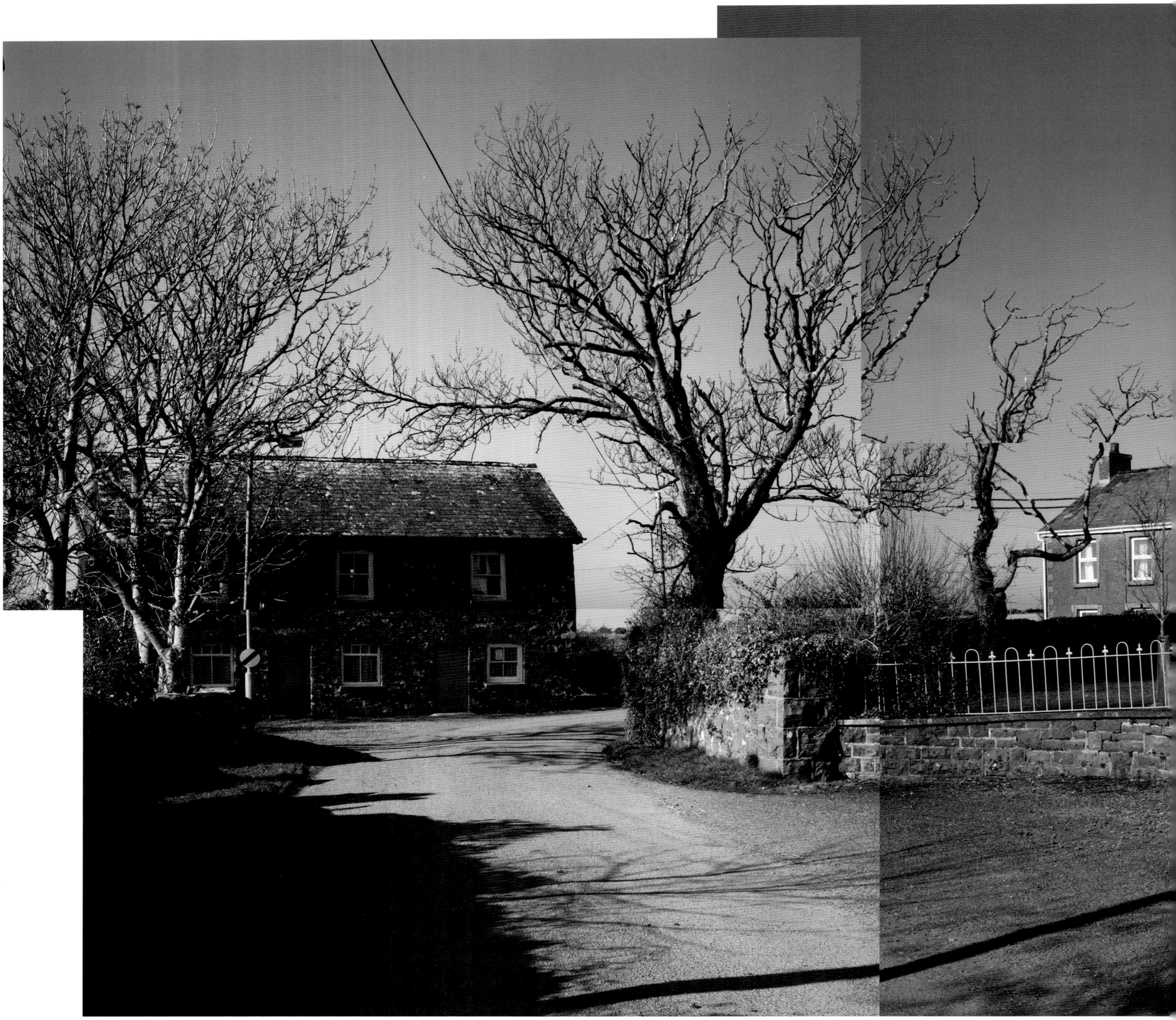

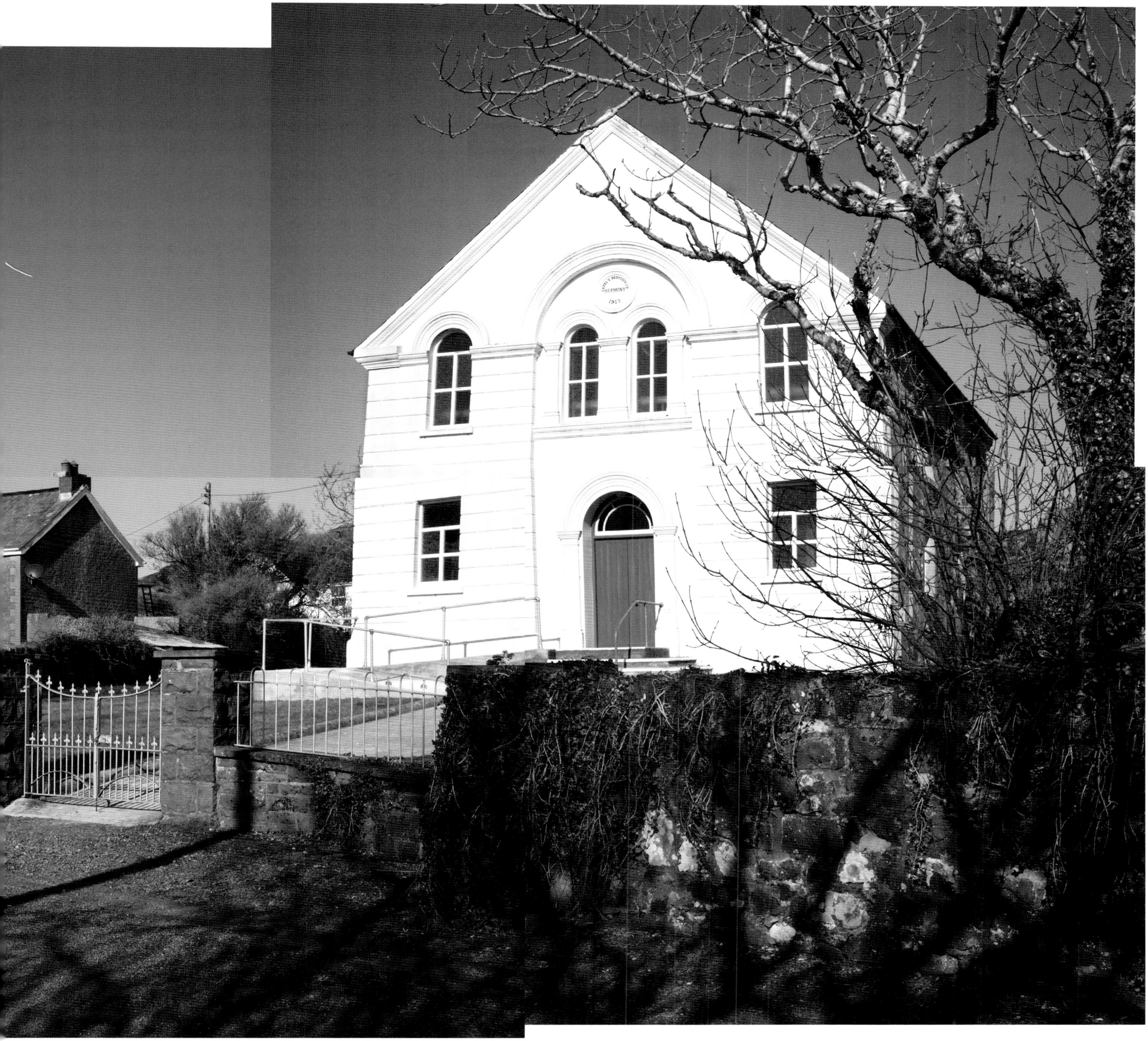
CAPEL Y BEDYDDWYR
HARMONY
1913

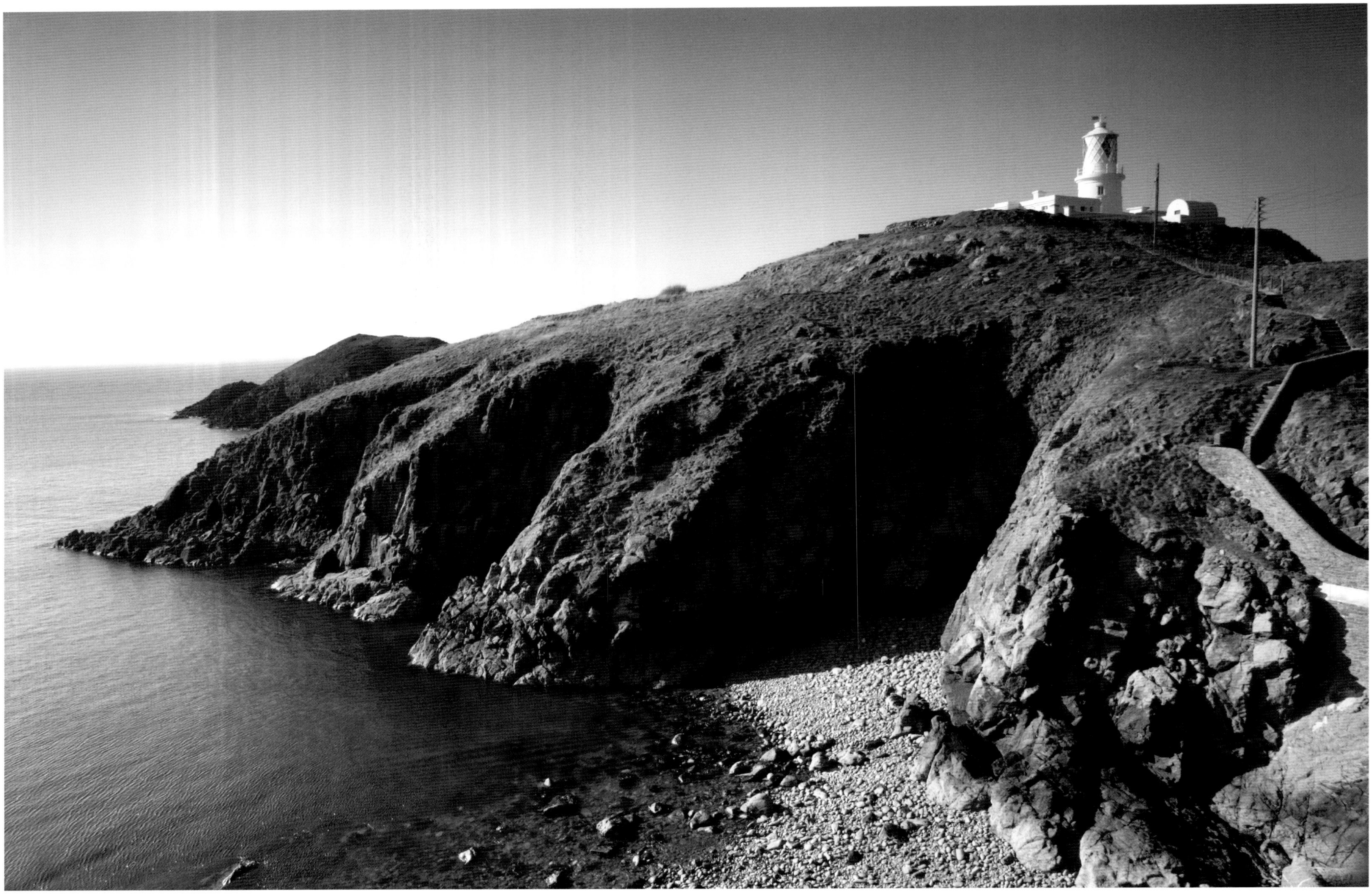

Above: Strumble Head Lighthouse

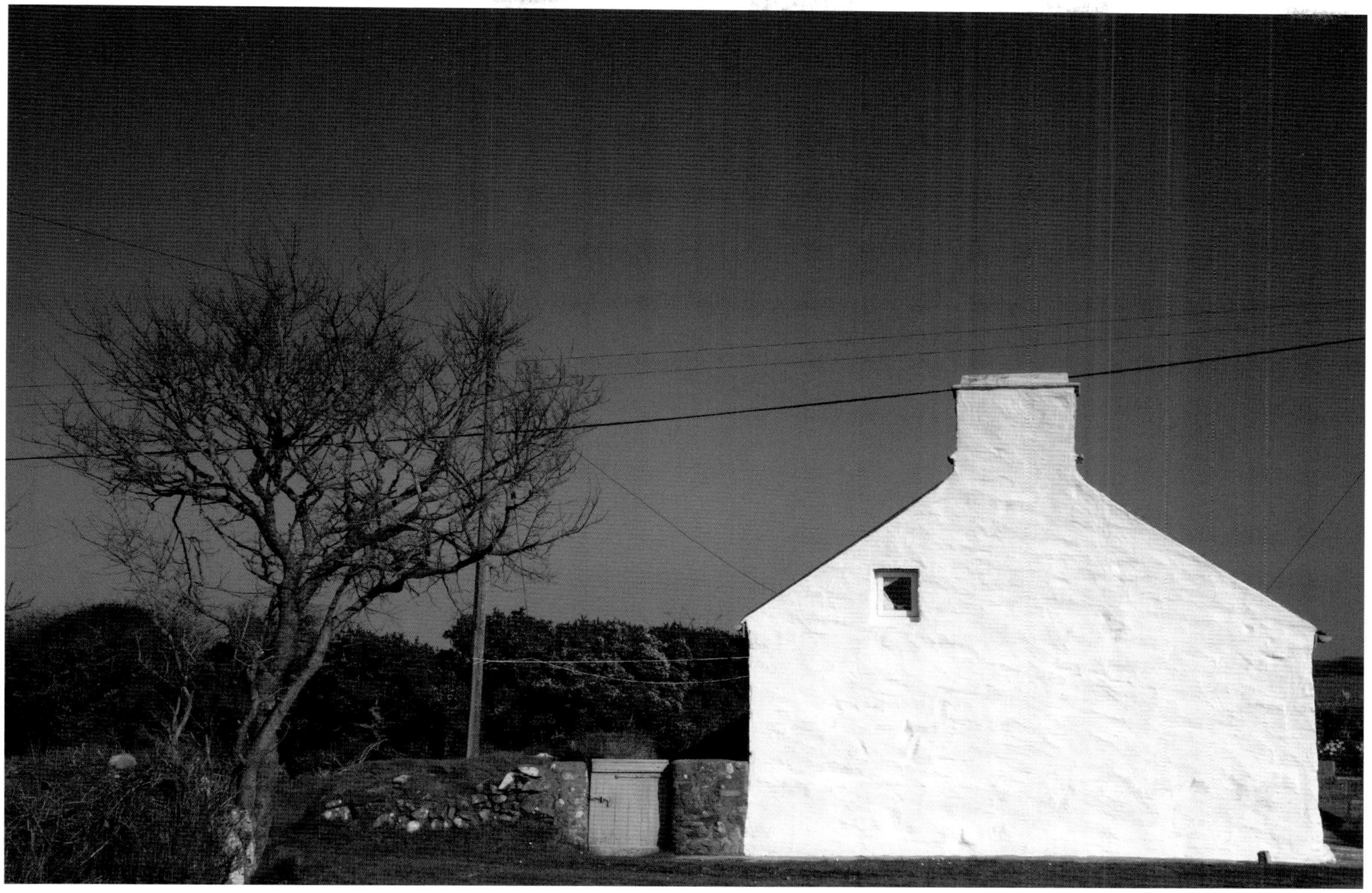

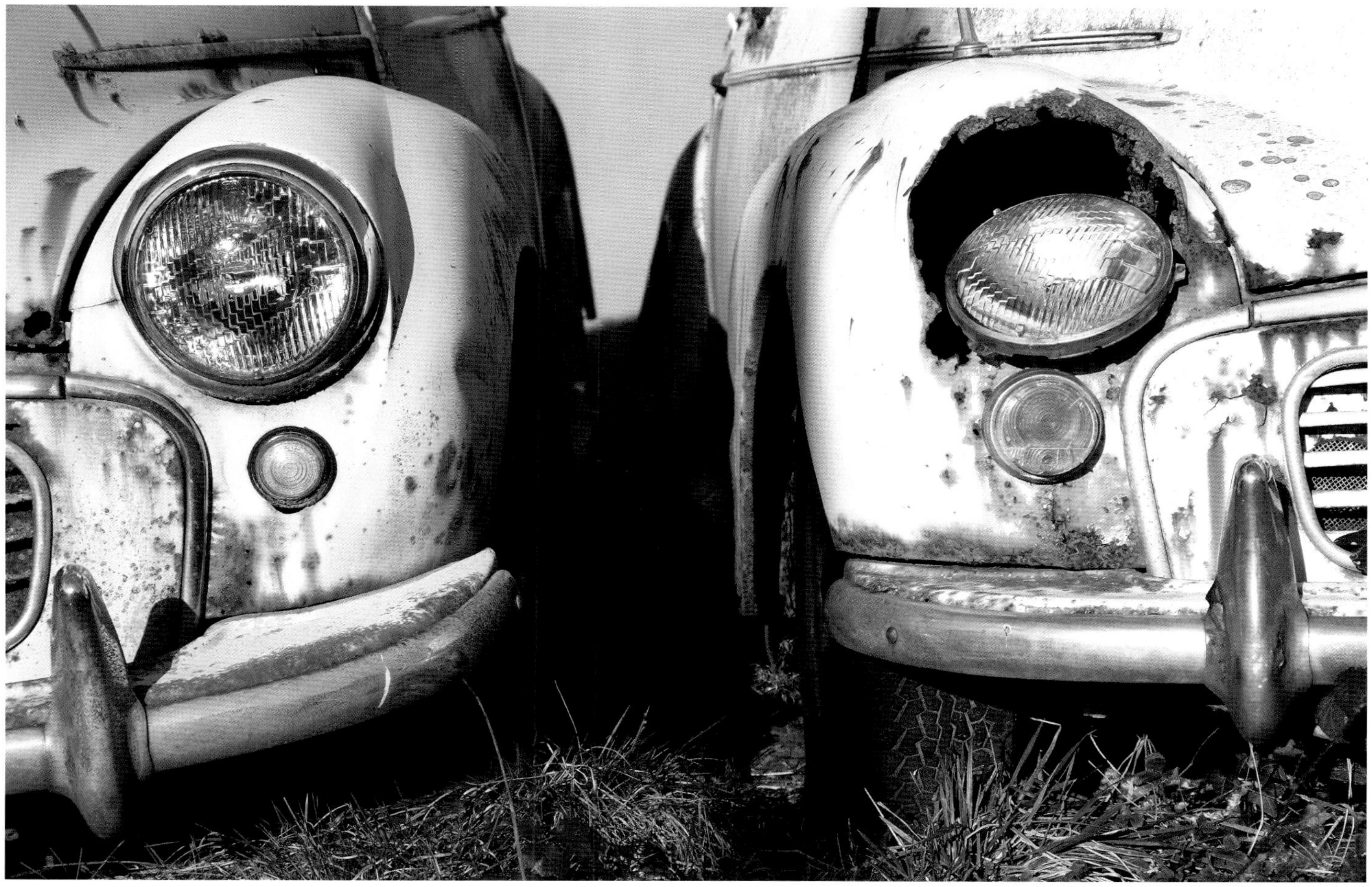

21 Strumble Head, Pembrokeshire

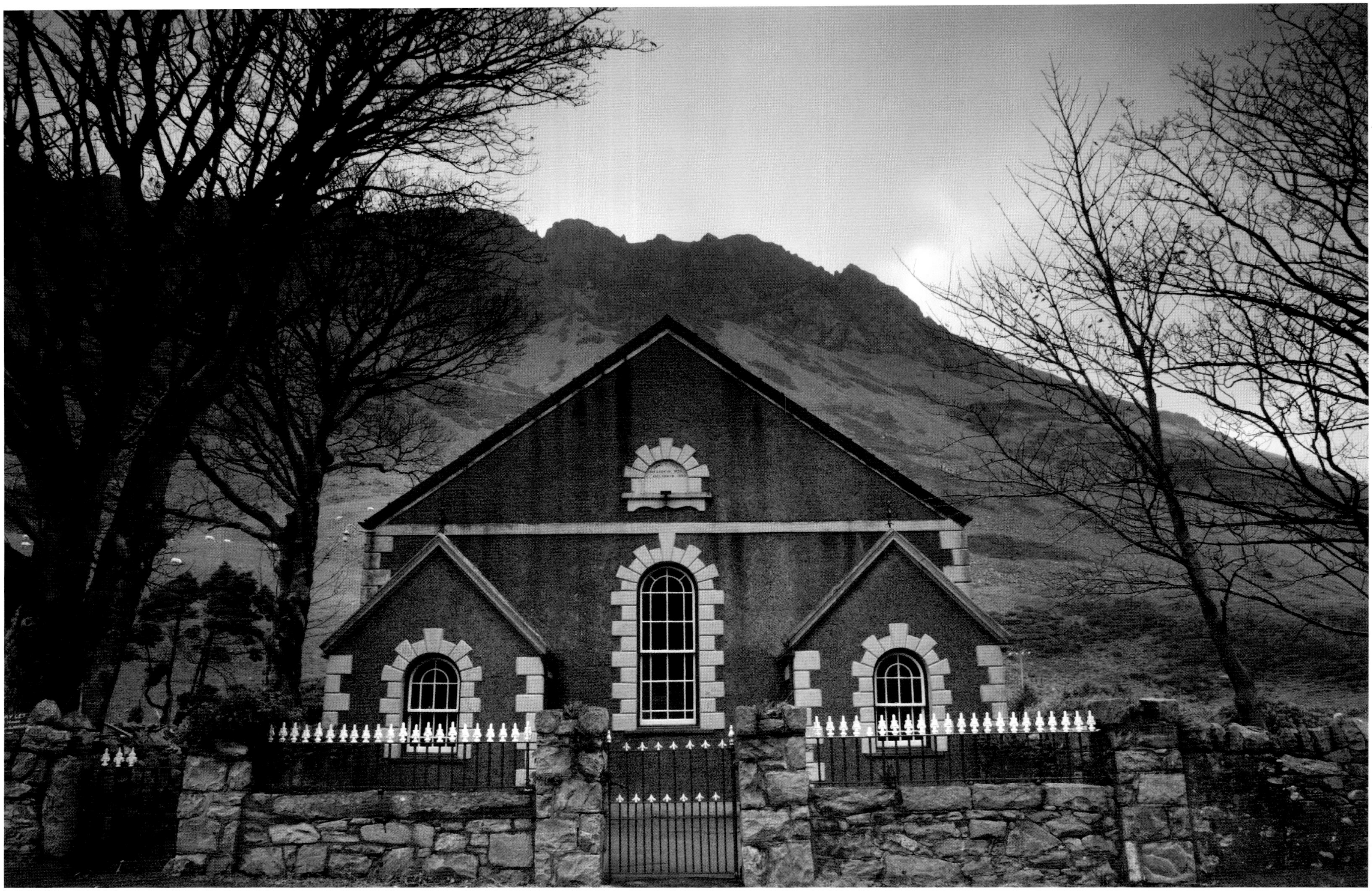

22 NANTLLE TO DRWS Y COED, SNOWDONIA

I once came across an image of a painting by one of the foremost landscape artists of the eighteenth century – 'Snowdon from Llyn Nantlle' by Richard Wilson (no relation – at least not that I am aware of!). When I embarked on this book I was determined to capture the scene looking across the lake and along Dyffryn Nantlle to Snowdon in the distance. I arrived on a crisp mid-November day with the peak already white and a wispy halo of cloud crowning the summit. It was amazing to think I was just one of many who over the centuries have striven to portray this timeless view.

Along Dyffryn Nantlle you head down an arrow-straight road towards Drws y Coed chapel, located in a tiny bottle-neck between the mighty ridges of Craig y Bera and its neighbour Clogwyn y Barcut.

In days gone by the congregation would have endured a damp, cold walk to chapel on this kind of winter's day – a torrential hail storm greeted my arrival. They toiled five and a half days a week in the local quarry and on Sunday, their only day of rest, chapel beckoned. With the slog required to get there, there was not much rest in the offing! (Map C2)

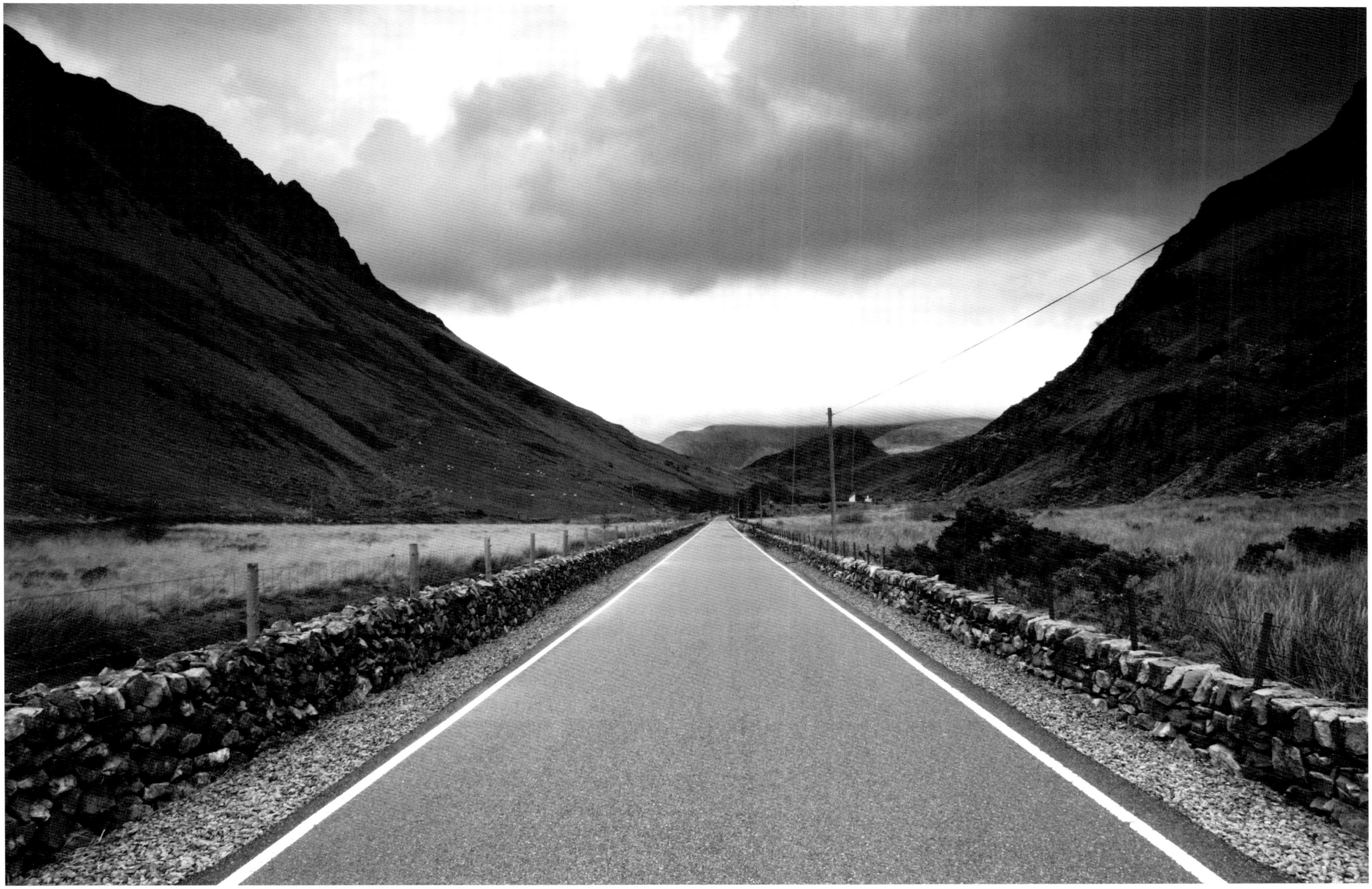

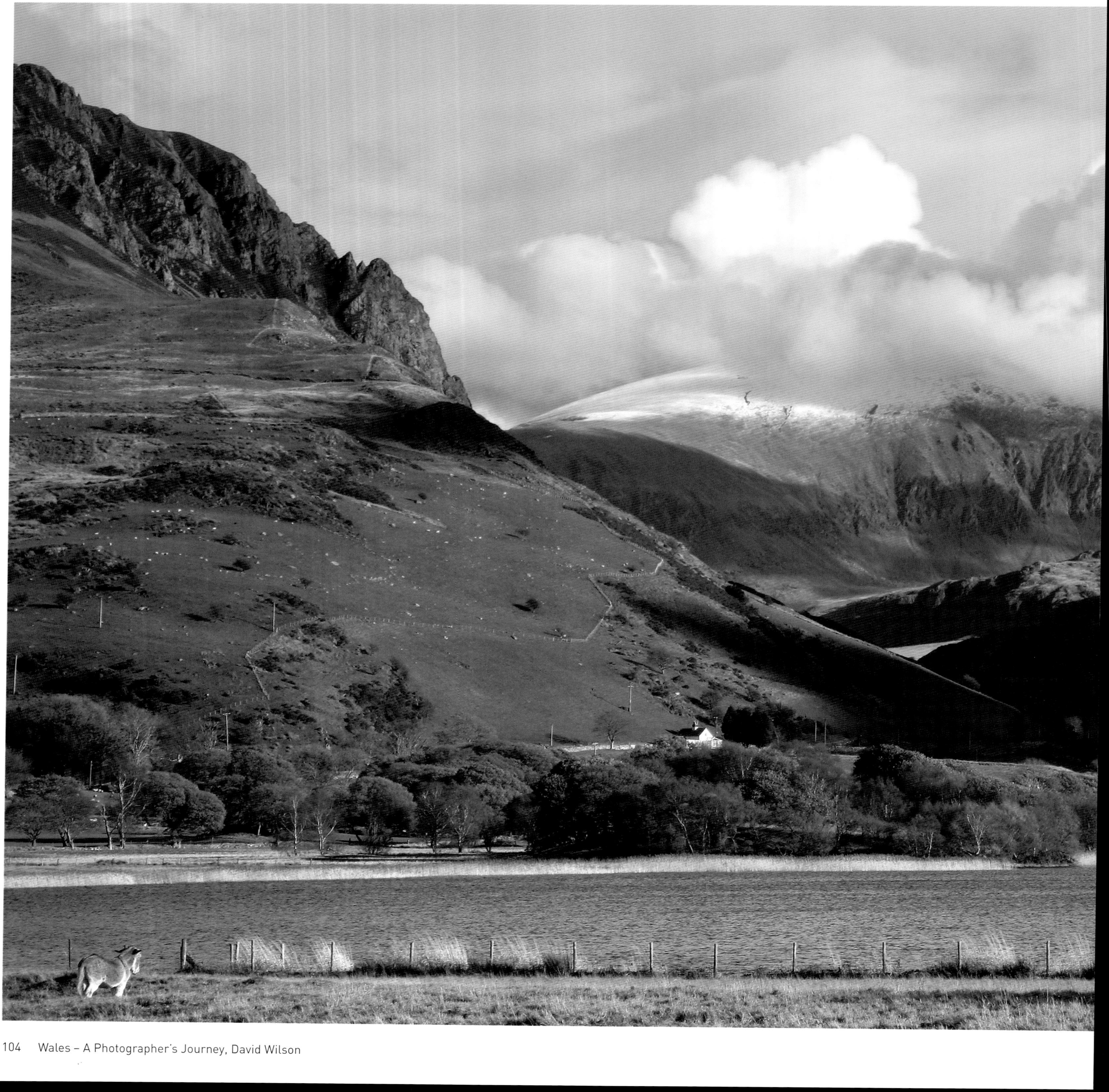

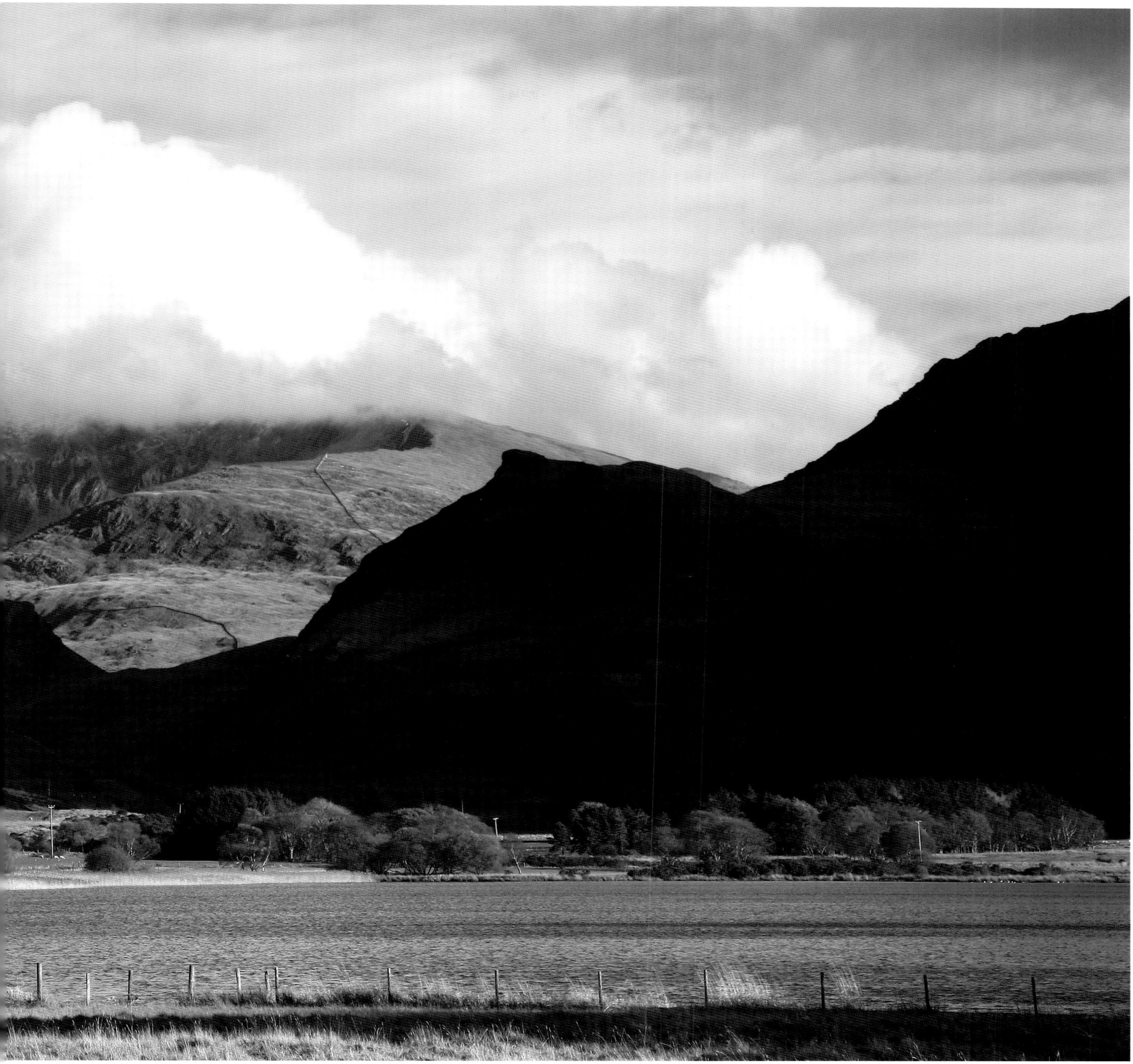

22 Nantlle to Drws y Coed, Snowdonia

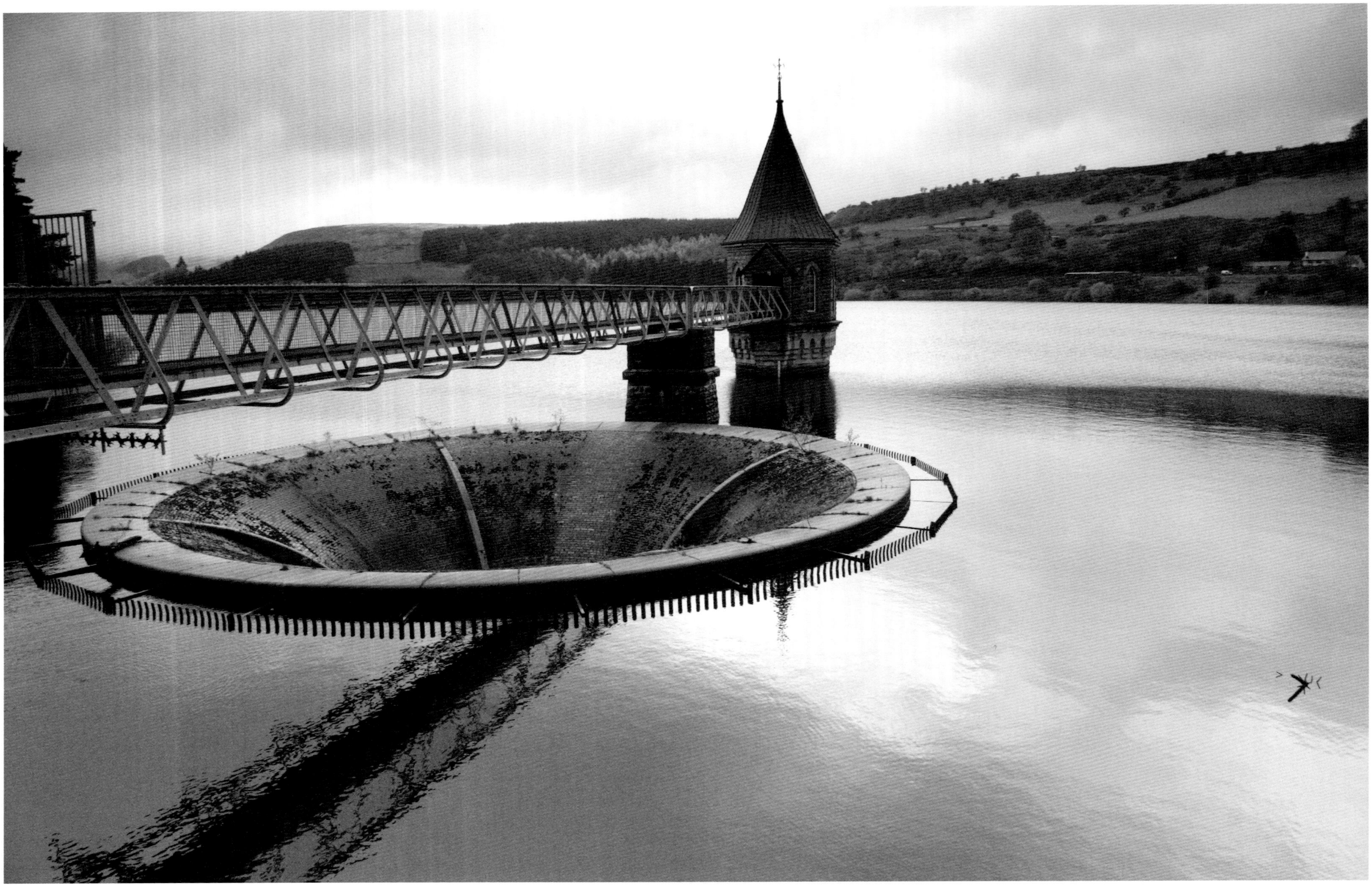

Pontsticill Reservoir

23 PONTSTICILL RESERVOIR TO TALYBONT-ON-USK, BRECON BEACONS

Aside from the nail-biting climax to the golf, spectators and competitors at the 2010 Ryder Cup (held at the Celtic Manor near Newport) will forever remember the rain! Living in Wales you get used to it, much like an Amazonian might factor in the odd downpour in their neck of the woods.

This day in the Brecon Beacons was certainly a damp one. Some photographers may be inclined to write off wet days as a non-starter, but I relish the odd rainy excursion. It is an element that can add so much atmosphere to an image.

Starting my journey at the Pontsticill Reservoir above Merthyr Tydfil, I made my way to the Upper Neuadd Reservoir where you can park and hike your way up to glorious vantage points of Pen y Fan.

I quickly dispensed with that idea as my camera is not an underwater model! Instead I used the tailgate of my car as cover while I shot into the gloom and driving rain along the road leading to the Upper Neuadd.

I then headed for Talybont-on-Usk, encountering a wet pony with an air of resignation and a pair of hardy walkers on the way. (Map D5)

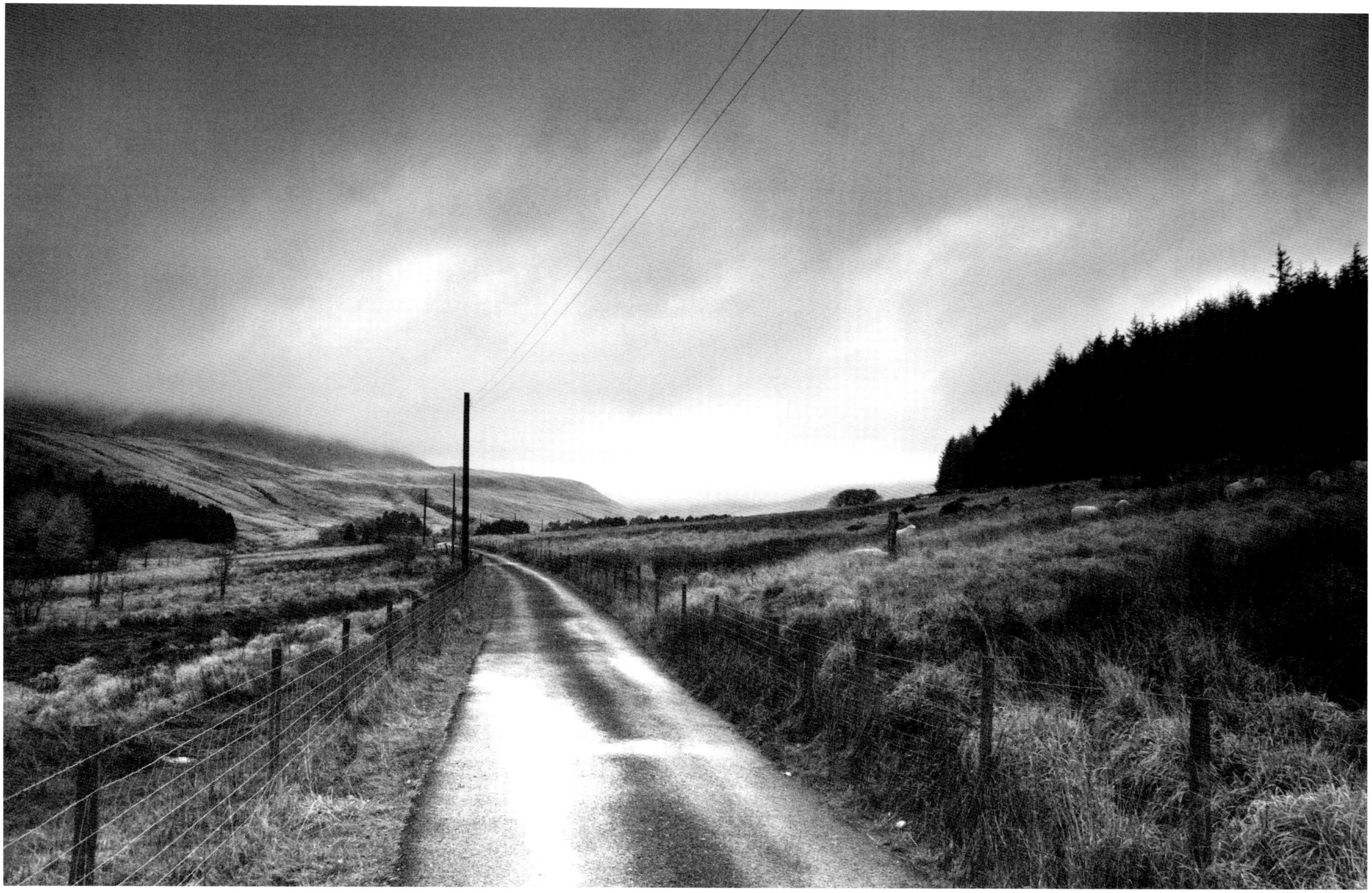

The road leading to the Upper Neuadd Reservoir

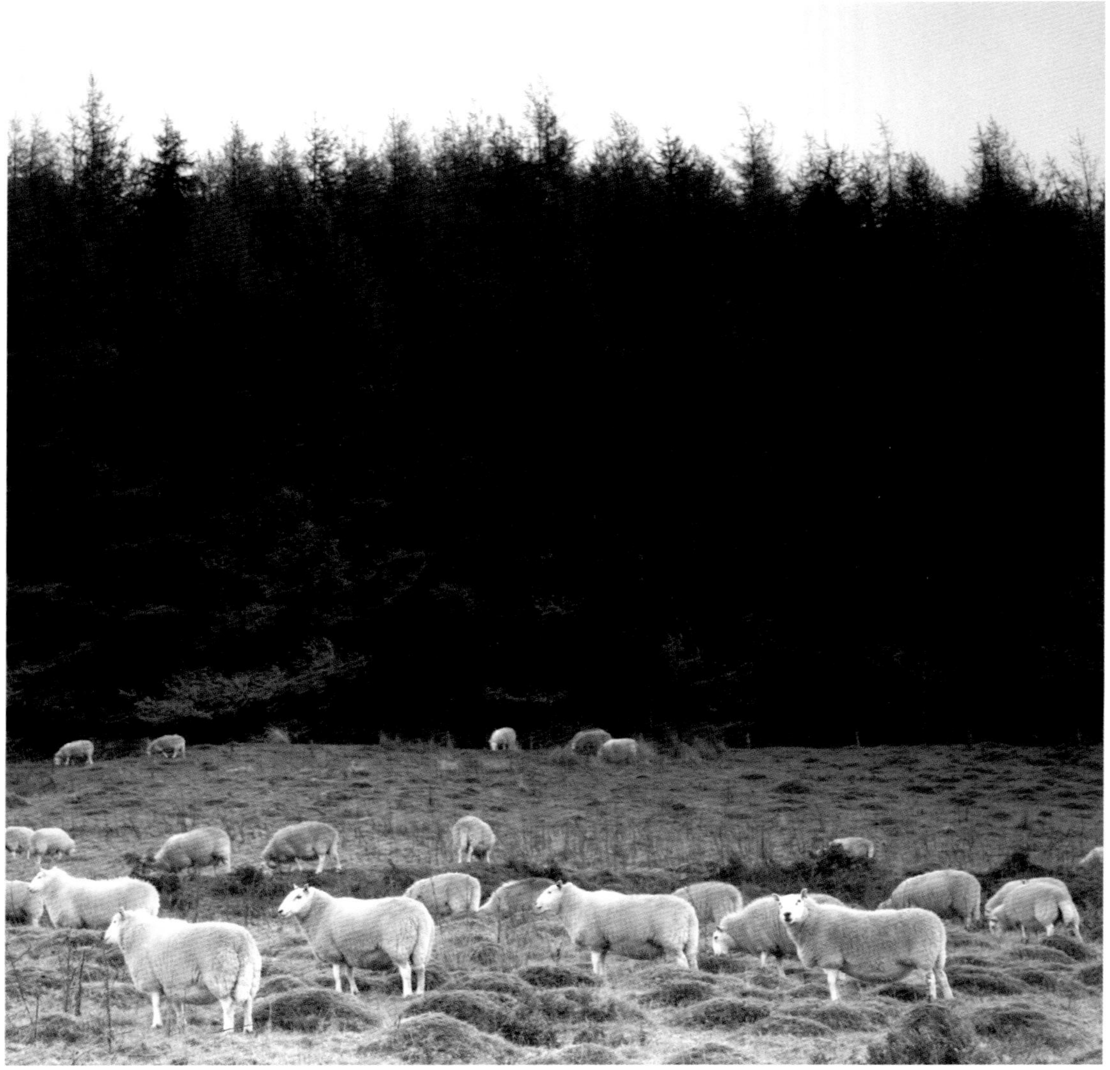

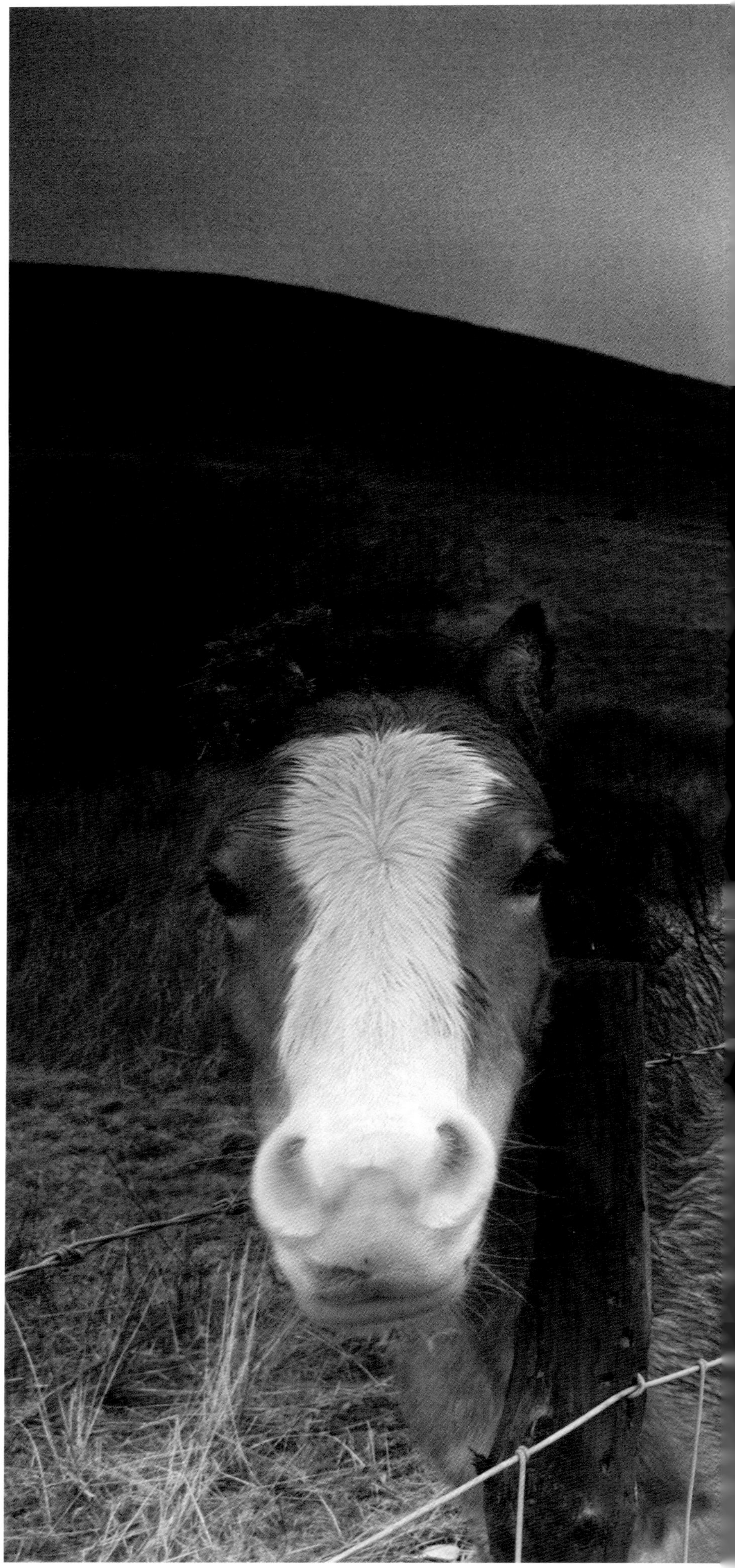

Above: On the journey to the Upper Neuadd Reservoir
Right / Overleaf: On the road to Talybont-on-Usk

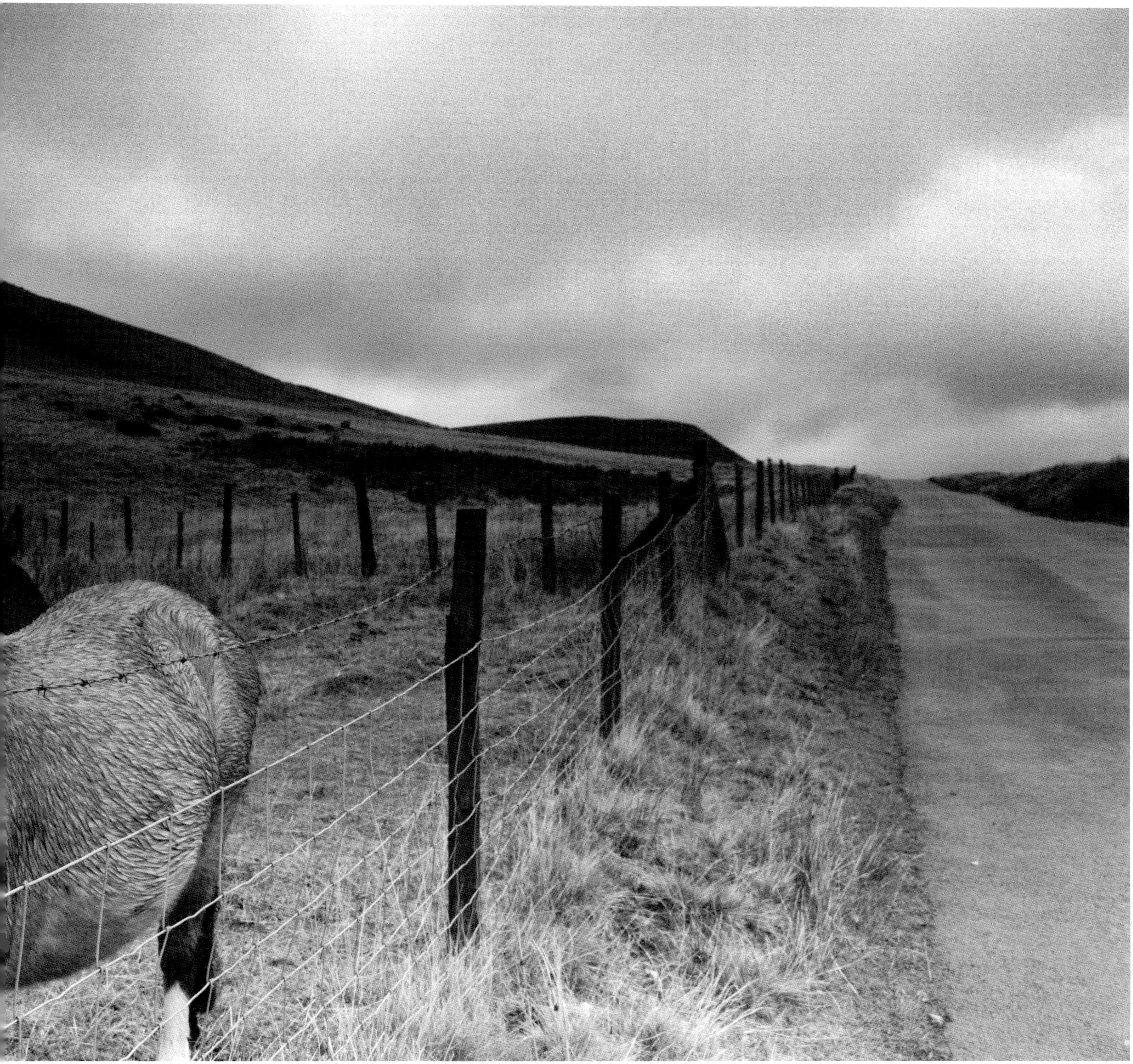

23 Pontsticill Reservoir to Talybont-on-Usk, Brecon Beacons

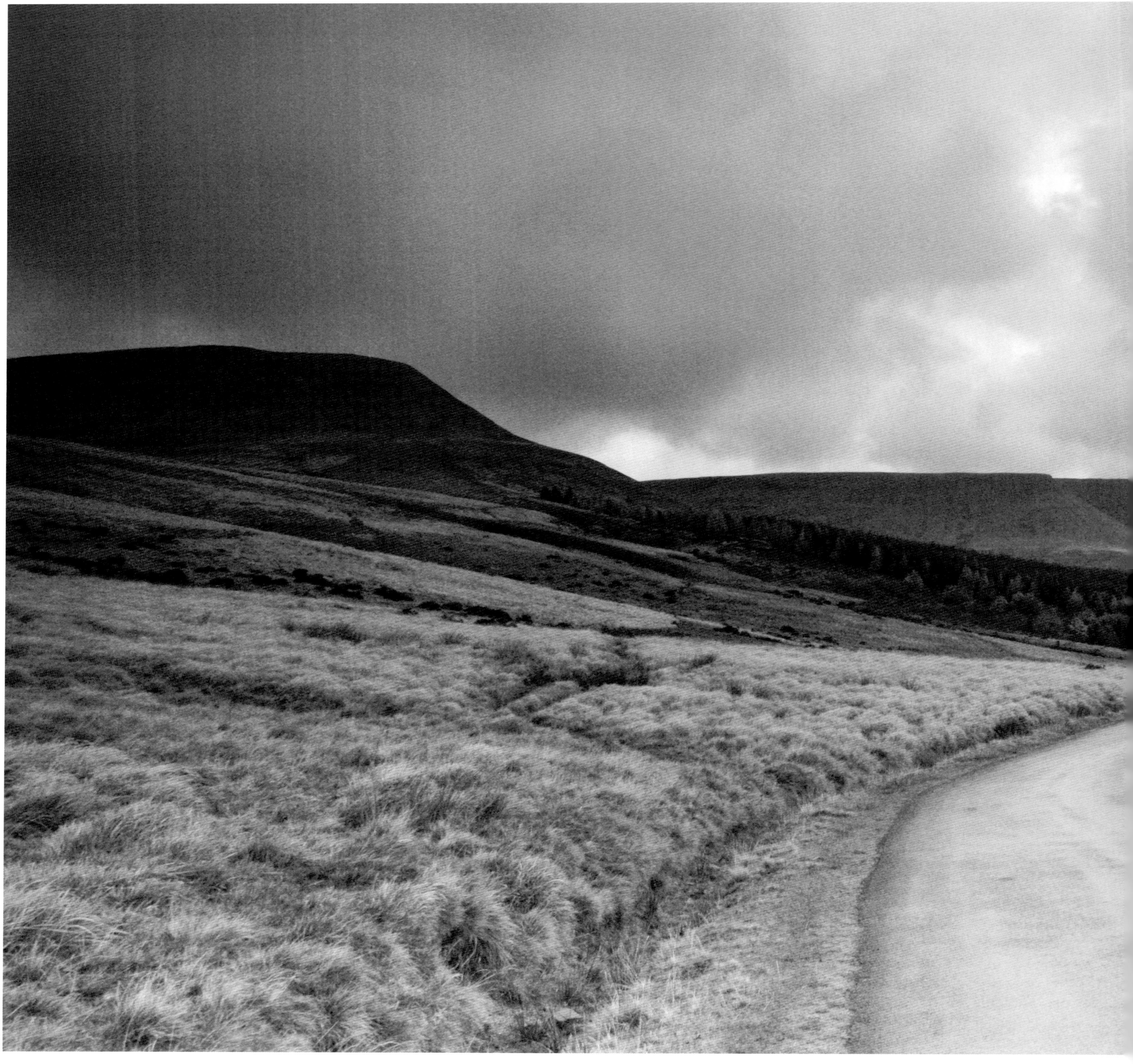

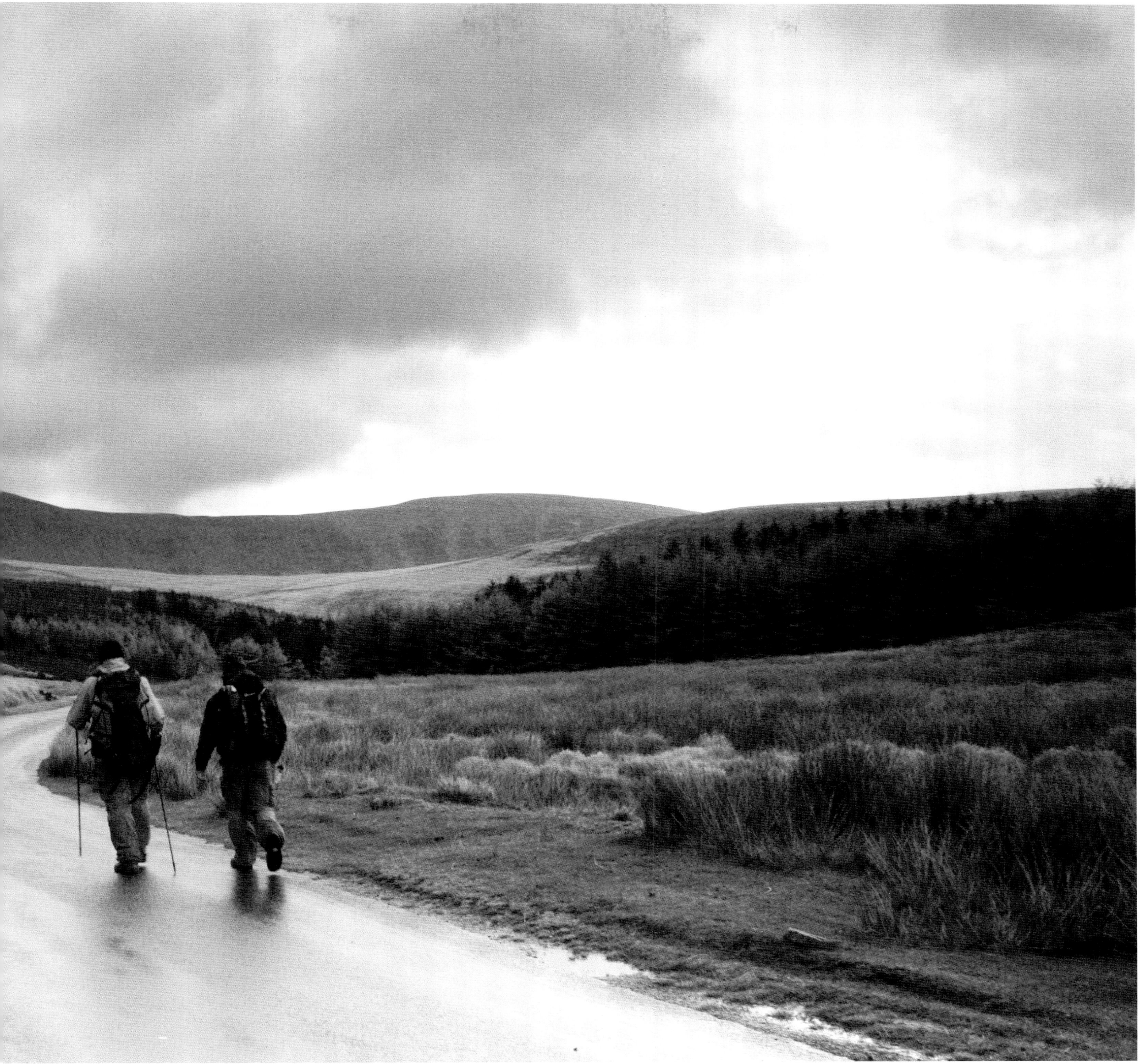

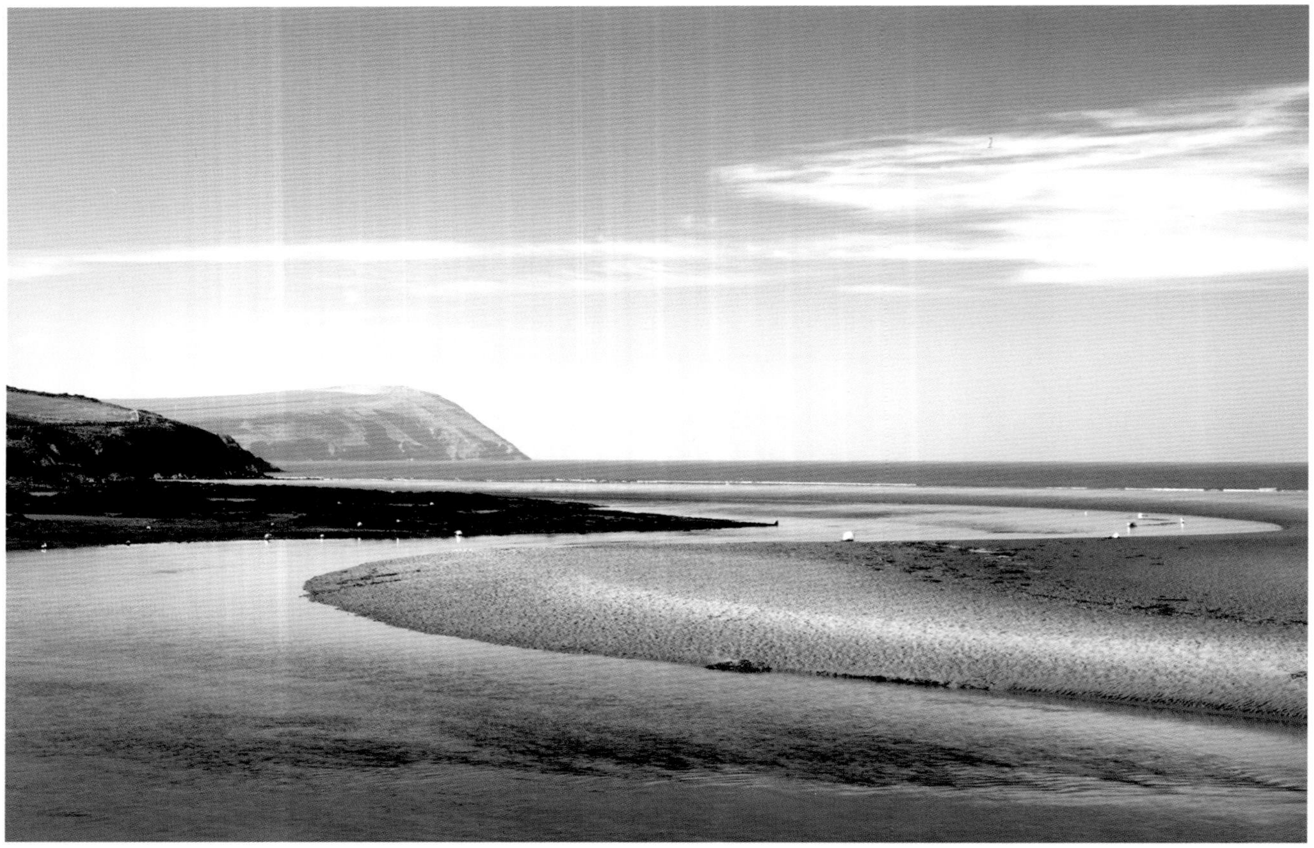

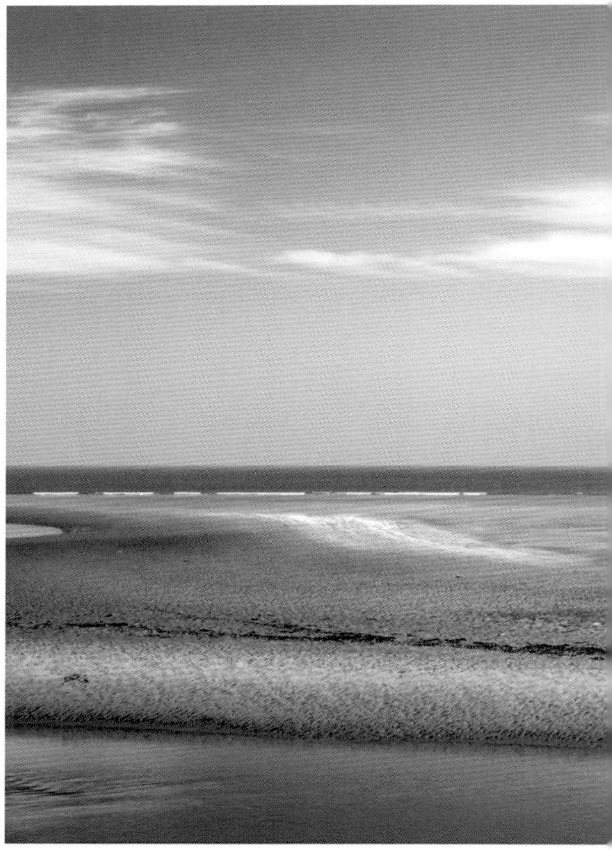

24 THE PARROG, NEWPORT, PEMBROKESHIRE

Approaching some of Pembrokeshire's more rugged beaches, with their contorted rock formations rupturing from sheer headlands, saturating the sands with minefields of huge boulders, requires something akin to mountaineering skills. The Parrog, by contrast, has broad sweeping lines and soft edges. When lit by the soft winter sun, as in this image, it is tranquillity itself. (Map B5)

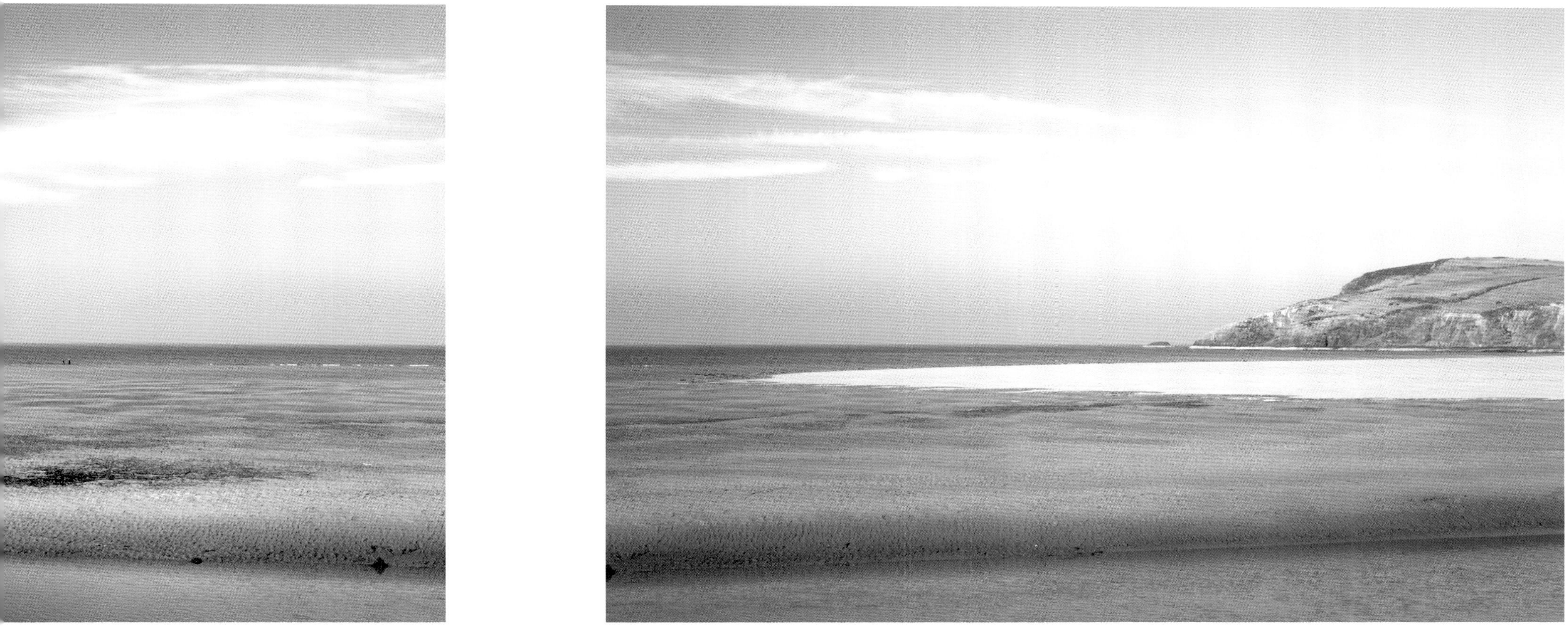

24 The Parrog, Newport, Pembrokeshire

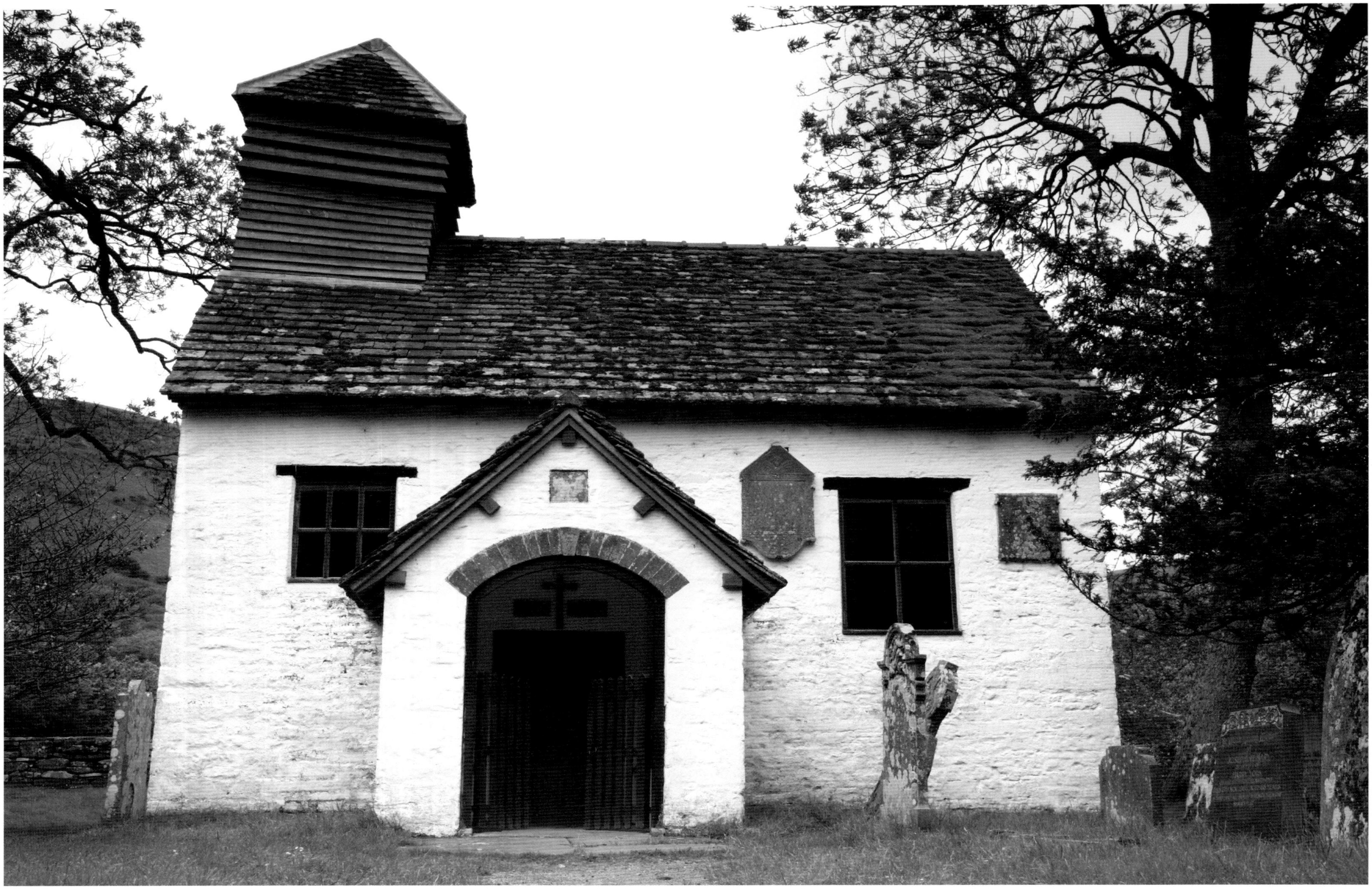

25 ST MARY'S CHURCH, CAPEL-Y-FFIN, EWYAS VALLEY

On my journeys throughout Wales I have stumbled across many an unexpected little gem. Happening upon St Mary's Church at Capel-y-Ffin in the Ewyas Valley was just such an occasion.

Surely one of the smallest churches in Wales, its tiny scale only added to its sense of intimate beauty. I tried the door and it opened, a wonderful affirmation of faith in human goodness. Anna was with me and she remarked on how peacefu. and serene it felt. She sat on a pew while I took photographs and said she could have stayed there for hours.

Such a simple and innocent building, with cows grazing just yards away from the windows, country flowers in a vase, and a delightfully eclectic mix of fixtures, fittings and paraphernalia. I got the feeling that the accoutrements on the altar table had been begged and borrowed rather than stolen!

It all felt very welcoming, well-used, and above all, loved. (Map D5)

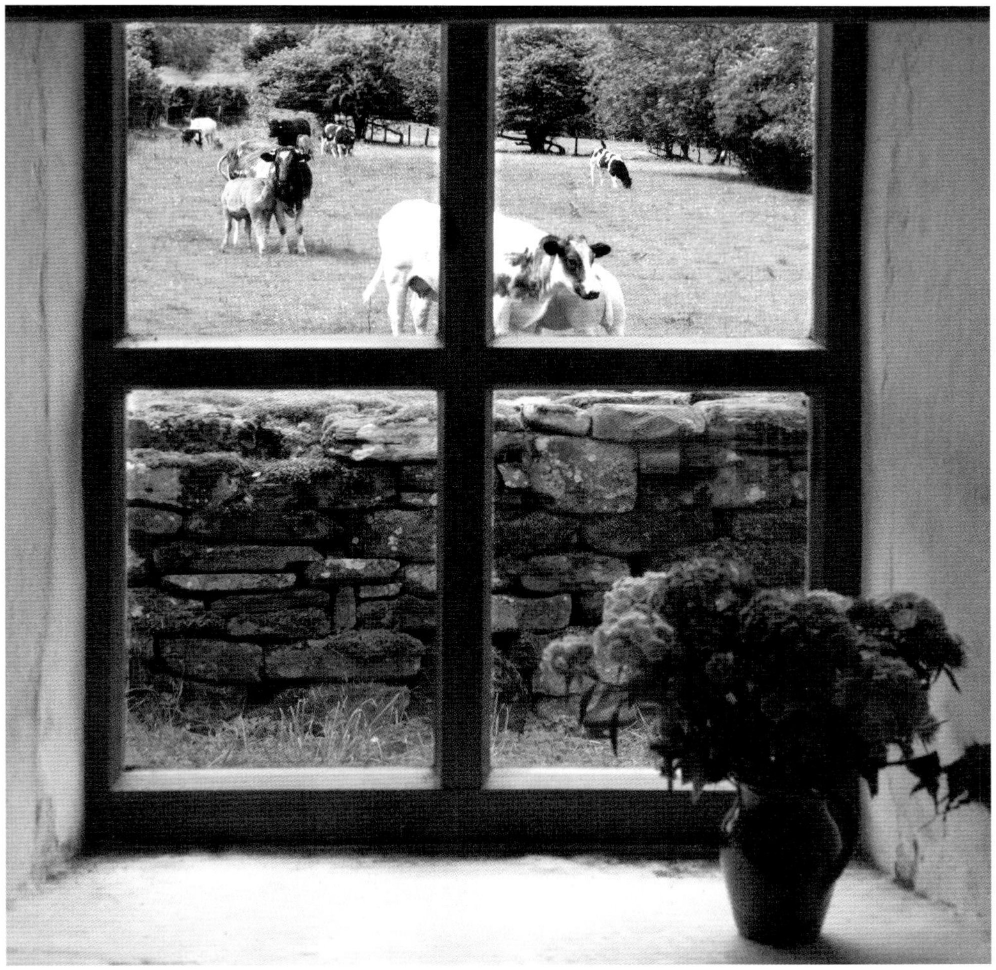

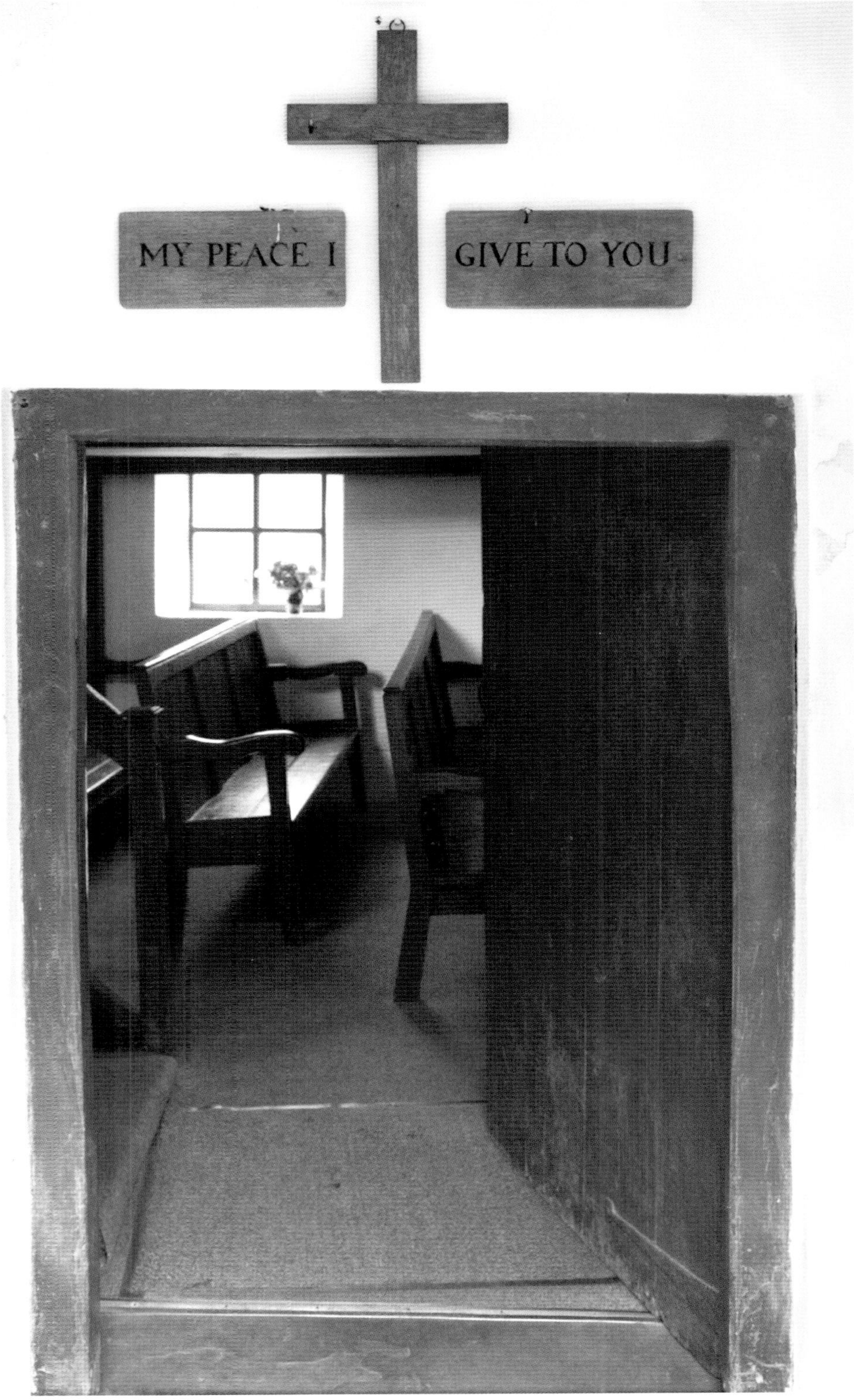
MY PEACE I
GIVE TO YOU

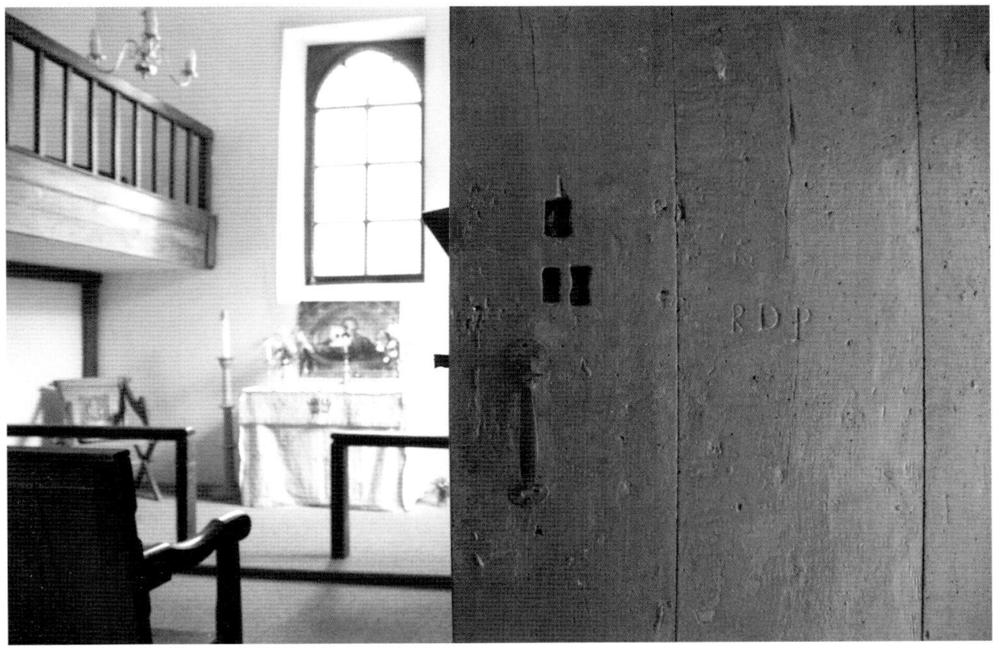
RDP

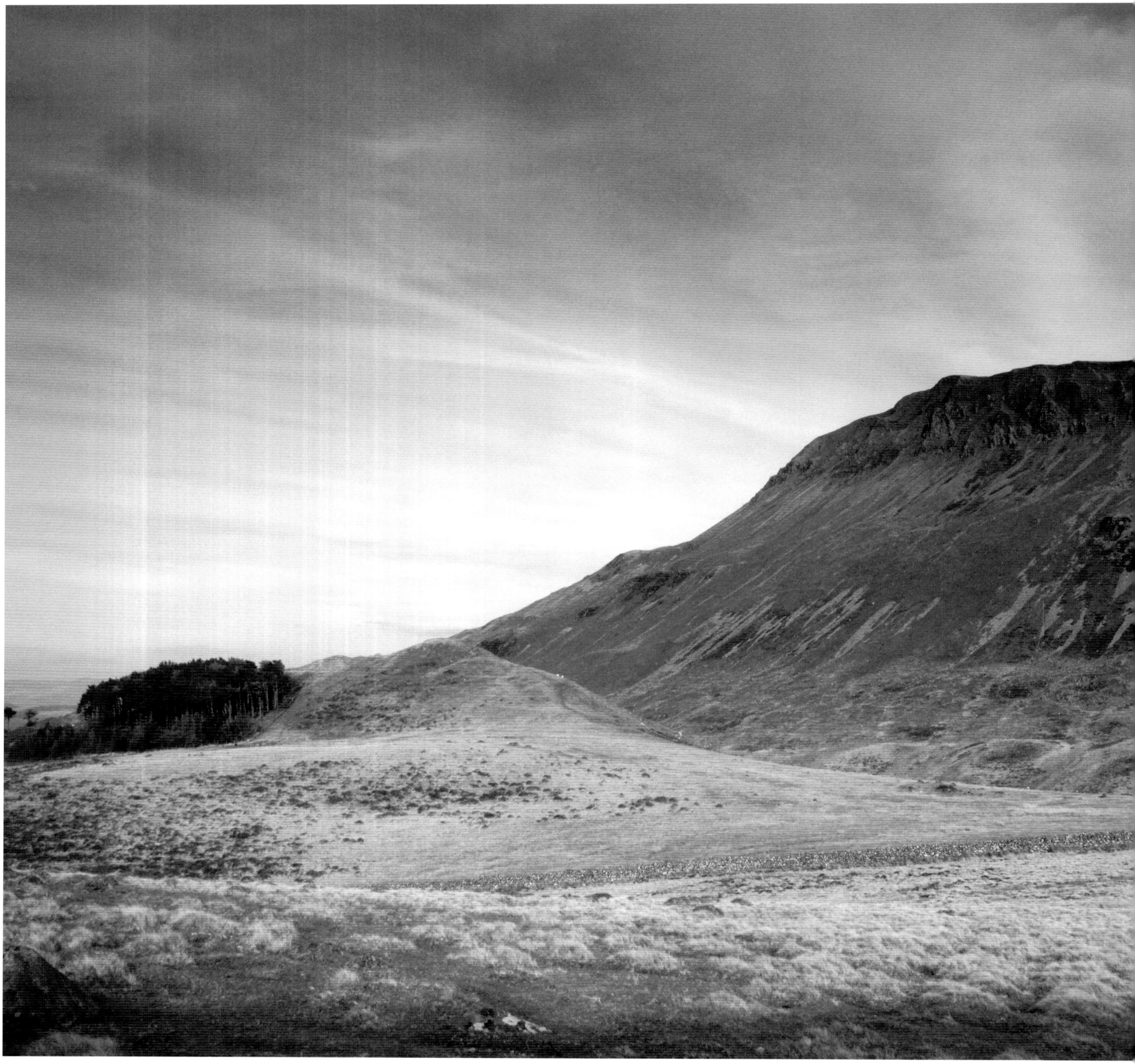

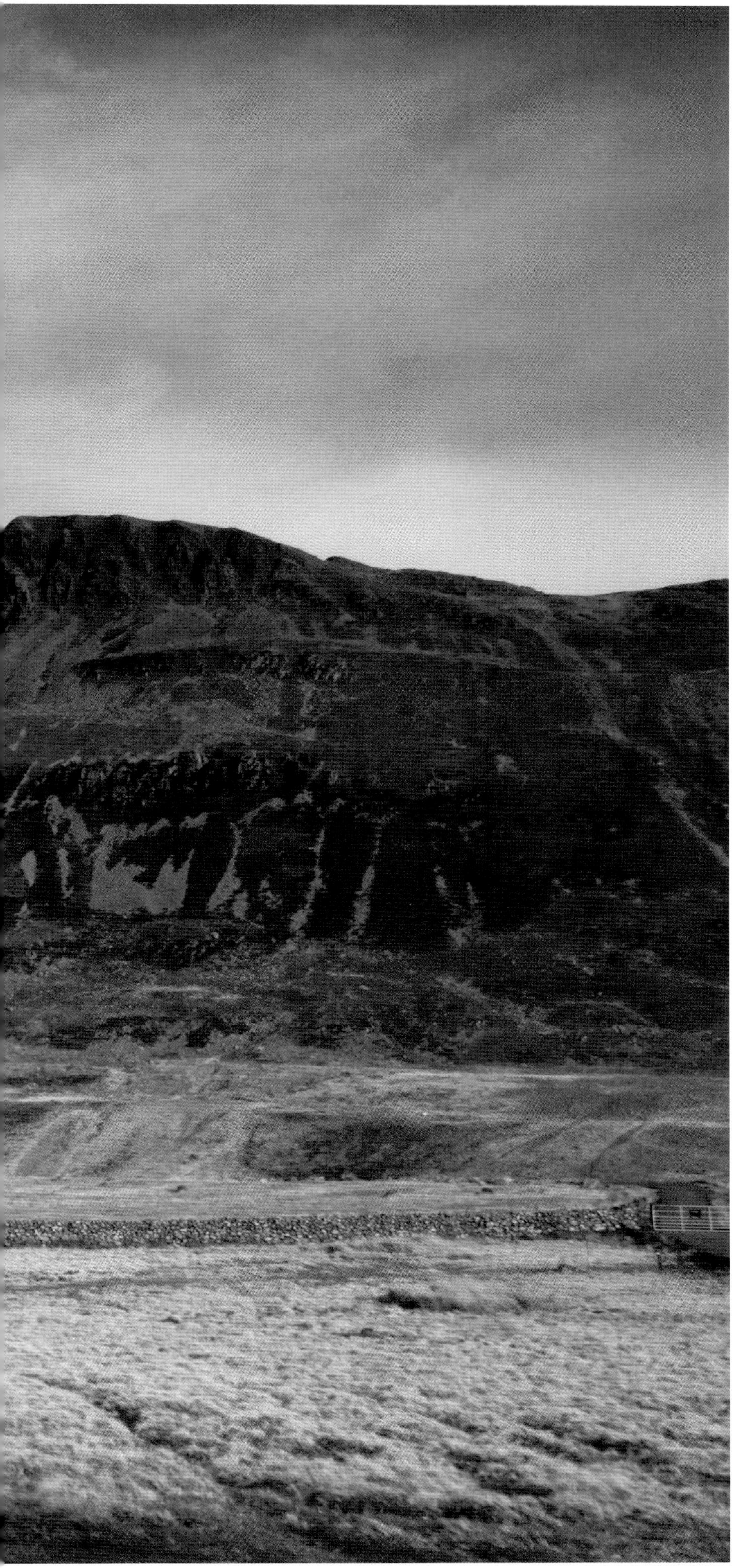

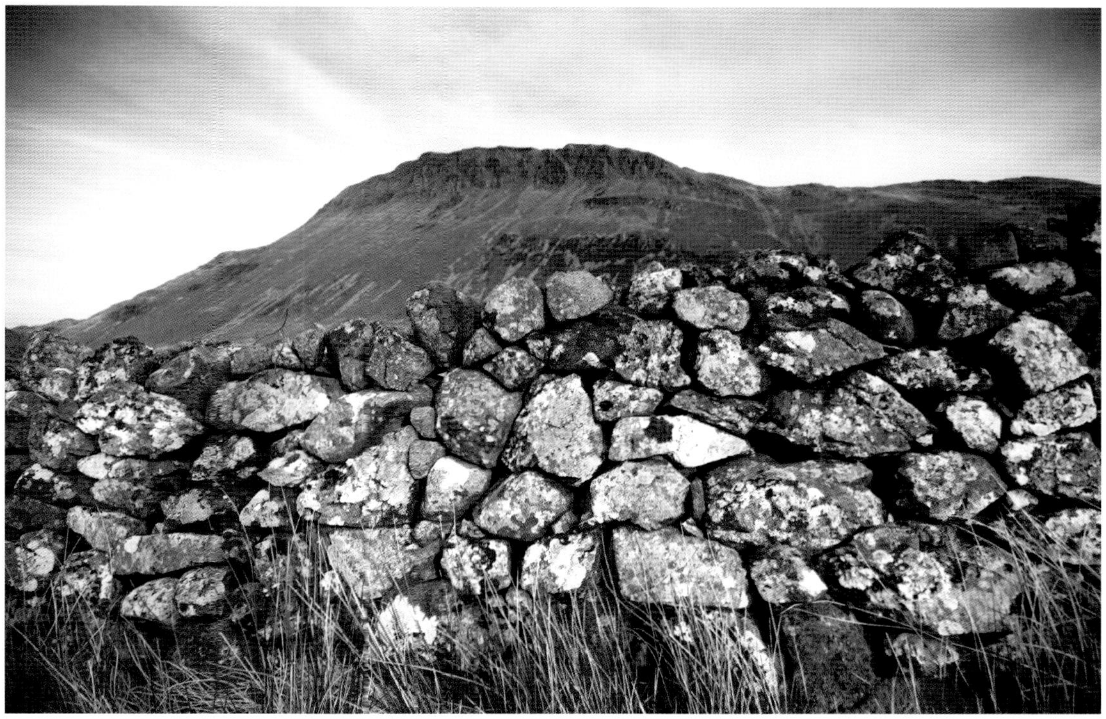

26 LLYNNAU CREGENNEN AND TYRRAU MAWR, SNOWDONIA

Approaching Arthog, on the road hugging the Mawddach Estuary (opposite Barmouth) there is a narrow lane off to the left. If you head through the woodland up steep twisting lanes, you emerge high up amid dry-stone enclosed pasture.

The road continues to climb ever more steeply. Suddenly you drive over the crest of a large hillock and, as the nose of the car drops down on the other side, a most impressive vista presents itself: Llynnau Cregennen with the monumental backdrop of the sheer Tyrrau Mawr soaring to 661 metres (2,168 ft). Run your eye along the ridge and you eventually arrive at Cadair Idris, one of the highest peaks in Wales at 893 metres (2,929 ft).

Photographing the panoramic image of the lake, I included what I assumed to be a boathouse in the foreground as a scaling device, to communicate the impressive grandeur of the peaks. The road skirts the edge of the lake before running adjacent to Tyrrau Mawr and eventually descending into Dolgellau. (Map C3)

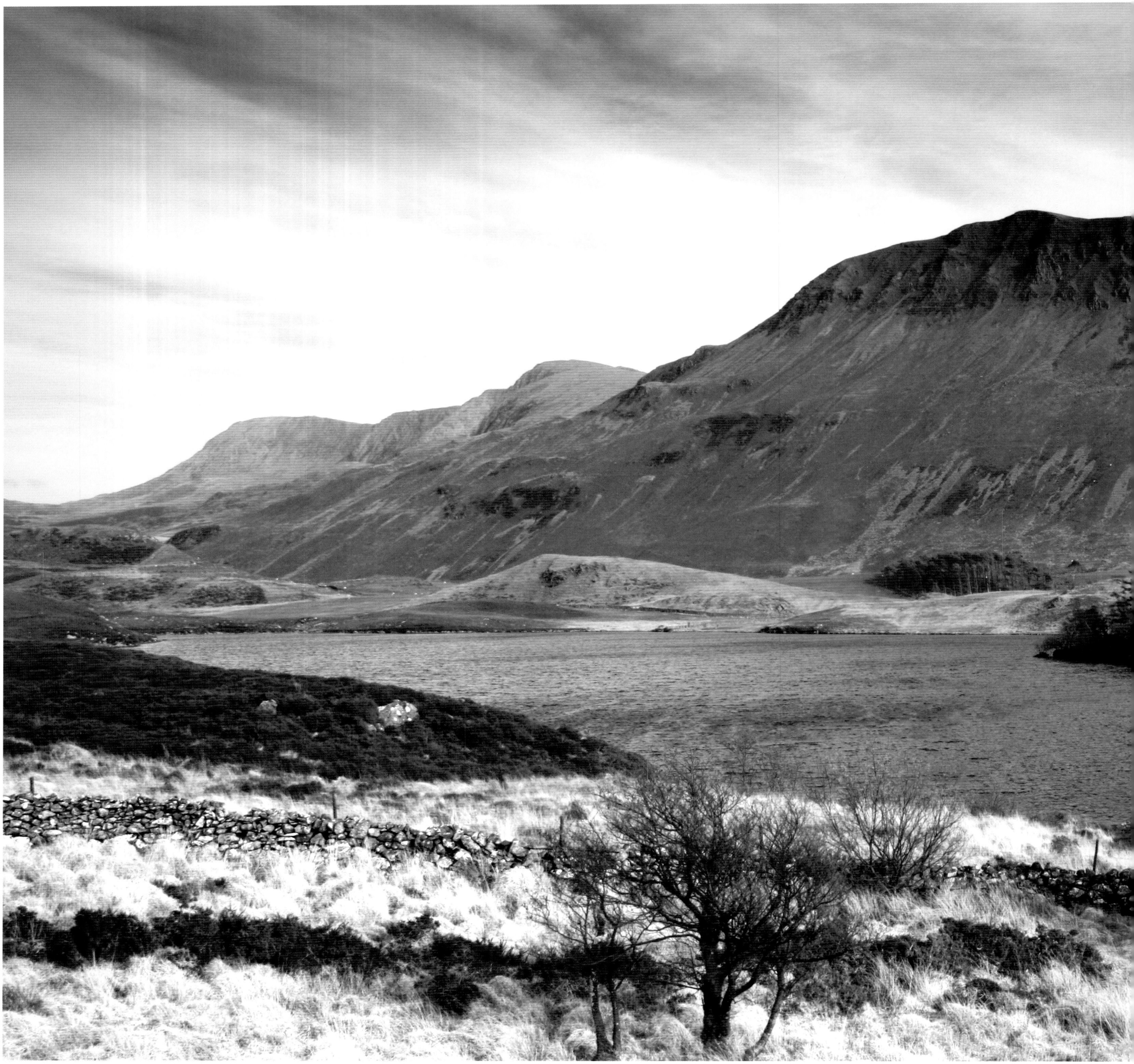

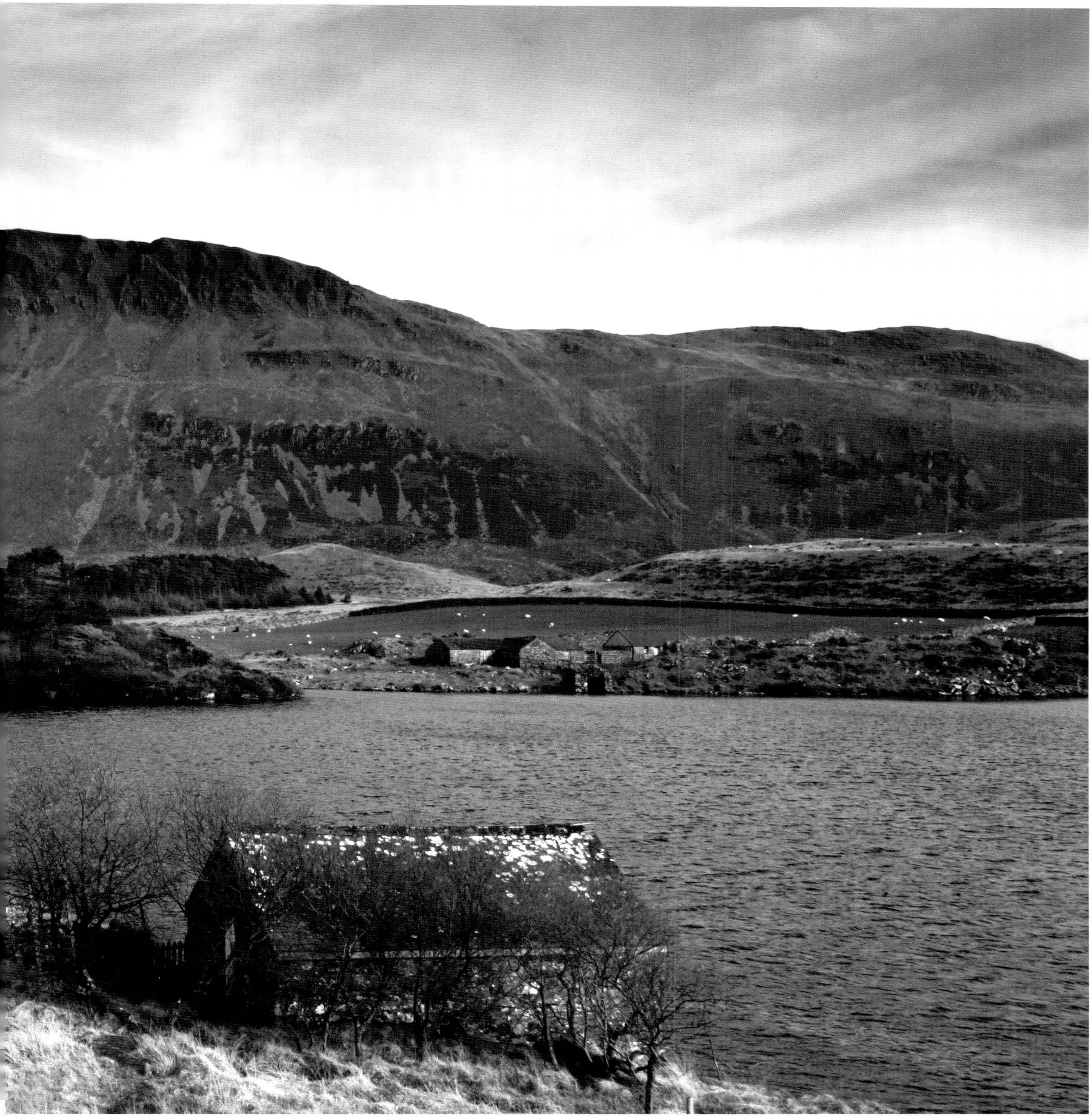

26 Llynnau Cregennen and Tyrrau Mawr, Snowdonia

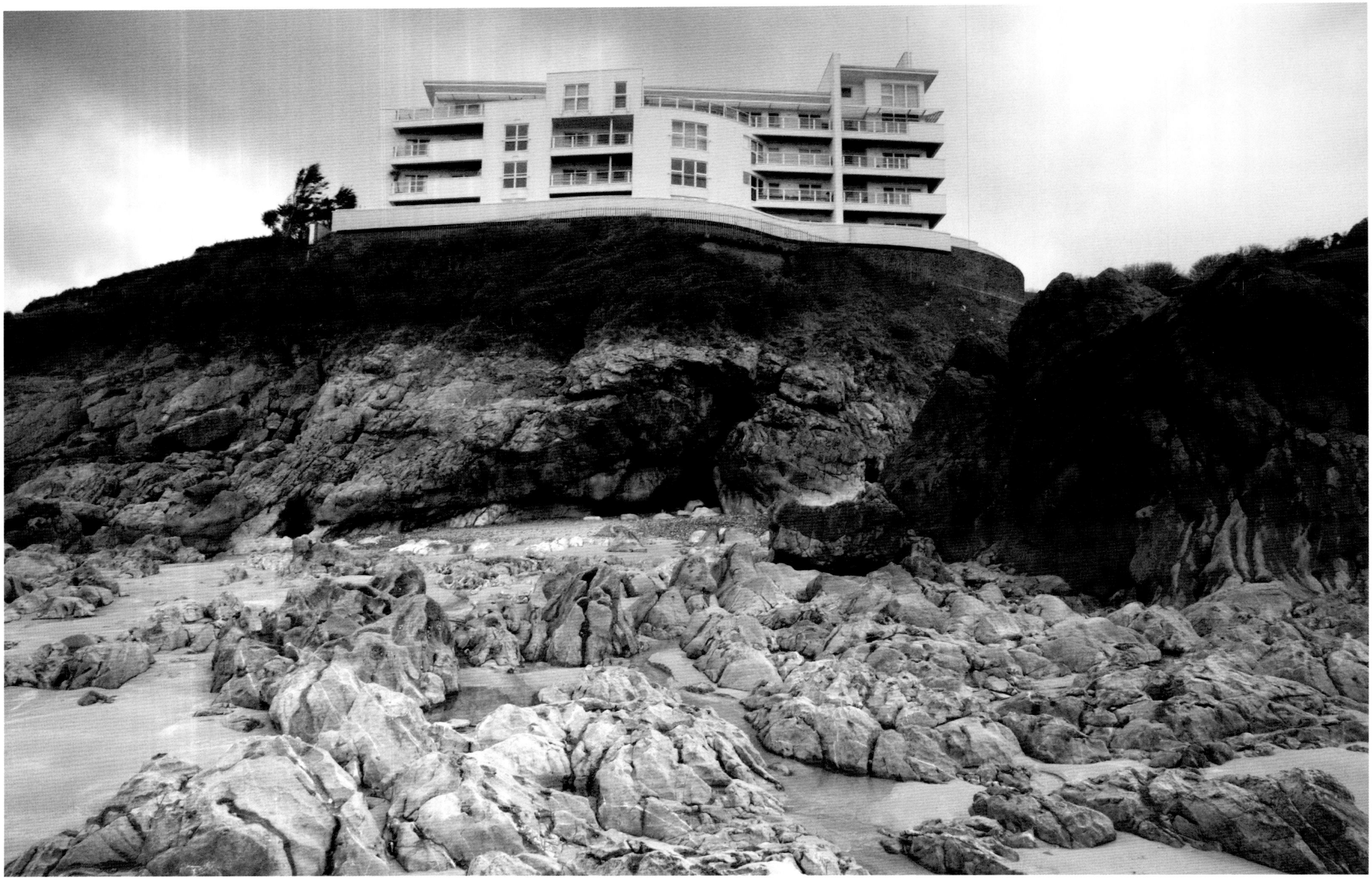

27 LANGLAND BAY, GOWER

Visiting a beach resort in the winter can be a more rewarding experience than in the summertime. It's easier to connect with its soul when all the frenetic hustle and bustle of the height of the season has been stripped away. And I have to say I very much warmed to Langland Bay in January. It had a quiet air of dignified slumber.

The beach was deserted except for what appeared to be the local dog walking society and their canines scampering back and forth at the sea's edge. It gave the heartening impression of a town that continues to thrive throughout the peaceful months when the tourists are absent.

The sweeping arc of beach-huts strung out along the sea-wall projected a certain poignancy; locked up and unattended. Dormant, perhaps, but only a couple of months away from being dusted down once again.

There was a hint of art deco in the sweeping curves of the apartments straddling the cliff-edge. I imagined myself sitting huddled up on the balcony with a steaming mug of coffee while a winter storm lashed the rocks below. Certainly more elemental than lying there on a sun-lounger during a stiflingly hot July day! (Map C6)

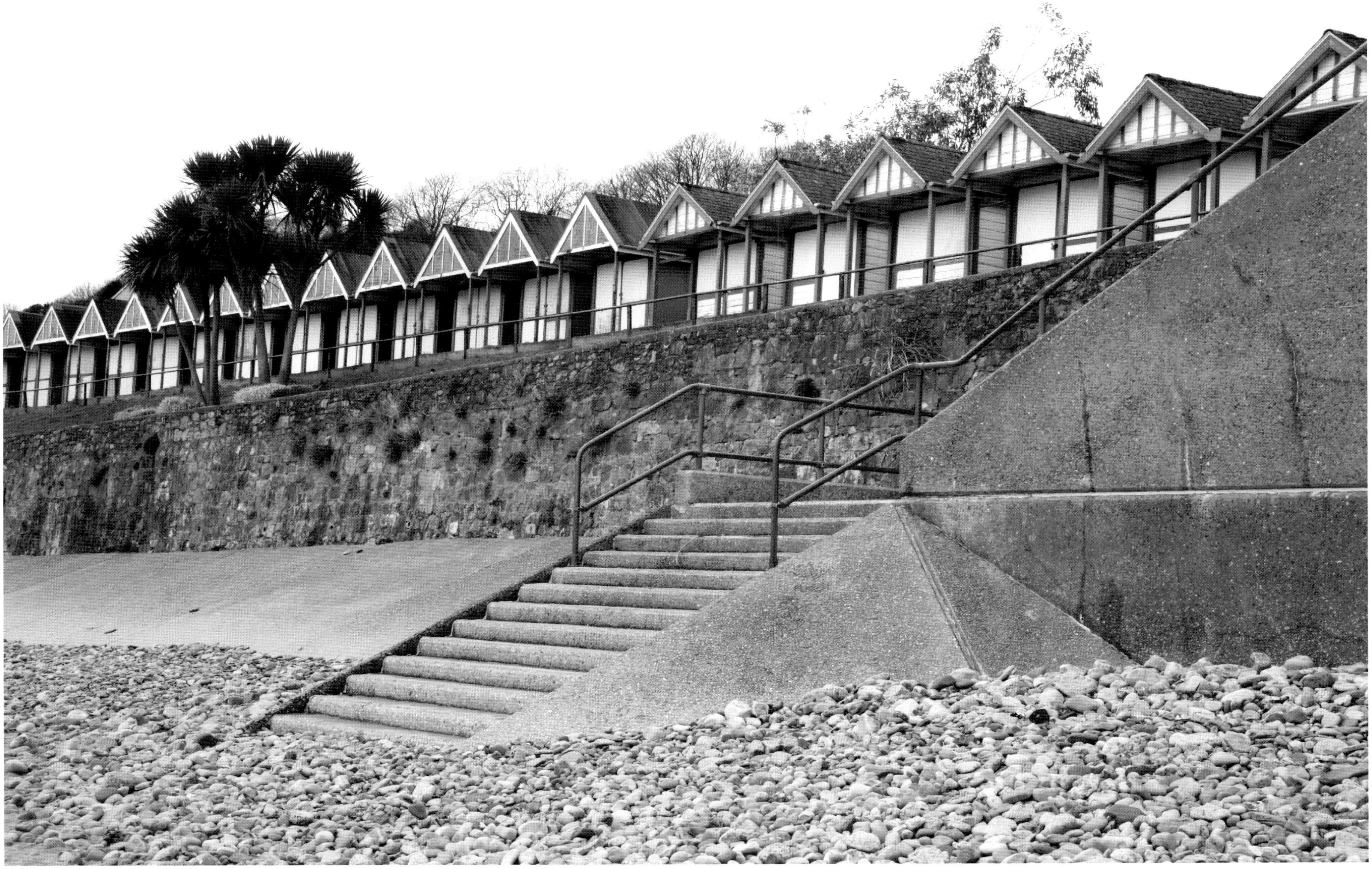

27 Langland Bay, Gower

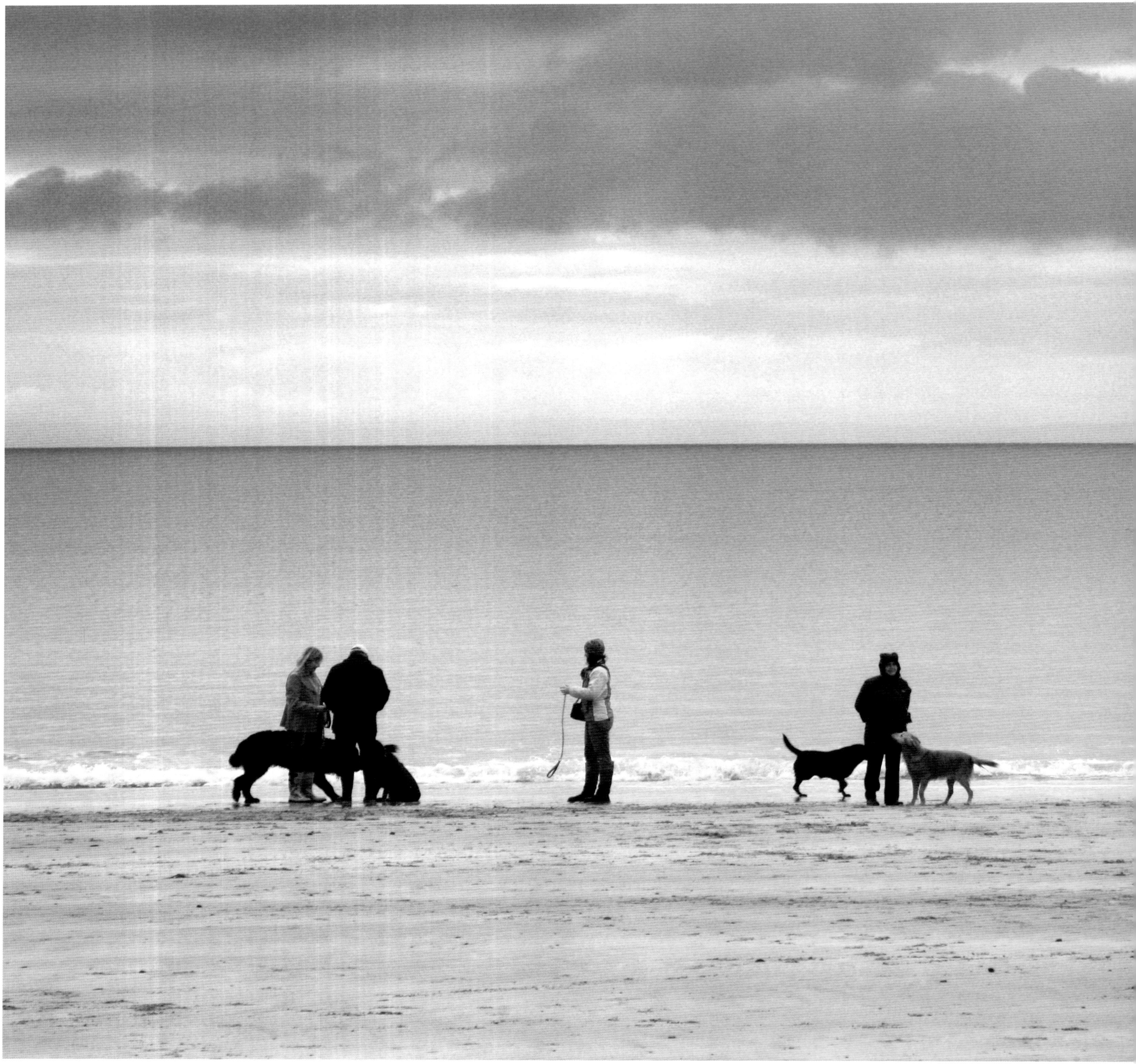

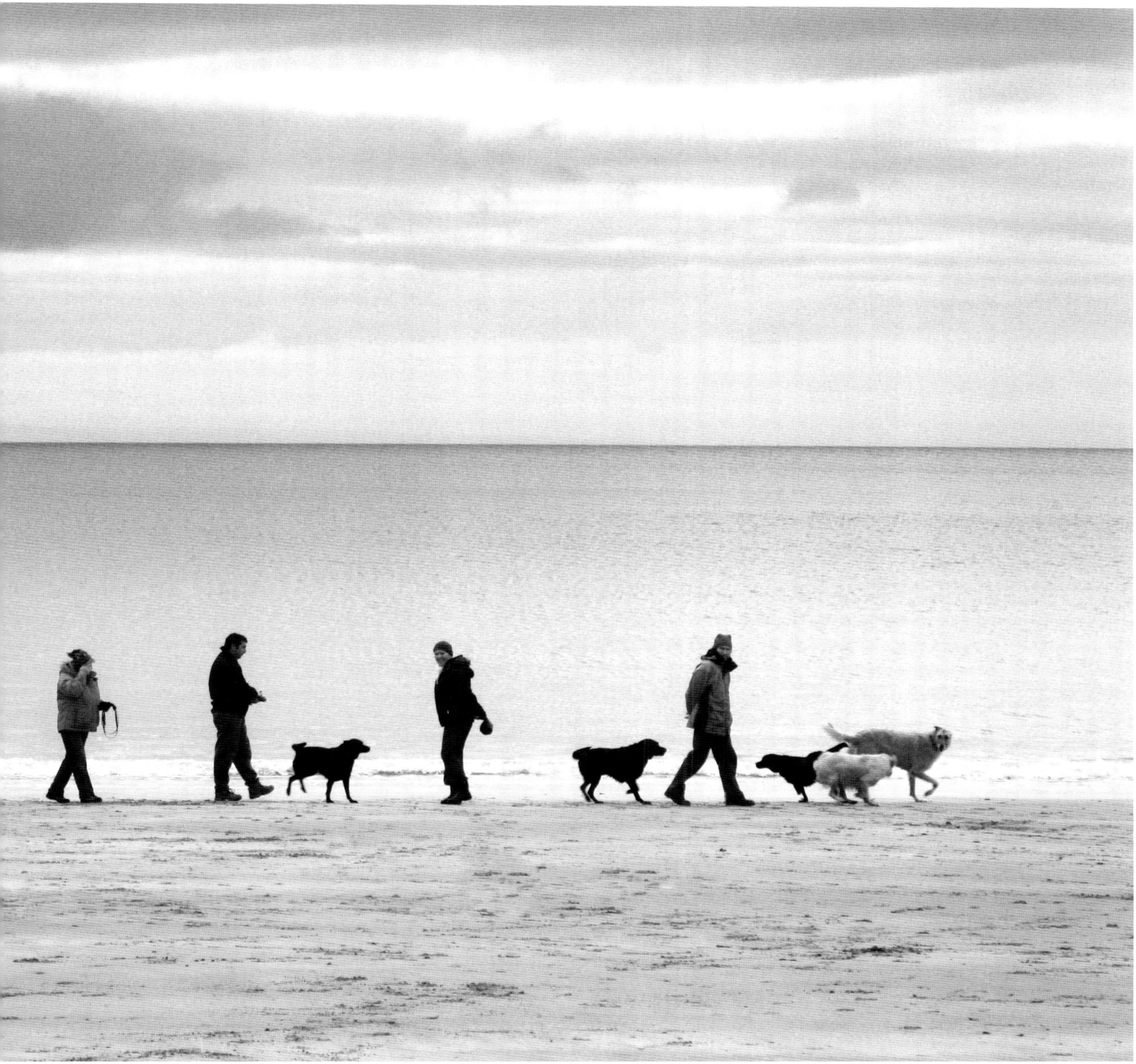

27 Langland Bay, Gower

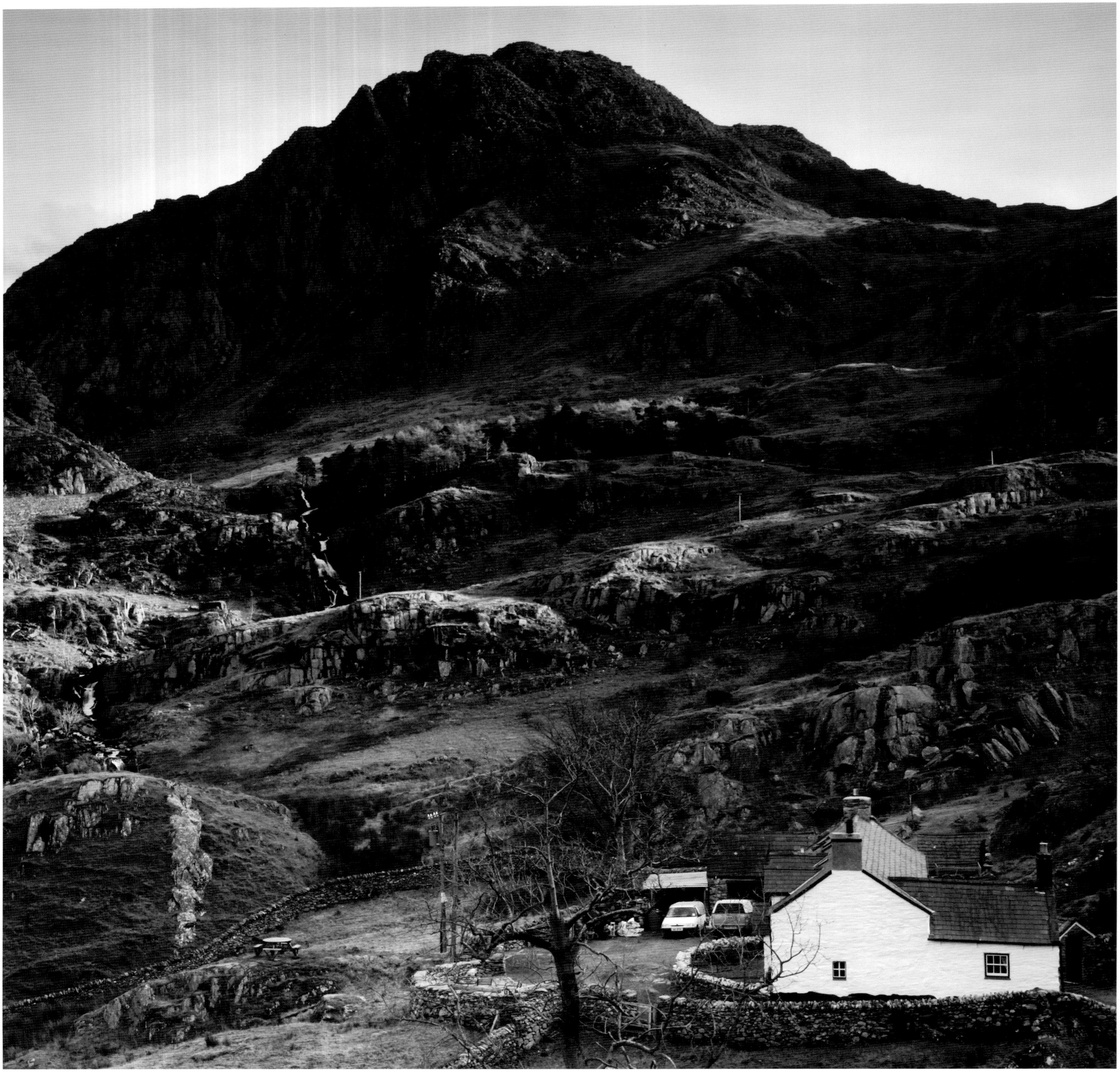

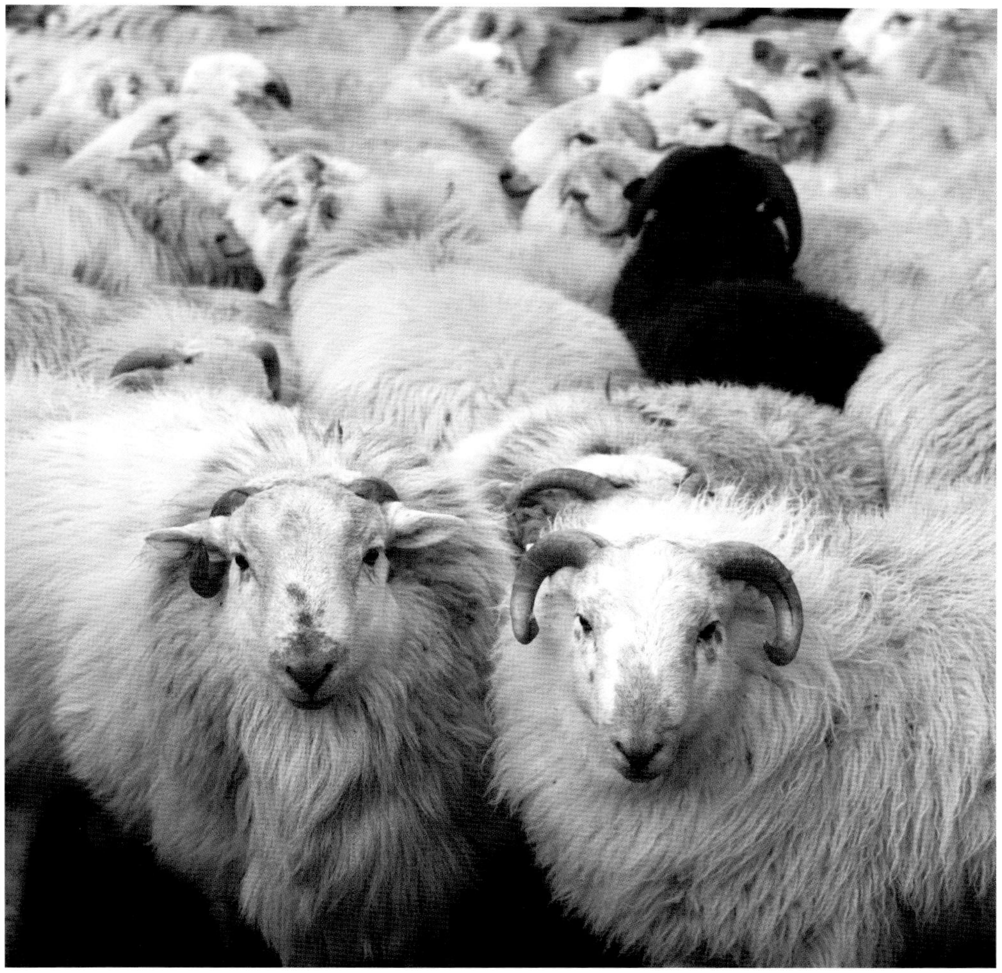

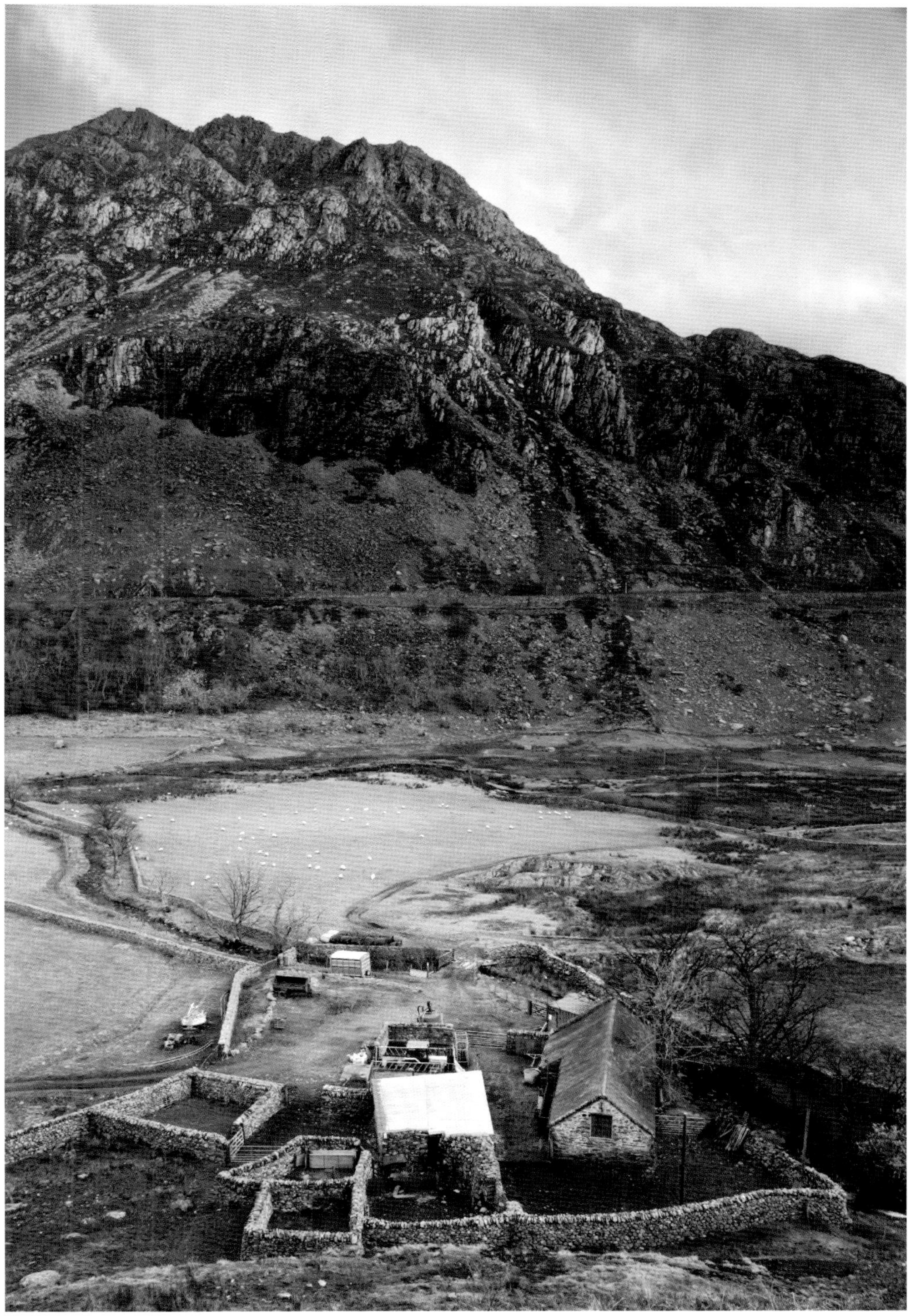

28 BLAEN Y NANT, OGWEN VALLEY, SNOWDONIA

Blaen y Nant nestles at the head of the Ogwen Valley, Snowdonia. Gwyn Thomas farms here. Indeed his family have cultivated this valley for countless generations. His father split slate in Penrhyn Quarry near Bethesda while somehow finding time to work the land. Gwyn has toiled tirelessly to transform his piece of the valley into a prized organic farm. He's particularly proud of the six miles (9.65 km) of dry stone walls which have been rebuilt. Parts of the farm have been returned to nature, enabling the return of a number of animal and bird species that had long since disappeared.

This is farming at the limit of human endeavour. The landscape surrounding the farm is brutal; it takes no prisoners. Hemmed in by the towering giants of Tryfan at 915 metres (3,000 ft) and Pen yr Ole Wen at 978 metres (3,208 ft) this is a farm with an epic backdrop. The landscape tolerates Gwyn and his farm, there being little scope for him to mould his surroundings. Winters here can be particularly harsh; he keeps his shovel indoors to dig himself out! (Map C2)

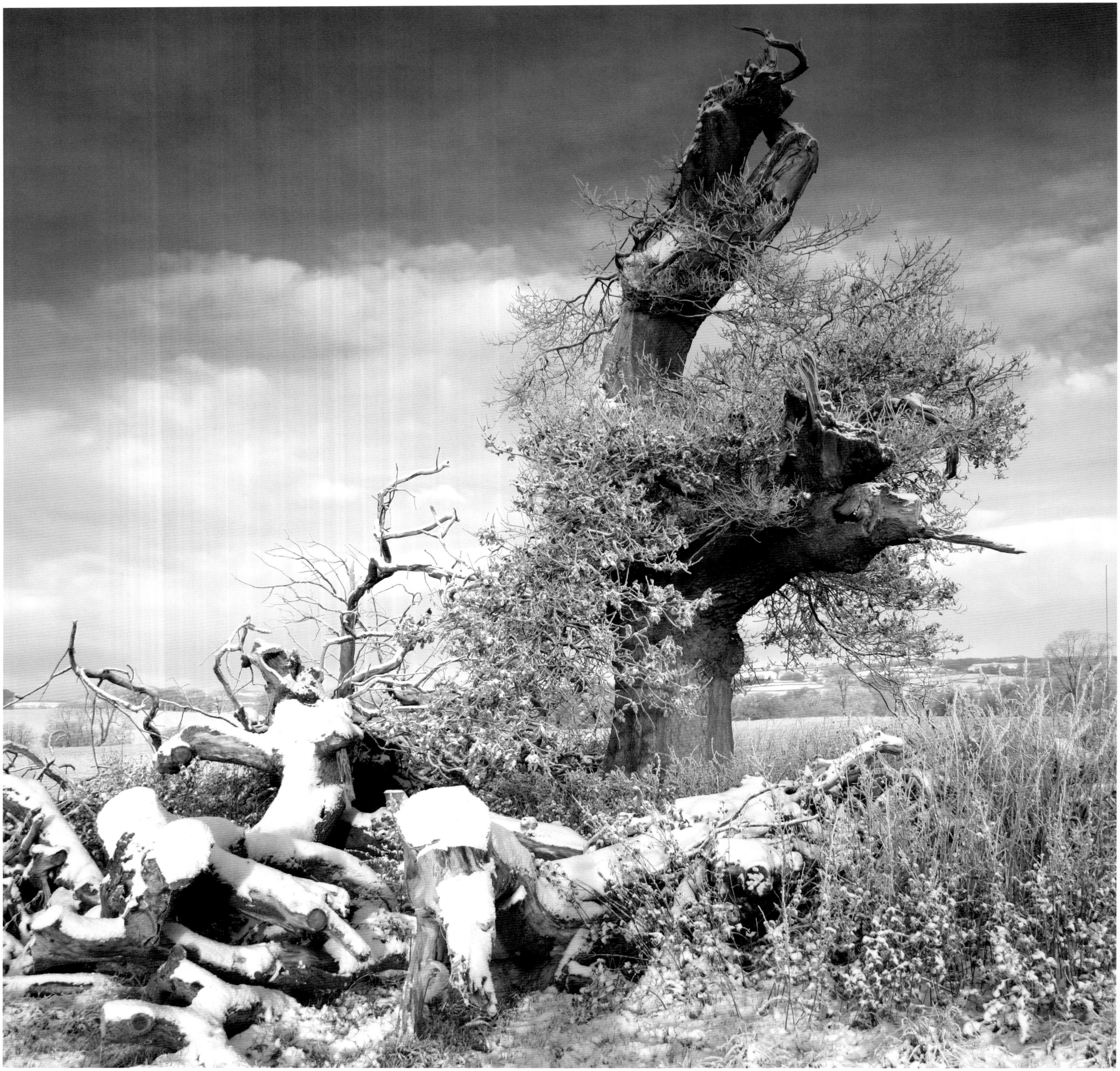

29 DINEFWR PARK, LLANDEILO, CARMARTHENSHIRE

Winter came early in 2010. The thermals saw action sooner than they may have imagined, and this was definitely a day for those extra layers. I had been to Dinefwr Park a couple of months earlier and made a mental note that a sprinkling of snow would bring the place to life. And so here I was in late November crunching through the snow, heading towards a dismembered tree on the horizon, surrounded by its once glorious branches. There was something almost sculptural about this pile of dead wood, as if each branch had been deliberately placed around the shorn trunk as a form of homage to a noble tree.

Alternatively, the image of a cluster of trees on another horizon projected a hearty vitality, albeit without their leaves. I was drawn to the upright starkness of the trunks set in contrast to the snow and the white sky. (Map C5)

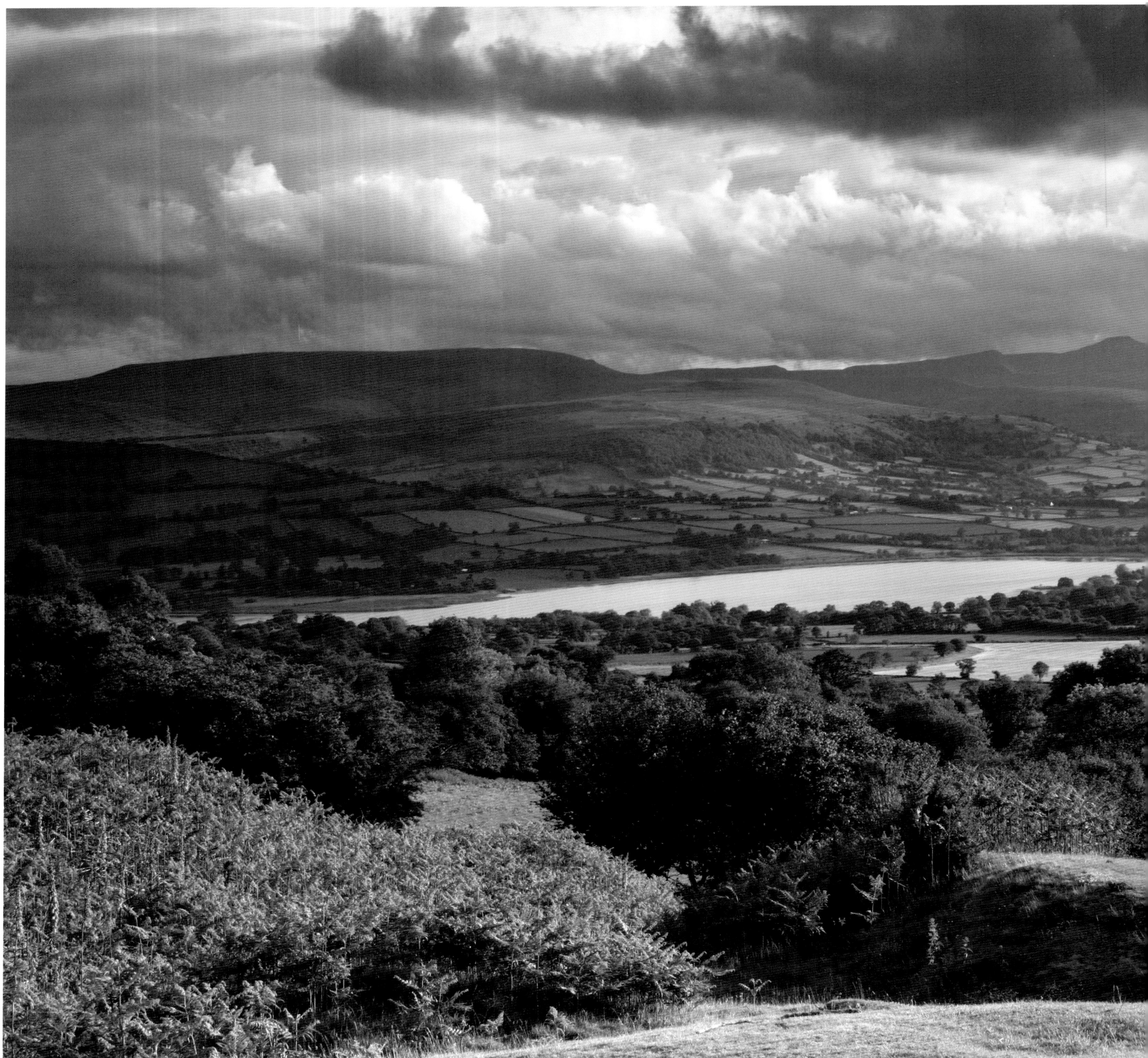

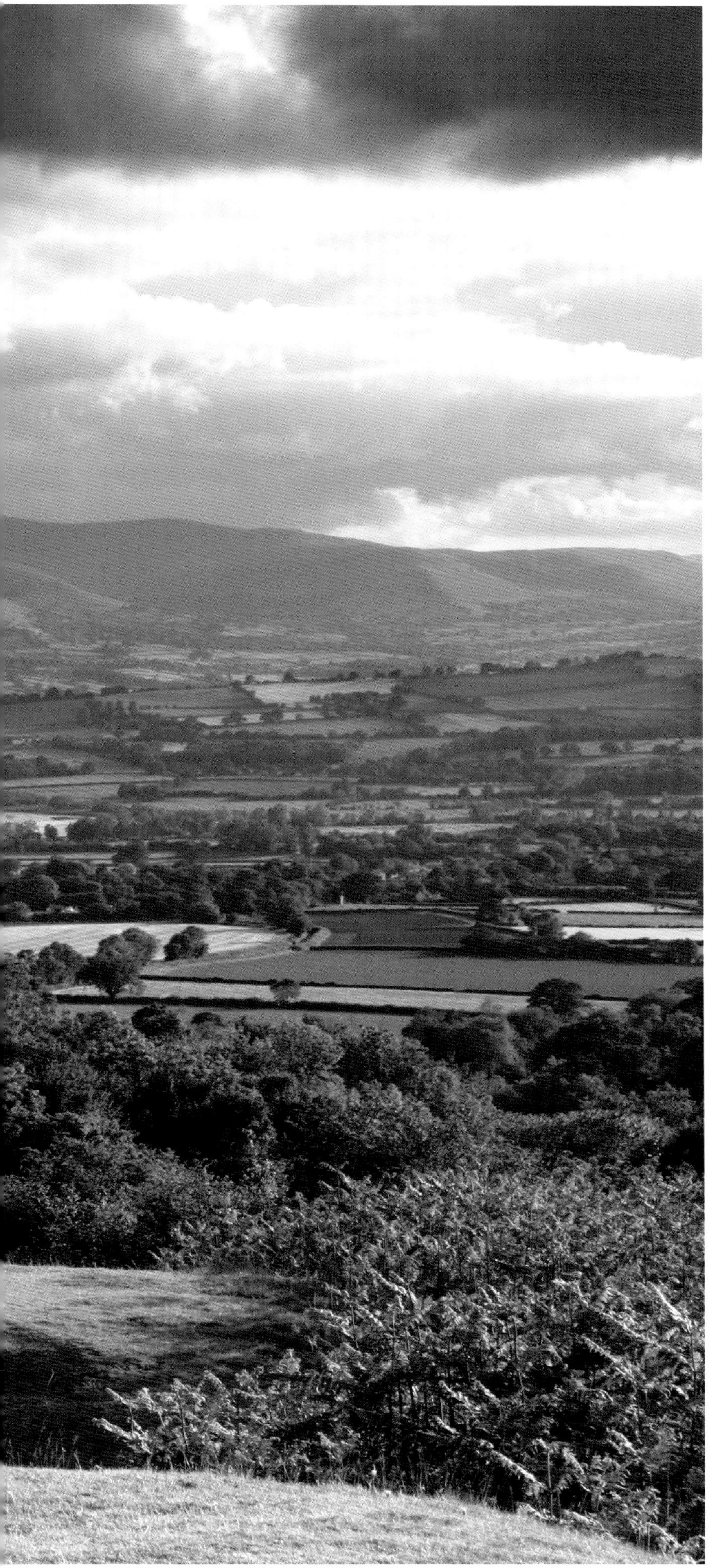

30 PEN Y FAN AND LLANGORS LAKE FROM COCKIT HILL, BRECON BEACONS

Taken late one afternoon in April this is an all-encompassing grand sweep of landscape. There are times when a photographer can get too close to a peak, losing the wider story and the context in which it dominates the landscape. Distance can often magnify its magnificence.

From afar you embark on a journey through the image, in this instance from foreground bracken, descending through hilly woods, over fields, across Llangors Lake and onwards to the distant Brecon Beacons. The stormy sky was an added bonus. (Map D5)

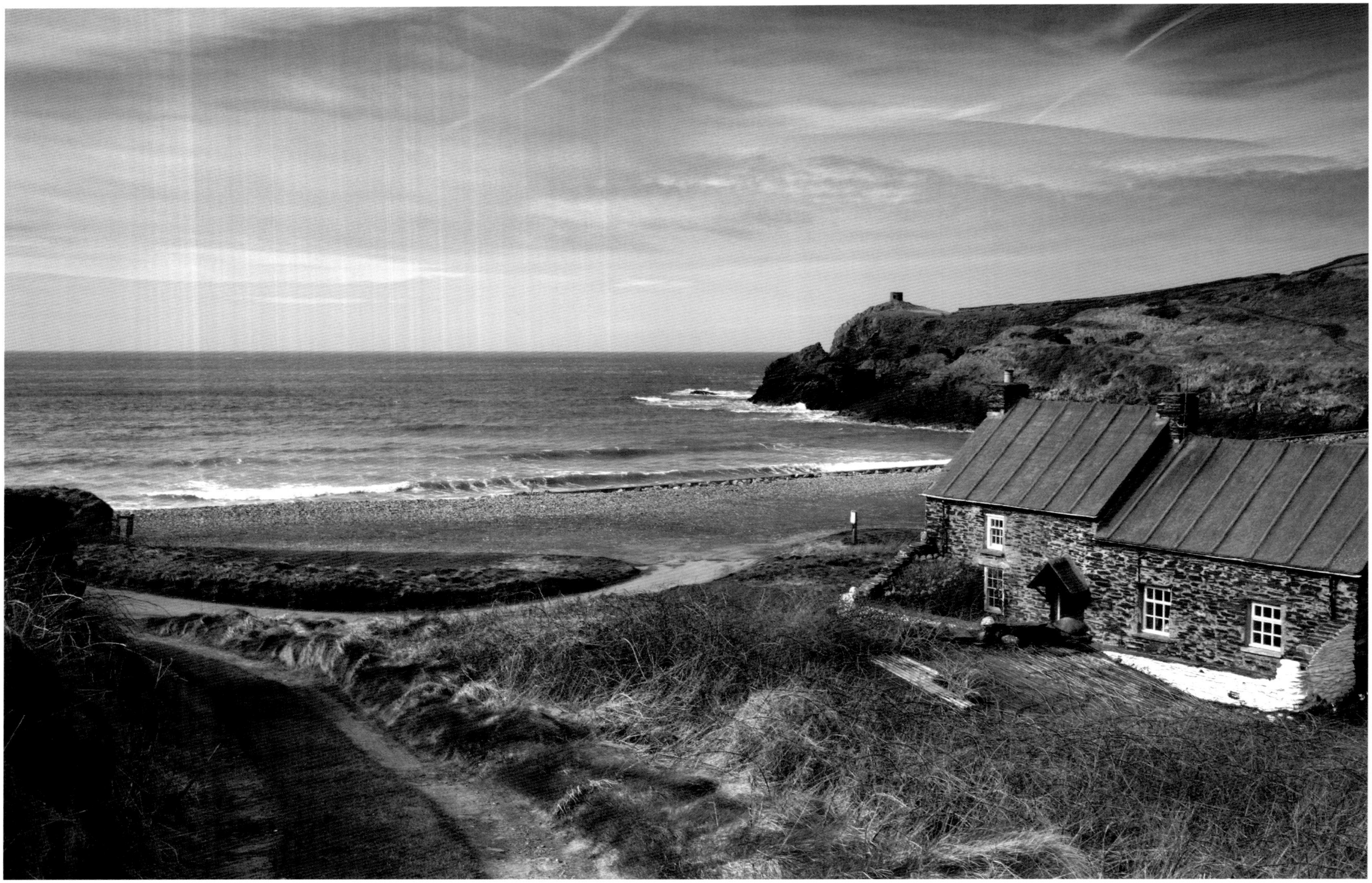

31 ABEREIDDI, PEMBROKESHIRE

The tiny cluster of cottages at Abereiddi huddle together a stone's throw from the water's edge. A substantial earth embankment offers some of the dwellings protection from the winter storms that lash this coast. They seem almost to cower behind it. Take away the odd car and the telegraph poles and you could imagine yourself hurtled back 150 years to when this was a thriving little community employed at the local open-cast quarry. The quarry closed many decades ago.

These precious buildings sit beautifully in the landscape. An ocean of long grass seems to wash around them, rooting them to the earth. The criss-cross of dirt tracks, traditional grouted roofs, and plentiful evidence of lime-wash and render offer an insight into a bygone era; a peep into the past, if you like. (Map A5)

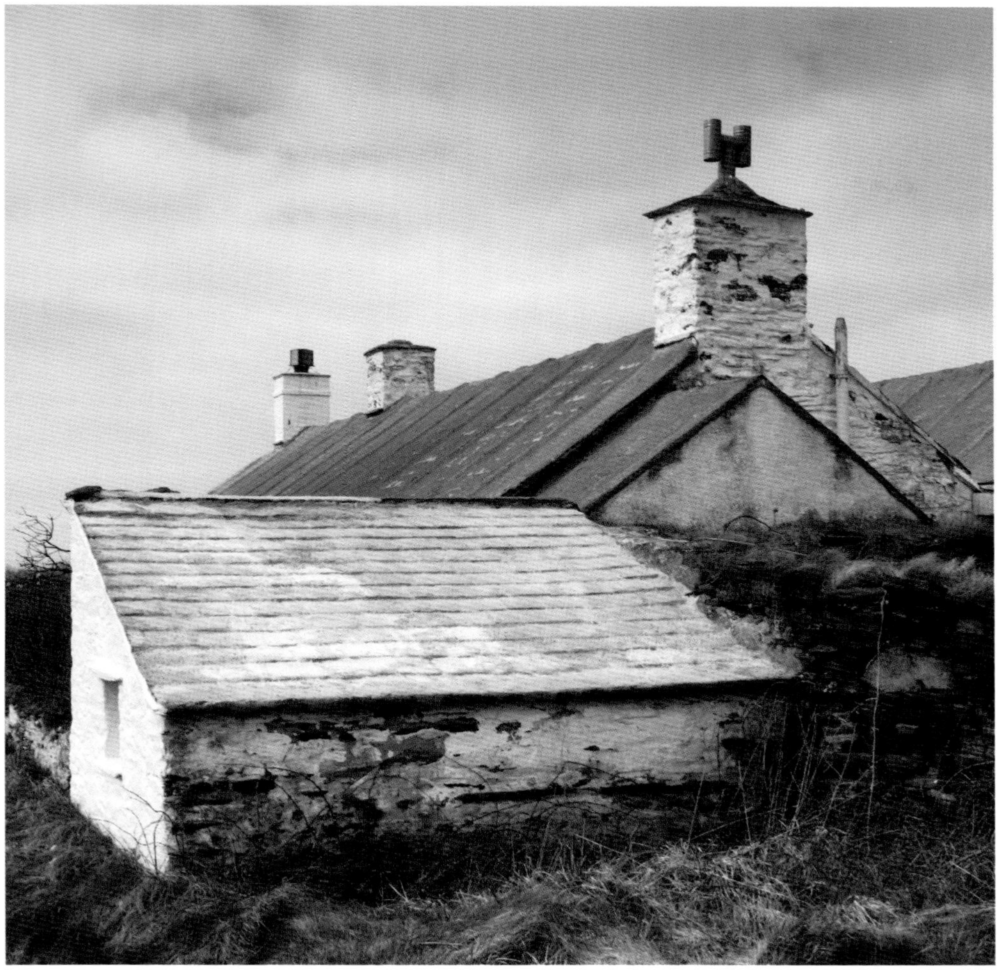

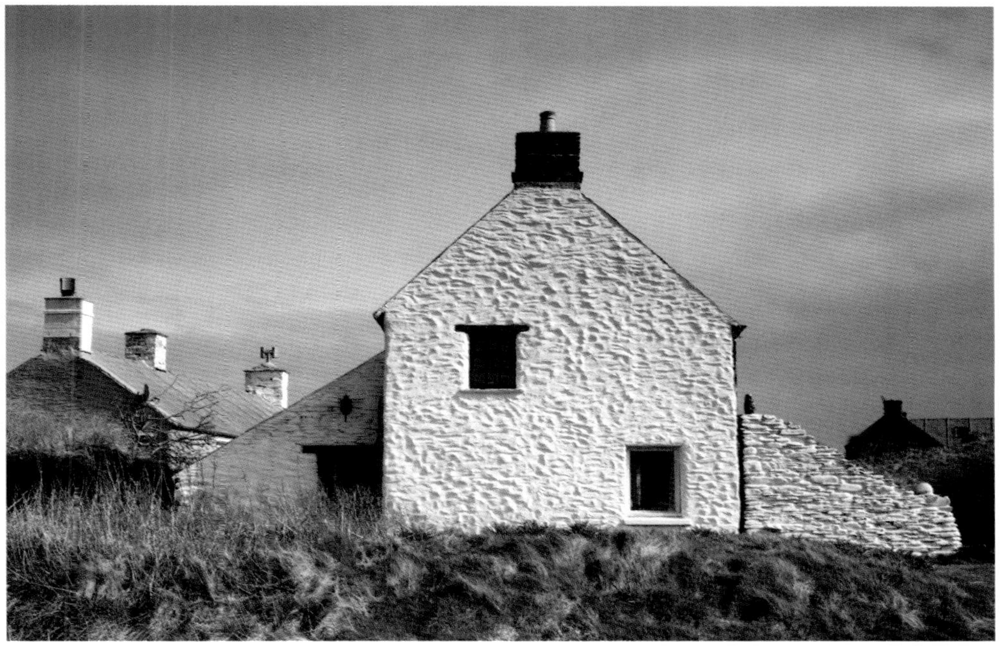

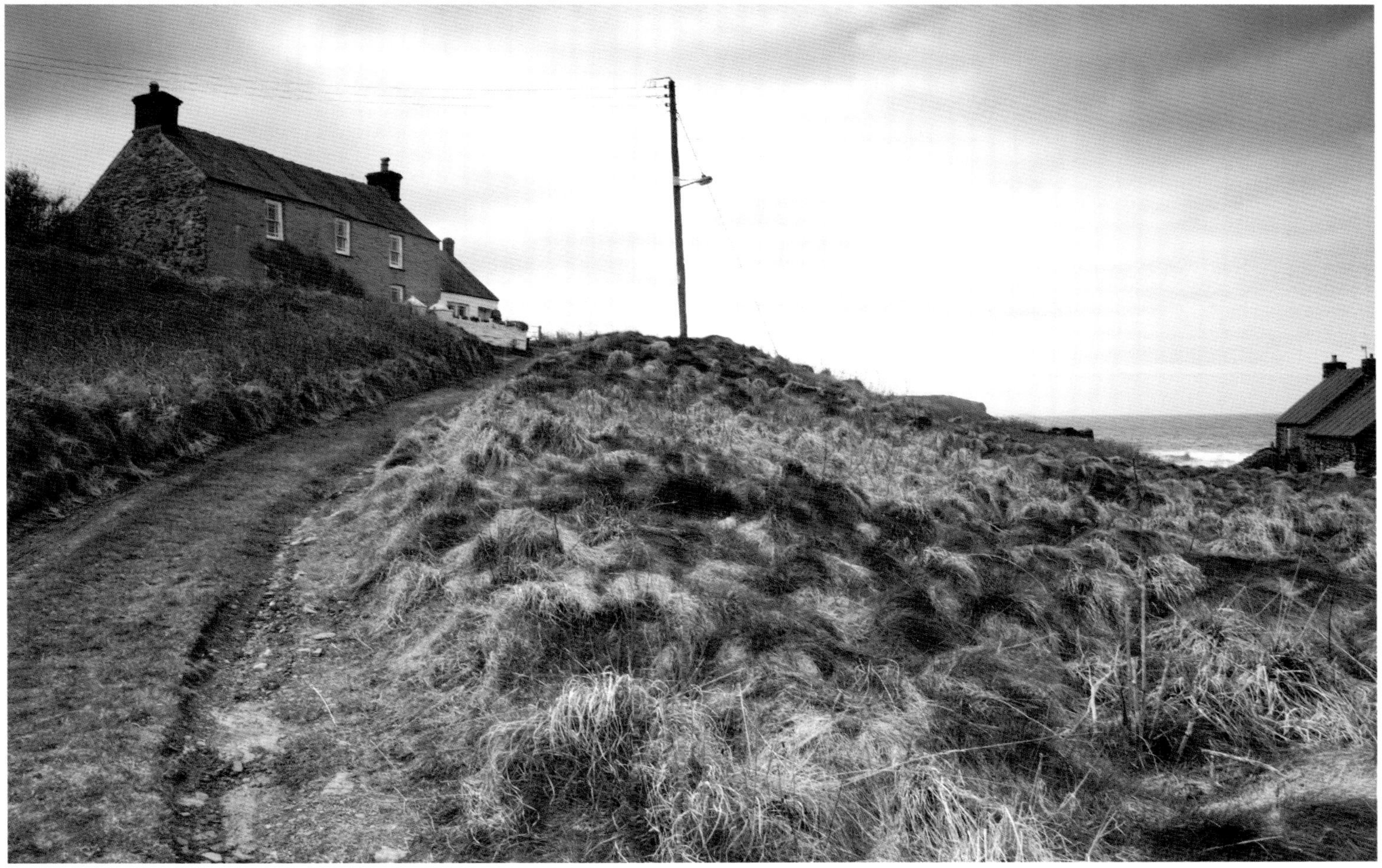

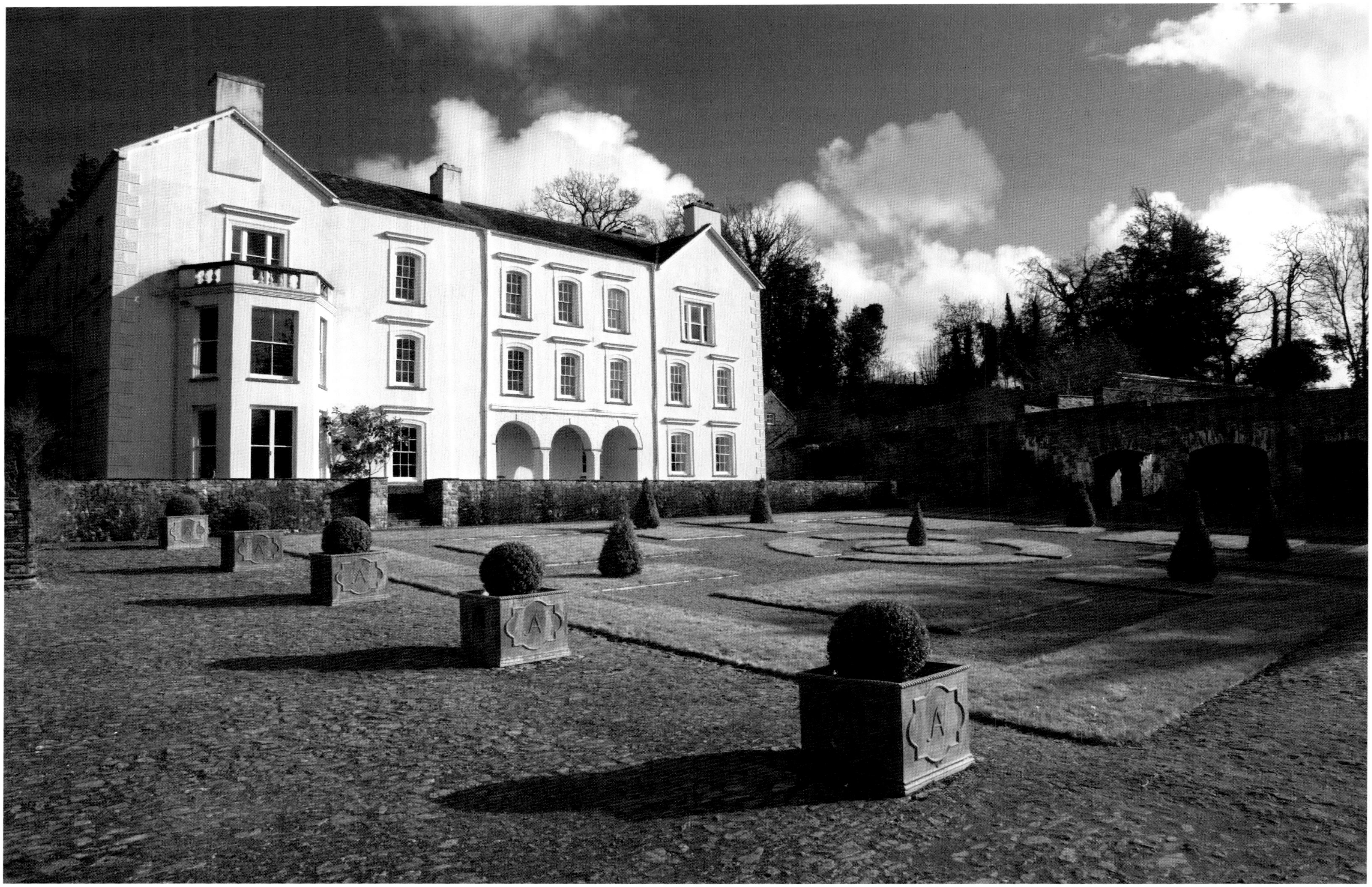

32 ABERGLASNEY HOUSE AND GARDENS, CARMARTHENSHIRE

Over the past fifteen years Aberglasney has been rescued from overgrown and dilapidated obscurity by a dedicated team of restoration experts and gardeners. The phrase 'a labour of love' is most definitely apt in this case.

I picked the perfect morning to photograph Aberglasney. True to its word, the weather forecast had predicted a lifting of the cloud and rain that had blighted the previous week and a return to winter sunshine. I arrived early as arranged to sneak in a couple of hours before the visitors arrived. I had the place all to myself, which was ideal for the shoot, though I had to stifle an urge to simply wander around aimlessly soaking up the solitary calm of these beautiful gardens. I don't pretend to have much knowledge of horticulture – it's probably on par with my grasp of nuclear physics – but the symmetrical, almost mathematical precision of some of the spaces brought a sense of serene contemplation. I had to crack on though while I had the skirting February sunlight to work with. (Map C5)

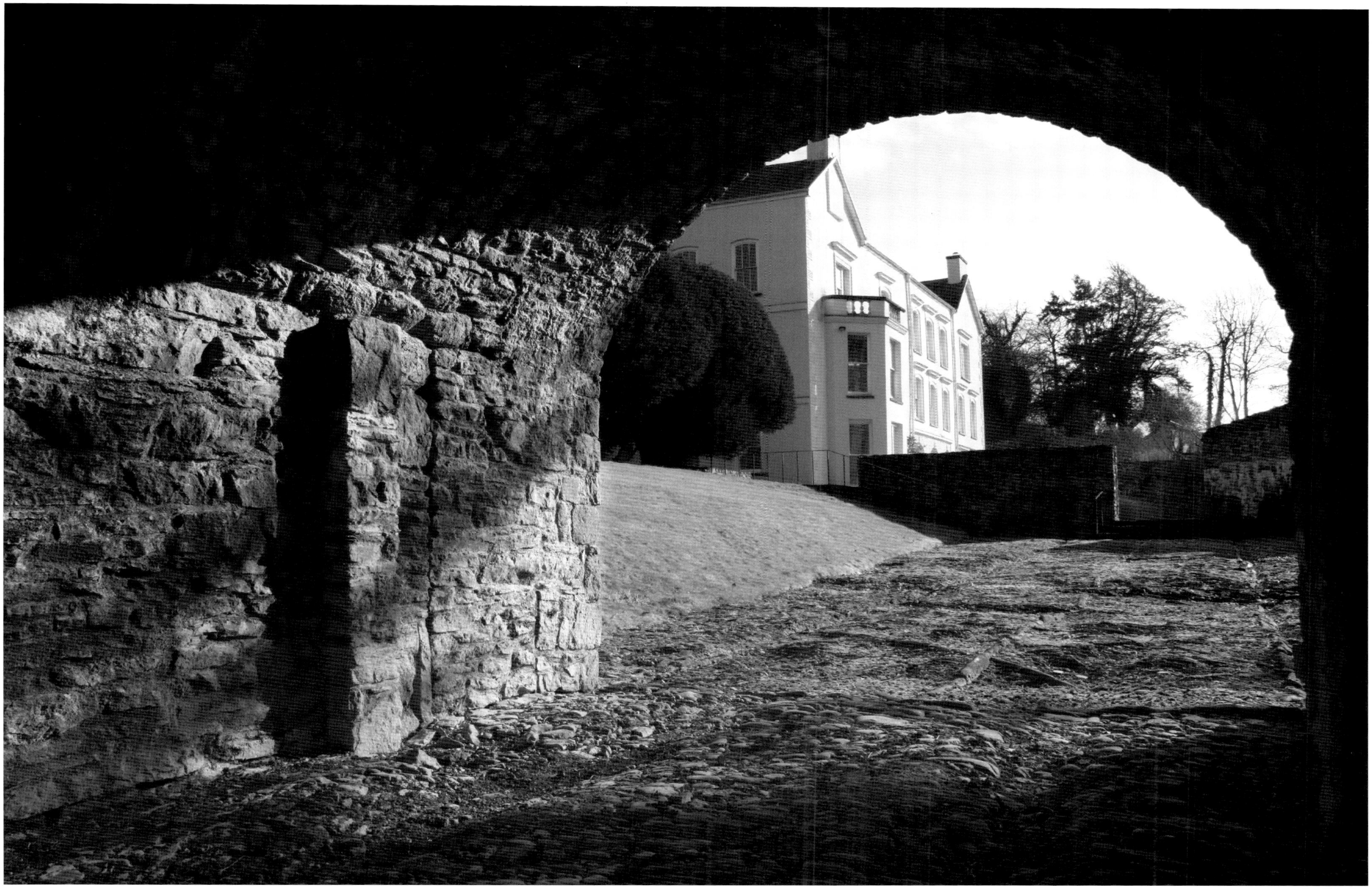

32 Aberglasney House and Gardens, Carmarthenshire

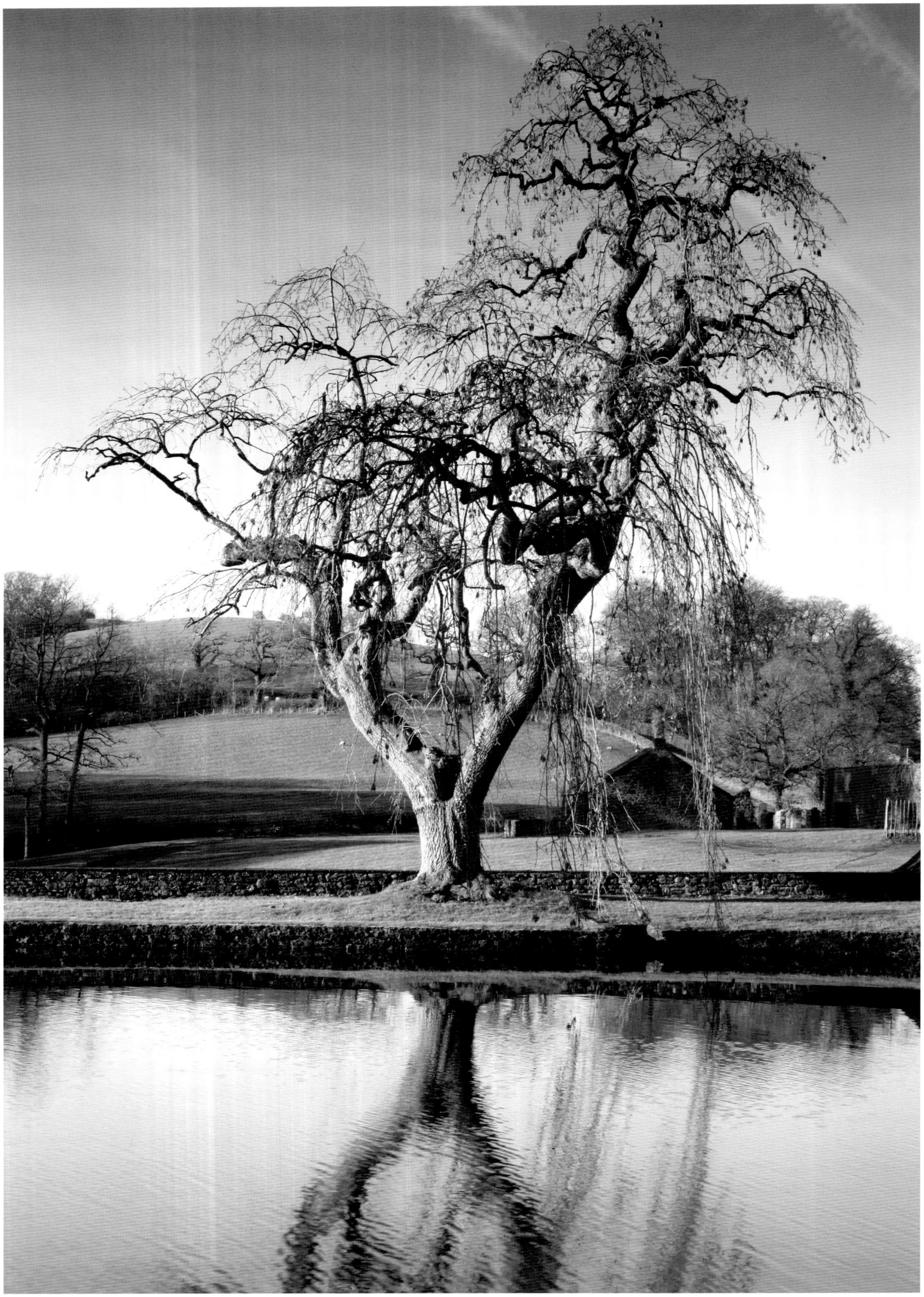

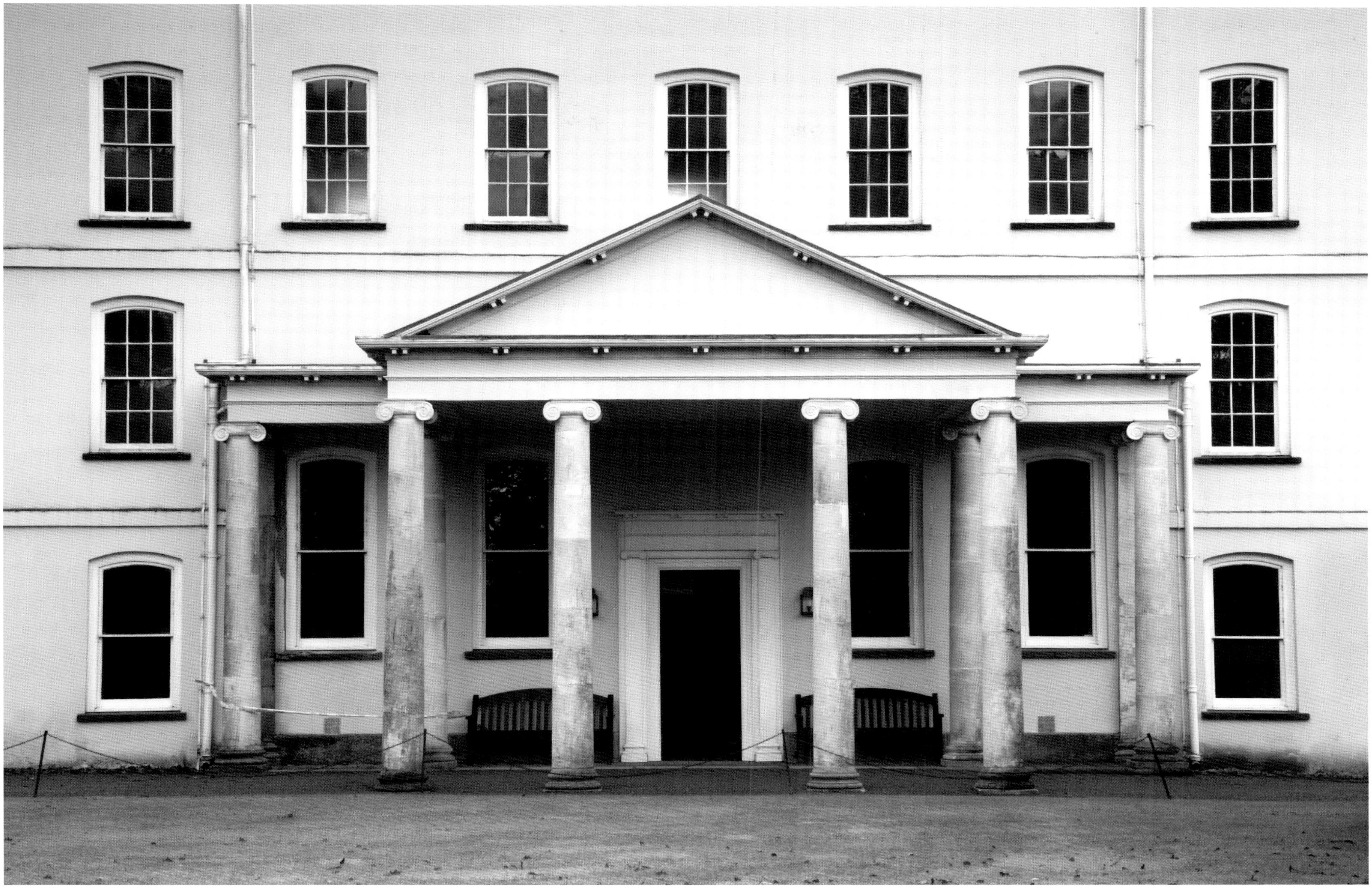

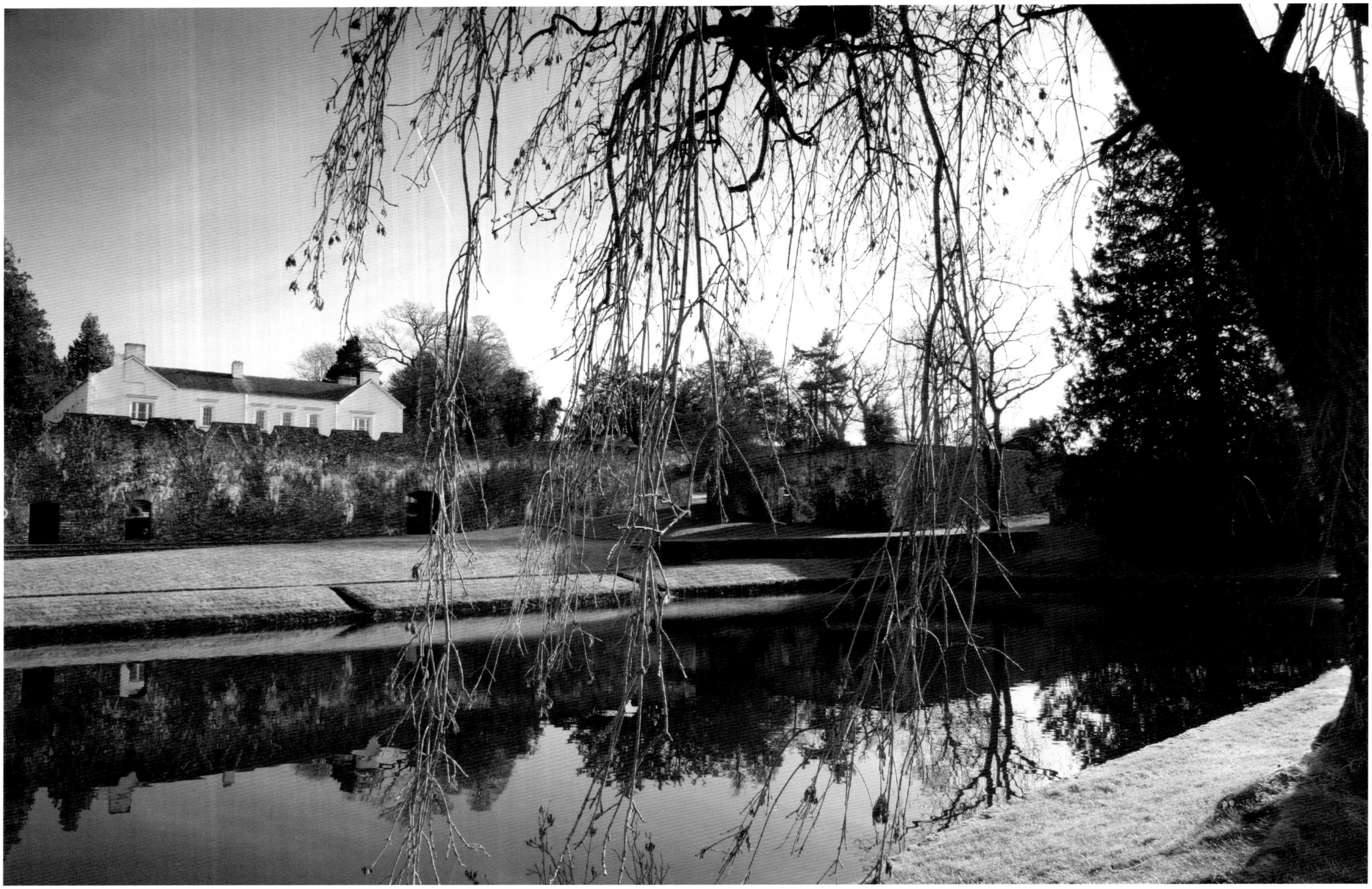

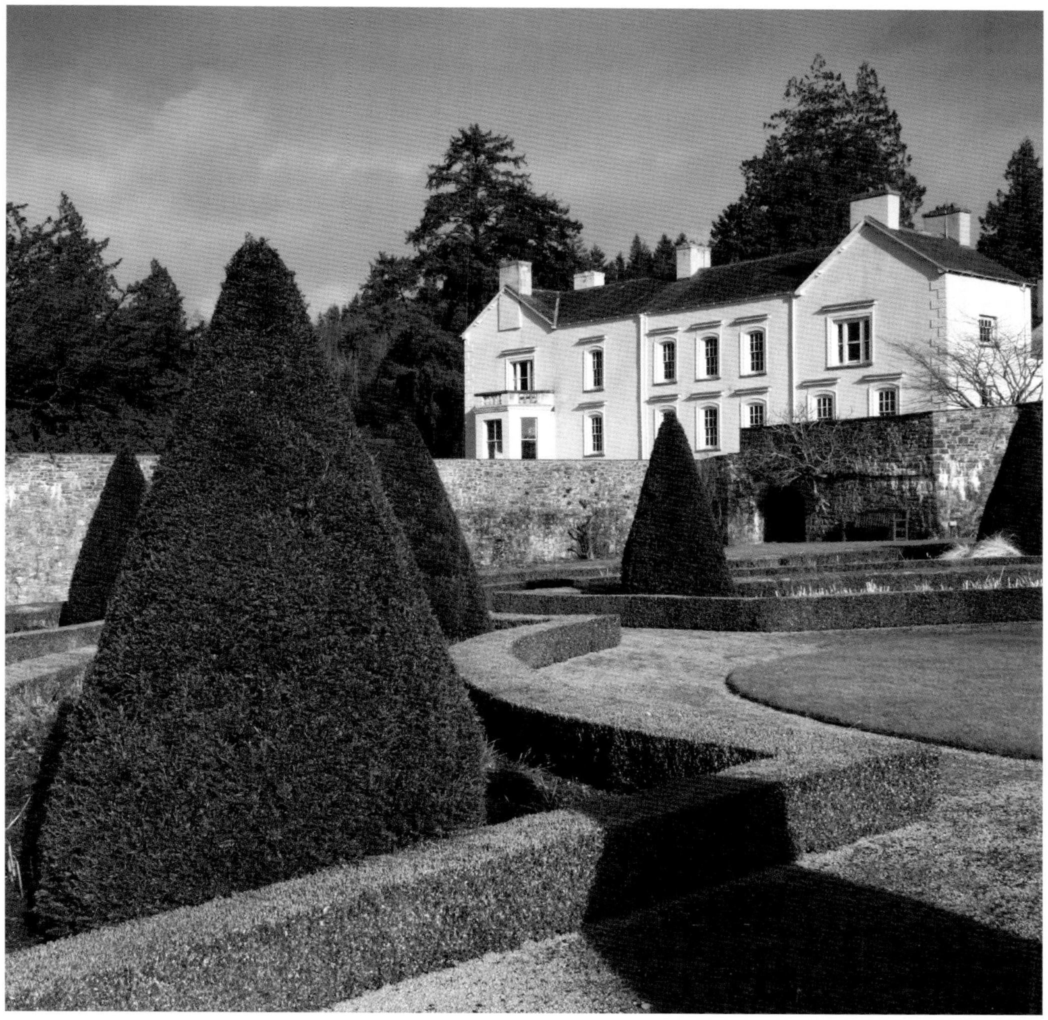

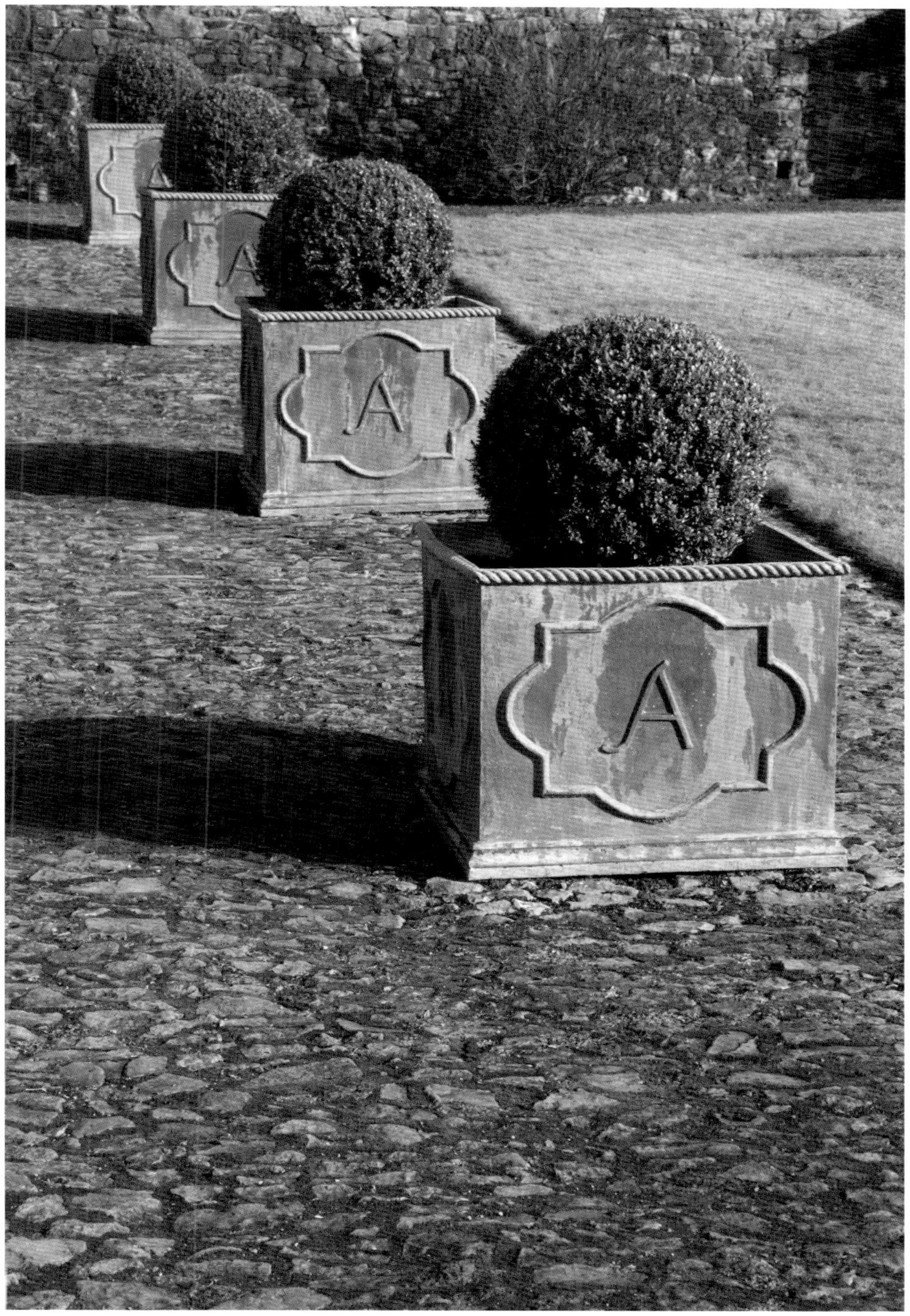

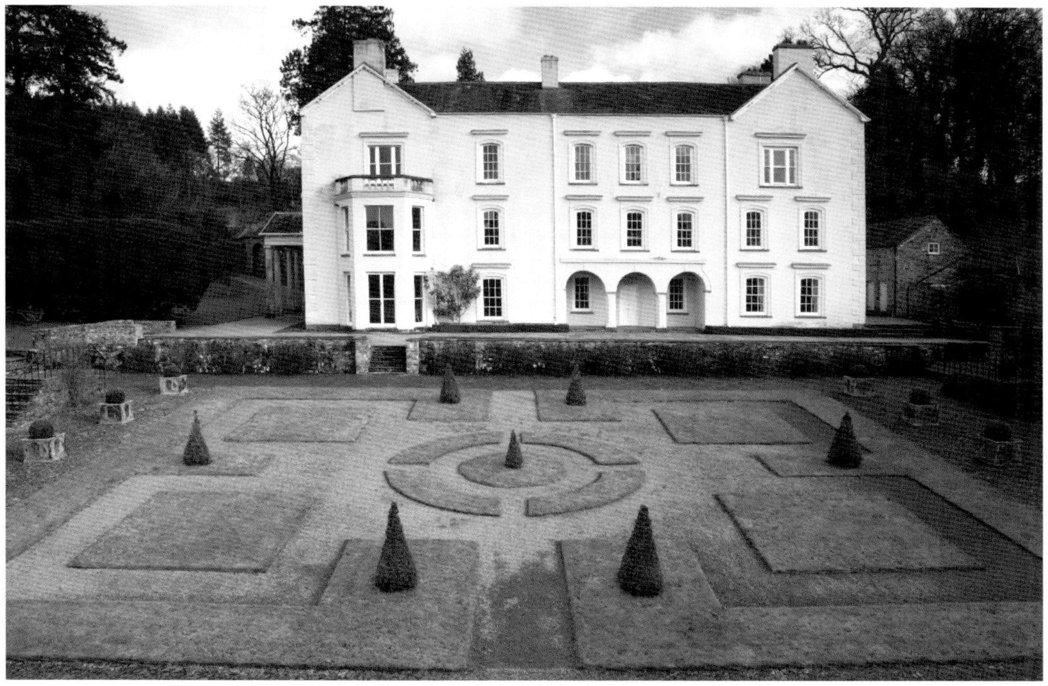

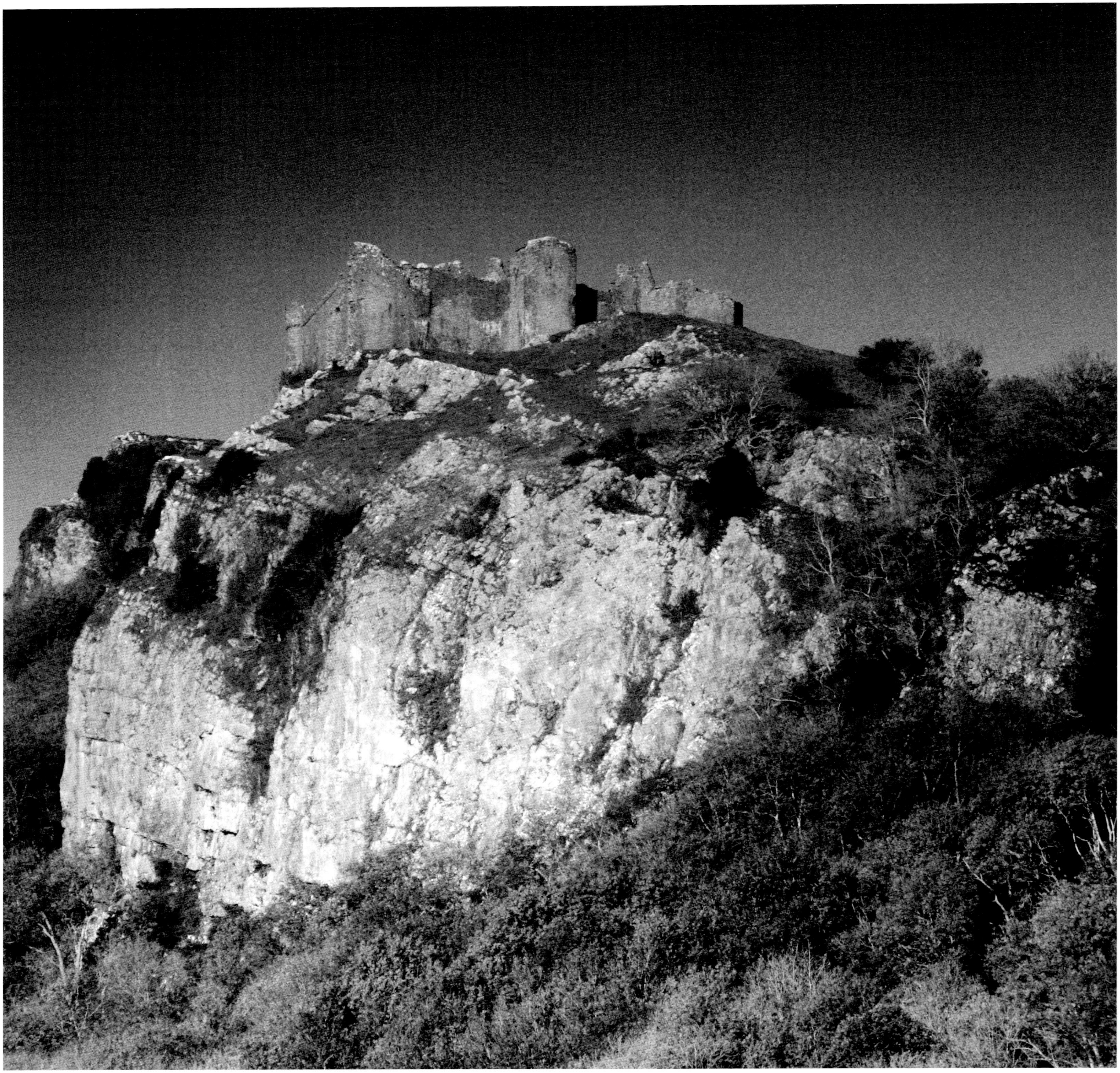

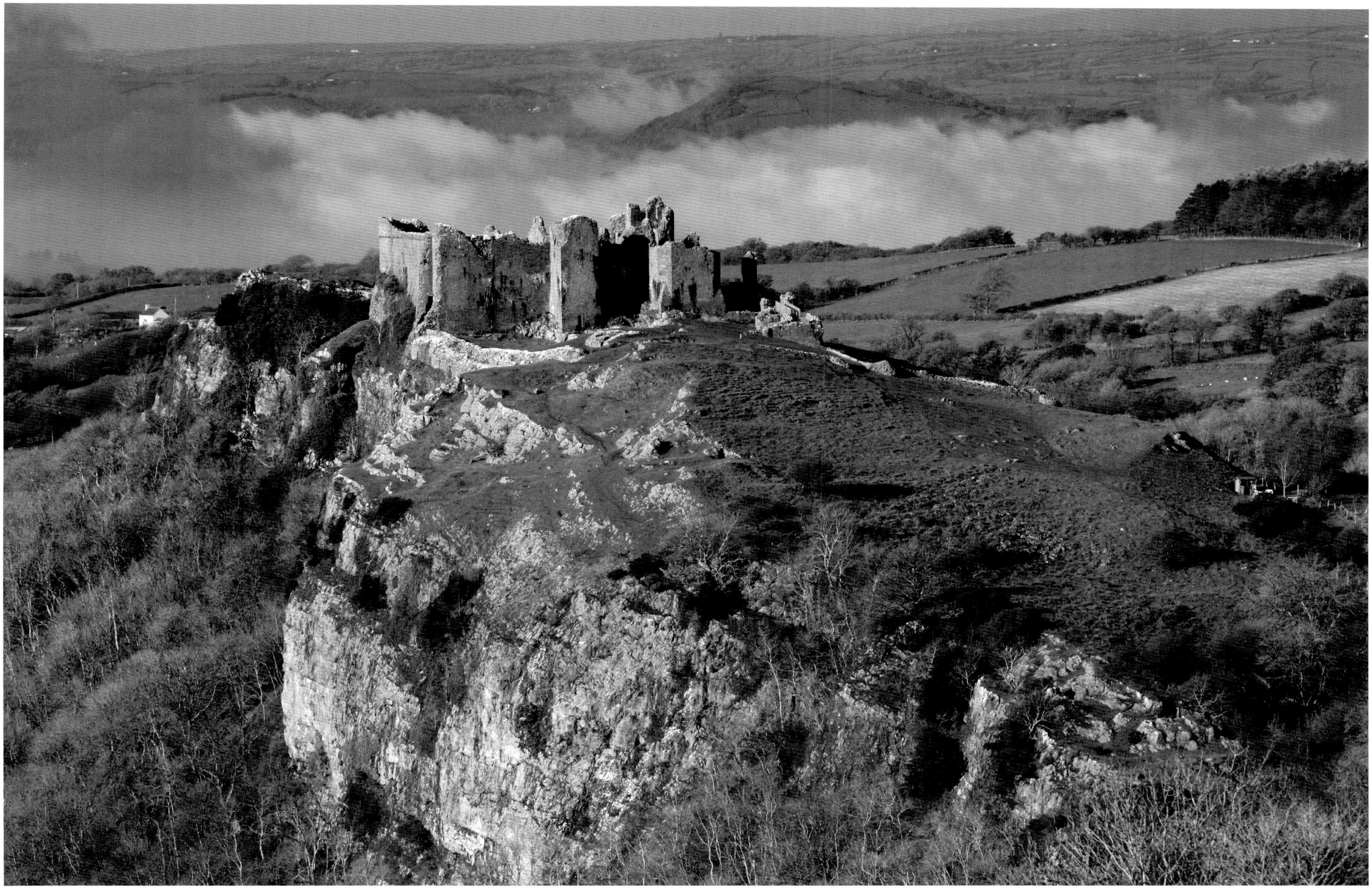

33 CARREG CENNEN CASTLE, CARMARTHENSHIRE

The early morning was veiled in mist that clung stubbornly to the Black Mountain above Carreg Cennen Castle. Reduced visibility gave the narrow twisting road through the mountain an eerie sense of isolation. Recalling the film *An American Werewolf in London*, I decided not to venture far from the tarmac!

The mist burnt off with the rising sun and I suddenly became aware of Carreg Cennen perched below on its rocky plateau. Voted one of the most romantic ruins in Britain, this imposing fortress would have had no rosy connotations when first built to deter any unwanted attention from the locals. The word impregnable could have been made for this castle. (Map C5)

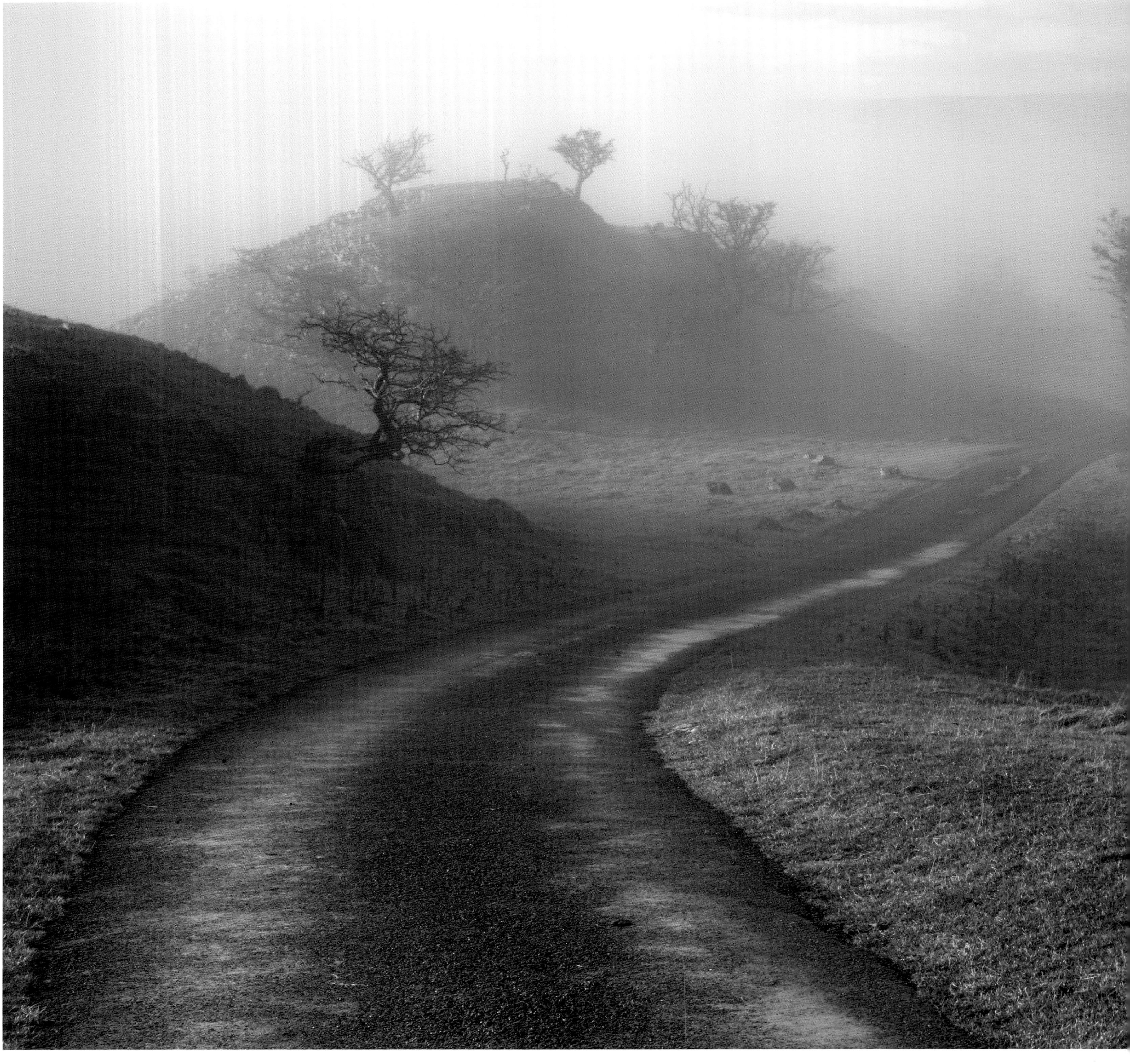

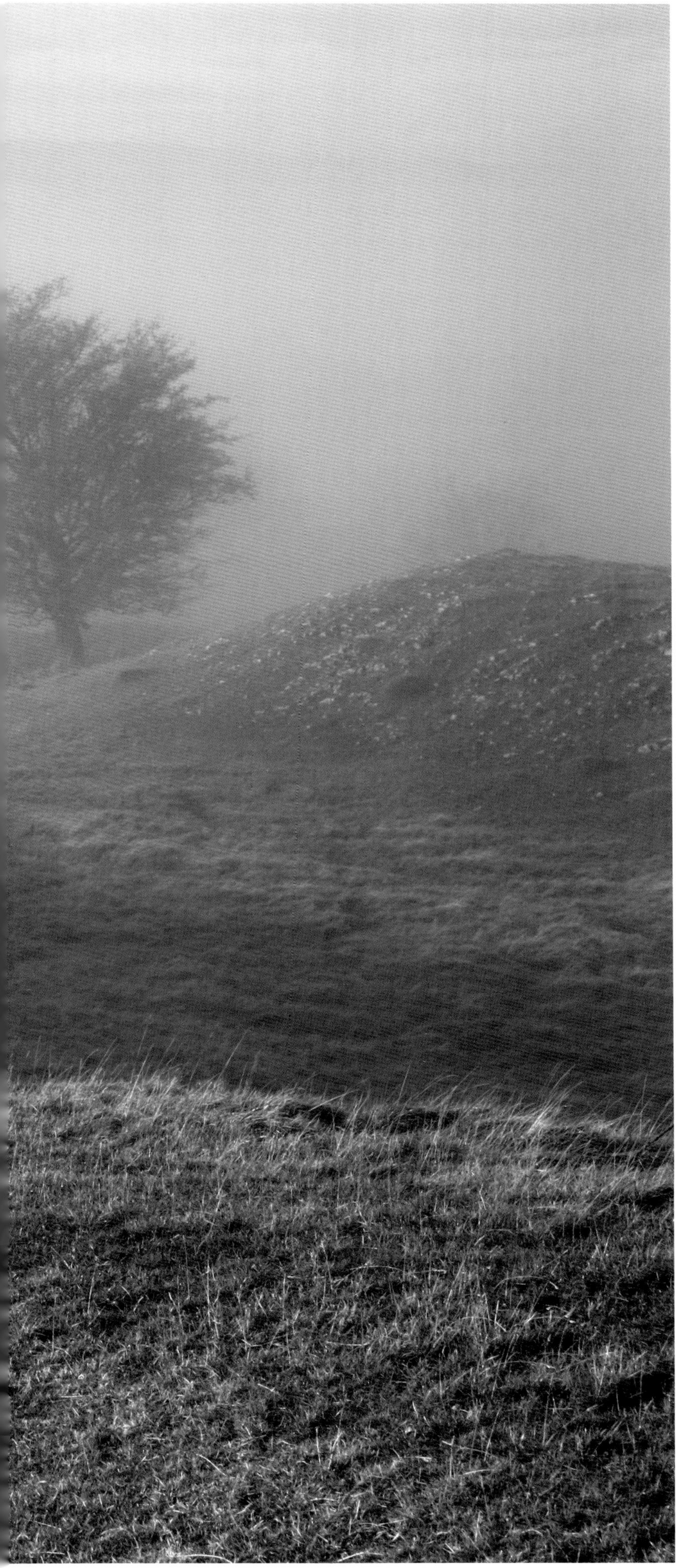

33 Carreg Cennen Castle, Carmarthenshire

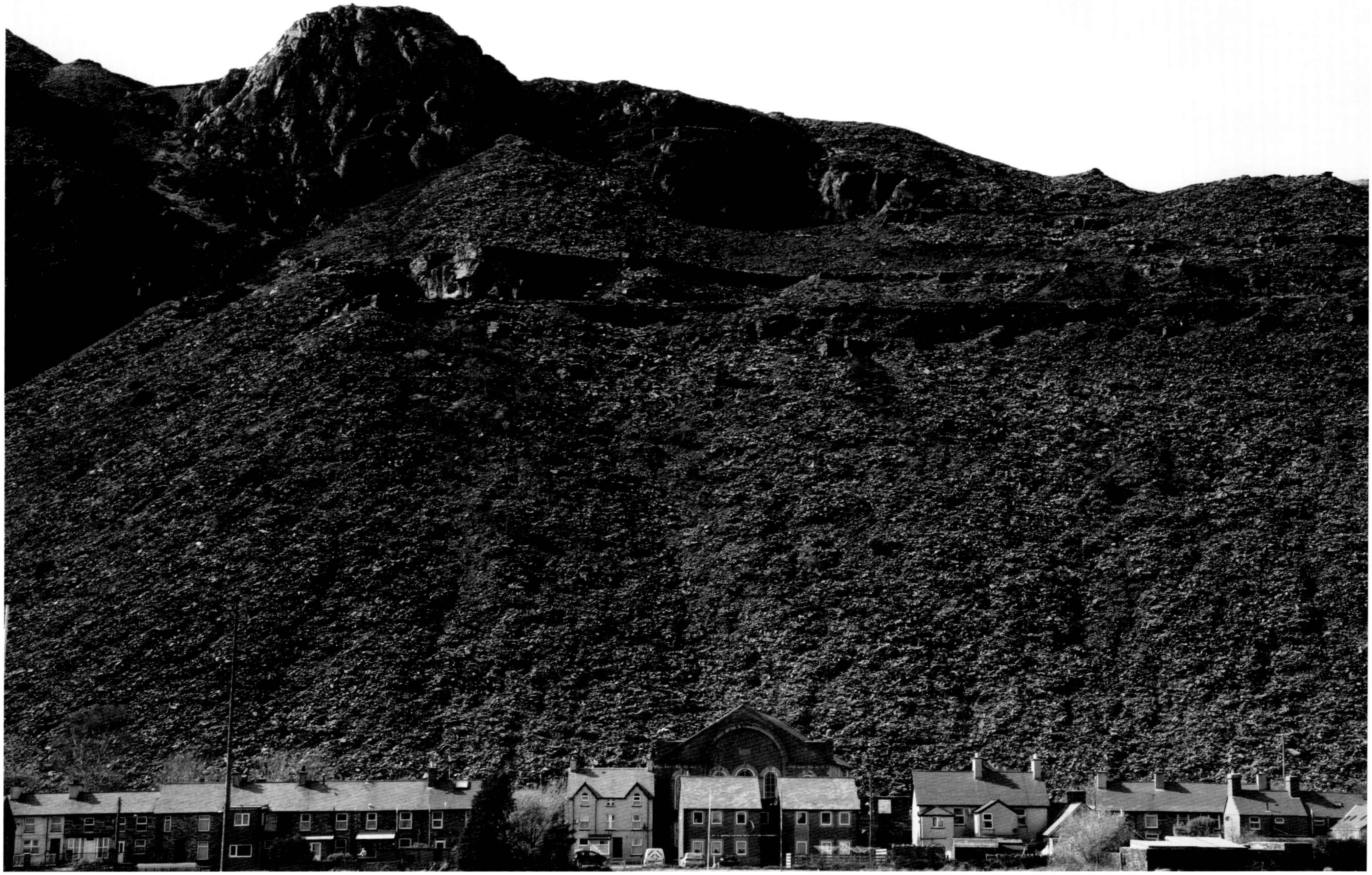

34 BLAENAU FFESTINIOG, GWYNEDD

Blaenau Ffestiniog was built on the back of the slate industry. In this area the slate tended to be mined rather than quarried, as it was with the Penrhyn operation at Bethesda. The industry has all but disappeared in recent years and these days the town exudes a faded majesty. Once great mines such as the Llechwedd slate caverns have re-invented themselves as tourist attractions, sustained by inquisitive visitors.

The railway line that once carried the slate from the town is now disused and overgrown, and rows of terraced houses sit beneath mountains of waste material, reminders of that bygone industry. In a few generations the town has gone from a thriving industrial centre to a sleepy relic of its past.

As I explored the back streets, I happened upon a sight which, although not unusual, has stayed with me. A man in his seventies, possibly eighties, was sweeping the pavement outside his terraced house, his civic pride still strong. This gentleman may have lived his whole life in Blaenau Ffestiniog. If so, he woulc have witnessed seismic changes in that time. (Map C2)

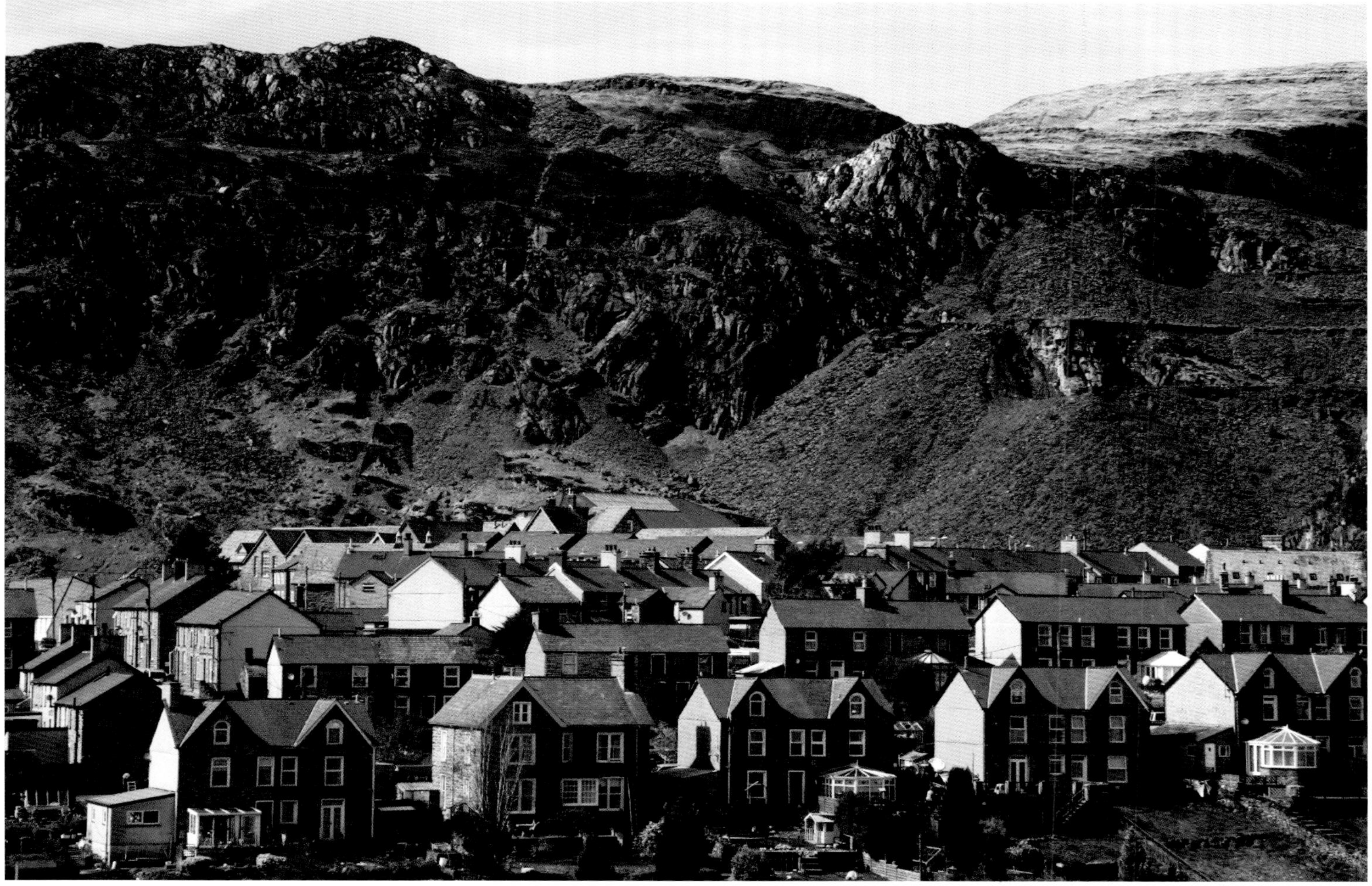

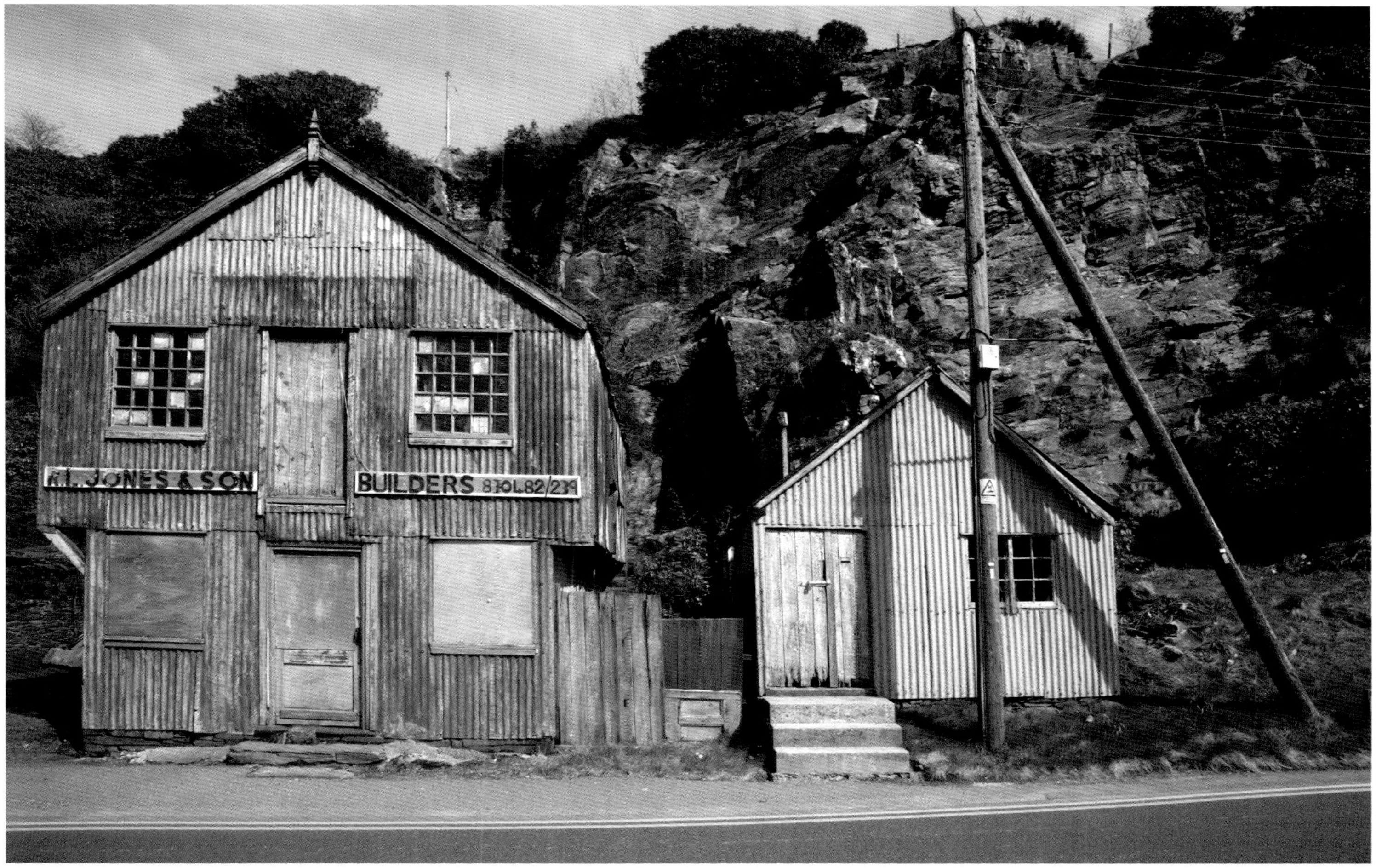
JONES & SON
BUILDERS

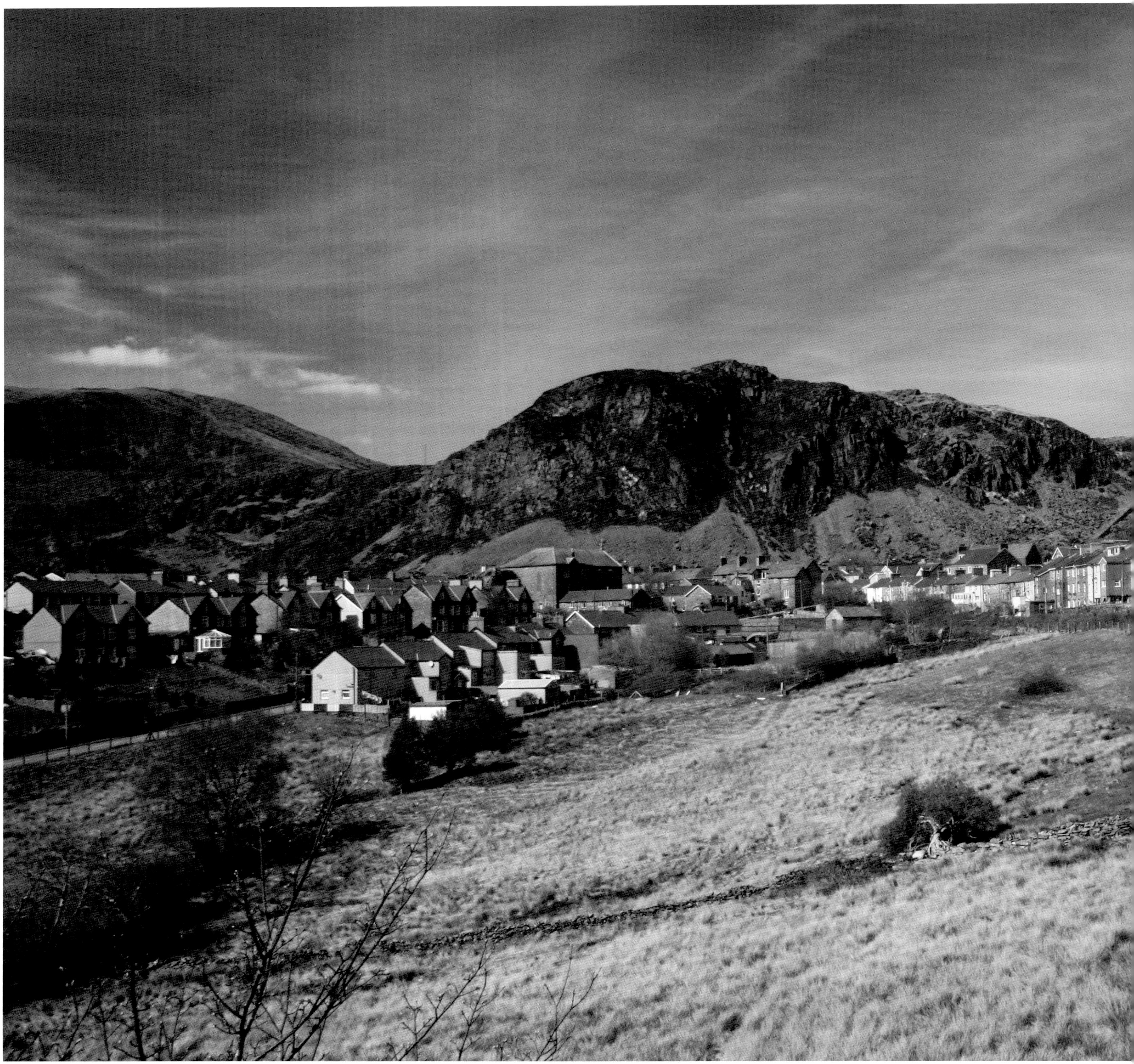

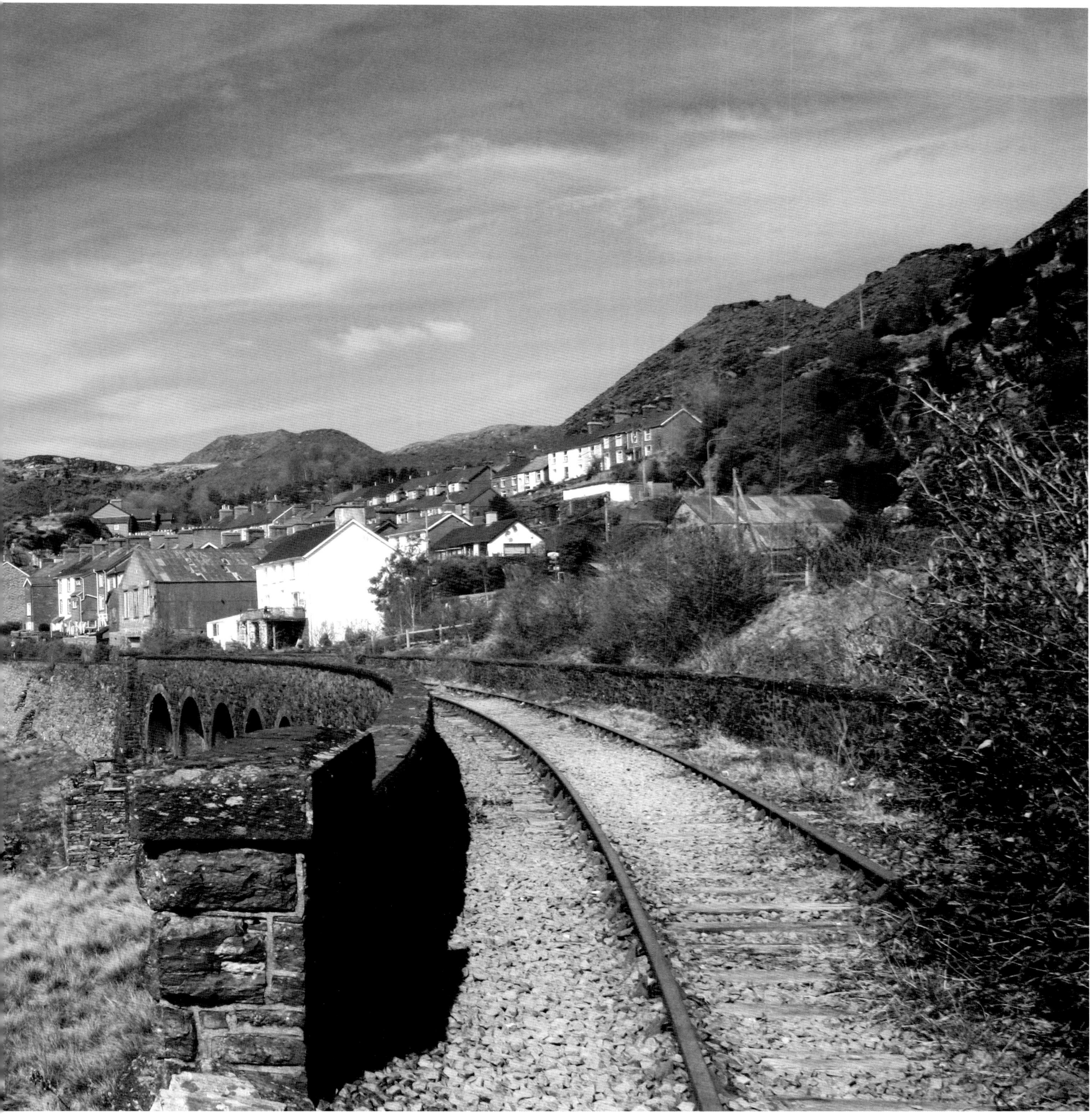

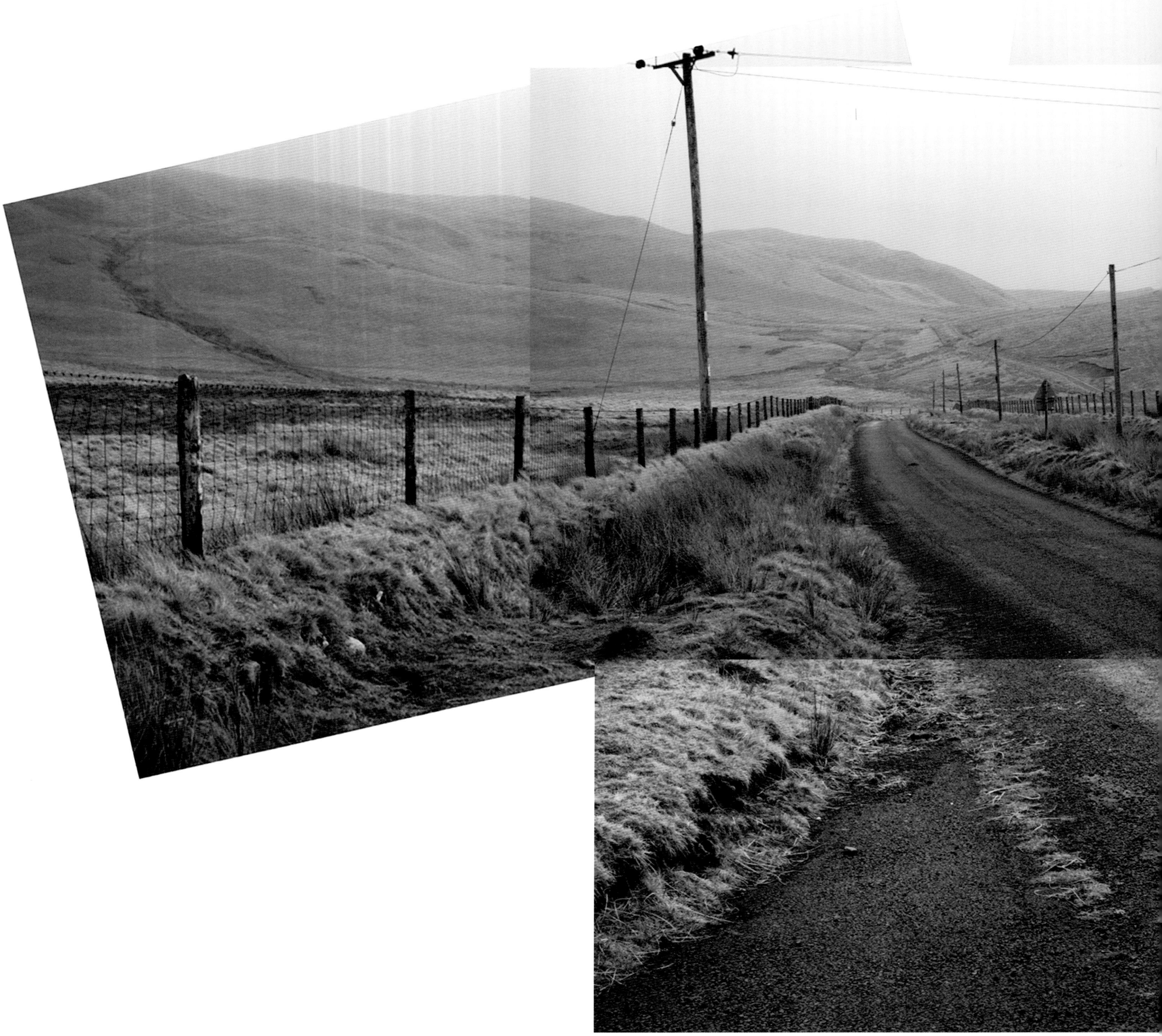

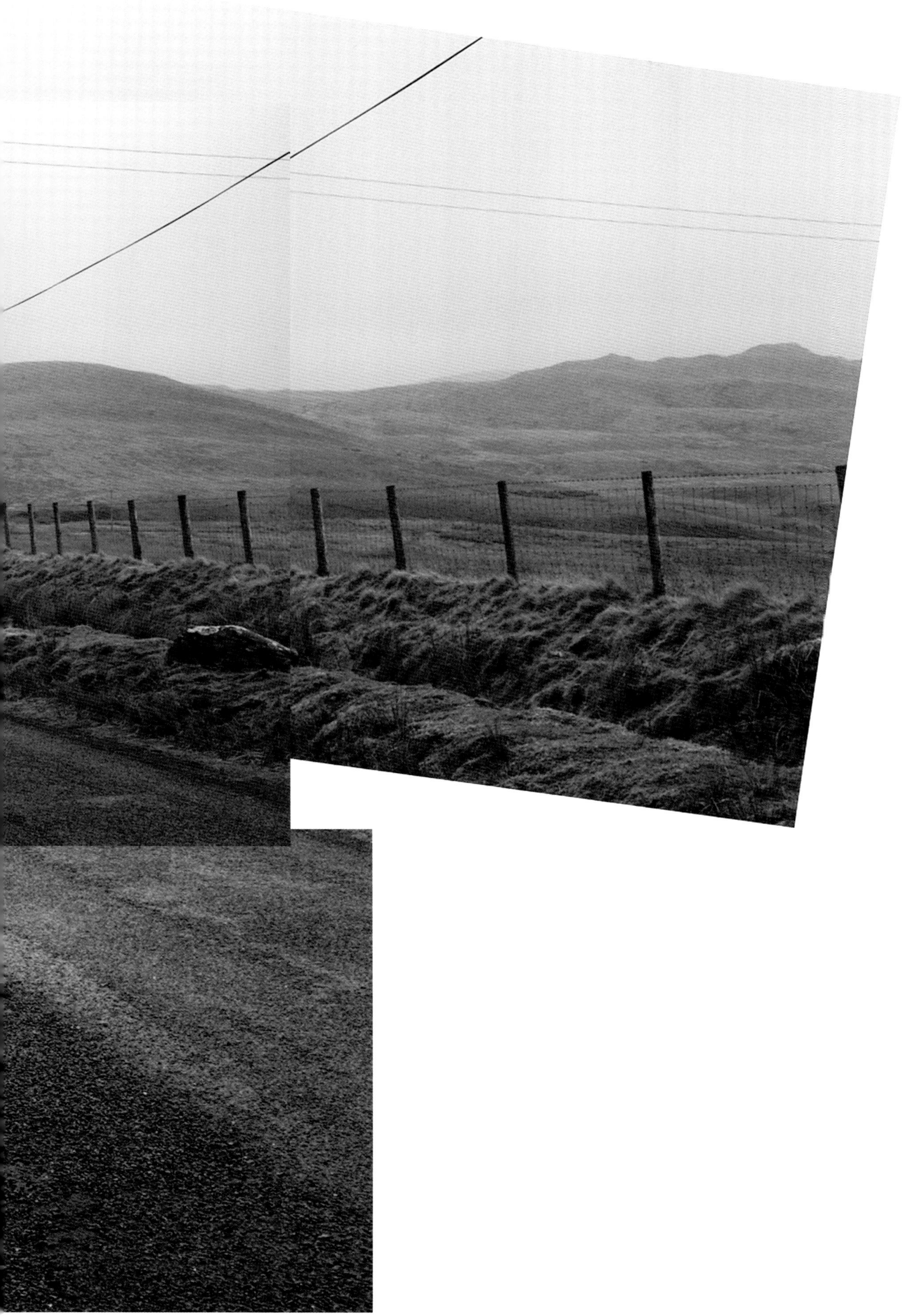

35 TEIFI POOLS, CEREDIGION

I followed the B4343 north from Tregaron and arrived at the village of Ffair Fach before turning right onto the narrow twisting road that took me into the heart of the Teifi Pools. Situated on the western edge of the Cambrian Mountains, the 'pools' comprise Llyn Teifi, the waters of which eventually meet the sea at Poppit Sands near Cardigan, Llyn Hir, Llyn Gorlan, and Llyn Egnant. As you edge ever further into this stark land, leaving behind the certainty of the cottages and farms around Ffair Fach, you become immersed in a treeless landscape of rolling grassy hills, the 'pools' dotted among the numerous peaks. I ventured off to take photographs, losing sight of the road in the process. The sense of disorientation was quite unnerving as there were no features in the landscape with which to fix my bearings. I knew I could not be far from the car but it was still a relief when I spotted it again. (Map C4)

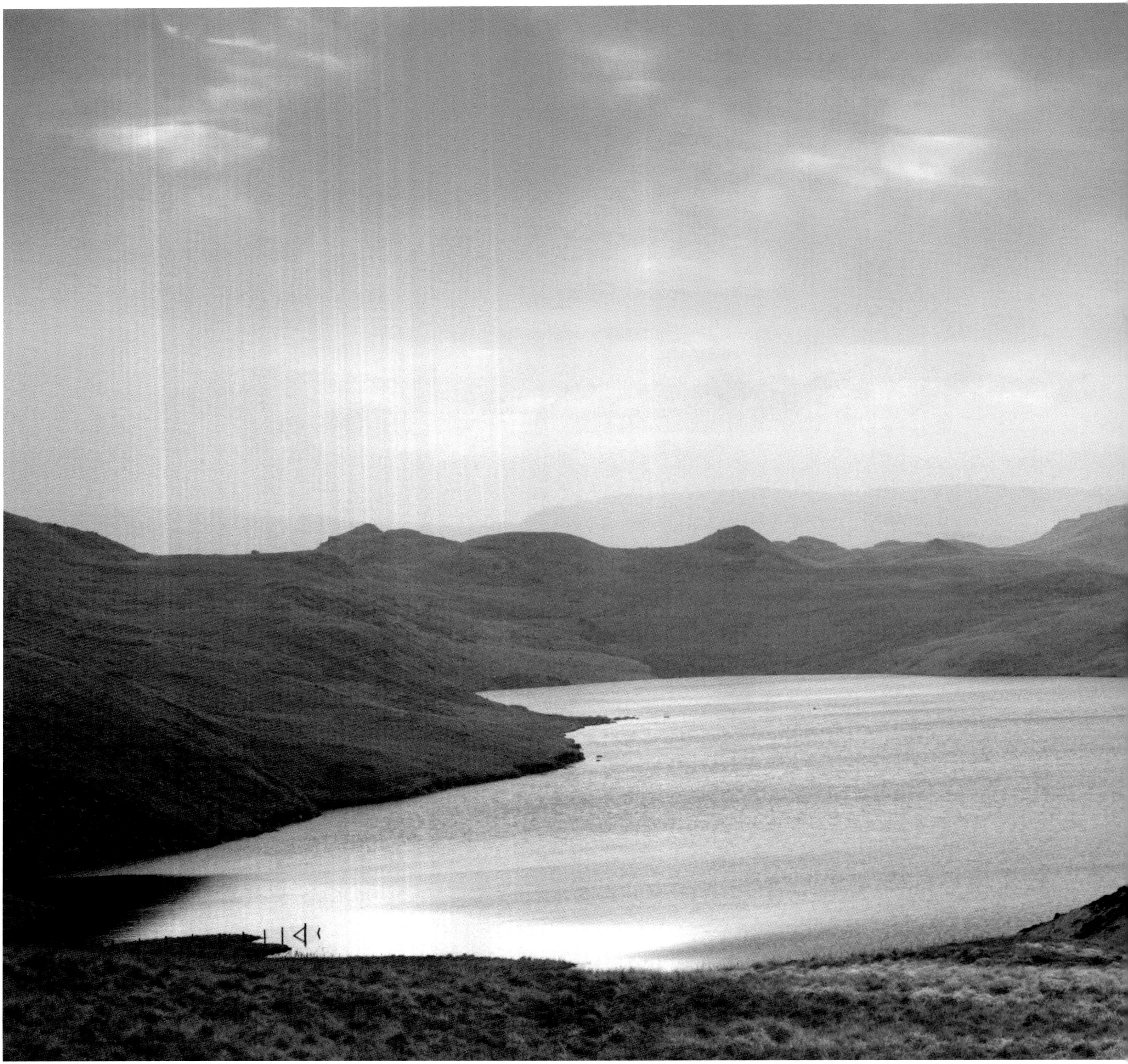

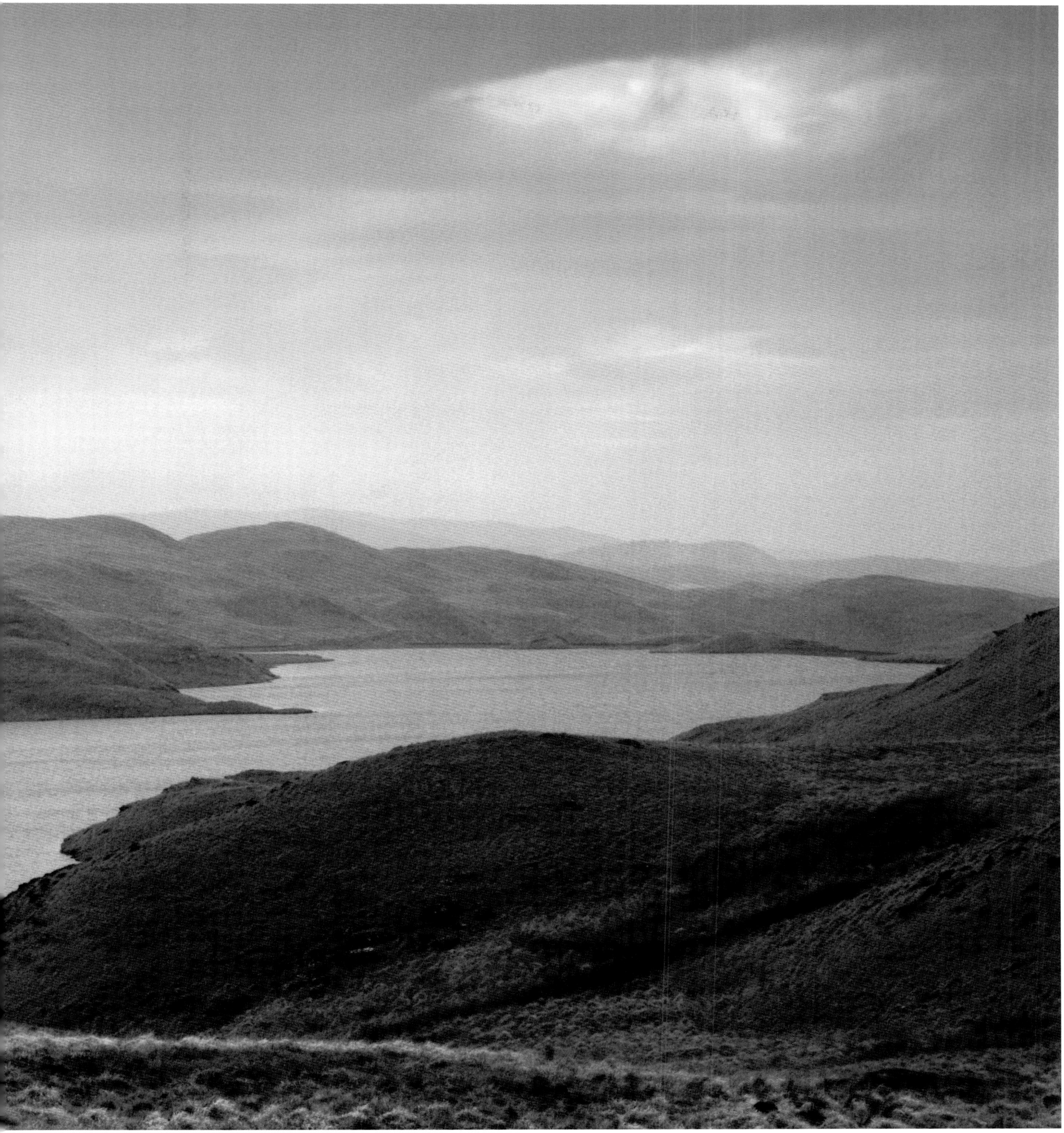

35 Teifi Pools, Ceredigion

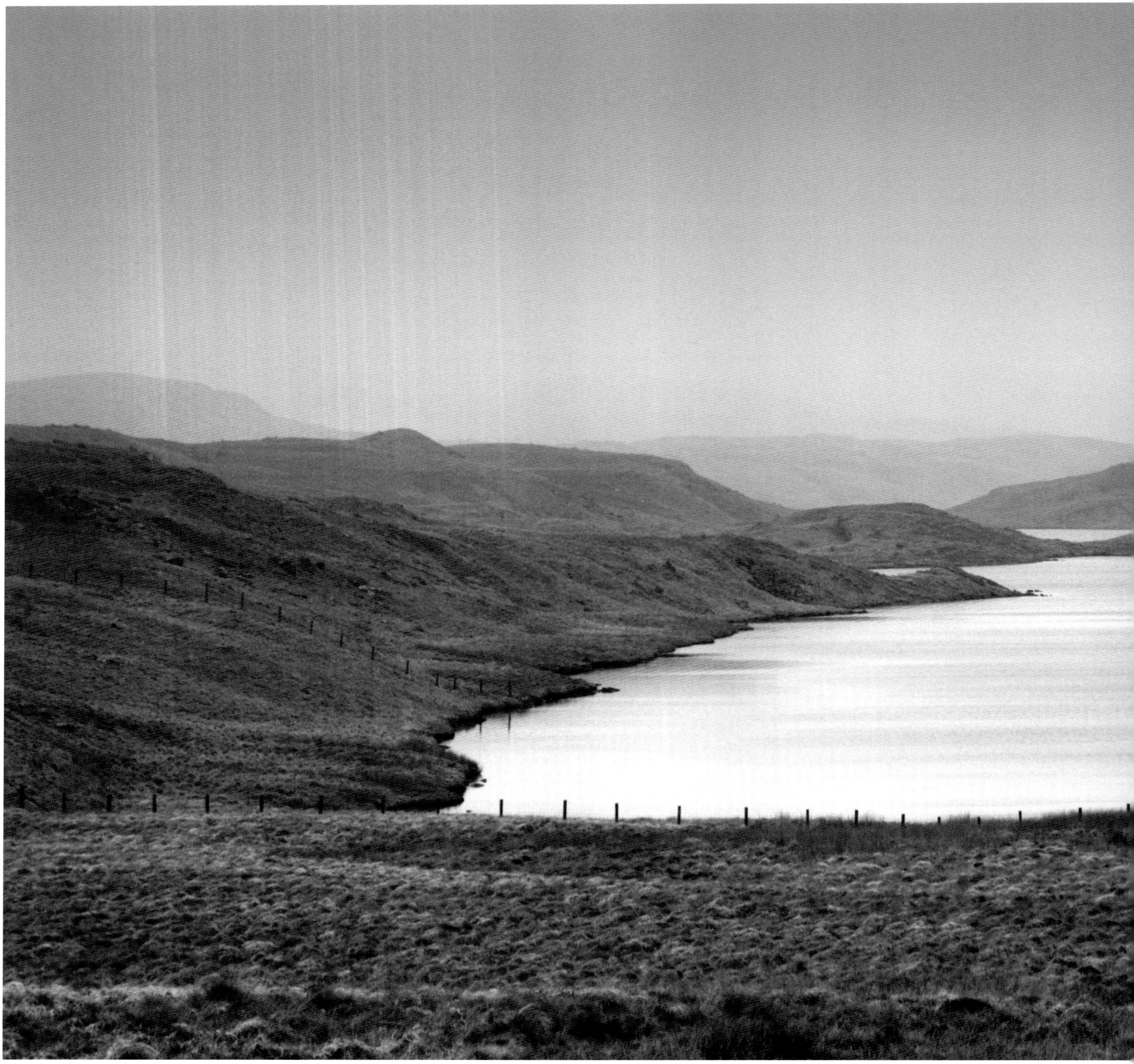

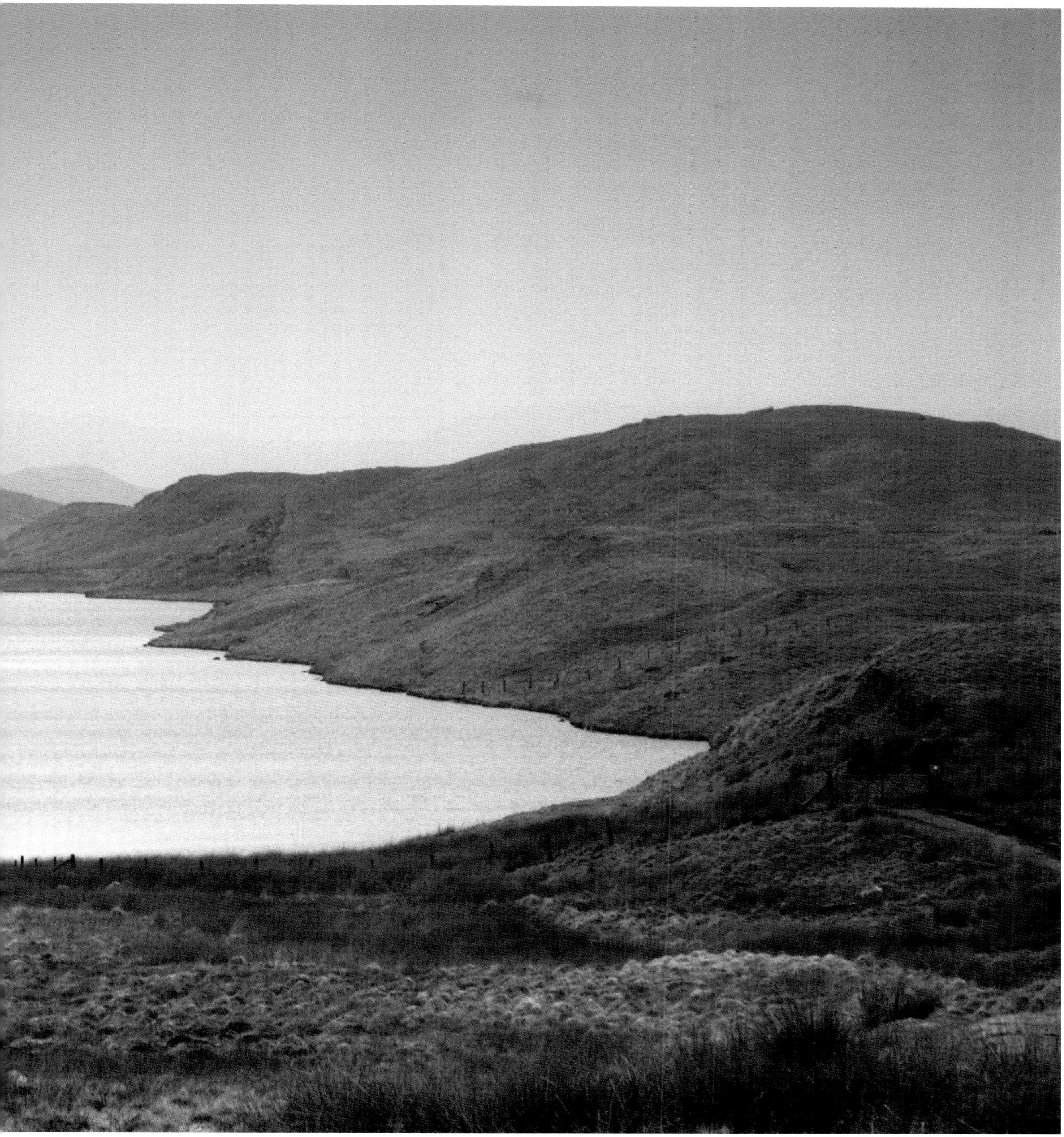

35 Teifi Pools, Ceredigion

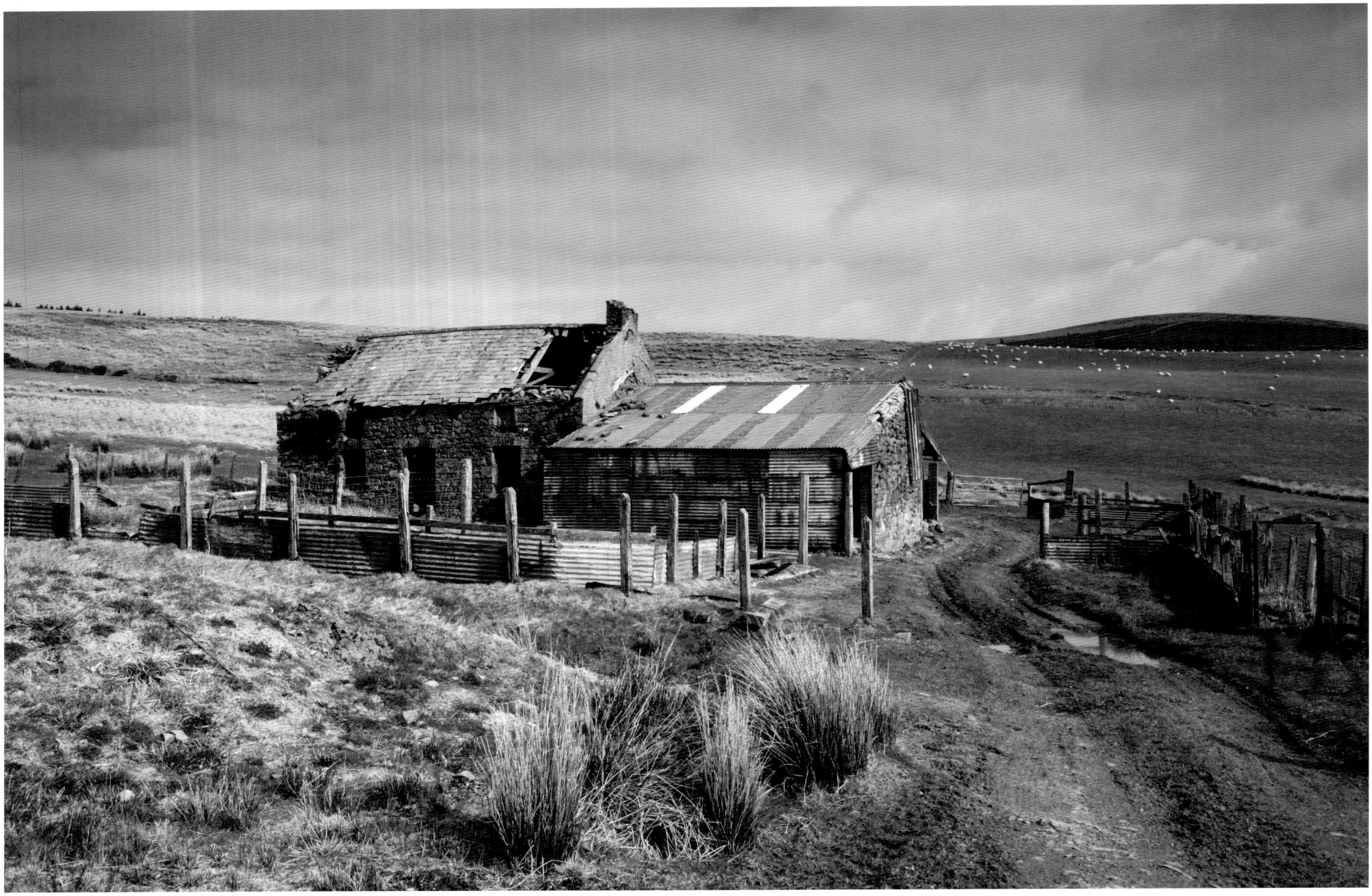

36 TRINANT, PRESELI HILLS, PEMBROKESHIRE

I have been visiting Trinant for the last five years, documenting its inexorable decline. It sits in a barren landscape devoid of shelter from the elements. The wind, rain and seasons are slowly dismantling this house slate by slate, stone by stone. Each time I visit, an ever-present wind rattles the corrugated iron and whistles eerily through the house. Yet up until just a few decades ago it was someone's home. The stream flowing by provided drinking water and the house gave protection from the elements that eventually began to destroy it.

A couple of years ago I had the good fortune to encounter a living link to its past. Anna and I went to register our son Harry's birth. After the formalities had been wrapped up the registrar unexpectedly enquired about Trinant. Her mum had been brought up there, and had fond memories of a childhood spent on that little isolated farm. A connection like that makes my visits all the more poignant, as I visualise a little girl running through the long grass or paddling in the stream. How many more seasons before the house simply gives up its futile struggle and collapses into the earth? (Map B5)

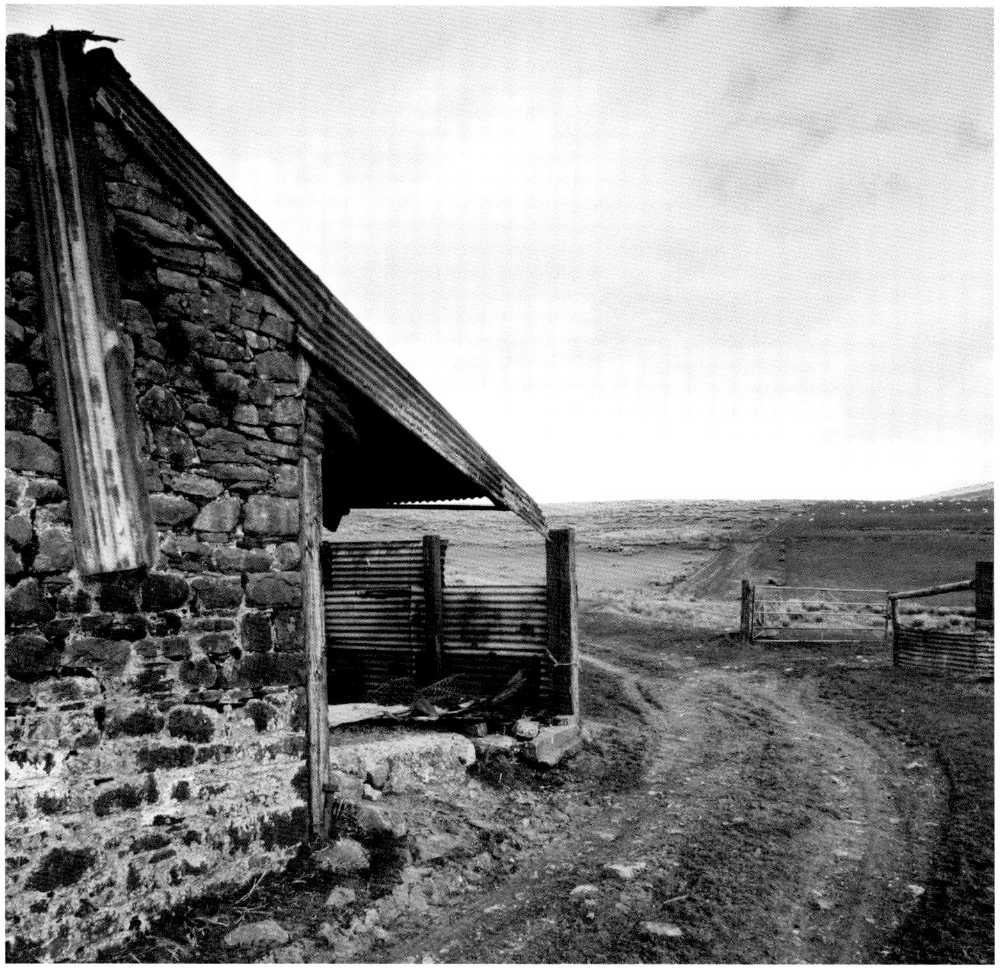

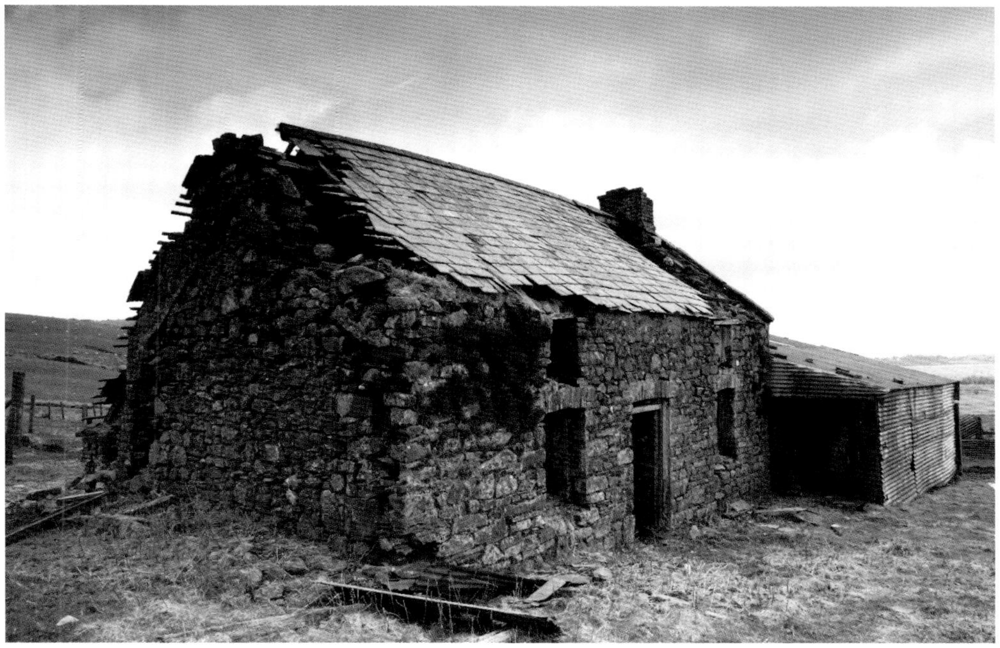

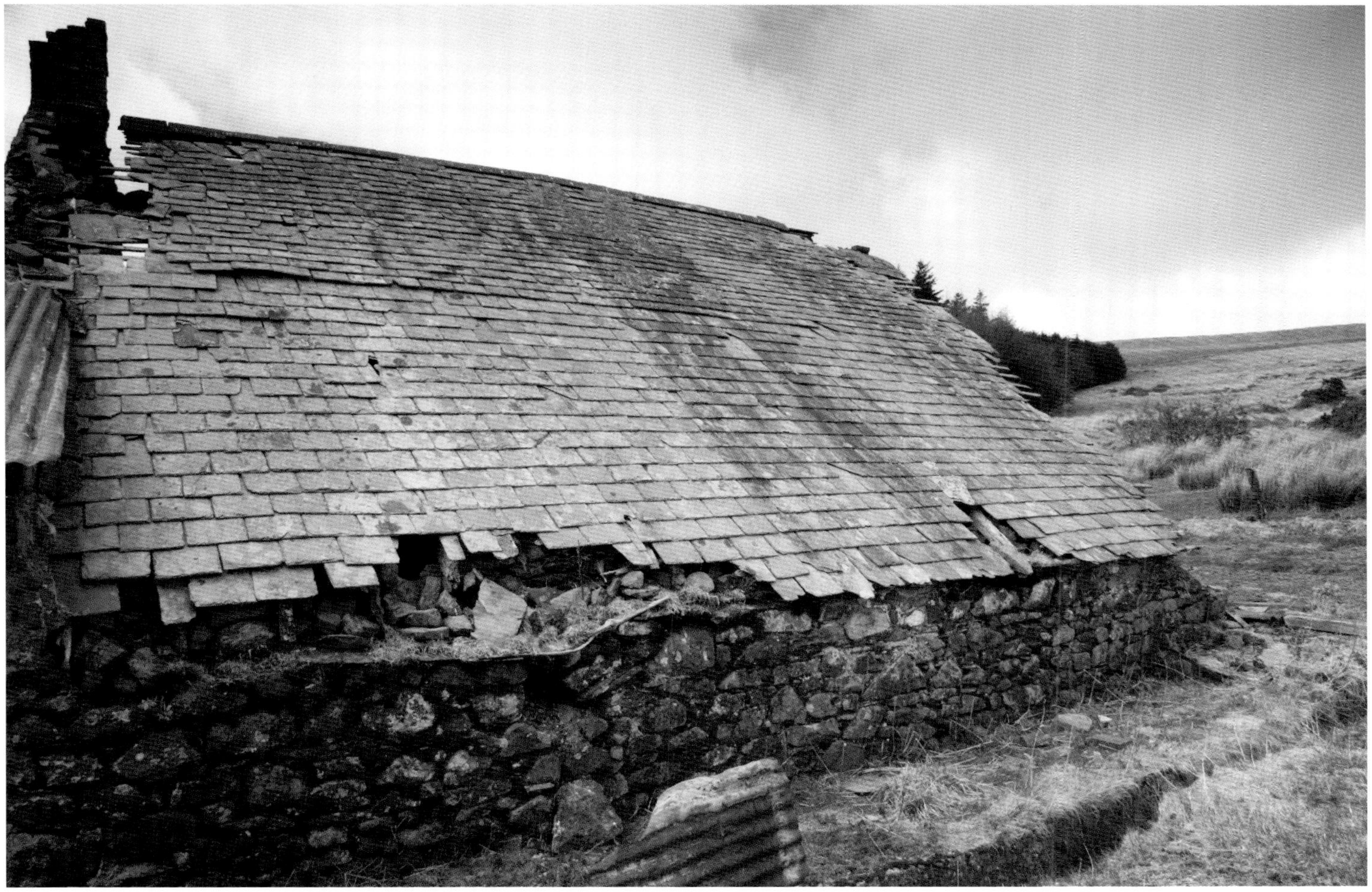

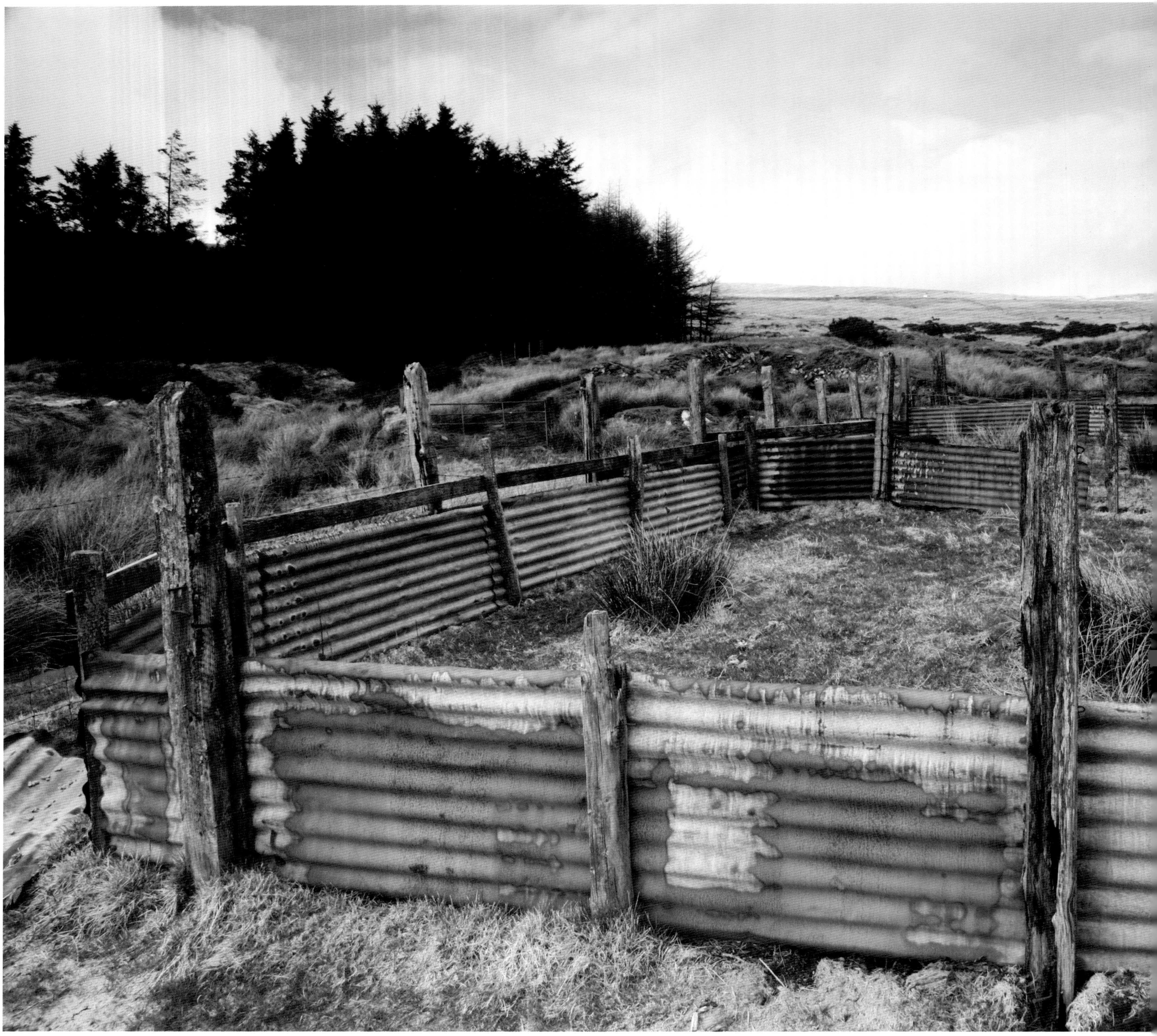

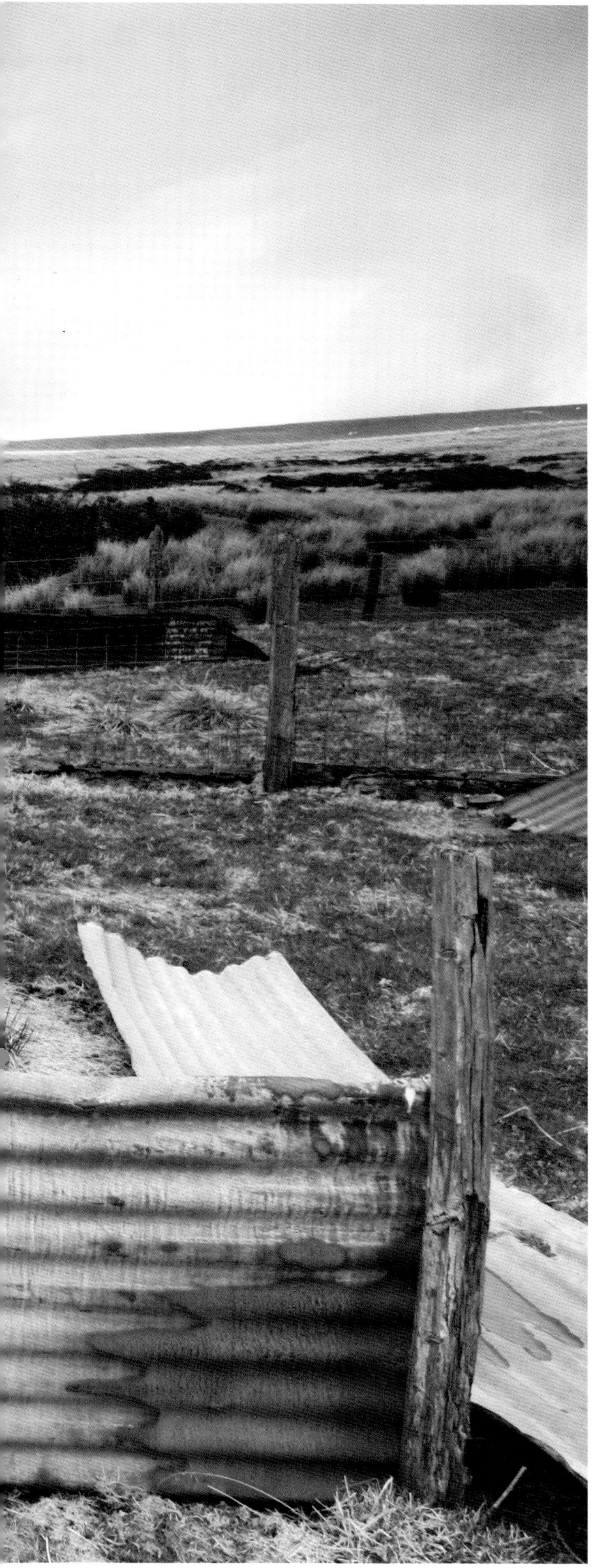

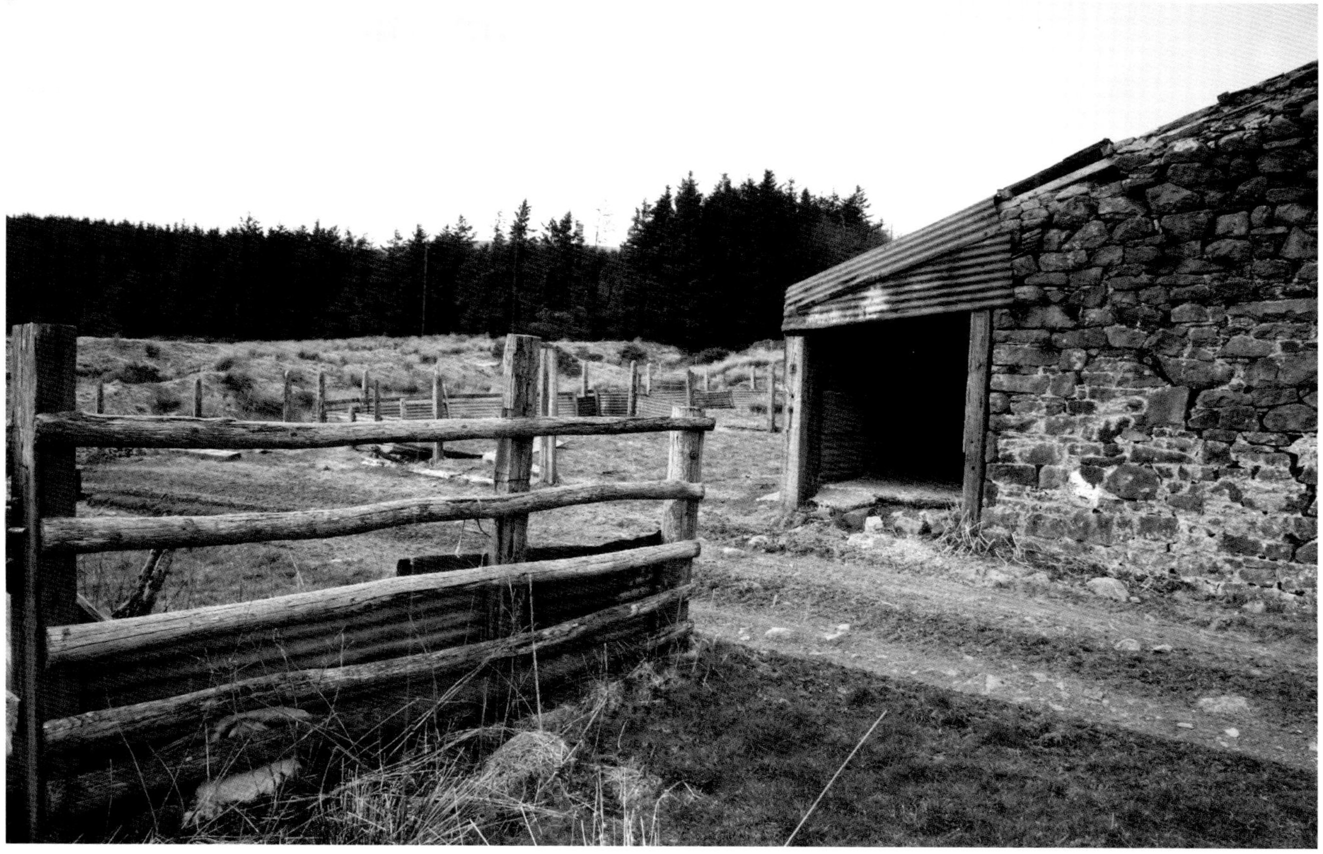

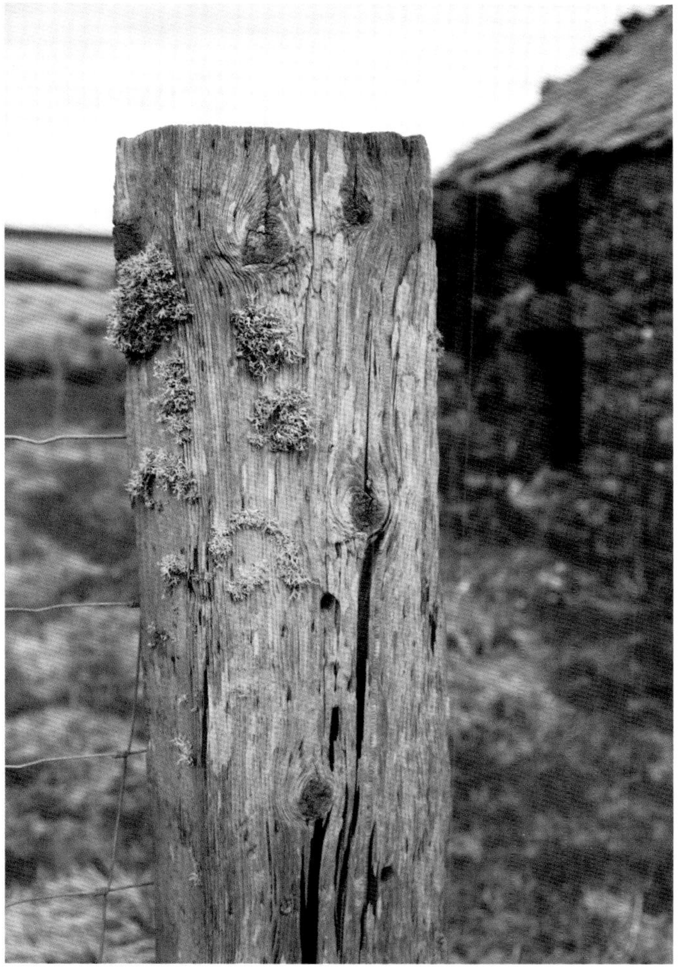

PHOTOGRAPHIC LOCATIONS

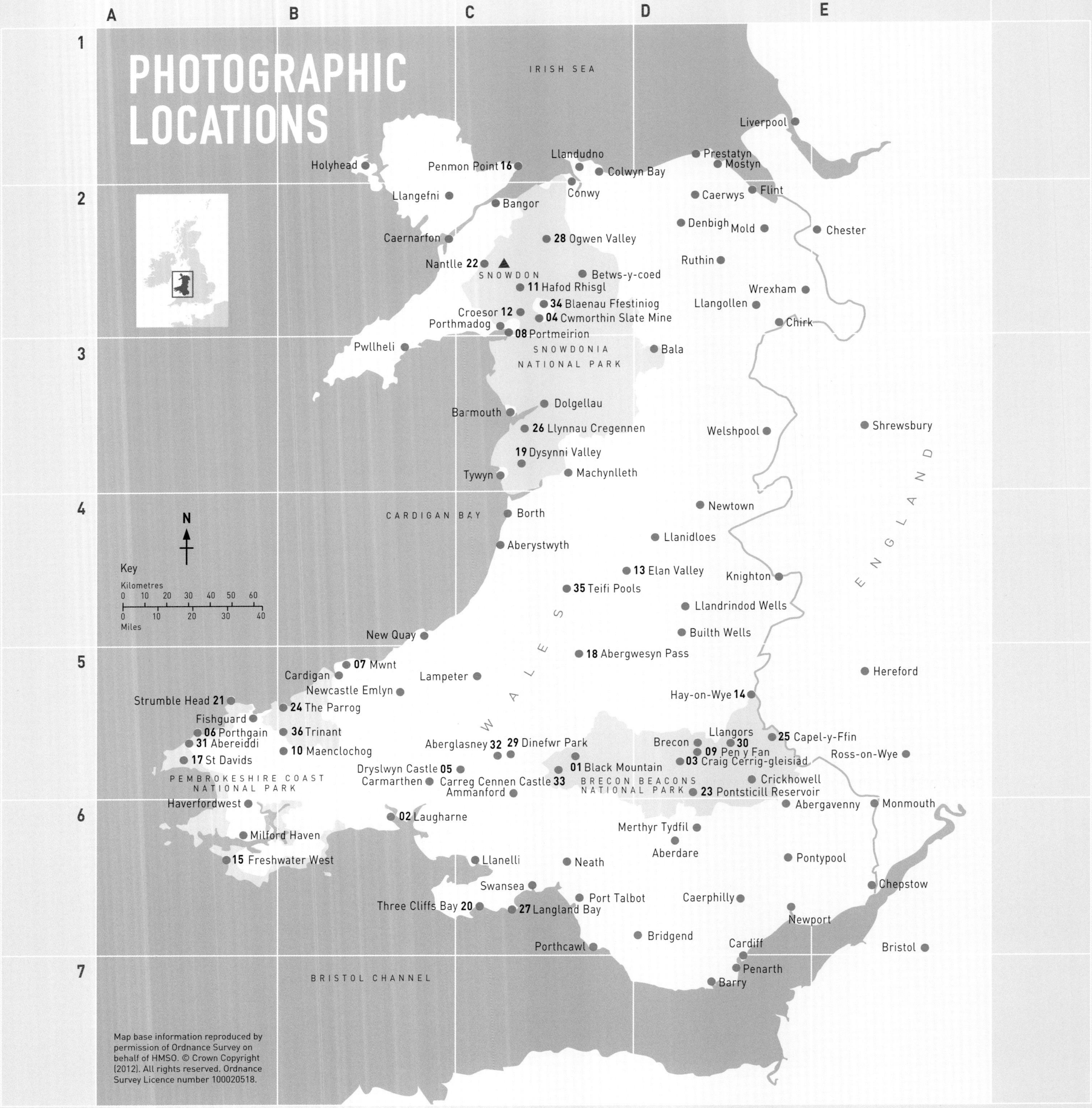

ACKNOWLEDGEMENTS

This book has come to fruition with the help, support and kindness of a host of individuals and organisations.

Foremost are my wife Anna, and young sons Charlie and Harry. Anna's unstinting help and encouragement have been invaluable, whether accompanying me on a trip (as chief bag carrier and, on wet days, official umbrella holder), offering constructive advice, or simply keeping me fed and watered. As for Charlie and Harry, they could offer nothing by way of practical help (they are only six and two years old after all) but they certainly kept my spirits up and enabled me to see the dim light at the end of what seemed like a pretty long tunnel on times.

I am indebted to Griff Rhys Jones for his scintillating and insightful foreword. His beautifully crafted words stir the emotions and perfectly encapsulate the essence of what I endeavour to portray in my work. Thank you, Griff.

I thank my publishers, Graffeg, for their continued belief in me and my photography. Their faith and backing has allowed me to produce a book of which I am immensely proud and I feel honoured to have worked once again with such a talented group of individuals.

To the Williams family of Hafod Rhisgl, Nant Gwynant, Snowdonia, many thanks for allowing me to photograph your handsome farm. Just a few miles away at the head of the Ogwen Valley, Gwyn Thomas of Blaen y Nant was equally hospitable. People such as Gwyn and the Williams family keep alive that old Welsh tradition of a warm and friendly welcome.

I would like to thank Portmeirion Village and in particular Robin Llywelyn for their kindness in allowing me to photograph that glorious venue.

The Dean of St Davids Cathedral kindly gave me permission to photograph the enchanting interior of the cathedral.

Aberglasney House and Gardens were equally as inviting, allowing me to enjoy yet another joyous day's photography.

Finally I would like to thank Wales herself for her disarming beauty and for presenting herself so confidently in my viewfinder.

PLATE INDEX 1–23

The plate index shows a selection of my favourite photographs – one from each location. The vast majority of my photographs are taken with the use of a tripod, an electronic cable-release and the mirror-up facility on my camera. I also use graduated neutral density filters and occasionally a polarising filter.

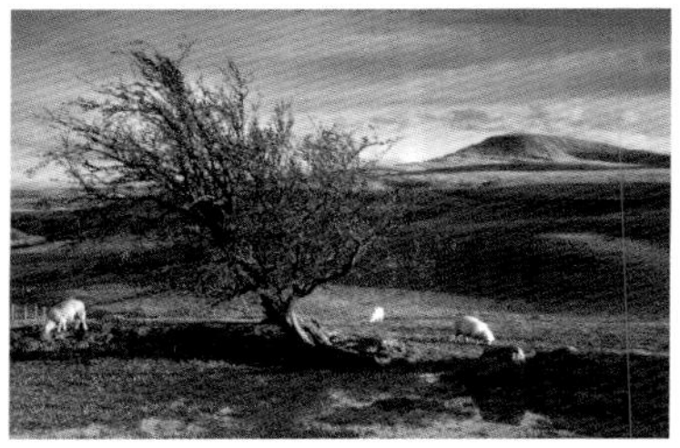

01 Black Mountain
Shutter Speed: 1/80
Aperture: 14.0
Focal Length: 58.0 mm
ISO Speed: 3200

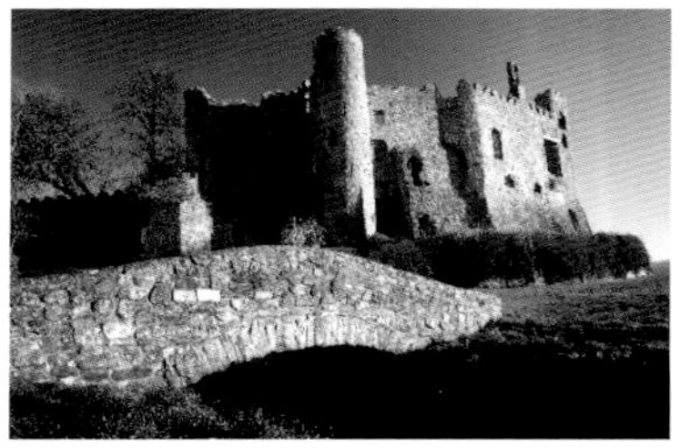

02 Laugharne
Shutter Speed: 1/8
Aperture: 16.0
Focal Length: 28.0 mm
ISO Speed:100

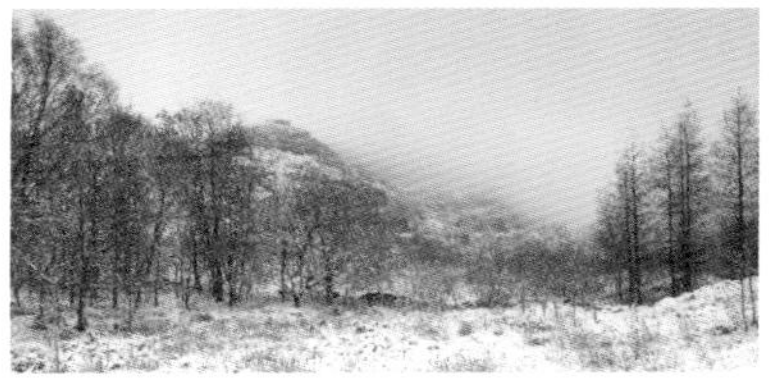

03 Craig-Cerrig gleisiad
Shutter Speed: 0.5
Aperture: 16.0
Focal Length: 50.0 mm
ISO Speed: 100

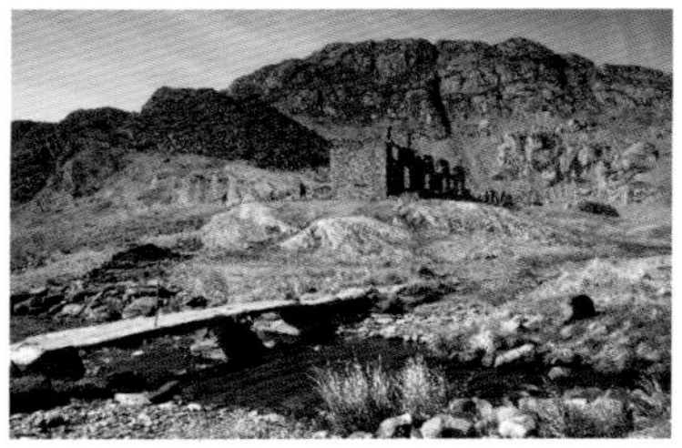

04 Cwmorthin Slate Mine
Shutter Speed: 1/20
Aperture: 18.0
Focal Length: 28.0 mm
ISO Speed: 100

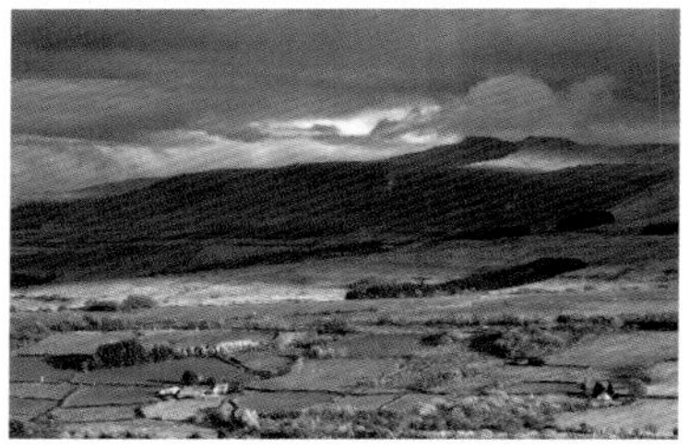

09 Towards Pen y Fan
Shutter Speed: 1/15
Aperture: 14.0
Focal Length: 160.0 mm
ISO Speed: 100

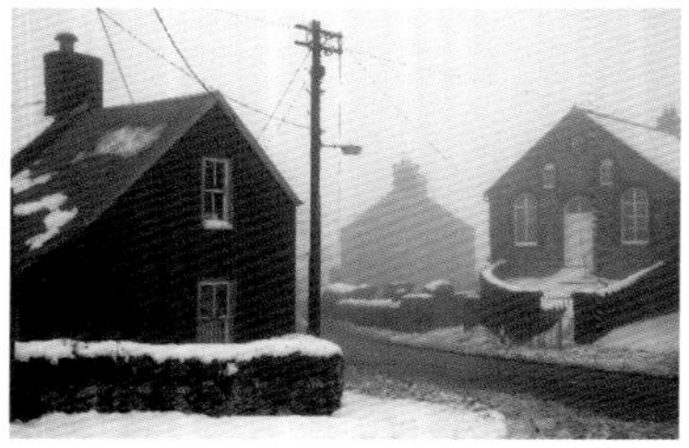

10 A Pembrokeshire Winter
Shutter Speed: 1/80
Aperture: 14.0
Focal Length: 50.0 mm
ISO Speed: 500

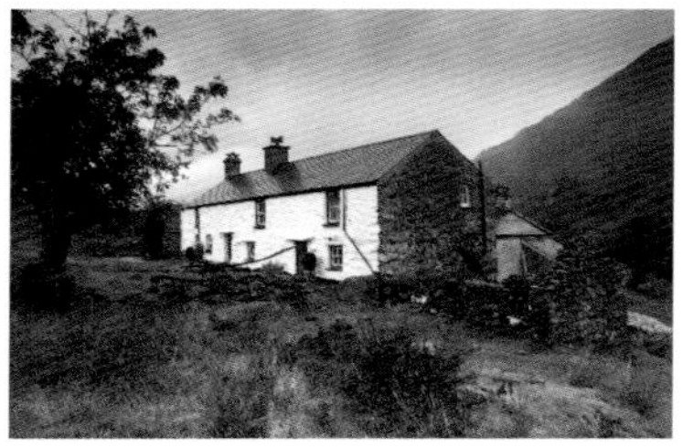

11 Hafod Rhisgl
Shutter Speed: 1/100
Aperture: 16.0
Focal Length: 24.0 mm
ISO Speed: 3200

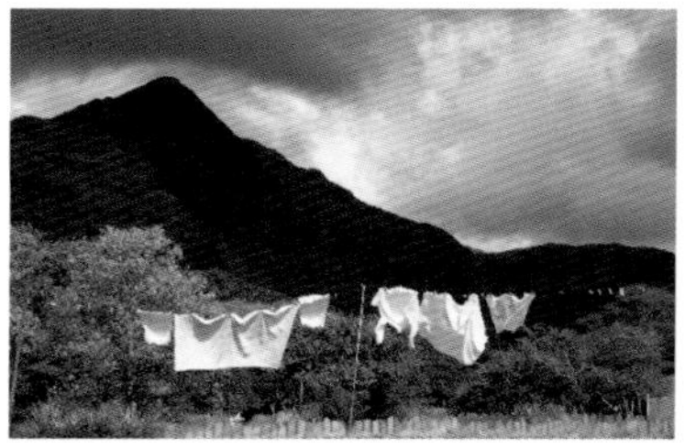

12 Mynydd Cnicht
Shutter Speed: 1/320
Aperture: 16.0
Focal Length: 70.0 mm
ISO Speed: 1000

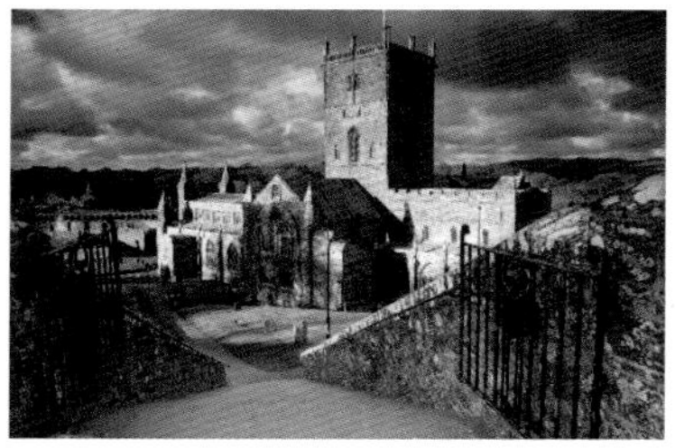

17 St Davids
Shutter Speed: 1/15
Aperture: 18.0
Focal Length: 28.0 mm
ISO Speed: 200

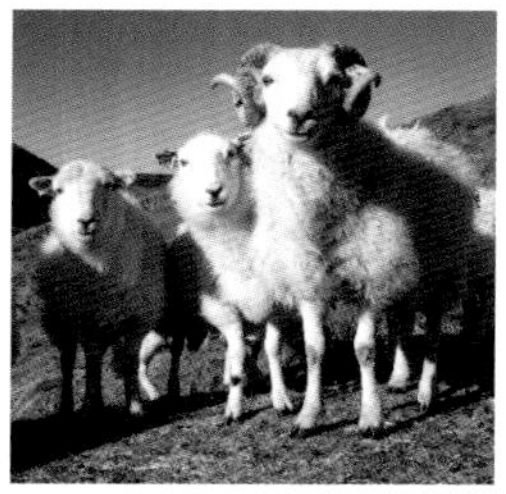

18 Abergwesyn
Shutter Speed: 1/800
Aperture: 14.0
Focal Length: 35.0 mm
ISO Speed: 1600

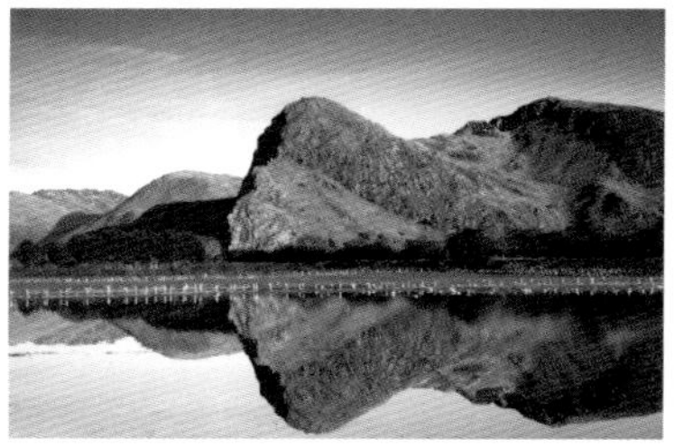

19 Dysynni Valley
Shutter Speed: 1/80
Aperture: 14.0
Focal Length: 70.0 mm
ISO Speed: 800

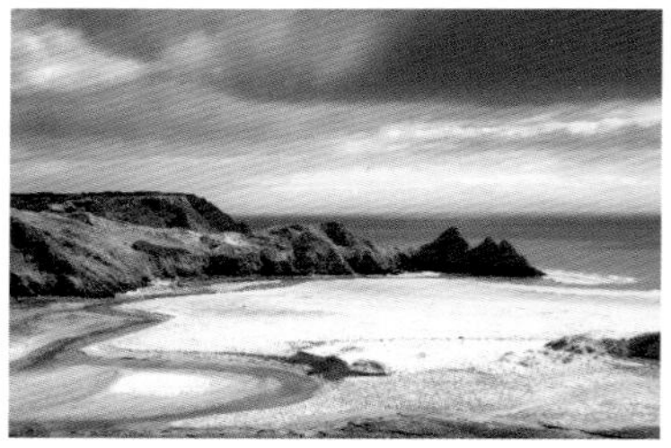

20 Three Cliffs
Shutter Speed: 1/13
Aperture: 16.0
Focal Length: 65.0 mm
ISO Speed: 100

ORDER PRINTS ONLINE

Limited edition prints of selected images by David Wilson
are available to order at **www.graffeg.com**

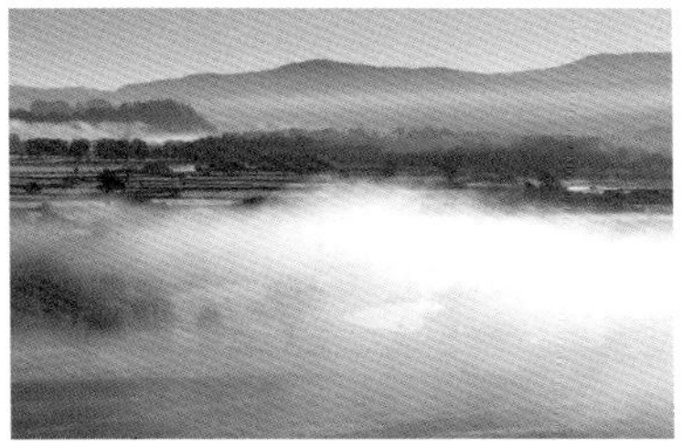

05 Towy Valley
Shutter Speed: 1/50
Aperture: 13.0
Focal Length: 120.0 mm
ISO Speed: 100

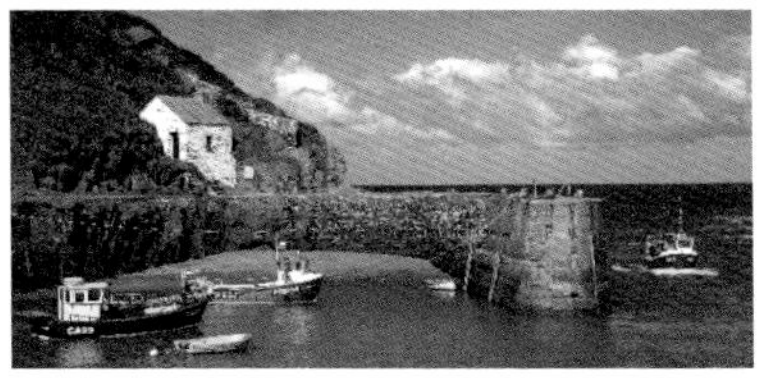

06 Porthgain
Shutter Speed: 1/640
Aperture: 16.0
Focal Length: 75.0 mm
ISO Speed: 800

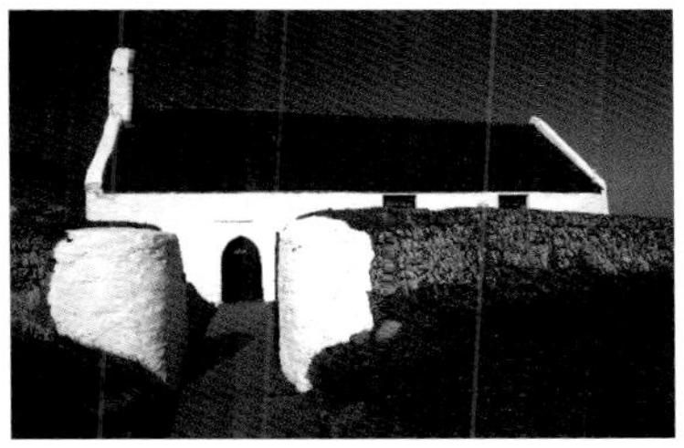

07 Mwnt
Shutter Speed: 1/200
Aperture: 16.0
Focal Length: 24.0 mm
ISO Speed: 400

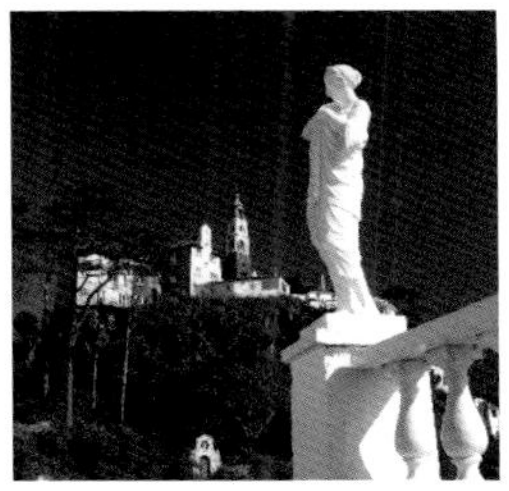

08 Portmeirion
Shutter Speed: 1/15
Aperture: 16.0
Focal Length: 24.0 mm
ISO Speed: 100

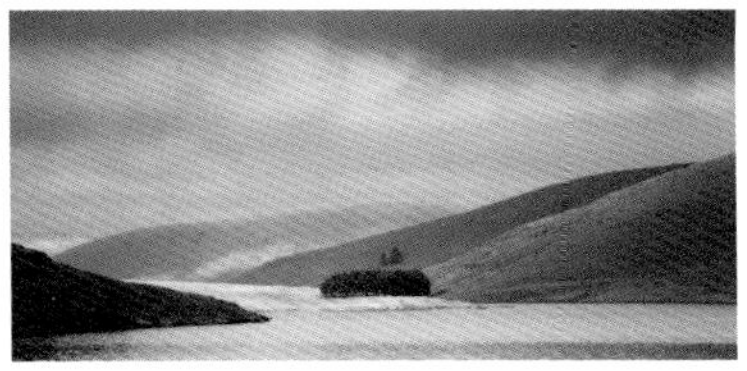

13 Elan Valley
Shutter Speed: 1/13
Aperture: 16.0
Focal Length: 105.0 mm
ISO Speed: 100

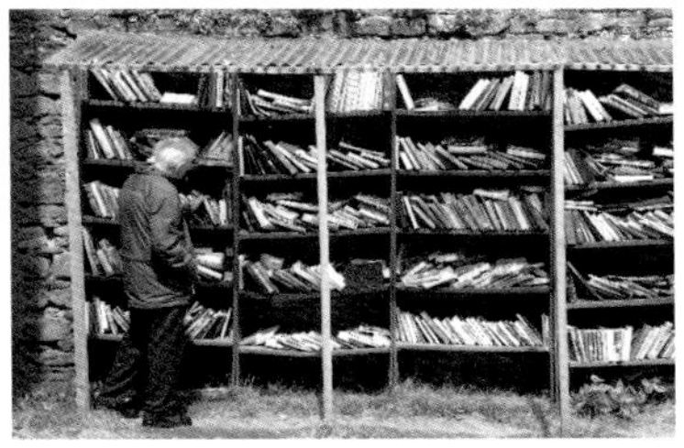

14 Hay-on-Wye
Shutter Speed: 1/160
Aperture: 11.0
Focal Length: 90.0 mm
ISO Speed: 400

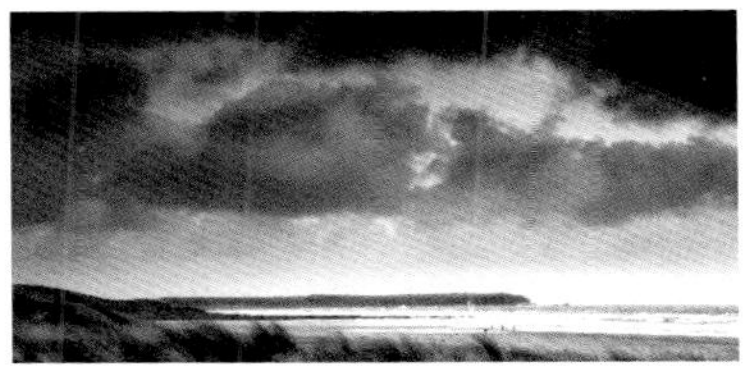

15 Freshwater West
Shutter Speed: 1/250
Aperture:16.0
Focal Length: 28.0 mm
ISO Speed: 3200

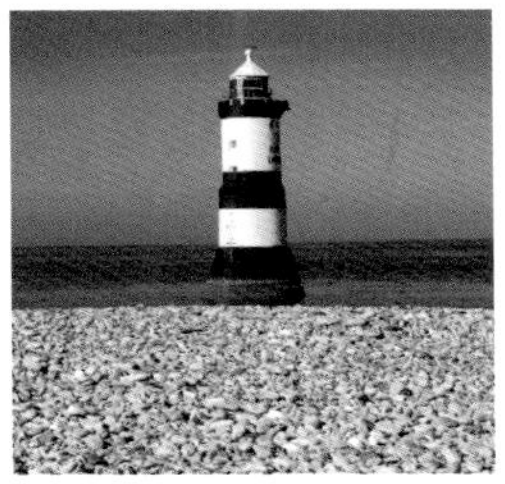

16 Penmon Point
Shutter Speed: 1/10
Aperture:18.0
Focal Length: 105.0 mm
ISO Speed: 50

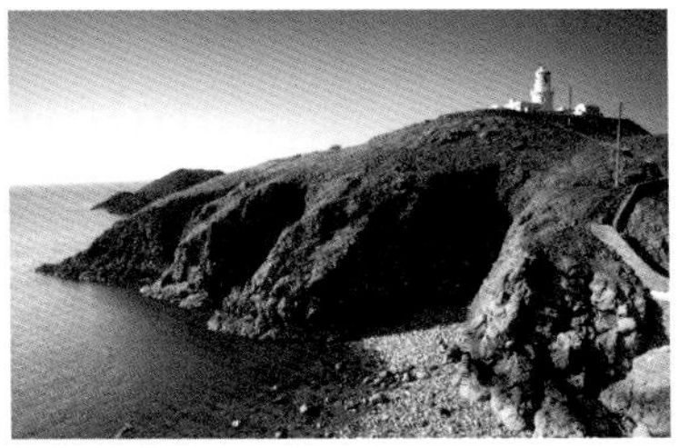

21 Strumble Head
Shutter Speed: 1/60
Aperture: 14.0
Focal Length: 24mm
ISO Speed: 800

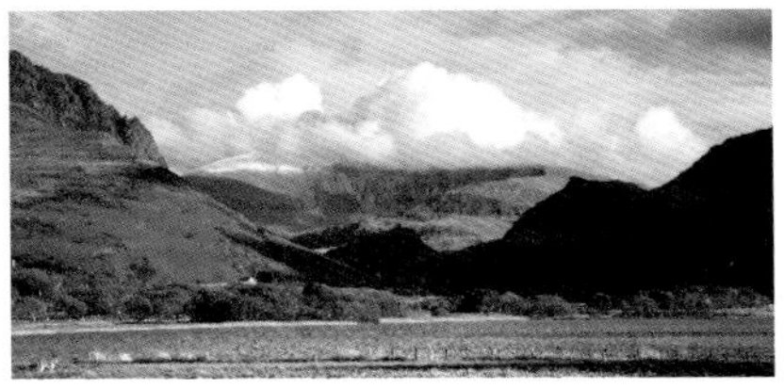

22 Nantlle
Shutter Speed: 1/13
Aperture: 16.0
Focal Length: 80.0 mm
ISO Speed: 100

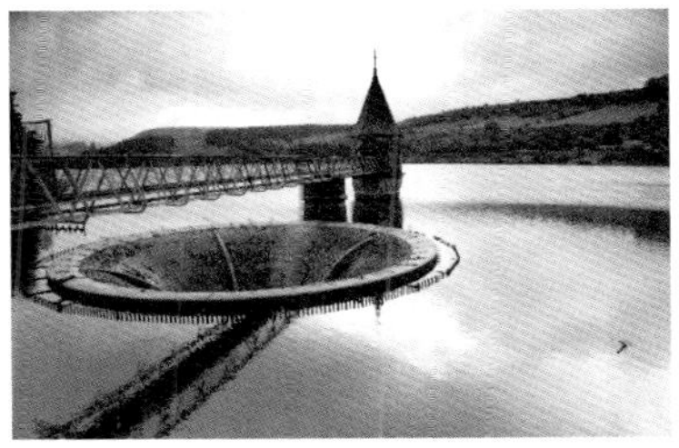

23 Pontsticill Reservoir
Shutter Speed: 1/125
Aperture: 13.0
Focal Length: 24mm
ISO Speed: 3200

24–36 >

PLATE INDEX 24—36

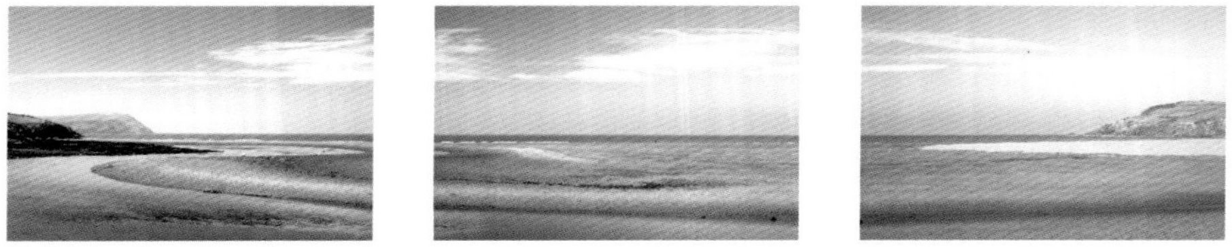

24 The Parrog
Shutter Speed:1/80
Aperture: 14.0
Focal Length: 70.0 mm
ISO Speed: 640

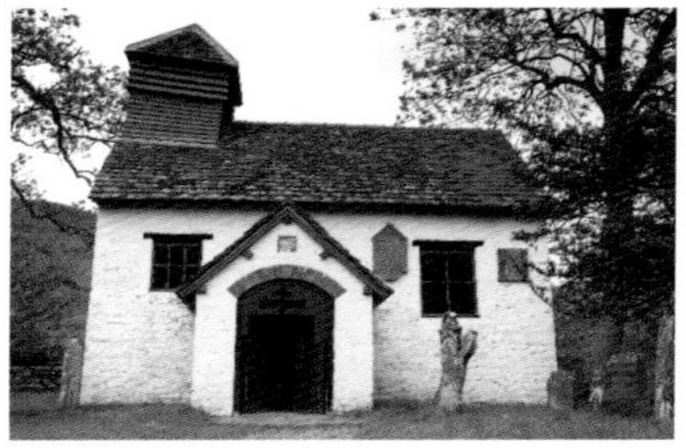

25 St Mary's Church
Shutter Speed: 1/50
Aperture: 16.0
Focal Length: 40.0 mm
ISO Speed: 400

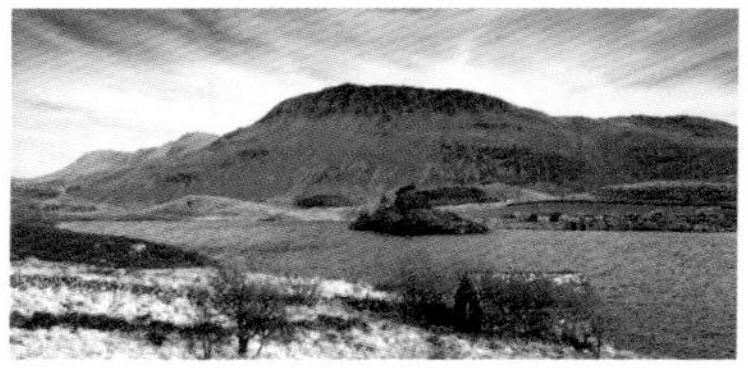

26 Llynnau Cregennen
Shutter Speed: 1/15
Aperture:16.0
Focal Length: 32.0 mm
ISO Speed: 100

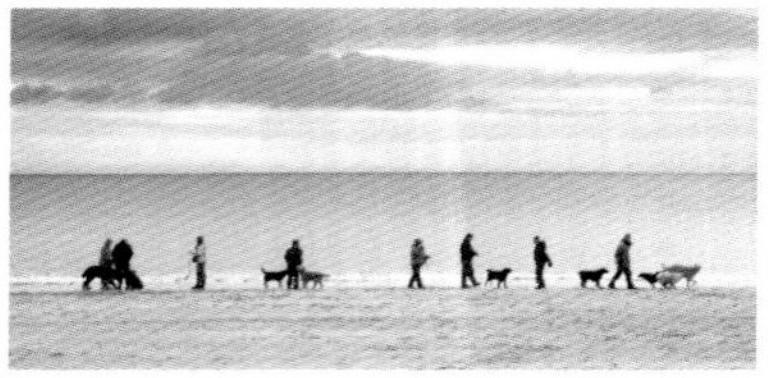

27 Langland Bay
Shutter Speed: 1/200
Aperture: 16.0
Focal Length: 105.0 mm
ISO Speed: 1250

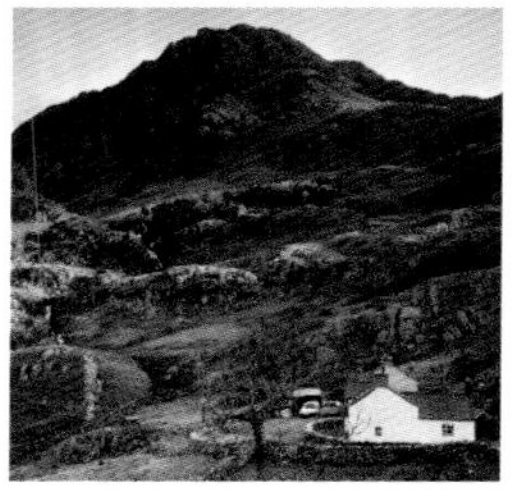

28 Blaen y Nant
Shutter Speed: 1/5
Aperture: 16.0
Focal Length: 50.0 mm
ISO Speed: 100

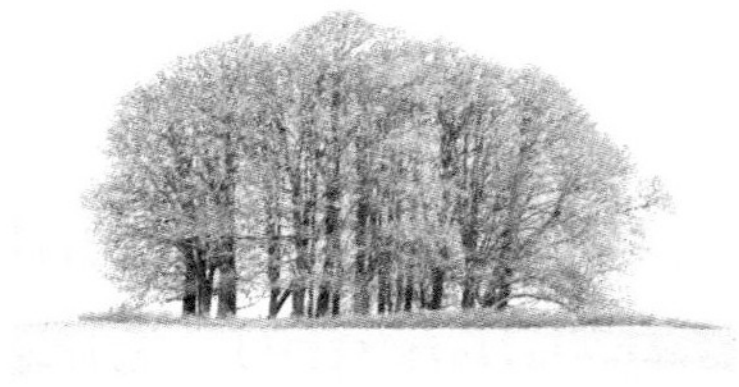

29 Dinefwr Park
Shutter Speed: 1/13
Aperture: 14.0
Focal Length: 90.0 mm
ISO Speed: 100

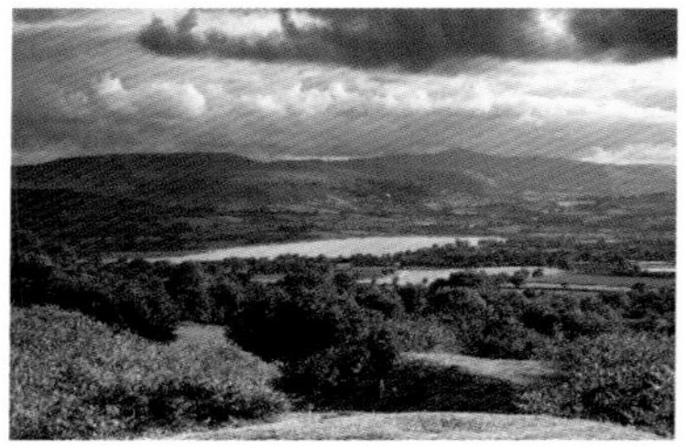

30 Pen y Fan & Llangors
Shutter Speed: 1/25
Aperture: 16.0
Focal Length: 58.0 mm
ISO Speed: 400

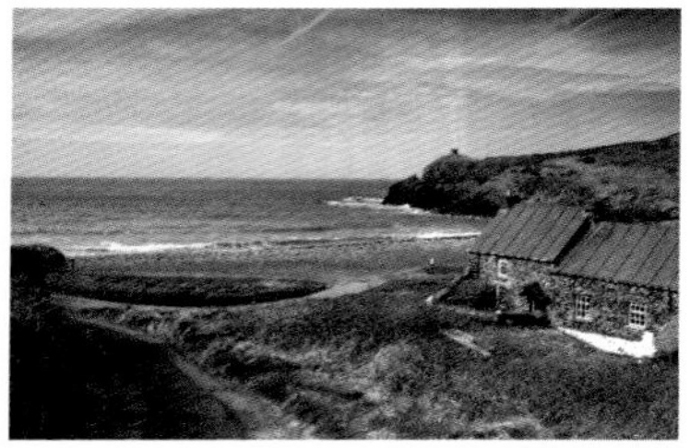

31 Abereiddi
Shutter Speed: 1/100
Aperture: 16.0
Focal Length: 35.0 mm
ISO Speed: 640

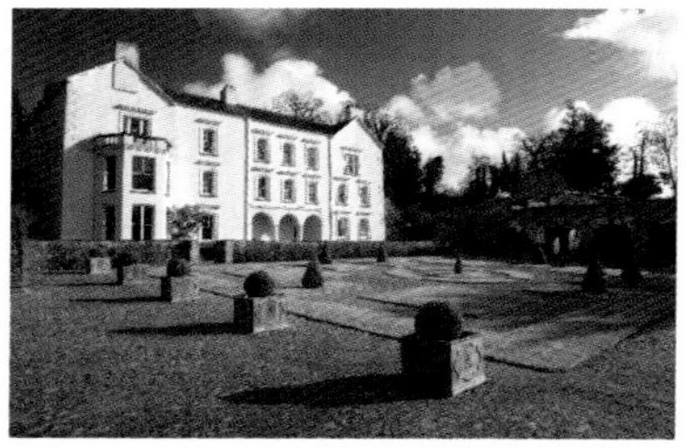

32 Aberglasney
Shutter Speed:1/320
Aperture: 14.0
Focal Length: 24.0 mm
ISO Speed: 1000

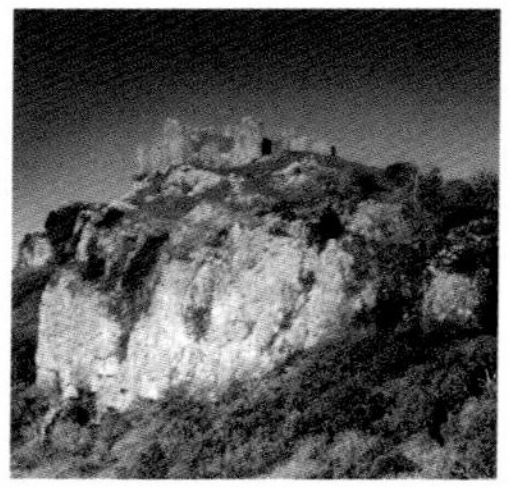

33 Carreg Cennen
Shutter Speed: 1/640
Aperture: 14.0
Focal Length: 105.0 mm
ISO Speed: 3200

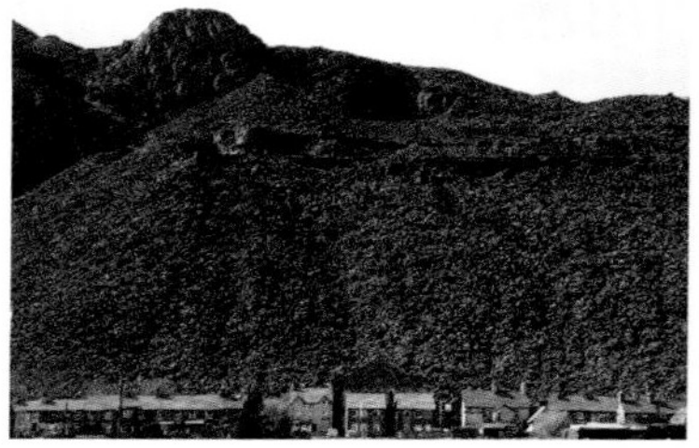

34 Blaenau Ffestiniog
Shutter Speed: 1/100
Aperture: 12.0
Focal Length: 70.0 mm
ISO Speed: 800

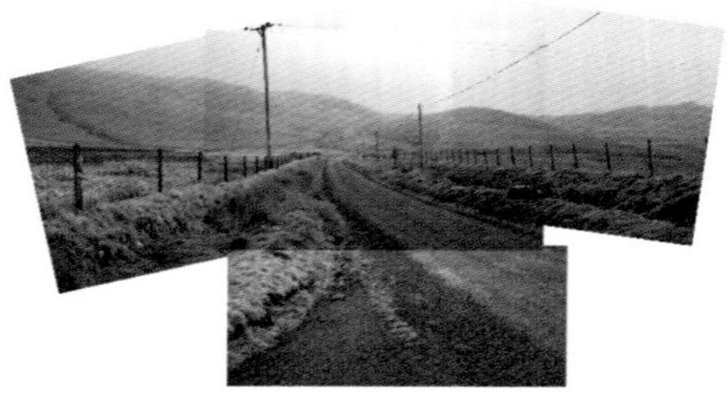

35 Teifi Pools
Shutter Speed: 1/160
Aperture:16.0
Focal Length: 70.0 mm
ISO Speed: 1600

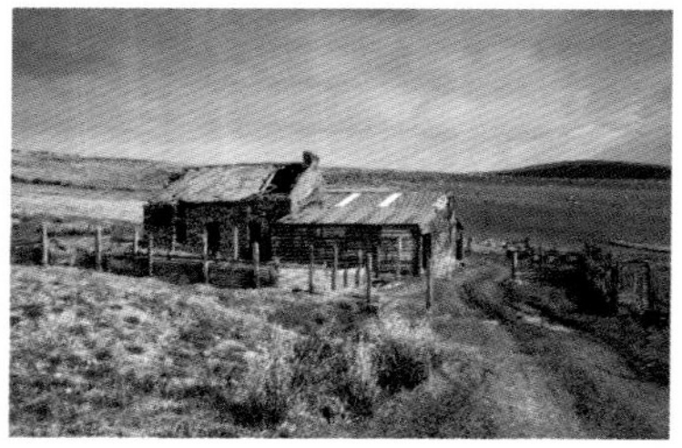

36 Trinant
Shutter Speed: 1/50
Aperture:18.0
Focal Length: 35.0 mm
ISO Speed: 200